COMMANDING
THE ARMY OF
THE POTOMAC

COMMANDING THE ARMY OF THE POTOMAC

Stephen R. Taaffe

To Bruce Steiner,
I'm doing my part to help you indulge
in your love of the Civil War

Stew Taaffe

University Press of Kansas

Published by the University Press of Kansas (Lawrence, Kansas 66045), which
was organized by the Kansas Board of Regents and is operated and funded by
Emporia State University, Fort Hays State University, Kansas State University,
Pittsburg State University, the University of Kansas, and Wichita State
University

Library of Congress Cataloging-in-Publication Data
Taaffe, Stephen R.
Commanding the Army of the Potomac / Stephen R. Taaffe.
p. cm. — (Modern war studies)
Includes bibliographical references and index.
ISBN 0-7006-1451-6 (cloth : alk. paper)
1. United States. Army of the Potomac—History. 2. Generals—United
States—History—19th century. 3. Command of troops—History—19th
century. 4. United States—History—Civil War, 1861–1865—Campaigns.
5. Virginia—History—Civil War, 1861–1865—Campaigns. I. Title. II.
Series.
E470.2.T23   2006
973.7'410922—dc22
2005026803

British Library Cataloguing in Publication Data is available.

Printed in the United States of America

10 9 8 7 6 5 4 3 2 1

The paper used in this publication meets the minimum requirements of the
American National Standard for Permanence of Paper for Printed Library
Materials Z39.48-1984.

CONTENTS

List of Maps   vii

Acknowledgments   ix

Introduction   1

1. "McClellan Is Not the Man": July 1861 to November 1862   6

2. Burnside's Unhappy and Insecure Tenure:
November 1862 to January 1863   60

3. Fighting Joe's Big Opportunity: January to June 1863   82

4. Meade Marks Time: June 1863 to March 1864   108

5. Grant as General in Chief: March 1864 to April 1865   143

Conclusions   208

Biographical Afterword   219

Notes   221

Bibliography   261

Index   271

Photograph section follows page 138.

MAPS

Theater of War, 1861–1865   3

The Peninsula Campaign, March–July 1862   14

Battle of Antietam, 17 September 1862   44

Battle of Fredericksburg, 13 December 1862   69

Battle of Chancellorsville, 29 April to 4 May 1863   92

Battle of Gettysburg, 1–3 July 1863   113

Battle of the Wilderness, 5–6 May 1864   153

Battle of Spotsylvania, 12 May 1864   158

Siege of Petersburg, June 1864–April 1865   166

ACKNOWLEDGMENTS

This book would not have been possible without the generous help of numerous people. My friend and colleague, Dr. Allen Richman, read through the manuscript and made many useful suggestions. Another friend, Ken Arbogast-Wilson, was gracious enough to take time out of his busy schedule to draw the book's maps for me. Stephen F. Austin State University's Office of Research and Sponsored Programs gave me a Faculty Research Grant to facilitate my progress. The folks at the University Press of Kansas were patient and accommodating from beginning to end. Last but not least, my wife, Cynthia, displayed her usual forbearance and understanding. Over the last five years my family has increased in size, and the knowledge that I will in all likelihood someday have to put them through college helped motivate me to finish this project. Therefore, I dedicate this book to my two good boys, John and Alexander, and the third—unexpected and as-of-yet-unnamed—girl still squirming in her mom's belly.

INTRODUCTION

Major General Daniel Butterfield was a self-confident and ambitious man, but not even he could have predicted his rapid rise through the Union army's hierarchy. The twenty-nine-year-old New York–born businessman had enlisted shortly after the Confederates fired on Fort Sumter, and in September 1861 he was appointed a brigadier general. He fought well enough afterward as a brigade, division, and corps commander, but his personal and political connections played as great a role as his performance on the battlefield in propelling him upward through the ranks. In January 1863, President Abraham Lincoln promoted Butterfield's friend, Major General Joseph Hooker, to lead the Army of the Potomac, and Hooker in turn asked Butterfield to become his chief of staff. Butterfield hesitated to accept a staff position, but he ultimately agreed. Although he was efficient and energetic in his new duties, many officers resented his imperious manner, which was all the more galling to some because he had so little prewar military experience.[1]

If Butterfield was brusque with some of his fellow officers, it was at least in part because of the responsibilities under which he labored. The Army of the Potomac was in deplorable shape in the winter of 1862–1863, and Butterfield worked hard to restore it in body and spirit. Among his most important innovations was the creation of flannel badges for each of the army's seven infantry corps. Butterfield borrowed the idea from his friend, Major General Philip Kearny, who had fashioned a red diamond patch for the men of his division before he was killed at the Battle of Chantilly in September 1862. Butterfield had suggested expanding the concept throughout the army to then Army of the Potomac commander Major General George McClellan, but McClellan had shown no interest. Once he was chief of staff, however, Butterfield had the clout to make his notion a reality. Butterfield believed that giving each corps its own patch would raise morale by providing the troops

1

with a greater sense of identity, and it would also encourage discipline by enabling officers to more easily round up and classify stragglers. He designed the badges himself, selecting distinctive and easily recognizable patterns. He chose a circle for the First Corps, a trefoil for the Second Corps and its large Irish-American contingent, a diamond for Kearny's old Third Corps, a Maltese cross for the Fifth, a Greek cross for the Sixth, a crescent for the Eleventh, and a star for the Twelfth. Hooker signed off on the idea in March 1863, and, as Butterfield had hoped, the patches were an immediate hit. Soon soldiers stitched them with pride not only on their kepi caps, but also on their tents, wagons, caissons, and all the other paraphernalia that was part and parcel of nineteenth-century warfare. Thanks in part to Butterfield's innovation, for most Army of the Potomac soldiers, loyalty to their corps became second only to loyalty to their regiments.[2]

The Army of the Potomac was the most important of the numerous field armies the Union deployed during the Civil War. Its initial missions were to defend Washington, D.C., and seize the Confederate capital of Richmond, Virginia, and it spent the entire war camping, marching, and fighting in the increasingly battle-scarred region between and around those two cities. Because of its high-profile location and assignment, it attracted a disproportionate amount of attention from the Union public. To most people, the Army of the Potomac was center stage, so at the beginning of the war prominent citizens and Regular Army officers aggressively sought commands in it. Not surprisingly, throughout the conflict various political factions tried to score points with the electorate by manipulating the army's officer corps. This, combined with the inevitable pressures and suspicions generated by civil war, made the Army of the Potomac the most politicized military force in U.S. history, so much so that at one point some people feared it might march on Washington and impose its will on the government. That it did not was a credit to its officers and men, who, whatever their political differences, shared a common devotion to the Union. This devotion ultimately saw them through to victory despite often wretched leadership and missed opportunities that cost tens of thousands of casualties in the woods and fields of Virginia, Maryland, and Pennsylvania. These staggering losses and heartbreaking defeats endowed the Army of the Potomac with a pathos and poignancy unique in U.S. military history.

The loyalty that most of the Army of the Potomac's soldiers felt toward their corps underscored the importance of these units to Civil War field armies. A corps consisted of between 10,000 and 30,000 men, and there were anywhere from three to seven of them in the Army of the Potomac at any given time. They were divided into three or four divisions, each of which contained three or four brigades of about five regiments apiece. Corps

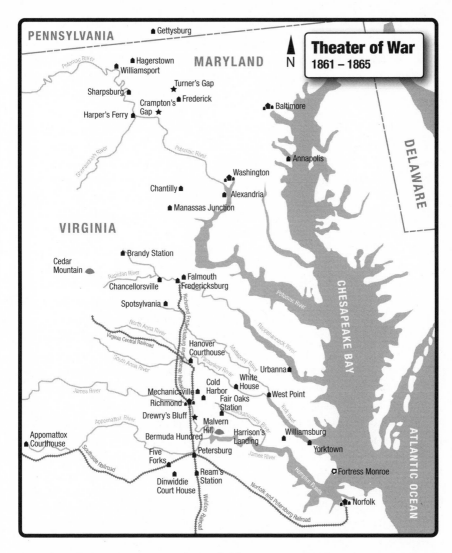

served as the primary pieces that a field army commander maneuvered and used to fight. Officers like Butterfield aspired to lead corps because of the size, status, and prominence of these units, but there was more to it than that. By providing officers with valuable training in managing large numbers of men in and out of combat, corps command could serve as a stepping-stone to bigger and better things. Indeed, three of the Army of the Potomac's four commanders gained experience at the corps level before ascending to the top spot. Furthermore, corps command was a place where ambitious officers could make names for themselves in ways not possible for their more numerous divisional and brigade counterparts. Such public recognition not only could lead to further promotion with greater responsibility but also could open up political, economic, and military opportunities after the war. Finally, corps commanders advised their superiors both informally and through councils of war, giving them opportunities to influence strategic, tactical, personnel, and administrative decisions that helped determine the conflict's outcome.

As commander in chief, President Abraham Lincoln reserved for himself the power to appoint corps commanders, but it was never that simple. Lincoln eventually realized that he lacked the time and expertise to propose officers for corps command, so he usually merely expressed his approval or disapproval of names his military advisers put forth. Lincoln normally consulted with the secretary of war, general in chief, and Army of the Potomac commander before he made his final decisions, and these men all lobbied for their favorite officers behind closed doors. Moreover, Army of the Potomac commanders and generals in chief learned that they could circumvent Lincoln when it served their purposes by assigning officers to "temporary" corps command for long periods of time, a procedure that did not require the president's consent. Lincoln tolerated this ploy when he had faith in his subordinates and when he wanted to avoid making controversial appointments. Lincoln and his advisers used numerous criteria in recommending and choosing corps commanders. The most significant factors were rank,[3] seniority, and availability. Perceived ability, personal relationships, and political connections were also important. As a result, Army of the Potomac corps commanders were not chosen arbitrarily. Instead, their selection was generally the result of informal negotiations between the president and his chief military policymakers based on both tangible and intangible standards.

As it was, Lincoln had plenty of opportunities to approve new corps commanders because their turnover rate was so high. During the war, thirty-six officers led corps in the Army of the Potomac as permanent or "temporary" commanders.[4] One reason for this was enemy fire that killed or incapacitated several of them. Others succumbed to the strain of leadership and had to relinquish their positions. Some corps commanders lost their posts because they performed poorly in battle, their outspoken politics alienated the Lincoln administration, they were transferred elsewhere, or they were unable to get along with their superiors. Finally, several disgruntled corps commanders resigned because they failed to get the recognition they felt they deserved. In short, corps command in the Army of the Potomac was no sinecure.

The officers who served as corps commanders in the Army of the Potomac were not a monolithic group. Instead, they fell into one of four overlapping categories. The first and most common was that of officers who sympathized with and supported Major General George McClellan, the Army of the Potomac's original leader. The army also contained a number of corps commanders who owed their positions primarily to President Lincoln. Some of them were Regular Army officers appointed by Lincoln to corps command over McClellan's objections, and his enmity forced them to fetter themselves to the president for their own protection. Others, however, were political generals with minimal prewar military experience selected by Lincoln to placate some constituency. Opportunists formed the third category of Army of the Potomac corps commanders. These ambitious and often unscrupulous officers allied themselves with any politician or general who could advance their careers, even those whose beliefs did not coincide with their own. Finally, as the Lincoln administration and the pressures of war gradually weeded out those generals who failed on the battlefield, officers who rose through the ranks primarily on the basis of merit began to assert themselves. By the end of the war these men supplied the bulk of the Army of the Potomac's brigade and divisional commanders, but only a few managed to lead corps.

The Civil War remains one of the defining events in U.S. history. Although ideological, economic, social, and political factors were important, the war was ultimately decided on the battlefield. Other Union field armies won more battles and seized more territory, but it was the Army of the Potomac that captured the Confederacy's capital and destroyed its premier army. By examining the selection and retention of its corps commanders, it is possible to gain a greater understanding of the military and political obstacles the Army of the Potomac faced on its rocky road to victory.

CHAPTER ONE

"McClellan Is Not the Man"
July 1861 to November 1862

McClellan Builds an Army

The rain that pelted Washington on 22 July 1861 matched the moods of those Unionists who knew that the rebels had defeated Brigadier General Irvin McDowell's army the previous day in the Battle of Bull Run at Manassas Junction, Virginia. Throughout the morning and afternoon exhausted, panicky, and disorganized soldiers streamed into Washington seeking refuge wherever they could find it, including on the open ground. As they slept or scrounged for food, President Abraham Lincoln met at the White House with his cabinet and his general in chief, Lieutenant General Winfield Scott. If the Bull Run debacle proved anything, it proved that the army needed new leadership, so McDowell had to go. In the discussion that followed, the secretary of the treasury, Salmon Chase, suggested Major General George McClellan as a replacement, and everyone agreed. McClellan then commanded the Department of the Ohio, and he had recently won two battles in western Virginia that had freed that pro-Union region from rebel control. These engagements had not been very big, and their strategic significance was relatively marginal, but no other Union general had fared any better. Lincoln ordered him to report to Washington at once, and McClellan was in the capital four days later.[1]

George Brinton McClellan had all the trappings of a man of destiny. The thirty-four-year-old Philadelphian had graduated second in his West Point class of 1846 and served with distinction as an engineer in the Mexican War. After the conflict he had returned to West Point as an instructor, and he had later participated in an exploratory expedition up the Red River in Arkansas. The War Department had sent him and two other officers to Europe to study military organizations there, and while overseas he had witnessed the tail end of the Crimean War. In 1857 he had resigned his commission to accept a job as chief engineer of the Illinois Central Railroad. His second career was every bit as successful as his first, and by the time the Confederates fired on Fort Sumter he was president of the Ohio and Mississippi Railroad.

McClellan was one of the most baffling figures ever to wear a United States Army uniform. In many ways he was an ideal commander. He certainly looked the part; he was handsome, martial, broad-shouldered, and muscular, a man whose very physical presence encouraged others to give their best. His subordinate officers appreciated his intelligence, friendliness, work ethic, physical courage, and apparent sincerity. He was a master of organization, administration, and drill, and very few details escaped his scrutiny. He understood the value of pomp and ceremony to a new army, and his extravagant grand reviews won the adoration of the rank and file even though he kept a certain distance from them. Indeed, shortly after his arrival one observer wrote, "The rapidity with which he has restored good order, strict discipline, and confidence, is almost miraculous. We are almost willing to look upon our repulse [at Bull Run] as a blessing in disguise, while considering this portion of its consequences."[2] It was McClellan—or Little Mac, as his soldiers called him affectionately—who turned the disorganized mob of bluecoats in and around Washington into the Army of the Potomac, and in that sense the army bore his imprint throughout the war.

Unfortunately for the Union, there was a dark side to McClellan that in the final analysis made him an ineffective general. The adulation and praise he received when he first came to Washington swelled his already healthy ego until he became convinced that he was God's principal agent for the Union's restoration.[3] He had small use for those he considered his intellectual, social, and moral inferiors, a list that eventually included almost everyone in the Lincoln administration. Indeed, he referred to the president as a "well meaning baboon" and "idiotic" in letters to his wife.[4] Most damning of all, McClellan lacked the moral courage to wage the kind of ruthless revolutionary war necessary to suppress the rebellion. Instead, he wanted a safe and limited conflict that would leave the country's social system intact.[5] As a result, he was unduly cautious and too eager to accept exaggerated estimates of Confederate troop strength. He was so devoted to the Army of the Potomac—*his* army—that he had difficulty accepting the fact that many of its soldiers had to die to preserve the Union. Time and time again he missed battlefield opportunities because he could not bring himself to launch the ferocious all-out attacks necessary to grind down the opposing Confederate army. His soldiers loved him for his obvious interest in their well-being, but in this case such concern did not translate into victory.

Considering McClellan's prickly personality, it was not surprising that he failed to get along with Winfield Scott, general in chief and commander of the entire United States Army. Scott was a Washington fixture with a long and illustrious career behind him as a War of 1812 and Mexican War hero, military diplomat, and 1852 Whig presidential candidate. But the years had taken their toll, and by 1861 the seventy-five-year-old general was so infirm that he could no longer mount a horse. Even so, he still maintained his intellect and pride. Scott and McClellan soon clashed over several issues, including the formation of corps. McClellan understood that the large field army the Union was deploying in and around Washington required corps, and he wanted to organize them as soon as possible. Scott resisted, however, because he believed that army regulations called for geographical divisions only. Besides, an army built around brigades had worked well enough in the Mexican War. This dispute was merely symptomatic of a bigger issue between the two men: control of the army. As McClellan saw things, Scott was too old, too out of touch, and too stupid to be entrusted with the responsibilities of general in chief during these trying times. As he put it in a letter to his wife, "He [Scott] understands nothing, appreciates nothing and is ever in my way."[6] As a result, McClellan increasingly isolated Scott by denying him important information about the Army of the Potomac. McClellan also enlisted the assistance of Radical Republican congressmen who saw Scott as an obstacle to the war's vigorous prosecution. Scott tolerated these affronts to his dignity, mostly because the president asked him to stay on, but on 31 October Lincoln finally accepted Scott's resignation. Lincoln and his cabinet agreed that McClellan should not only replace Scott as general in chief but also continue as the Army of the Potomac's commander. The president worried that this might be too much work and responsibility for one man, but Little Mac blithely responded, "I can do it all."[7] Early on the morning of 2 November, McClellan and his staff saw the old general off on a train to New York in the driving rain. McClellan later wrote to his wife, "The sight of this morning was a lesson to me which I hope not soon to forget. I saw there the end of a long, active, and ambitious life—the end of the career of the first soldier of his nation—and it was a feeble old man scarce able to walk—hardly any one there to see him off but his successor."[8]

Although McClellan won his power struggle with Scott, his victory exposed him to attacks from far more formidable foes than one frail old man. As the months slipped by and the Army of the Potomac continued to drill and train around Washington, Radical Republican congressman such as Benjamin Wade, Zachariah Chandler, and George Julian grew increasingly frustrated with McClellan's inaction. These Radicals were abolitionists who wanted to wage a violent revolutionary struggle to crush the South and end its evil slave system once and for all. They were not a majority in Congress, but they made up for their lack of numbers with their energy, determination, and the courage of their convictions. They initially took their anger out on Scott, but they redirected their fire at McClellan once he became general in chief. To get the conflict on track and on schedule, in December 1861 the Radicals played a key role in organizing the Joint Committee on the Conduct of the War to investigate any and all aspects of the Union's war effort. Like any congressional committee, the Committee on the Conduct of the War had the power to subpoena, and its Radical members used this to compel testimony from officers as part of its campaign against those who seemed to lack sufficient enthusiasm for the Union cause. By autumn 1861, they included McClellan on that list, and in January they were so unhappy that they urged Lincoln to replace McClellan with Irvin McDowell, who seemed more sympathetic to their viewpoints. McClellan was well aware of these assaults on his character and motives, which he interpreted as part of a Radical plot to make the war about slavery and cement Republican control of the government.[9]

Not only was McClellan losing support among members of Congress, but some within Lincoln's own administration were beginning to have doubts about him. In January 1862, Lincoln appointed noted attorney Edwin Stanton as secretary of war in place of the corrupt and inefficient Simon Cameron. Stanton was a mercurial, energetic, and often duplicitous man whom McClellan initially counted as a friend and supporter. Once Stanton assumed office and became responsible for the War Department, however, he lost confidence in McClellan and made common cause with the Radicals. He was not the only skeptical cabinet member; Secretary of the Treasury Chase and Secretary of the Navy Gideon Welles were also losing faith in McClellan. As for Lincoln, he continued to defend his new general in chief despite the numerous snubs to which Little Mac subjected him. For example, in mid-November, McClellan refused to see Lincoln and Secretary of State William Seward when they called upon him at his home. Lincoln was well aware of the growing clamor for action, but he also understood McClellan's need for time to train and prepare his army adequately. Even so, he was a keen judge of men, and he was getting a pretty good idea of McClellan's weaknesses and limitations.[10]

The selection of Army of the Potomac corps commanders became part of the increasing struggle between McClellan and the Radical Republicans. Now that he was general in chief, McClellan decided not to immediately divide his army into corps. He recognized that leading a corps was a big responsibility, so he was reluctant to entrust officers with the position until they had proven themselves to him in battle. Radical Republicans, on the other hand, contended that the army could not go to war until it had corps and commanders for them, and they based their arguments on testimony provided by officers such as McDowell and quartermaster general Brigadier General Montgomery Meigs before the Committee on the Conduct of the War. Throughout January and February 1862, the Committee repeatedly pressed Lincoln to pressure McClellan to organize the army into corps, but the president resisted because he feared that McClellan might resign and create a public relations disaster for his administration.[11]

Regrettably, McClellan did very little to restore his relations with the Lincoln administration and the Radicals. In particular, he refused to disclose his military plans to the president. In December, McClellan came down with typhoid fever, rendering him bedridden for three weeks and leaving the Union army rudderless. Lincoln did not visit him, but at Meigs's suggestion he instead consulted with some of McClellan's subordinates—McDowell and Brigadier General William Franklin—about strategy. McClellan was outraged when he discovered what was going on behind his back, and he rose from his sickbed to attend a tense 13 January 1862 meeting at the White House with Lincoln and several cabinet members and officers. Lincoln did not insist that McClellan divulge his designs, but he was instead content to learn that McClellan had fixed a date for the Army of the Potomac to advance. Even so, he continued to pressure Little Mac to take the offensive as soon as possible. On 11 March, he relieved McClellan as general in chief so he could focus his undivided attention on the Army of the Potomac's operations. Three days earlier, on 8 March, the president arbitrarily and without warning divided the Army of the Potomac into four corps and assigned them to its four senior subordinate officers: Brigadier Generals Irvin McDowell, Edwin Sumner, Samuel Heintzelman, and Erasmus Keyes.[12]

Although he could not know it, Irvin McDowell's Civil War career had already peaked. He was a forty-three-year-old Ohioan who had graduated in the middle of his West Point class of 1838. He had served on the Canadian border and had later seen action in Mexico, but he had spent most of his prewar career as a staff officer. It was in that capacity that he attracted Winfield Scott's attention, and both Scott and Salmon Chase successfully lobbied Lincoln to appoint McDowell to command the conglomeration of soldiers who gathered in and around Washington after hostilities began. He marched on the rebel army in northern Virginia against his better judgment and suffered defeat at Bull Run as a result. Almost everyone acknowledged that McDowell was a capable man who knew how to drill and discipline troops, but he also possessed less admirable qualities that doomed him as a combat general. He often acted in an abrupt, tactless, and haughty manner toward his subordinates, and he proved unable to inspire affection, devotion, or even respect from the rank and file. Moreover, there was something strange about the man. He was both a teetotaler and a glutton, and he campaigned in the field wearing a peculiar straw hat of his own design. One young officer who dined with McDowell remembered that he ate a large meal and then polished off an entire watermelon for dessert. McDowell never made the transition from peacetime staff officer to wartime leader, which no doubt contributed to the bad luck he experienced throughout the conflict. Even so, he retained the confidence of many in the Lincoln administration who understood that he had done his best under trying and unfair conditions at Bull Run. Radicals saw him as an alternative to McClellan, demonstrating for the first but not last time their proclivity for backing militarily incompetent officers for political reasons.[13]

Edwin Sumner was nicknamed "Old Bull" in the prewar army for his plain, unsubtle, and straightforward manner. He was born in Boston late in the previous century, entered the army in 1819, and saw extensive service in Mexico and along the frontier during his long climb up the military ladder. He was famous among junior officers as a martinet and strict disciplinarian, and he epitomized the courageous, conscientious, indomitable, and duty-bound old soldier. Beneath the surface, however, Sumner was an amiable, gentle, and kind officer who cared deeply about his men. He was promoted to brigadier general shortly after the war began, thanks to his friendship with both Scott and the president, and many in the Lincoln administration admired the white-haired and bearded Sumner for his simple bravery. Those who served in the field with Sumner, however, recognized that he was beyond his prime and out of his depth. Sumner had no experience commanding large numbers of men, and he treated his corps like an oversized regiment. He had trouble seeing the big picture, and he was slow to adapt to the accelerating changes in nineteenth-century warfare. To make things worse, in the winter of 1861–1862 he was thrown from his horse while crossing a field, severely injuring his lungs and shoulder. He had not completely recovered when Lincoln appointed him a corps commander.[14]

Like Sumner, Samuel Heintzelman was an old career soldier with plenty of experience out on the frontier. Unlike Sumner, however, Heintzelman impressed neither his superiors nor subordinates. One person described him as "a little man, almost black, with short coarse gray hair and beard, his face one mass of wrinkles, he wears the most uncouth dress and gets into the most awkward positions possible. He talks way down in his throat too, having lost his palate, so that one can hardly understand him. I was much disappointed in him; could not see any signs of a great man."[15] He was not alone in his assessment; others depicted Heintzelman as an unoriginal, grim, uninspiring, and ossified officer who had been promoted beyond his ability. All this was true, but Heintzelman was also generous, brave, and competent in an ordinary sort of way. He was often oblivious to the political machinations around him, but he was also surprisingly shrewd and perceptive in his assessments of others. Although he had been severely wounded leading a division at Bull Run, he owed his new position in the Army of the Potomac to his seniority more than anything else.[16]

Erasmus Keyes shared Sumner's and Heintzelman's long years of service in the prewar army, but the similarities ended there. Keyes had spent comparatively little time on the frontier, and he had missed the Mexican War entirely. He owed his ascent through the army's hierarchy instead mostly to his relationship with Scott as his aide and military secretary. In addition, whereas Sumner and Heintzelman were basically nonpartisan, Keyes was a well-known Republican in an officer corps full of Democrats. He counted Chase among his correspondents, and he was more than willing to use his connections to advance his career. He was well aware that his political views made him unpopular among War Democrats such as McClellan, and this enhanced Keyes's natural caution. He led a brigade at Bull Run and was commended for his performance there, but he was not cut out for corps command. Although he was kind and friendly to his subordinates, observers noted that he was also irresolute and unaggressive.[17]

Lincoln's decision to appoint these four men to corps command was based primarily on expediency. Choosing anyone else would have caused all sorts of problems that the president undoubtedly hoped to avoid. For one thing, it would have alienated McDowell, Sumner, Heintzelman, and Keyes, all important men in the old army, and at least two—McDowell and Keyes—with powerful Republican patrons whom Lincoln did not want to antagonize. Moreover, the Army of the Potomac had yet to fight a major battle, so Lincoln could not judge its generals on the basis of their performance in recent combat, even if he possessed the expertise to do so. Picking corps commanders by any other criteria would have led to charges of favoritism, bringing dissension to an officer corps full of large and fragile egos. By using seniority as his guide, Lincoln was merely taking the path of least political resistance.

In the long run, Lincoln's selections did little to advance the Union war effort. Although his reasoning was understandable, he set a bad example by overtly promoting on the basis of seniority instead of proven talent. McDowell, Sumner, Heintzelman, and Keyes were all brave and diligent, but the latter three men in particular were relics from a bygone era. It was one thing to administer a small professional army and lead it in limited combat against remote American Indian tribes out on the frontier, but it was something else to master the rapidly evolving technology, tactics, and strategy of a civilian army engaged in large-scale warfare. To make things worse, instead of working together as a team, all four corps commanders distrusted one another's motives and abilities. McDowell was the youngest of the four, but he was promoted to major general first, much to Sumner's chagrin. As far as Sumner was concerned, McDowell's advancement was due more to his political connections than to his military aptitude. Heintzelman and Sumner had been rivals for years, and the war did little to change that. Keyes did not believe that either Sumner or Heintzelman was up for his job, and he said as much in his correspondence. Finally, all four had their doubts about McClellan. They all increasingly questioned Little Mac's estimates of enemy strength, and three of them—McDowell, Sumner, and Heintzelman—went on record against McClellan's initial plan to attack Richmond.[18]

McClellan's estimation of his new corps commanders was not much better than their opinion of him. Ever since he had taken charge of the Army of the Potomac, McClellan had systematically seeded its growing number of divisions and brigades with as many of his supporters as possible, and he had hoped to tap into this pool for his future corps commanders. He conferred frequently with his allies on strategic and administrative matters, but he ignored men such as McDowell, Sumner, Heintzelman, and Keyes whom he did not count among his friends. He was angry that Lincoln made such important appointments without consulting him, and many of his subordinates were unhappy that the president had passed them over. Within weeks, McClellan was complaining that his new corps commanders were interfering with the army's management. Nor was he pleased when three of them came out against his strategic plans. McClellan in particular despised McDowell. He believed that McDowell was conspiring with the Lincoln administration and Radical Republicans against him in both strategic and organizational matters. Certainly McDowell made himself available to those who disliked McClellan, but there is no evidence that he was intent on replacing him. McClellan had kept McDowell around despite his defeat at Bull Run, and he had even endorsed McDowell's promotion to major general, but he believed that in return McDowell had repaid him with ingratitude and disloyalty. As for Sumner, Heintzelman, and Keyes, McClellan doubted they could handle the responsibilities of corps command, despite their prewar achievements. But, like it or not, they were his top lieutenants now, and he had to rely on them when he finally went off to war.[19]

The Peninsula

McClellan's original plan called for the Army of the Potomac to mount an amphibious landing at Urbanna, Virginia, to outflank the Confederate army

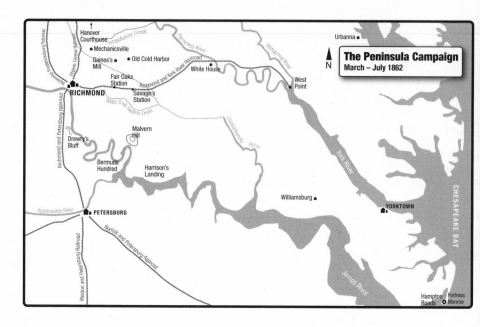

dug in around Centreville. On 9 March, however, the rebels suddenly pulled up stakes and fell back to the Rappahannock River in central Virginia, destroying the bridges as they retreated. McClellan led his army to Centreville and back to claim victory, but the expedition generated more ridicule than applause from the public. The Confederate withdrawal negated any advantages an offensive from Urbanna might gain, but McClellan still liked the idea of using Union naval supremacy to his advantage. Mulling things over, McClellan decided to take his army to the peninsula between the York and James rivers in southeastern Virginia. Union forces already controlled Fortress Monroe on the peninsula's tip, the roads there were reportedly good, and the navy could protect the Army of the Potomac's flanks as it marched the 70 miles toward Richmond. Most important, an advance up the peninsula would enable McClellan to avoid any big battles until he reached the Confederate capital. Once there, McClellan could carry out a methodical and scientific siege to occupy Richmond and, he hoped, end the war. Lincoln reluctantly approved the plan, but only on the condition that McClellan would leave behind sufficient forces to protect Washington. In mid-March, McClellan began the largest amphibious operation in U.S. history to that date. For three weeks nearly 400 vessels shuttled 121,000 men and all their supplies, equipment, and weaponry from Alexandria to Fortress Monroe with an ease that befitted McClellan's reputation as a first-rate organizer.

On 4 April, the Army of the Potomac began its ascent up the peninsula. Unfortunately, no sooner had it gotten under way than McClellan received two pieces of bad news. First, probing Union patrols had discovered that the rebels had established a line of fortifications across the peninsula around the old Revolutionary War battlefield at Yorktown. Second, Lincoln had decided to strip McClellan of McDowell's corps. To be sure, Lincoln had his reasons. McClellan had declared that he had left 73,000 troops behind to protect Washington, well over the 40,000 men his corps commanders thought necessary. When Lincoln counted noses, however, he discovered that very few of those soldiers were actually manning the Washington defenses. Lincoln knew better than anyone the incalculable damage the Union would sustain if the Confederates seized Washington, so he decided to keep McDowell's 38,000 soldiers in northern Virginia. Whatever his feelings toward McDowell, McClellan was outraged to lose such a large chunk of his army before he even engaged the enemy. He later argued that his reduced strength forced him to besiege Yorktown because he now lacked the muscle to carry out an amphibious landing at West Point that would have outflanked the rebels and driven them back to Richmond. While his men entrenched and hauled up the heavy artillery necessary to conduct a siege, McClellan demanded reinforcements. By now McClellan was so convinced that McDowell was his enemy that he no longer wanted him in the Army of the Potomac. Instead, he asked for the corps' components, especially the division commanded by his friend William Franklin. Lincoln agreed, and Franklin's division arrived on 22 April. This would not be the last time McClellan dealt with a corps commander he disliked by taking away his troops, not his command.[20]

The Union siege of Yorktown dragged on for a month, during which time Lincoln grew increasingly frustrated with McClellan's dilatoriness. Little Mac's slowness, moreover, stood in stark and unflattering contrast with the spate of Union victories that late winter and spring. Out in the remote Transmississippi, for example, Brigadier General Samuel Curtis's victory at the Battle of Pea Ridge on 7–8 March secured Missouri for the Union and opened the door for further operations into Arkansas. About a month earlier, at the other end of the war, Brigadier General Ambrose Burnside flexed the Union's amphibious muscles by storming Roanoke Island off the North Carolina coast. Burnside followed up his success by besieging and occupying New Bern, North Carolina, on 14 March. These accomplishments, impressive though they were, paled compared to Union successes in the Mississippi River basin. In February, Brigadier General Ulysses Grant's army seized Fort Donelson along the Cumberland River, thus bringing most of Kentucky into the Union fold and exposing Tennessee to Union invasion. In the wake of Grant's victory, the rebels abandoned Nashville to Major General Don

Carlos Buell's army, lost Island Number Ten on the Mississippi River to a Union force under Major General John Pope, and surrendered New Orleans to Rear Admiral David Farragut's fleet. Although the Confederates launched a ferocious surprise assault on Grant's army at Pittsburg Landing in the Battle of Shiloh on 6 April, the Union troops beat off the attack in two days of bloody fighting and then began a slow and ultimately successful advance toward the vital Confederate railroad junction at Corinth, Mississippi. The Union tide, it seemed, was flowing inexorably forward everywhere—everywhere, that is, except on the peninsula.

Finally, just hours before McClellan ordered his artillery to begin a massive bombardment on the rebel positions at Yorktown, the heavily outnumbered Confederates evacuated their lines on the night of 3–4 May and slipped northwestward toward Richmond. The Army of the Potomac set out in pursuit the next day, and on 5 May the Union advance clashed with the rebel rear guard at Williamsburg. All day long Union and Confederate soldiers slugged it out, often in the driving rain, across the wet fields and roads. Sumner, Heintzelman, and Keyes all had men there, but no one was really in charge, so it was hardly surprising that a small number of units bore the brunt of the fighting while others stood idly by. The press awarded Brigadier General Winfield Scott Hancock, a brigade commander in Keyes's Fourth Corps, the sobriquet "Hancock the Superb" for his actions that day. In reality, however, Brigadier General Joe Hooker's division in Heintzelman's Third Corps did most of the fighting. Although McClellan learned of the encounter that morning, he did not get to the battlefield until evening. The rebels broke off contact during the night, leaving behind 1,682 casualties. Union losses were much heavier, totaling 2,283.

McClellan claimed victory at Williamsburg, but he was not nearly as satisfied as his initial reports to Washington indicated. Although McClellan himself did not witness the battle, some of his favorite subordinates, such as divisional commander Brigadier General William "Baldy" Smith, did, and they were quick to damn Sumner in particular for his lack of leadership there. To McClellan, the Williamsburg brouhaha was more evidence that the corps commanders Lincoln had appointed were unfit for their jobs. On 8 May he telegraphed Stanton: "I respectfully ask permission to reorganize the army corps. I am not willing to be held responsible for the present arrangement, experience having proved it to be very bad, and it having very nearly resulted in the most disastrous defeat. I wish either to return to the organization by division or else be authorized to relieve incompetent commanders of army corps."[21]

Lincoln's reaction was swift, astute, and twofold. In an official communiqué to McClellan, he wrote that he did not want the corps system disrupted, but he was willing to tolerate any temporary reorganization that Mc-Clellan considered militarily necessary. In a private letter, however, the president attempted to explain the political consequences of McClellan's proposed course of action. Lincoln noted that McClellan had recently alienated one of his own strongest supporters in the Senate by relieving Brigadier General Charles Hamilton from command of his division for insubordination and disrespect. Firing three of the prewar army's most politically powerful officers would generate an even greater uproar that would reverberate all the way back to Washington. As it was, there were already rumors in the capital that McClellan had given preferential treatment to such friendly officers as William Franklin and Brigadier General Fitz John Porter while ignoring Sumner, Heintzelman, and Keyes. Lincoln did not know whether or not these reports were true, but their mere existence would expose McClellan to charges of favoritism should he move against his corps commanders. Lincoln asked if Sumner, Heintzelman, or Keyes had disobeyed any orders, implying that he needed specific evidence of military misconduct for him to agree to McClellan's request. Having given Little Mac a crash course in the realities of waging civil war in a democracy, Lincoln concluded by asking, "Are you strong enough, even with my help—to set your foot upon the necks of Sumner, Heintzelman, and Keyes all at once? This is a practical and very serious question for you."[22]

McClellan did not press the issue, but he quickly seized the opportunity Lincoln's official communiqué presented him. On 17 May, he created two new, "provisional" corps—the Fifth and Sixth—out of the other three and placed two of his favorite officers, Brigadier Generals Fitz John Porter and William Franklin, in charge of them. Both men were among the first brigadier generals Lincoln had appointed, so they had plenty of seniority in an army in which McClellan was currently the only major general. This put nearly half of Little Mac's army under men he could trust when he fought the climactic battle for Richmond. Moreover, both corps—they would become permanent in July—quickly gained reputations as the most pro-McClellan units in the army. Sumner, Heintzelman, and Keyes retained their commands, but at reduced strength that matched their declining influence. Unfortunately, McClellan's decision ultimately did substantial damage to the Army of the Potomac. For one thing, it reduced the combat power of each corps. For the next two years the Army of the Potomac would be plagued by too many small corps that lacked the muscle to carry out their missions. Any talk of eliminating or combining them inevitably caused considerable angst among officers and men who proudly identified themselves with their corps. Worse yet, finding officers with sufficient rank and competence to command all those corps became very problematic. Finally, in assigning Porter and

Franklin to their corps, McClellan introduced into the army's high command two officers who, whatever their talents, eventually brought everyone considerable grief.

No one was surprised that McClellan appointed Fitz John Porter to a corps command. The two men were close friends, and McClellan consulted with him frequently on military matters big and small. The New Hampshire–born Porter was related to the famous naval family of the same name, but he went to West Point and graduated eighth in his class in 1845. He fought under Winfield Scott in Mexico and was brevetted twice for gallantry. Afterward he taught at West Point and served in Utah. Almost everyone admired Porter. He was a brave, graceful, dignified, soldierly looking man with a keen intellect, just the kind of officer who appealed to McClellan. McClellan valued his good judgment and administrative ability so much that he made him Director of the Siege at Yorktown. During the siege Porter was nearly killed when the balloon from which he was observing the rebel lines broke free of its moorings and floated away, but he managed to force its descent by climbing 8 feet into the netting to reach the gas valve. Within two weeks after he had assumed command of the Fifth Corps, Porter justified McClellan's confidence in him by winning the hard-fought Battle of Hanover Courthouse, north of Richmond. Small wonder that years later McClellan wrote, "Take him for all in all, he was probably the best general officer I had under me."[23]

Like Porter, William Franklin was a close McClellan confidant. The thirty-nine-year-old Pennsylvanian had graduated first in his West Point class of 1843, a testament to his universally acknowledged intelligence. He surveyed the Great Lakes, fought bravely at the Battle of Buena Vista in the Mexican War, and was overseeing the construction of the new Capitol dome when the southern states seceded. He commanded a brigade at Bull Run, and he was one of the officers Lincoln consulted on strategy in the winter of 1861–1862, although McClellan did not hold that against him. Franklin was a candid officer who impressed most people, and McClellan was well pleased with his performance after his division arrived on the peninsula. Unfortunately, Franklin also possessed a penchant for conspiracy and an inability to understand the chain of command. Even worse, he lacked the aggressiveness and initiative a successful combat officer requires, so he was never able to translate his unquestioned talents into successful generalship. Instead, he brought misfortune almost everywhere he served.[24]

McClellan undoubtedly appreciated the support and advice he received from friends like Porter and Franklin, but he paid a price for his overt favoritism. Although the Army of the Potomac's officer corps as a whole remained very loyal to its commander, pockets of discontent were already forming, and nowhere was this truer than in Heintzelman's Third Corps. The crusty Heintzelman was not an especially happy man as May wore on, and the Union army continued its slow and methodical crawl up the peninsula. Heintzelman believed correctly that his corps had done the bulk of the fighting at Williamsburg, but McClellan had initially failed to acknowledge its contribution. Although Little Mac eventually rectified the record after Heintzelman complained, the slight still rankled. Nor did Heintzelman approve of the formation of two new corps that reduced his strength and elevated Franklin, with whom he had a running dispute over seniority. Rumors that McClellan was holding up Heintzelman's promotion to major general seemed like more evidence that his commander was playing favorites. Finally, Heintzelman had continuing doubts about McClellan's military ability. As he saw things, the Army of the Potomac could have stormed the Confederate defenses at Yorktown and avoided a time-consuming siege had McClellan shown some initiative.[25]

Heintzelman's grievances paled compared to those of his two divisional commanders, Brigadier Generals Philip Kearny and Joseph Hooker. Kearny was the scion of a rich New York family. As a child he was fascinated with the military, but his relatives prevented him from going to West Point. Once he gained his inheritance, however, he got a commission in 1836. His immense wealth afforded him the luxury of entering and leaving the army several times. Over the years he had fought with the French in Algeria and Italy, served as Winfield Scott's aide, recruited and commanded a cavalry unit in the Mexican War, and campaigned against the Rouge River Indians in California. In Mexico he had exclaimed that he would sacrifice his arm for the opportunity to lead a cavalry charge against the enemy, and he had gotten his wish at the price he pledged at the Battle of Churubusco. His personal life was every bit as colorful as his professional one; he abandoned his first wife for another woman whom he later married in an era when divorce was extremely rare and scandalous. McClellan gave Charles Hamilton's old division to Kearny after the Army of the Potomac arrived on the peninsula, and he led it well at Williamsburg. Indeed, Kearny enjoyed combat more than almost anything else, though his strategic and tactical abilities were limited. He was an impulsive, passionate, opinionated, and recklessly courageous man whose example inspired his soldiers. At Williamsburg the rebels yelled at him, "Come on you damned Yankee!" Kearny responded by shaking his fist at them and crying, "I'm coming you devils, and you'll be sorry enough to see me there!"[26] His wealth contributed to an independent mindset that interpreted orders as suggestions. His generosity, energy, chivalry, and charisma attracted other officers who under normal circumstances would have abhorred him for his disreputable marital past.[27]

Hooker shared Kearny's rashness, outspokenness, physical courage, and personal magnetism, but his background was more conventional and plebian. The Massachusetts-born bachelor had graduated in the middle of his West Point class of 1833, and afterwards he had been stationed in Florida and later along the Canadian border. He had served primarily as a staff officer in the Mexican War, but this had not prevented him from winning a brevet promotion for gallantry at the Battle of Monterrey. Unfortunately for Hooker, he alienated Winfield Scott by siding against him in his power struggle with Gideon Pillow. Hooker resigned in 1853 to try his hand at farming in California, and there his life degenerated into sloth and indolence. He hurried to Washington to offer his services to the Union after the Confederates fired on Fort Sumter, but Scott's continuing enmity stymied him until an interview with Lincoln led to Hooker's appointment to brigadier general. His division did most of the fighting and suffered most of the casualties at Williamsburg, and his performance there earned him promotion to major general and the nickname "Fighting Joe," which he disliked. Almost everyone commented on Hooker's impressive physical appearance; he was a handsome man with auburn hair, bright clear blue eyes, a florid complexion, and a clean-shaven face in a much-bearded army. He was also self-confident, critical of others, unscrupulous, and inordinately ambitious.[28]

Kearny and Hooker were by nature contentious men, so their discontent was hardly surprising. Neither had much respect for their superiors up to and including McClellan. They both believed that McClellan had elevated other, less qualified, officers at their expense—men such as William Franklin. In addition, they deeply resented the fact that McClellan did not initially give them sufficient credit for their actions at Williamsburg, which prompted Kearny to write to a friend with typical hyperbole, "Excuse this egotistical effusion but I am the first general that has ever been defrauded by his commanding officer."[29] Their common grievances united them in outward friendship, though in private Kearny denigrated Hooker's military ability. Such disgruntlement among generals was disturbing enough, but Kearny's and Hooker's charisma attracted to their standard other unhappy Third Corps officers who, for whatever reason, were angry with McClellan and his clique. Kearny and Hooker were both War Democrats, but their allies within the Third Corps included officers such as Brigadier Generals David Birney and Hiram Berry, who had close connections to the Lincoln administration. Nor was Kearny's and Hooker's influence limited to the officer corps. Both men were popular with the rank and file, and they effectively cultivated the press. They also used their political connections to undermine McClellan by reaching out to policymakers already hostile to the Army of the Potomac commander. Oddly enough, although McClellan's antennae were finely tuned to detect enemies both real and imagined, he never recognized this growing cancer in the Third Corps, and he continued to praise Kearny and especially Hooker even as they denounced him with increasing fury and vehemence behind his back.[30]

By the end of May, the Army of the Potomac was so close to Richmond that soldiers could hear the city's church bells pealing. McClellan hoped to approach the Confederate capital along the south side of the Chickahominy River, but other considerations forced him to alter his plan. Lincoln was considering sending the remainder of McDowell's corps to the Army of the Potomac overland from Fredericksburg, so McClellan had to keep forces on the Chickahominy's north bank to link up with that corps, should it arrive. As a result, McClellan split his army, deploying Sumner's Second, Porter's Fifth, and Franklin's Sixth Corps north of the river and Heintzelman's Third and Keyes's Fourth Corps to the south. Normally the Chickahominy was not much of an obstacle, but spring rains had caused it to overflow its banks and flood the surrounding area. McClellan could do little but build bridges across it and hope that Lincoln would order McDowell to join him as soon as possible.

On 31 May, the Confederates took advantage of the divided Union army to assault Heintzelman's and Keyes's isolated corps south of the Chicka- hominy. Their initial attack crumpled Brigadier General Silas Casey's raw Fourth Corps division, but Keyes's other division, under Brigadier General Darius Couch, managed to withstand the pressure at first with assistance from Heintzelman's men. Gradually, however, the rebels forced the Yankees back. McClellan did not cross the river himself to take a firsthand look at the battle but instead directed Sumner's Second Corps over to help. Al- though Old Bull had his troops ready to go even before he got his instruc- tions, the fast-flowing Chickahominy threatened to wash out the bridges Sumner needed to get to Heintzelman and Keyes. When an engineering of- ficer informed Sumner of this, he roared, "Impossible! Sir, I tell you I *can* cross. I am ordered."[31] Sumner sent his men over, and fortunately the weight of all the soldiers and their equipment secured the flooring, so the Second Corps was able to enter the fighting and steady the Union lines. Next day the engagement seesawed back and forth, but the rebels finally drew off and left the battlefield to the Army of the Potomac. The Battle of Fair Oaks—or Seven Pines, as the Confederates styled it—was over. Union losses totaled 5,031, less than the 6,314 casualties suffered by the rebels. Confederate army commander Joseph Johnston was among the wounded, and he was replaced by the officer who would be responsible for many of the Army of the Po- tomac's subsequent woes: Robert E. Lee.

Even though Fair Oaks was a Union victory, it still generated plenty of finger-pointing within the Army of the Potomac. Most officers blamed Silas Casey for the Union setback the first day because he had failed to adequately prepare his inexperienced soldiers for combat. McClellan saw it that way, and he asked Stanton to quietly transfer Casey to a noncombat position. When Stanton was not forthcoming, McClellan took matters into his own hands, assigned Casey to command the supply deport at White House Landing, and gave Casey's division to Brigadier General John Peck. Some officers, however, argued that Casey's sins were symptomatic of Keyes's insufficient and lackluster leadership. Keyes was aware of the criticism, which he attributed to his unpopular Republican party affiliation. Keyes aggressively defended his performance at Fair Oaks by claiming that reports of a Fourth Corps rout were inaccurate and exaggerated. McClellan seemed sympathetic to Keyes's plight, but he signaled his lack of confidence in his lieutenant by placing him under first Heintzelman's, and then Sumner's, orders. Keyes's resentment festered, and within weeks he asked Salmon Chase to use his influence to secure him a new position away from the Army of the Potomac.[32]

Keyes had his woes, but Heintzelman and Sumner were basking in the glow of their finest Civil War hours. Officers throughout the army praised them for repelling the ferocious rebel assault. This included the normally critical McClellan, who commended both generals to the War Department. Indeed, McClellan showed his new confidence in Sumner by putting him in charge of the three corps now south of the Chickahominy. Heintzelman did not like this one bit, and he complained repeatedly about Sumner's interference until McClellan moved his headquarters across the river and assumed command on 12 June.[33]

Heintzelman was no doubt unhappy taking orders from his old rival, but he had other problems that June that further detracted from his Fair Oaks laurels. No sooner had the smoke cleared than he preferred charges against Brigadier General David Birney for disobeying orders. Heintzelman believed that Birney had failed to bring his brigade forward during the recent battle as instructed, so he placed him under arrest until a court martial could meet to determine his fate. Birney, however, insisted that he had followed every directive he had received. Unfortunately for Heintzelman, the Third Corps' officers rallied to Birney's defense. Kearny wrote to Heintzelman to vouch for Birney, and his division's officers all signed a petition supporting him. At the mid-June court martial, the prosecution's own witnesses testified in Birney's favor. Indeed, even Heintzelman admitted that he had no firsthand knowledge that Birney defied his authority. The court cleared Birney of all charges before he even had a chance to call witnesses in his defense. Heintzelman tried to put the best face on the incident and assured Birney that there were no hard feelings, but he did not mean it. As for Birney, he was now free to continue his climb up the chain of command. This otherwise insignificant incident further united the Third Corps' officers behind leaders such as Kearny, thus increasing the potency of the anti-McClellan sentiment that had been boiling since Williamsburg.[34]

Throughout June, McClellan continued his laborious preparations for his final advance on Richmond. Accumulating supplies, building roads and bridges, and deploying troops all took time. McClellan wanted things done right, particularly because he was mistakenly convinced that the Confederate army heavily outnumbered his own. To lessen the odds that he was sure were stacked against him, he continued to badger Lincoln for the balance of McDowell's corps around Fredericksburg. Lincoln would have been happy to send it, especially if doing so would get his sluggish Army of the Potomac commander moving. Unfortunately, Confederate machinations in the Shenandoah Valley made the president reluctant to dispatch the corps, although he did eventually order one more of its divisions to the peninsula. McClellan kept Porter's reinforced Fifth Corps north of the Chickahominy just in case McDowell ever put in an appearance, but he transferred his remaining troops southward. Finally, on 25 June, McClellan moved toward Richmond. He directed Hooker's division to probe rebel defenses around Oak Grove in a day-long engagement that gained little ground. Although McClellan did not know it, it was his last offensive on the peninsula.

The next day the rebels, reinforced by General Thomas "Stonewall" Jackson's forces summoned from the Shenandoah Valley, launched an all-out attack on the Army of the Potomac in what would be called the Seven Days Battle. Lee threw the bulk of his troops at Porter's isolated Fifth Corps north of the Chickahominy. Confronted with the vicious Confederate onslaught that threatened his supply depot at White House Landing, McClellan decided to shift his logistical base to the James River and pull his army back there. Over the next few days, some 100,000 Union soldiers with their supplies and equipment marched through the peninsula swamps and bogs southward toward the James while fighting off increasingly desperate and fierce rebel assaults at Mechanicsville, Gaines's Mill, Savage's Station, Glendale, and Malvern Hill. On 2 July, the Army of the Potomac reached the relative safety of Harrison's Landing, about 30 miles southeast of Richmond.

McClellan could take pride in surviving the gauntlet run from the Chickahominy to the James with his army more or less intact. Indeed, the Army of the Potomac had on the whole fought well, inflicting more than 20,000 casualties on the rebels while suffering 15,850 in return. Among the casualties, however, were some of the army's most promising young officers. Brigadier General John Reynolds, for example, was captured after the Battle of Boatswain's Swamp. Brigadier Generals George Meade and John Sedgwick were wounded at Glendale, and Colonel Gouverneur Warren was injured at Gaines's Mill. Except for Gaines's Mill, the bluecoats repelled every major rebel assault, including the climactic Confederate charge at Malvern Hill. Despite such tactical and statistical successes, however, the fact was that the Seven Days Battle was a Union strategic defeat. Lee not only removed the Army of the Potomac as an immediate threat to Richmond but also threw McClellan onto the defensive. For the first time since the Union army had landed on the peninsula, the rebels had the strategic initiative.

McClellan was among the casualties of the Seven Days Battle, but his wounds were psychological rather than physical. Once he had ordered the Army of the Potomac to withdraw to the James, he had abdicated his tactical responsibilities and left his corps commanders to their own devices. In fact, he had witnessed almost none of the fighting. Despite unclear orders and confused chains of command, they got the job done. Porter performed particularly well in transferring his corps across the Chickahominy and later in repulsing the rebel assault at Malvern Hill. For his part, McClellan spent much of the battle sending increasingly mercurial and strident messages to Washington demanding reinforcements for his supposedly outnumbered army, justifying his actions, and shifting the blame for his defeat—although he did not exactly call it that—onto the Lincoln administration. For example, after the Confederate breakthrough at Gaines's Mill he telegraphed Stanton:

> I have lost this battle because my force was too small. I again repeat that I am not responsible for this and I say it with the earnestness of a General who feels in his heart the loss of every brave man who has been needlessly sacrificed today. I still hope to retrieve our fortunes, but to do this the Gov[ernmen]t must view the matter in the same earnest light that I do—you must send me very large reinforcements, and sent them at once. . . . If I save this Army now I tell you plainly that I owe no thanks to you or any other persons in Washington. You have done your best to sacrifice this Army.[35]

Fortunately for McClellan, neither Lincoln nor Stanton saw the last two insubordinate sentences because the telegraph office operator excised them before forwarding the rest of the message.

Lincoln did his best to reassure the panicky McClellan, but he also made it clear that McClellan's demands for substantial reinforcements were hopelessly unrealistic. As if McClellan's reports were not alarming enough, Lincoln got more bad news from Stanton. The secretary of war had been talking to Brigadier General Randolph Marcy, McClellan's chief of staff and father-in-law. McClellan had sent Marcy to Washington right after the Seven Days Battle to plead his case, and Marcy suggested that the Army of the Potomac might have to surrender. Such reports distressed Lincoln, and he concluded that he had to go to Harrison's Landing for a firsthand look. The president arrived on 8 July and stayed for two days assessing the situation and consulting with McClellan and his subordinates. McClellan presented the president with a letter outlining his current views on the war. In it he argued that Lincoln should refrain from making the war one to end slavery; instead he called for a limited conflict between armies that would not upset the country's social structure. Lincoln read the letter without comment and put it away. As for the military situation, McClellan again stated that he needed heavy reinforcements to resume the offensive, and he tried to force Lincoln's hand by arguing that withdrawing the army from Harrison's Landing would be extremely difficult. Most of his chief subordinates more or less agreed. Sumner, Heintzelman, and Porter said that the army was perfectly safe for now, but they believed that abandoning Harrison's Landing would be militarily unwise and politically disastrous. Although Keyes noted that the army's current sanitary conditions were deteriorating, he felt the army could hold out with reinforcements and leave if necessary. Oddly enough, only McClellan's friend Franklin argued unequivocally in favor of redeploying the army to northern Virginia.[36]

Lincoln scarcely knew what to make of these contradictory and qualified reports. A big part of the problem was his lack of military experience. Ever since Lincoln had relieved McClellan as general in chief, he and Stanton had attempted to run the Union war effort on their own, resulting in considerable confusion. Once he returned from Harrison's Landing, however, Lincoln moved to rectify this. He had consulted with Winfield Scott and Major General John Pope, the new commander of the Army of Virginia. Both men recommended as general in chief Major General Henry Halleck, current head of the Department of the Mississippi. Nicknamed "Old Brains," on paper Halleck looked like a good choice. He had graduated third from his West Point class of 1839, and afterward he had acquired considerable experience in engineering, civil and military administration, legal affairs, and military theory. He resigned from the Army in 1854 and made a fortune in California writing, investing, and practicing law. When the war began he returned east, and in November 1861 he replaced John Frémont as commander of the Department of the Missouri. Most of the Union's victories since then—the capture of Forts Henry and Donelson, the Battle of Shiloh, the seizure of Island Number Ten, the fall of Nashville, and the occupation of Corinth, Mississippi—had occurred in his theater and on his watch, and Halleck was quick to claim much of the credit. With such a good résumé and record of success, he seemed a logical choice for general in chief, so on 11 July Lincoln ordered him to Washington to assume the post.[37]

Unhappily, there was less to Halleck than his record indicated. Although he initially tried to exert his authority over the Union armies, his failures ultimately made him indecisive. In a short time he became reluctant to assume responsibility for major decisions or to initiate any actions that might be traced back to him should things go wrong. Instead, he frustrated subordinate commanders seeking direction with an endless stream of platitudes and clichés. Lincoln himself eventually described Halleck as little more than a first-rate clerk, not the commander of armies he had hoped for when he had summoned him to Washington. The president was adept at accepting men as they were, however, and he quickly realized that Old Brains had his uses. Halleck served as Lincoln's and Stanton's military adviser, explaining to them the army's way of doing things. He also translated their wishes into orders that officers could understand. Finally, he used his considerable bureaucratic and administrative skills to keep flowing the paperwork upon which the Union war effort depended. Unfortunately, Halleck's personality made it difficult for people to appreciate these talents. He was a sardonic, unfriendly, passionless, and suspicious man. He had a habit of facing visitors in profile and looking at them from the corners of his eyes, fishlike, while rubbing his elbows. As one officer later wrote,

> When I beheld his bulging eyes, his flabby cheeks, his slack-twisted figure, and his slow and deliberate movements, and noted his sluggish speech, lacking in point and magnetism, I experienced a distinct feeling of disappointment which from that day never grew less. I could not reconcile myself to the idea that an officer of such negative appearance could ever be a great leader of men. He might be a great lawyer, a great student, a great theorist, but never an active, energetic, and capable commander in the field.[38]

One of Halleck's first major tasks was to decide what to do about the Army of the Potomac. On 25 July, he traveled down to Harrison's Landing to consult with McClellan. McClellan suggested an attack on Petersburg, through which ran most of Richmond's rail connections, but Halleck quashed the idea as too risky. McClellan said he was willing to resume the offensive to the Confederate capital, but he wanted 30,000 more troops first. Halleck responded that there were only 20,000 additional men available, and he recommended that McClellan discuss the matter with his subordinates. Sumner and Heintzelman wanted to stay on the peninsula and fight, but Keyes, Porter, and Franklin favored redeploying the army to Washington to start afresh. McClellan mulled over this divided counsel, and next day he told Halleck he was willing to assault Richmond from the peninsula even with the limited number of reinforcements Old Brains offered. Halleck agreed in principle, but after he returned to Washington he received intelligence that Confederate forces were concentrating against Pope's army in northern Virginia. Clearly Pope needed all the help he could get, so Halleck and Lincoln decided to recall the Army of the Potomac. On 3 August, Halleck ordered McClellan to evacuate his men as rapidly as possible to northern Virginia. The Peninsula campaign was over.[39]

Major General Ambrose Burnside was among the men who attended McClellan's informal war council at Harrison's Landing, but he was not yet a member of the Army of the Potomac. Although the Indiana-born Rhode Islander had graduated from West Point in 1847 in time to go to Mexico, he had seen little action there. He resigned his commission in 1853 to concentrate on building a breech-loading rifle for the Army, but his company went bankrupt when the expected government contract failed to materialize. Fortunately, his good friend George McClellan secured him a job with the Illinois Central Railroad. He was active in the Rhode Island militia, and when the war broke out he led the state's first unit sent to Washington, where he befriended President Lincoln. He fought at Bull Run, and late in 1861 he was appointed commander of an expedition to the North Carolina coast. He performed well there, securing Roanoke Island and much of the North Carolina littoral, which enabled the Union to twist the blockade that much tighter. When McClellan ran into trouble in the Seven Days Battle, Lincoln ordered Burnside to take some of his troops—they were designated the Ninth Corps on 22 July—to reinforce his old friend. It was hard to miss Burnside; he was a manly and picturesque person with an extravagant set of whiskers. Moreover, almost everyone liked him for his amiability, modesty, generosity, and sincerity. Burnside was not without ability, but he himself recognized that there were definite limits to it.

Burnside's presence at Harrison's Landing was no accident. His friendship with both the president and McClellan made him an increasingly rare commodity, so he was the ideal go-between. Burnside undertook several trips to Harrison's Landing on Halleck's behest, and he managed to alleviate temporarily some of the tension between the Lincoln administration and McClellan. Unfortunately, in the long run and through no fault of his own, Burnside contributed to McClellan's ever growing loathing of his superiors. In Burnside, Lincoln and Stanton saw a successful and cooperative commander, so they sounded him out about replacing McClellan, who possessed neither trait. Burnside refused because he believed that his old friend was the most qualified for the post, but word of the offer leaked out. Although

McClellan appreciated Burnside's loyalty, the news did little to sweeten his disposition toward the Lincoln administration.[40]

As the days turned into weeks at Harrison's Landing, the Army of the Potomac fought a continual battle with boredom, malaise, and disease. Illness left many men weak and lethargic, and officers applied for sick leaves in increasing numbers. Bull Sumner still suffered from the fall he had taken the previous winter, and his condition was not improving. Malaria and dysentery sidelined William Franklin, Hiram Berry, Henry Slocum, Baldy Smith, Darius Couch, and hundreds of others. Officers such as Brigadier General Daniel Sickles finagled leaves of absence to escape the squalor. With little to do beyond the usual day-to-day drudgery of soldiering, discontent festered. Stanton tried to raise morale by nominating many officers for promotion, including all the corps commanders, but this instead resulted in infighting over seniority and comparative worthiness.[41]

Not surprisingly, dissatisfaction was especially obvious in the Third Corps. Heintzelman recognized that McClellan had been outgeneraled, but he was horrified by rumors that Lincoln planned to appoint the incompetent Keyes as new Army of the Potomac commander. Although Heintzelman managed to view the overall situation with a dispassion born of years of old army service, the same could not be said of Kearny and Hooker. Both men believed that the Union army could have seized Richmond with proper leadership, but instead McClellan's ineptitude had stranded it in its Harrison's Landing pesthole. Hooker was so disgusted that he talked of resigning his commission. Kearny was even more vitriolic, though he seemed as concerned with his own future as that of the Union. He was convinced that Heintzelman and McClellan were conspiring to deny him the credit he deserved, and in fact he wrote, "I am the first General officer, whose feats in arms have been ignored by all. Cheated of prestige by the falsity of McClellan, not thanked by Congress, passed over in promotions."[42] As it was, Kearny received a promotion to major general on 25 July, but this did little to improve his negative attitude that so many high-ranking Third Corps officers shared. Indeed, David Birney even questioned McClellan's courage.[43]

Third Corps officers such as Kearny and Hooker had been disgruntled ever since the Army of the Potomac landed on the peninsula, but others were also increasingly unhappy with the army's plight. This dissatisfaction infected even McClellan's clique. Fitz John Porter had fought well during the Seven Days Battle, and it was his corps that had repulsed the final ferocious rebel assaults on Malvern Hill. Afterward Porter recommended that the army take advantage of the Confederate bloodletting to resume the offensive, but McClellan turned him down. Comparing his efforts with the results, it was hardly surprising that Porter was depressed. Although Porter retained his faith in McClellan, the same could not be said for Baldy Smith. The Peninsula campaign had so soured him on Little Mac's military talent that he predicted that the Confederates would capture the entire Army of the Potomac, in which case he said he planned to escape down the James River in a skiff.[44]

Smith was a chronic malcontent, but he might have taken some comfort knowing that McClellan was as demoralized as anyone by the Army of the Potomac's plight. Of course, McClellan had no intention of accepting any responsibility for the current unhappy military situation. As far as he was concerned, he was a victim of a Lincoln administration plot to discredit him by deliberately depriving him of sufficient manpower to fulfill his mission. Halleck might not be a conscious member of the conspiracy, but McClellan interpreted Halleck's elevation to general in chief as the first step in removing McClellan as Army of the Potomac commander. Indeed, rumors that Lincoln and Stanton had offered Burnside the position stoked his fears. McClellan not only disagreed with Halleck's strategic thinking, but he also had little respect for Old Brains as an individual. Years later he wrote, "Of all men whom I have encountered in high position Halleck was the most hopelessly stupid. It was more difficult to get an idea through his head than can be conceived by any one who never made the attempt. I do not think he ever had a correct military idea from beginning to end."[45] Nor had McClellan's opinion of Lincoln and Stanton improved since he left for the peninsula. McClellan viewed Lincoln with a kind of bemused and exasperated contempt, but by now he absolutely detested the secretary of war. With venom that would have done even Kearny proud, McClellan expressed his feelings to his wife:

> So you want to know how I feel about Stanton, and what I think of him now? I will tell you with the most perfect frankness. I think that he is the most unmitigated scoundrel I ever knew, heard or read of; I think that (and I do not wish to be irreverent) had he lived in the time of the Savior, Judas Iscariot would have remained a respected member of the fraternity of the Apostles, and that the magnificent treachery and rascality of EM Stanton would have caused Judas to have raised his arms in holy horror and unaffected wonder.[46]

As the weeks at Harrison's Landing dragged on and the results of the Peninsula campaign sank in, McClellan also began to cast a jaundiced eye at some of his closest subordinates. This did not include Porter, in whom McClellan continued to have unparalleled confidence for his performance from Yorktown to Malvern Hill. In fact, he warmly recommended Porter's promotion to Stanton, noting,

The energy, ability, gallantry and good conduct displayed throughout the eventful period of this campaign through which we have just passed by Brig. Genl. F. J. Porter, desires the marked notice of the Executive and the nation. From the very commencement his unwearied assiduity in his various duties, his intelligent and efficacious assistance which he has rendered me under all circumstances, his skilful management of his command on the march, in the siege and on the field of battle and his chivalric and soldierly bearing under fire, have combined to render him conspicuous among the many faithful and gallant spirits in this Army.[47]

On the other hand, McClellan was increasingly unhappy with William Franklin. He and Franklin had publicly disagreed on whether or not the army should return to northern Virginia, but Little Mac seemed more disturbed by Franklin's lassitude. He complained to his wife,

Franklin ought to have been off [to northern Virginia] nearly by this time, but he and Smith have so little energy that I fear they will be very slow about it. They have disappointed me terribly. I do not doubt Franklin's loyalty now, but his efficiency is very little. I am very sorry it has turned out so. The main, perhaps the only cause is that he has been and still is sick—and one ought not to judge harshly of a person in that condition.[48]

As for Smith, McClellan dismissed him by stating, "Smith WF went off today. I don't think he intends on returning, and don't think he was as sick as many who remained. He had not even the decency to bid me good bye after all I have done for him! Such ingratitude. I no longer expect such a feeling. I don't care to have him come back."[49] Oddly enough, McClellan made no attempt to blame his woes on those in the army who were not beholden to him for their commands. Sumner, Heintzelman, and Keyes all escaped serious censure, and McClellan even continued to praise Hooker.[50]

North to Maryland

By the end of the summer, the Union war effort had sputtered to a discouraging halt. Although Union forces had seized the strategic railroad junction at Corinth, Mississippi, in late May, logistical difficulties, Halleck's dispersal of Union soldiers, coordination problems, and rebel resistance had stymied Union operations thereafter. Rebel General Braxton Bragg had taken advantage of Union quiescence to shift the bulk of his forces to eastern Tennessee for an invasion of Kentucky, compelling Don Carlos Buell's Army of the Cumberland to backtrack in pursuit. To the west, additional Confederate forces had concentrated against Ulysses Grant's soldiers in northern Mississippi. After months on the strategic defensive, the rebels had everywhere seized the initiative.

While McClellan and the Army of the Potomac huddled in their Harrison's Landing refuge, events were rapidly unfolding in northern Virginia. On 26 June, Lincoln ordered Major General John Pope to take charge of the hodgepodge of Union forces scattered from Fredericksburg to the Shenandoah Valley. Pope was a forty-year-old West Pointer who had spent most of his prewar career as an engineer. After the conflict began, he was appointed a brigadier general and assigned to Missouri. He commanded the expedition that seized strategically vital Island Number Ten on the Mississippi River on 8 April, and he later spearheaded Halleck's drive on Corinth in northern Mississippi. Chase and Stanton lobbied Lincoln to bring Pope east as a counterweight to McClellan, and the president, who by now looked kindly upon any officer who showed some aggressiveness, agreed. Unfortunately, although Pope was an energetic man, he was also a vain, pompous, and arrogant blowhard. He quickly alienated many of his troops by comparing them unfavorably to those he had led out west, and his hard war pronouncements angered officers who still wanted a limited conflict with the rebels. His force, eventually dubbed the Army of Virginia, consisted of three corps under Major Generals McDowell, Franz Sigel, and Nathaniel Banks.[51]

Lee and his rebel army had not been idle since the Seven Days Battle. The shrewd Confederate general surmised the Union plan to ship the Army of the Potomac back to northern Virginia soon after Halleck issued the orders to do so. Lee decided to take advantage of the divided Union forces by striking at Pope before McClellan could reinforce him. Pope had deployed his army along the Rappahannock River, but Lee simply went around the Union right flank and plunged northward, severing the Army of Virginia's communications and supply lines. Pope backpedaled in an effort to run the rampaging rebels to the ground and unite with McClellan's troops, but in the process he rapidly exhausted and disoriented his entire army. Rebel and Union soldiers clashed in a series of disjointed engagements, most prominently at Groveton on 28 August, where Brigadier General John Gibbon's inexperienced brigade fought Stonewall Jackson's elite Confederate soldiers to a bloody standstill.

While Pope's tired and confused soldiers trudged back and forth along the dusty north Virginia roads in search of Lee, McClellan concentrated on evacuating his army from the peninsula. Transporting nearly 100,000 soldiers and all their weapons and equipment on such short notice was logistically difficult and time consuming, but McClellan was in his element. Even so, Halleck complained that he was not moving fast enough. Burnside's Ninth Corps reached Aquia in early August and moved to Falmouth. Burnside remained there while two divisions under Brigadier General Jesse Reno marched on 13 August to reinforce Pope. Porter's Fifth Corps arrived at Aquia on 22 August, the same day Heintzelman's Third Corps docked at Alexandria. Five days later Sumner's Second Corps disembarked at Aquia, and the last of Franklin's Sixth Corps landed at Alexandria on 29 August. As for McClellan, he came ashore at Aquia on 24 August and moved his headquarters to Alexandria two days later.[52]

Erasmus Keyes was not among the tens of thousands of officers and men plodding down the gangways at Aquia and Alexandria. Although McClellan later praised Keyes for his performance on the peninsula, he seized the opportunity presented by the Army of the Potomac's redeployment to rid himself of his Fourth Corps' commander. On 20 August, McClellan ordered Keyes and much of his corps to remain on the peninsula at Yorktown. To add insult to injury, Little Mac also stripped Keyes of Couch's division and sent it to Alexandria on 30 August, leaving Keyes with a reduced force. McClellan informed Keyes that garrisoning the peninsula was of vital importance, but Keyes recognized the demotion for what it was. Even before McClellan issued these new orders, Keyes had been lobbying his political friends to secure him a transfer, and now he redoubled his efforts. He did not get along with Halleck, so on 25 August he wrote directly to the president to ask for a new command commensurate with his rank. Keyes complained that it was a waste of resources to leave the remainder of his corps to occupy what was now a military backwater. He assured Lincoln of his political support, and he defended his conduct during the campaign. Unfortunately for Keyes, Lincoln apparently saw no reason to help him, so Keyes remained on the peninsula in Major General John Dix's Department of Virginia with his depleted corps. The following year he quarreled with Dix and was assigned to a retirement board. Keyes resigned his commission in May 1864, moved to California, and prospered as a businessman until his death in 1895. As for his Fourth Corps, the War Department disbanded it in August 1863.[53]

Keyes could have taken some comfort in the knowledge that Halleck was doing to McClellan what McClellan was doing to him. Halleck had promised McClellan that Pope's forces would fall under his command once the Army of the Potomac and the Army of Virginia united, but it was not turning out that way. Instead, Halleck sent the Army of the Potomac's units off to join Pope as soon as they disembarked, leaving McClellan to cool his heels at Alexandria. Halleck tried to coordinate events by telegraph from his War Department office, but by the end of August it was clear that no one in the Union Army had an accurate picture of the increasingly fluid military situation in northern Virginia. It was, however, obvious to McClellan that although the Lincoln administration had not removed him as commander of the Army of the Potomac, it had instead removed the Army of the Potomac from him and given it to Pope. Small wonder that he wrote his wife,

> I feel too blue and disgusted to write any more now, so I will smoke a cigar and try to get in better humor. They have taken *all* my men from me—I have even sent off all my personal escort and camp guard and am here with a few orderlies and the aides. I have been listening to the distant sound of a great battle in the distance—my men engaged in it and I away! I never felt worse in my life.[54]

This was all the more galling for McClellan because he had so little respect for Pope as a soldier and a man. To McClellan, character was fate, so he believed that Pope's defeat was inevitable. As early as 10 August he wrote his wife, "I have a strong idea that Pope will be thrashed during the coming week—and very badly whipped he will be and ought to be—such a villain as he is ought to bring defeat upon any cause that employs him."[55] McClellan was not the only officer in the Army of the Potomac who felt this way. Indeed, anger toward Pope included both McClellan's enemies and friends. After a few short days in the field, Third Corps officers such as Heintzelman, Hooker, and Kearny were shaking their heads in disbelief at Pope's bungling. Porter felt much the same way, and he complained about Pope to Burnside—who by now had been ordered to Washington—in a series of telegrams. On 27 August, he wired Burnside, "I believe they [Confederates] have a contempt for this Army of Virginia. I wish myself away from it, with all our old Army of the Potomac, and so do our companions."[56] Unfortunately for Porter, he did not realize that Burnside was forwarding these messages to the War Department. Porter incorporated these digs at Pope in his official military dispatches, and Burnside did not think that he had the right to censor or stop them. As a result, Lincoln read them with growing concern. He asked McClellan to telegraph Porter and urge him to cooperate with Pope, and McClellan did so. Porter responded by pledging to do his utmost for the common cause, but his incautious statements ultimately did his career irreparable harm.[57]

On 29 August, Pope finally came to grips with Lee's army at Manassas in the Second Battle of Bull Run. Throughout the day Pope's army—McDowell's, Heintzelman's, Reno's, and Sigel's commands—bravely assaulted the Confederate lines without success. The Fifth Corps arrived in the morning to reinforce the Army of Virginia, and Pope directed Porter to move to the

Union left flank and attack the rebels from that direction. Porter, however, concluded correctly that there were large numbers of Confederates in his way and that it was too late in the day to act, so he did not carry out the order. Pope redeployed Porter's corps and planned to resume the offensive the next day. Unfortunately, on 30 August, all those rebels whose presence Porter suspected struck the exposed Union left flank and drove Pope's army from the field toward Washington. As the Yankees scurried northward, a disgusted Kearny fell in with John Gibbon, whose brigade was helping to cover the Union retreat. "I suppose you appreciate the condition of affairs here, sir?" Kearny roared. "It's another Bull Run, sir, it's another Bull Run!" When Gibbon responded that he hoped the situation was not that bad, Kearny exclaimed, "Perhaps not. Reno is keeping up the fight. He is not stampeded. I am not stampeded, you are not stampeded. That is about all, sir, my God that's about all!"[58]

Unfortunately, Kearny did not live to see the Union Army rebound from its latest defeat. On 1 September, Lee attempted to head off the retreating bluecoats, but Pope dispatched Kearny's division and a division in the Ninth Corps under Brigadier General Isaac Stevens to intercept them. That evening, Kearny's and Stevens's men clashed with the rebels in a torrential thunderstorm at the Battle of Chantilly. During the engagement Kearny mistakenly galloped toward the Confederate lines and was killed as he tried to get away. "Poor Kearny," said a rebel general later as he gazed at the muddy one-armed corpse. "He deserved a better death than that."[59] Stevens also went down, shot in the head. Even so, the Union soldiers succeeded in stopping the rebels before breaking contact to rejoin their comrades for the dreary trek back to Washington. Pope's campaign cost the Union 14,500 casualties, substantially more than the 9,200 men the Confederates lost.

Back in Washington, these dismal events in northern Virginia galvanized McClellan's enemies in Lincoln's cabinet. Stanton was convinced that McClellan's failure to forward troops to Pope fast enough to stave off the Confederate onslaught indicated downright treason. Ever the good lawyer, the secretary of war began to build a case against McClellan by asking Halleck for data that McClellan had not acted promptly enough in getting the Army of the Potomac back from the peninsula. Halleck responded next day—30 August—with a letter complaining that McClellan had not obeyed his orders with sufficient alacrity. With this evidence in hand, Stanton wrote a memo to Lincoln calling for McClellan's dismissal. To increase its potency, he tried to get all the members of the cabinet to endorse it. Secretary of the Treasury Chase by now believed that McClellan should be shot— he did not say with or without a fair trial—so he came on board quickly enough, as did Secretary of the Interior Caleb Smith. The attorney general,

Edward Bates, had already gone on record in favor of McClellan's removal, so he signed too. Secretary of State William Seward was out of town—a bit too conveniently, thought some—and Stanton and Chase did not want to approach Postmaster General Montgomery Blair until they talked with Secretary of the Navy Welles first. Welles agreed that McClellan should be fired for military incompetence and was more than willing to say as much to Lincoln, but he did not think that the cabinet should try to dictate policy to the president. Stanton put away his memo, but the hostility toward McClellan remained. On 2 September, the cabinet met at the White House. Chatting among themselves while waiting for Lincoln to arrive, there was a clear consensus among those cabinet members present that McClellan had to go.[60]

Lincoln entered the room soon after, and he announced that on Halleck's advice he had placed McClellan in command of Washington's defenses. Although rumors to that effect had been swirling around for the past few days, the cabinet was shocked. Chase exclaimed that McClellan was untrustworthy, so putting him in charge of the capital was tantamount to surrendering the city to the rebels. Besides, he continued, Hooker or Sumner or Burnside was just as qualified to carry out the assignment. Everyone else agreed except for Bates, who kept quiet. Lincoln was clearly distressed, but he defended his decision. Thousands of defeated and disorganized Union soldiers were retreating toward Washington, and someone had to sort, arrange, and reinvigorate them. Whatever his faults, McClellan was a first-rate organizer and an inspiration to most officers and men. As Lincoln later put it, "We must use what tools we have. If he can't fight himself, he excels at making others ready to fight."[61] Lincoln admitted that he had serious doubts about McClellan. He too believed that McClellan wanted Pope to fail, but he attributed this to the general's deep-rooted jealousy, envy, and spite, not to treason. He acknowledged that there were other officers available for the task, but none except for perhaps Burnside possessed the skills now needed. In fact, Halleck had approached Burnside again about assuming command, but he had again demurred. Lincoln's logic was persuasive, but no one was happy about it. Montgomery Blair best summed up the problem at a subsequent cabinet meeting by commenting, "McClellan is not the man, but he is the best among the major generals. The War Department must hunt up greater men, better military minds, than these to carry on successful war."[62]

Blair had a good point, but Lincoln's position that McClellan could restore the defeated Union forces proved correct. McClellan had been badgering Lincoln and Halleck for days to clarify his status, and on 31 August Old Brains ordered him to Washington. The next day McClellan arrived to receive instructions from Halleck and Lincoln to take command of the capital's defenses, but not of the troops still in the field. McClellan returned to his headquarters and contemplated refusing unless Lincoln fired Stanton and Halleck first, but Burnside argued persuasively that he had no right to make such demands on the government. On 2 September, McClellan rode out to greet the retreating soldiers. He was conspicuous in his yellow sash, and he exulted to a fellow officer, "Well, General, I am in command again!"[63] The results were electric. As word of McClellan's reinstatement spread up and down the long dusty blue columns, the troops cheered and shouted with joy. Indeed, McClellan's mere appearance went far toward restoring the army. One officer reported, "That night and the next day we marched toward Washington and received news that General McClellan had been put in command again. The effect was like magic on the whole army. Men who had been straggling along, blue and dispirited, fell into place in their ranks with new vigor and new life, and with renewed determination and courage."[64] Even officers such as Baldy Smith, who doubted McClellan's abilities, welcomed his return because he was so preferable to the beaten and despised Pope.[65]

Despite his organizational and administrative skills, McClellan had his hands full sorting out and squaring away all the soldiers streaming back toward the capital. Untangling the confused Union command structure presented an equally challenging problem. Pope's status in particular was now unclear. McClellan's hatred for Pope had not abated, and in fact he blamed him for the Second Bull Run debacle that had killed or wounded so many bluecoats for no good reason. The officer corps as a whole felt the same way. Pope himself was thoroughly disgruntled because McClellan had taken his Army of Virginia and scattered it all around Washington without consulting him, so he had no idea where his soldiers were. Moreover, he believed that McClellan and his clique—specifically, Porter, Franklin, and Brigadier General Charles Griffin, an outspoken Fifth Corps brigade commander—had intentionally obstructed and denigrated his operations in northern Virginia, and he said as much to Lincoln and the cabinet. On 5 September, Pope sent to Halleck for orders. Old Brains informed him that the Lincoln administration was combining the Army of Virginia and the Army of the Potomac under McClellan's command. Halleck also noted that Pope's poor relationship with McClellan made it impossible for Pope to serve in the Army of the Potomac, so he directed him to report to Stanton for new orders. Pope did so, and within a month he found himself stationed in St. Paul, Minnesota, riding herd over Sioux Indians as commander of the Department of the Northwest. He stayed in the army after the war and oversaw various departments in the Reconstruction South and out west until he retired in 1886. He mellowed as he aged, which enabled him to write one of the war's more thoughtful memoirs; he died in 1892.[66]

Lincoln's decision to sacrifice Pope was based on hard military realities. Lincoln believed that Pope had done his best under adverse circumstances, and he was inclined to attribute his defeat to professional rivalries and jealousies among McClellan and his clique. Most of his cabinet agreed, except for Montgomery Blair, who dismissed Pope as a braggart and liar. Even so, Pope was expendable, and McClellan currently was not, so Pope had to go. The president did not, however, intend to let the bad behavior he perceived among some officers go unpunished. On 5 September, he relieved Porter, Franklin, and Griffin of their commands pending an investigation into their conduct during the Second Bull Run campaign.[67]

Pope was not the only high-ranking officer who suffered from his association with the unfortunate Army of Virginia. Like Pope, Irvin McDowell also found his career on the chopping block. He too possessed a defeat-laden record and McClellan's enmity. Moreover, for some reason soldiers believed that he was disloyal, and they muttered loudly whenever he rode by wearing his distinctive straw hat. Halleck and Lincoln recognized that McDowell's usefulness as a field commander was over, but the president hesitated to fire him outright, probably because he believed that McDowell's misfortunes were not of his own making. On 5 September—the same day he pulled the rug out from under Pope—Lincoln asked Chase to suggest to McDowell that he request a court of inquiry to clear his name. McDowell hesitated because no one had leveled any formal charges against him that required adjudication, but he changed his mind after a night's sleep. A senator had recently received a letter from a mortally wounded cavalry officer who claimed that he was a victim of McDowell's treachery, so McDowell used this incident to justify his demand for a formal hearing. He turned his letter over to Chase, who took it to Lincoln. Lincoln asked to see it, and Chase, thinking the president wanted to make a copy, gave it to him. Later that day Chase discovered to his consternation that Lincoln had used McDowell's request as a pretext to accept his resignation from command. When McDowell learned the news he complained plaintively to Chase, "I did not ask to be relieved—I only asked for a court," but it was too late.[68] In February 1863, a court of inquiry exonerated McDowell of any suspicion of treason, but this vindication came too late to salvage his military reputation, a situation for which he blamed McClellan. McDowell spent the remainder of the war commanding various backwater departments, and after the conflict ended he remained in the army. He retired in 1882 and died three years later.[69]

While Pope and McDowell were watching their careers grind to a halt, the war entered a new phase. On 4 September, Lee's Confederate Army of Northern Virginia crossed the Potomac River about 40 miles upstream from Washington and invaded Maryland. By then McClellan had whipped the defeated Union army back into shape, vindicating Lincoln's confidence in his organizational abilities. On 7 September, McClellan left the capital to lead the Army of the Potomac northwestward into Maryland to intercept Lee. He later claimed that he did so without orders from the confused Lincoln administration. In fact, McClellan said that he believed that if he had lost the upcoming battle with Lee, the Lincoln administration would have court-martialed him and sentenced him to death for assuming authority without orders. Halleck, however, afterward testified that he and Lincoln had spent several days discussing who should command the Army of the Potomac in the field. On the morning of 6 September, they visited McClellan at his house, and there Lincoln verbally directed McClellan to take charge of the army and pursue Lee.[70]

As the Army of the Potomac lurched into motion, McClellan got busy filling the various holes in its command structure. Doing so, however, required Halleck's and Lincoln's approval. One of McClellan's first priorities was to return Porter and Franklin to their corps. They were his two most loyal subordinates, and although McClellan had had his doubts about Franklin, he still wanted both men by his side when he squared off against Lee for the battle that might well determine the war's outcome. On 6 September, McClellan appealed to Lincoln and Halleck to reinstate the two men, as well as Charles Griffin. He justified his request on the basis of military urgency and necessity, and he noted that Stanton promised him that the administration would cooperate on such personnel matters. Neither Lincoln nor Halleck wanted to interfere with McClellan's efforts at this critical time, so they agreed, and Porter, Franklin, and Griffin got their commands back.[71]

Now that Lincoln had relieved McDowell, supposedly at his own request, the First Corps needed a new leader. Halleck wished to appoint Jesse Reno, even though numerous other officers in the army had seniority, but McClellan balked because he had other plans for him. Instead, McClellan urged Joe Hooker for the post. It was an obvious choice. Although Hooker was not elevated to major general until late July, the Lincoln administration had backdated his appointment to the Battle of Williamsburg so that he was now senior to all of the Army of the Potomac's other division commanders. There was more to it than that, however. Hooker had emerged from the Peninsula campaign with a reputation as the Army of the Potomac's best combat general. People in and out of the Army admired him, and he had generated considerable press that put him in the public eye. Indeed, he had come to Chase's attention, and the treasury secretary was already touting him as a possible McClellan replacement. McClellan had great confidence in Hooker—the feeling was not, however, mutual, although Hooker granted that McClellan was preferable to Pope—and believed that Fighting Joe had the experience and ability to undo the damage that McDowell had probably inflicted on the First Corps during its tenure in northern Virginia. Lincoln was well aware of Hooker's accomplishments and had slated him to take over the Fifth Corps, but this was no longer necessary now that McClellan had gotten Porter reinstated. On 6 September, McClellan asked Lincoln to assign Hooker to the First Corps, and Lincoln agreed the same day. Hooker saw the assignment as no more than his due, and he eagerly hopped onto an ambulance and rode over to his new command.[72]

There were other gaps. Major General Nathaniel Banks was one of Lincoln's political generals, and he led a corps under Pope. Banks was an ambitious, pleasant, and superficially intelligent man. Over the course of his long career he had served Massachusetts as a state legislator, congressman, speaker of the House of Representatives, and governor. During his political ascent he had gravitated from the Democratic party to the new Republican party, and he counted Chase and Seward among his many friends and supporters. In short, Banks had considerable political clout that Lincoln had to respect. Unfortunately, Banks's generalship did not match his aspirations. The rebels had run rings around him in the Shenandoah Valley earlier in the year, and he had lost the hard-fought Battle of Cedar Mountain on 9 August. Neither Halleck nor McClellan thought much of Banks, so on 7 September McClellan assigned him to command the Washington defenses. This was not exactly a demotion—in fact, the job suited Banks's talents—but it removed him from any role in the upcoming showdown with Lee's army.[73]

McClellan had planned to replace Banks with Major General John Sedgwick, a Second Corps divisional commander in whom Little Mac had considerable confidence. Sedgwick, however, apparently declined the offer, so McClellan instead turned to newly arrived Major General Joseph Mansfield. Mansfield was an old Army fixture. He had graduated from West Point in 1822 and had spent most of the following years constructing coastal fortifications in the south Atlantic states. He had fought with distinction in the Mexican War at Fort Brown, Monterrey, and Buena Vista, and later he had served as the army's inspector general. After the war began he found himself in the Department of Virginia, and he participated in the bloodless occupations of Norfolk and Suffolk. In early September, he asked Halleck for a more active assignment, and Old Brains obliged by sending him to the Army of the Potomac. Once there, McClellan had to find a slot for him worthy of his rank, so he gave him the newly available Twelfth Corps. Under normal circumstances Mansfield was a fussy, quarrelsome, and fault-finding man with limited intellect. In combat, however, he was famous for his fire and passion. He stopped in Washington on his way to join the Army of the

Potomac and visited his old neighbor Gideon Welles, and when they parted he noted prophetically that they might not meet again.[74]

The Army of the Potomac advanced into western Maryland in search of Lee along three roughly parallel roads. To accommodate this, McClellan divided his army into three wings. He placed Burnside in command of the Ninth and Hooker's First Corps, Sumner in charge of the Second and Twelfth Corps, and Franklin at the head of his Sixth Corps and Darius Couch's orphaned Fourth Corps division. Oddly enough, although Sumner retained control of his own corps, McClellan assigned newly promoted Major General Jesse Reno to take over the Ninth Corps while Burnside assumed his larger duties. There were several Army of the Potomac officers senior to Reno—Couch, Israel Richardson, Henry Slocum, George Morrell, Baldy Smith, and John Sedgwick—but McClellan opted for Reno, who also had Halleck's support. Although Lincoln had originally slated Reno for the First Corps, McClellan wanted to keep him in the Ninth because he had been running the unit on and off ever since it landed at Aquia in early August after its adventures along the North Carolina coast. Reno had graduated from West Point in 1846 and had then seen action with Scott in Mexico. In the 1850s he had taught at the Military Academy, served on various military boards, conducted surveys, and overseen arsenals. He had led a division capably on Burnside's North Carolina expedition, and his conduct during Pope's mismanaged campaign had won even Kearny's praise. Although he was quick-tempered, everyone liked Reno for his cheerfulness, confidence, energy, and frankness. He counted not only McClellan and Burnside among his admirers, but also John Pope.[75]

Heintzelman and Porter were conspicuously absent from McClellan's initial calculations as the Union army advanced into Maryland. Lincoln and Halleck were as usual hypersensitive to Washington's safety, so they kept Heintzelman's Third, Porter's Fifth, and Franz Sigel's newly numbered Eleventh Corps behind to defend the capital. All three units had suffered heavily in their recent operations in northern Virginia, so resting them would give them time to recover. On 9 September, Lincoln and Halleck put Heintzelman in charge of Washington's defenses south of the Potomac River. McClellan protested his appointment, but in all likelihood he did so more because he feared it might put the Third Corps beyond his reach than because he wanted Heintzelman under his command. McClellan as usual believed that he was heavily outnumbered, so he sought every soldier he could get his hands on, including those in Washington. Lincoln refused to strip the capital bare, but on 11 September he agreed to send Porter's Fifth Corps. Heintzelman remained behind with his Third and Sigel's Eleventh Corps, and although he did not know it, his days with the Army of the Potomac were over.[76]

Lee expected that it would take some time for Union forces to recover from the drubbing he had inflicted on them on the peninsula and at Second Bull Run, so he decided to divide his army to encircle and gobble up the Union garrison at Harper's Ferry before he continued his offensive northward. On 13 September, however, two Yankee sergeants resting near Frederick, Maryland, stumbled upon Lee's carelessly lost orders for the Harper's Ferry operation and the invasion of Maryland, and soon they were in McClellan's hands. McClellan now knew where the scattered rebel forces were and where they were going. Indeed, Union troops were now closer to the various pieces of Lee's dispersed army than the rebels were to each other. McClellan had a once-in-a-lifetime opportunity to destroy the Confederate Army of Northern Virginia in detail if he moved fast enough. Unfortunately, celerity was not an integral part of McClellan's make-up, and he did not demand it of his subordinates. On 14 September, the Army of the Potomac marched westward and ran into rebels defending the South Mountain passes in an effort to buy Lee time to reunite his army. To the south, Franklin managed to force Crampton's Gap with Major General Henry Slocum's division, but he did not follow up on his victory quickly enough to prevent the surrender of the 12,000-man Harper's Ferry garrison the next day. In the north, Burnside's wing assaulted Confederate positions at Turner's Gap and pried the rebels out after a grueling battle up the mountainsides that required elements from both the First and Ninth Corps. About 2,300 bluecoats fell in the day's fighting, compared to 2,700 Confederate casualties. Regrettably, Jesse Reno was among the dead. He was mortally wounded in the evening by a stray bullet as he rode along the front line, and he died that night.[77] Despite these losses, the Army of the Potomac had won its first offensive victory since Williamsburg, and next day thousands of Union troops poured across South Mountain and approached Sharpsburg on the Potomac River. Lee drew up his army there behind Antietam Creek, but McClellan did not attack that day or the next, even though he heavily outnumbered the still-gathering rebels. Instead, he spent 16 September reconnoitering, positioning his troops, and preparing for battle.

McClellan had originally planned to deploy Burnside's wing—the First and Ninth Corps—to the southern, or left, end of the Union line. Hooker, however, did not like the idea of going into battle under Burnside's command, so he campaigned for a more independent role. McClellan obliged him by moving his corps to the opposite end of the line, above Sumner's wing. To complicate matters further, McClellan also put the Twelfth Corps under Hooker's general direction, so it was unclear whether the newly arrived Mansfield was subject to Hooker's or Sumner's orders.[78]

Hooker's departure left Burnside with only the Ninth Corps, now led by right of seniority by divisional commander Brigadier General Jacob Cox.

Cox was an Ohio lawyer, politician, abolitionist, and one of the founders of the state's Republican party. He had close political connections with the Lincoln administration that had helped secure him a general's commission. He had not impressed McClellan at all when they had served together in western Virginia the previous year, but the truth was that Cox was a competent, precise, and inquisitive man with a good understanding of people and politics. He would become one of the Union's most able political generals, with a long distinguished combat record in just about every theater to prove it. Halleck had transferred Cox's so-called Kanawha division eastward to the Ninth Corps when McClellan ran into trouble on the peninsula, and Cox successfully lobbied Old Brains for permission to accompany it. He and his men participated in the fight at Turner's Gap, and his performance there and elsewhere earned McClellan's respect. McClellan even welcomed Cox into his inner circle, despite their very different political views. Cox was nothing if not practical, and after Hooker departed he suggested that Burnside resume direct command of the Ninth Corps. Cox argued that he himself lacked sufficient staff for the responsibility, but Burnside stood on his pride and insisted that Cox retain his position. As a result, the Ninth Corps went into battle with two commanders, neither of whom was certain of his authority with respect to the other.[79]

McClellan based his decision to split Burnside's wing at least in part on his estimation of the men involved. He had great confidence in Hooker—the feeling, of course, was not mutual—so it made sense to him to give Fighting Joe a role commensurate to his star billing. On the other hand, McClellan had increasing doubts about Burnside. This was the first time in the war that the two old friends had worked together, and as far as McClellan was concerned, Burnside simply was not measuring up. During the advance into Maryland, McClellan complained about Burnside's sluggishness, and in fact McClellan informed Burnside of his feelings in a written reprimand. He also grumbled that it took Burnside too long to get into position along the Antietam. Perhaps McClellan was frustrated with Burnside's performance, but there was probably more to it than that. It was by now common knowledge that the Lincoln administration had offered the Army of the Potomac to Burnside at least once, and it would have been natural for McClellan to resent and envy his designated successor. Burnside and McClellan got along well enough when they were together, but McClellan's jealousy bubbled to the surface when the two men were not in personal contact. For his part, although Burnside continued to speak favorably of McClellan, he complained about some of those surrounding and influencing his boss.[80]

The Battle of Antietam, fought on 17 September, was the bloodiest single-day engagement in U.S. military history. About 12,400 Yankees and

10,700 rebels were killed, wounded, or missing by sundown. McClellan's plan called for Hooker's First and Mansfield's Twelfth Corps, supported by Sumner's Second Corps, to assault the rebel left flank, followed by an attack by Burnside and Cox's Ninth Corps at the other end of the line. McClellan hoped to use his remaining forces—elements of Porter's Fifth and Franklin's Sixth Corps—to exploit any gains developed and deliver the coup de grâce. Unfortunately, instead of a closely synchronized sequence of knee-buckling assaults, McClellan's offensive degenerated into a series of uncoordinated and unsupported lunges that gave the outnumbered rebels time to shuttle their limited reserves from one threatened point to another.

At dawn Hooker launched a furious assault with his First Corps through the soon-to-be-infamous Cornfield toward the Dunker Church. The battle seesawed back and forth with terrible ferocity until a Confederate counterattack drove the bluecoats out of the Cornfield for good. Hooker went down with a bullet in the foot, but before he left the field he recommended to McClellan that Brigadier General George Meade, a First Corps division commander, take his place. Meade had led a Fifth Corps brigade on the peninsula and had been seriously wounded at Glendale, but he had recovered soon enough to fight at Second Bull Run. He had impressed almost everyone, including Porter, McDowell, and McClellan, with his combat skills. McClellan confirmed Hooker's request, but by the time he sent word back, Brigadier General James Ricketts, the First Corps' senior division commander, had already taken charge of the unit. Fortunately, Ricketts respected Meade as much as everyone else, so he gave way to let Meade sort out the scattered remnants of the First Corps.[81]

Before Hooker was wounded, he ordered up Mansfield to help his beleaguered First Corps. Mansfield was his usual fussy and nervous self as he led his Twelfth Corps forward, but he had little opportunity to demonstrate the passion for combat for which he was famous because he was mortally wounded just as his men entered the battle. Authority devolved on Brigadier General Alpheus Williams, the senior division commander. Williams was a well-traveled Yale graduate, lawyer, politician, and newspaper owner from Michigan who had seen service in the Mexican War. He had fought at Cedar Mountain, and he went on to become one of the war's best divisional leaders. Williams drove the two Twelfth Corps divisions forward through the Cornfield toward the Dunker Church, but he too was halted by a Confederate counterattack. The Twelfth Corps managed to hold onto some of the ground it gained, but it could do no more than that. Although some in the Army of the Potomac saw the First and Twelfth Corps as second-rate outfits because they had not accompanied McClellan to the peninsula, both units fought very well that day.

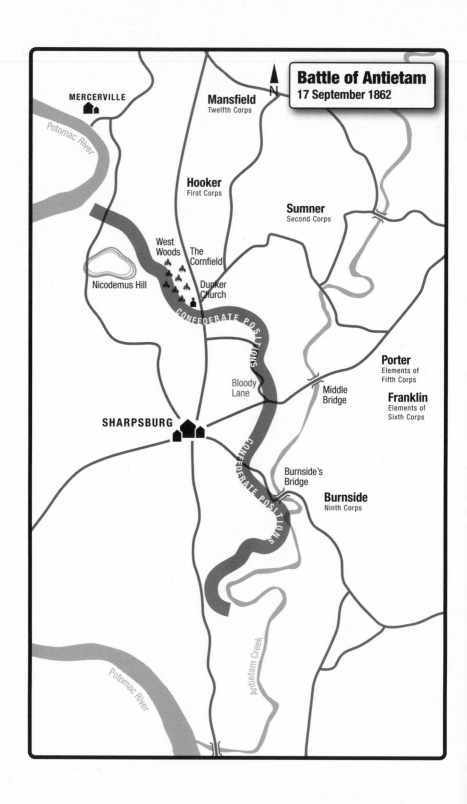

Sometime after 7:30 A.M., McClellan directed Sumner to join the offensive with his Second Corps. Sumner rode out front at the head of Sedgwick's division, so he quickly lost contact with his other two divisions. Sedgwick's division marched in compact formation through the backwash of the First and Twelfth Corps, and it looked to Sumner as if both units had all but gone out of existence. Near the West Woods, the Confederates ambushed Sedgwick's division from three sides, shooting down nearly half of its soldiers in scarcely fifteen minutes. Sumner was slightly wounded, and Sedgwick sustained injuries severe enough to put him out of action for two months. The bluecoats scurried away as fast as they could and took no further part in the battle. Alpheus Williams watched the bloodletting and later noted that Sedgwick's men "seemed to melt into the earth—so rapidly and mysteriously did they disappear from sight."[82]

To the south, Sumner's other two divisions also engaged the enemy. Brigadier General William French's division assaulted rebels positioned behind a sunken road that would become known as Bloody Lane. The Confederates repulsed the attack, but they were not as fortunate when Major General Israel Richardson brought up his division. Richardson was a West Point graduate who had seen service against the Seminoles in Florida and in Mexico before leaving the army in 1855 to become a Michigan farmer. He was a slovenly, absentminded, and unsocial man whom his soldiers called "Fighting Dick." He made up for his lack of decorum, however, with a keen mind and ample common sense. Many of his brother officers disliked him for his plebian ways, but McClellan thought enough of him to give him a division for the Peninsula campaign, and now his decision paid off. Richardson aggressively pushed his men forward, seized Bloody Lane, and shattered the Confederate line, opening the way for the coup de grâce McClellan hoped to deliver. Unfortunately, Richardson was mortally wounded as he reorganized his men, and no other officer present had the skill and clout to take advantage of the opening.[83]

Certainly Sumner would not provide the needed support. Old Bull had seen a lot in the course of his long army career, but none of his previous experiences had prepared him for the holocaust he witnessed that morning near the West Woods with Sedgwick's division. As far as he was concerned, the entire Union right flank had gone to pieces, so his men were in no condition to renew the fight. Franklin arrived with orders to attack with his corps, but Sumner on his own authority canceled the proposed assault. When one of McClellan's staff officers inquired about the current situation, Sumner exclaimed, "Go back, young man, and tell General McClellan I have no command. Tell him my command, Banks' [Mansfield's] command and Hooker's command are all cut up and demoralized. Tell him General

Franklin has the only organized command on this part of the field!"[84] Mc-
Clellan rode over for a firsthand look, and there he met with Smith, Sumner, Slocum, Franklin, and others for a hasty conference under enemy
artillery fire. Although Franklin was not known for his aggressive instincts,
he recommended renewing the offensive, but Sumner demurred. McClellan
looked things over and concluded that Sumner was right to be cautious, so
Richardson's breakthrough went unexploited.[85]

Meanwhile, the third act of McClellan's disconnected Antietam play
was underway. At 8:00 A.M., McClellan ordered Burnside to attack the rebel
right, or southern, flank. To do so, the Ninth Corps had to cross the 50-foot-
wide Antietam Creek. The creek was fordable at almost any point, but for
some reason Burnside became fixated on advancing over a stone bridge that
eventually bore his name. It took three assaults and a good deal of time to
seize the bridge and drive off the few rebels overlooking it. As the morning
turned into afternoon, McClellan grew increasingly frustrated with Burnside's lack of progress. He sent message after message urging haste, and finally Burnside said testily to one of McClellan's aides, "McClellan appears
to think I am not trying my best to carry this bridge; you are the third or
fourth one who has been to me this morning with similar orders."[86] Once
across the creek, elements of the Ninth Corps pushed on toward Sharpsburg
against scattered but limited enemy resistance. Before they could seize the
village, however, a sharp Confederate counterattack by rebels who had just
arrived from Harper's Ferry crumpled the Union left flank, killed divisional
commander Brigadier General Isaac Rodman, and drove Burnside's men
back to the Antietam. Burnside wanted to retire across the creek, but Mc-
Clellan ordered him to stay put. Throughout the entire day, Burnside never
managed to commit more than one of his four divisions to combat at any
given time.[87]

Burnside's debacle ended the day's fighting, leaving both sides battered
but unbowed. That night the Army of the Potomac received substantial reinforcements that compensated for all the casualties it had sustained
throughout the day, including Couch's and Brigadier General Andrew
Humphreys's divisions. Next day both Burnside and Franklin urged McClellan to resume the battle, but Little Mac hesitated. He believed that a defeat
would expose Washington to capture, and he was not prepared to run that
risk until he was good and ready. Instead, he spent the day reconnoitering,
redeploying his units, and mulling over the situation. Finally, he ordered an
attack for the following morning, but by then Lee's bloodied army had retreated back across the Potomac to safety.[88]

Tactically, Antietam was a drawn battle, but strategically the Union
could justly claim victory. The battle stopped Lee's invasion of Maryland,

and it enabled Lincoln to issue his Preliminary Emancipation Proclamation threatening to free all the slaves in Confederate-held territory unless the rebels returned to the Union by the end of the year. For the Army of the Potomac, Antietam was a dismal example of failed leadership and missed opportunities. There was plenty of blame to go around—Sumner and Burnside in particular deserved censure—but ultimately McClellan was responsible for the botched engagement. Throughout the day he had displayed the same hands-off attitude that he had exhibited on the peninsula. Indeed, he often acted more like an interested spectator than a general commanding an army. He committed his units to combat piecemeal, squandered his numerical superiority by leaving large numbers of his men unengaged, and failed to provide the drive necessary to exploit the opportunities his subordinates developed. McClellan later told his wife that some of his colleagues called his conduct masterful, but this was far from the truth. Although most of the corps that saw the heaviest action at Antietam were new to the Army of the Potomac—the First, Ninth, and Twelfth Corps—the rank and file fought well as usual. The battle demonstrated, however, that the Yankees deserved better than McClellan and many of his high-ranking officers.[89]

"We Shall Ever Be Comrades"

For all its tactical mismanagement, Antietam was still a Union victory that yielded significant strategic benefits. The engagement was one of several Union successes that autumn. In Kentucky, Braxton Bragg squandered his brilliant Confederate offensive into Kentucky at the fitful Battle of Perryville on 8 October, and his army retreated into central Tennessee. To the southwest, Confederate efforts to destroy Grant's forces in northern Mississippi collapsed at the Battles of Iuka and Corinth. Nowhere did Union arms achieve a decisive victory—in fact, Union generalship in all these engagements rivaled McClellan's dismal performance at Antietam—but the end result was that the Union had regained the strategic initiative.

McClellan did not immediately pursue the Confederate army after Antietam. Instead, he remained north of the Potomac River for what he considered good reasons. The Union army had just gone through a horrific battle, and it needed time to rest, refit, and recover from its ordeal. There were shortages of almost everything, including boots, blankets, canteens, uniforms, tents, and especially horses. Moreover, McClellan continued to believe that he was heavily outnumbered, so he wanted as many reinforcements as possible before he grappled with the enemy again. Finally, he needed time to fill the gaps the rebels had put in his high command at

Turner's Gap and Antietam. Both the First and Twelfth Corps required new leaders, and in fact casualties were heavy throughout the officer corps. The Second Corps alone had lost 134 officers at Antietam, including four generals—in addition to the more than 5,000 enlisted men who had fallen.[90] As a result, he squandered the good autumn weather, and he did not cross the Potomac to begin a new campaign in the Shenandoah Valley until 26 October.

Although Joe Hooker's injuries were not life threatening, he needed time to recuperate, so McClellan had to find a temporary leader for the First Corps. McClellan had placed George Meade in charge of it, even though James Ricketts had seniority. Ricketts was a forty-five-year-old New Yorker and West Point graduate who had served in the Mexican War and had been wounded and captured at First Bull Run. Not surprisingly, he was unhappy with Meade's elevation at his expense. Ricketts asked McClellan for an explanation even before the guns at Antietam had cooled. McClellan had more important things on his mind just then, but he promised to look into Ricketts's grievance. After a couple of weeks of silence, Ricketts rode over to McClellan's headquarters to reiterate his complaint. There McClellan patiently explained that Hooker had recommended Meade's appointment to First Corps command, and he put Ricketts on the defensive by asking if he had done anything to antagonize Fighting Joe. Ricketts said no, unless it was his awareness of Hooker's dubious personal life. In reality, McClellan doubted Ricketts's ability to lead a corps, in part because he was dismayed by the amount of straggling reported in his division. McClellan's reassurances initially appeased Ricketts, but he became disenchanted when nothing came of them. He eventually demanded and received a transfer out of the Army of the Potomac.[91]

Unfortunately for Meade, Ricketts's elimination from contention did not secure him command of the First Corps. Instead, on 29 September, McClellan gave the outfit to another First Corps divisional commander: Brigadier General John "Josh" Reynolds. Reynolds was one of McClellan's favorite officers. In fact, Little Mac had specifically asked then Secretary of War Cameron to transfer Reynolds to the Army of the Potomac the previous September. Through no fault of his own, Reynolds had missed Antietam. Five days before the battle, Pennsylvania's governor, Andrew Curtin, had asked Stanton to dispatch Reynolds to Harrisburg to organize the state militia gathering there to meet the Confederate invasion. Both McClellan and Hooker had objected to losing such a valuable officer at such a critical time, but Halleck overruled them. Now that the rebel threat was over and the First Corps was up for grabs, Reynolds hurried back to the Army of the Potomac to claim it. He and Meade were friends, and they went together to see McClellan. McClellan explained to them that he would have to assign the corps temporarily to Reynolds while Hooker recovered because Reynolds had seniority. Of course, by that logic, the unit should have gone to Ricketts. In all likelihood, McClellan simply believed that Reynolds was the better officer, but he did not want to offend Meade by saying so. McClellan may also have been unhappy with reports that Meade's division, like Ricketts's, had suffered heavily from straggling during Antietam. There were other officers in the Army of the Potomac available for the position who ranked Reynolds—Ricketts, Darius Couch, Henry Slocum, George Morrell, Baldy Smith, John Parke, Jacob Cox, and George Stoneman—but McClellan opted to promote from within the First Corps family. Although McClellan tried to mollify Meade by informing him that he had recommended him for a major generalship, he was only partially successful. Meade accepted his demotion with as much grace as he could muster, but he confided in his wife that he wished Reynolds, friend or not, had stayed in Pennsylvania.[92]

Despite his disappointment, Meade remained on good terms with Reynolds, but this was not hard to do. Indeed, Josh Reynolds was among the most liked and respected officers in the entire Army of the Potomac. He had graduated from West Point in 1841 in the middle of his class, and thereafter he had seen service at various garrisons throughout the country, in the Mexican War—he was brevetted twice for gallantry, once at Monterrey and again at Buena Vista—against Rouge River Indians, and on the Utah expedition. He was commandant of cadets at West Point when the Confederates fired on Fort Sumter, and he did a good enough job so that he noted wryly that he was certain that the cadets would be happy to see him go off to war. Reynolds was close to Franklin and Baldy Smith, but no one held his relationships with past and present members of McClellan's clique against him. For one thing, Reynolds kept his opinions about politics and personalities to himself, so he was a hard man to know. In fact, few people realized that he was engaged to a Catholic girl from New York City. For another, he was an intelligent, pleasant, thoroughly competent, and generous man to whom leadership came naturally. He had commanded a brigade on the peninsula and had been captured at Gaines's Mill. After an unhappy stay at Libby Prison in Richmond, he had been exchanged in time to participate in the Second Bull Run campaign. He had won kudos from Porter and McDowell, but he had yet to truly distinguish himself on the battlefield. Even so, he was a temporary corps commander for now, and almost everyone agreed that the First Corps was in good hands.[93]

In his never-ending search for someone to replace McClellan, Secretary of Treasury Salmon Chase left no stone unturned. Even after Antietam, he continued to tout Bull Sumner as a possible candidate. In reality, however, Sumner was a tired old man worn out by war. Antietam had taken a physical and psychological toll on him, so on 8 October he acquired a leave of absence and did not return to the army for a month. He also asked about a transfer to a less stressful job, perhaps commanding a department somewhere. McClellan admired Sumner for his simple courage and devotion to duty but was disappointed with his performance at Antietam and elsewhere, so he embraced the opportunity to put someone else in charge of the Second Corps. He endorsed Sumner's request to Halleck, stating,

> From his age, state of health, and the many exposures he has undergone, I think that it is very doubtful whether he [Sumner] can stand the fatigues of another campaign. His long and faithful service and the extreme gallantry he has so often displayed during this war alike entitle him to the most favorable consideration of the Government. I would regard it as an act of official justice, as well as a personal favor, if the wishes of General Sumner can be complied with.[94]

While Sumner's fate was being determined, McClellan looked for a temporary leader for the hard-fighting Second Corps. In this instance, he chose not to promote from within the corps, probably because all three of its divisional commanders were brigadier generals new to their positions. In fact, two of them—Winfield Scott Hancock and Oliver Otis Howard—had replaced Richardson and Sedgwick after Antietam. Instead, on 7 October, McClellan turned to Major General Darius Couch, the Army of the Potomac's senior division commander. The New York–born Couch had graduated from West Point in 1846, the same year as McClellan. He had seen action at Buena Vista in the Mexican War, done garrison duty mostly along the Atlantic coast, and then secured a leave of absence in 1853–1854 to collect zoological specimens for the Smithsonian in northern Mexico. He had resigned his commission in 1855 and taken a job with the Taunton Copper Company in Massachusetts, but he rejoined the Army after the war began. His old friend McClellan gave him a brigade, and by the time the Army of the Potomac reached the peninsula he led a division in Keyes's Fourth Corps. Although some criticized him for his performance at Fair Oaks, McClellan was not among them. In fact, Couch emerged from the Peninsula campaign with a promotion to major general. McClellan could have left Couch with Keyes on the peninsula after Halleck recalled the Army of the Potomac to northern Virginia, but he did not. Instead, he attached Couch and his division to Franklin's Sixth Corps, so he did not participate in Second Bull Run or Antietam. Couch was a quiet, sensible man with a low-key sense of humor who, according to one observer, dressed more like a Methodist minister than a general. He was handicapped by chronic bad health from his Mexican War days, and in fact he tried to resign from the army while at Harrison's Landing because of it, but McClellan valued his services and talked him out of it.[95]

Alpheus Williams had taken charge of the Twelfth Corps at Antietam after Mansfield was mortally wounded. He had done a good job, coming within an ace of breaking the rebel line. After the battle he had hoped to retain command of the corps, but he knew it was unlikely. Williams was a realistic man already well versed in army politics, with a wry sense of humor and a good understanding of human nature. He recognized that he was only a brigadier general in an army full of ambitious major generals who would relish the opportunity to lead a corps. In addition, Williams was neither a West Pointer nor a McClellan man. He had not participated in the Peninsula campaign, so he was still a stranger to the Army of the Potomac. Williams had political connections, but they were not substantial enough to compel the Lincoln administration to act on his behalf. Despite the long odds, Williams did what he could to bolster his case. He secured promises from Sumner and Banks to lobby for him, and to generate some favorable publicity he even leaked his report on Antietam to a friend for publication. Unfortunately, neither Sumner nor Banks carried much weight with McClellan. To make things worse, an inspection of Williams's division uncovered all sorts of problems and deficiencies, and it was probably no coincidence that soon afterward, on 15 October, McClellan appointed Major General Henry Slocum commander of the Twelfth Corps. There is no record that Lincoln formally approved Slocum's assignment to command the unit, though it is possible McClellan cleared his decision with the president when he visited the army in early October. All things considered, McClellan's actions were hardly surprising; the wonder was that it took him so long to make his decision. Williams returned to his division and led it with distinction for the rest of the war in both the eastern and western theaters, but he never received either a permanent corps command or a second star.[96]

Henry Slocum had had an eclectic career. He had been a teacher for several years until the Mexican War piqued his interest in the military, so he had obtained an appointment to West Point, where he stood out because of his vocal opposition to slavery. He had graduated seventh in his class of 1852 and then had been posted in Florida and later in South Carolina. In 1855, he had resigned his commission to practice law in Syracuse, New York. He was also active in politics and served in the state legislature as a Democrat. His militia connections helped to secure him command of a regiment when the war began, and he was wounded at First Bull Run. He led a Sixth Corps division on the peninsula, where his performance impressed Franklin, Porter, and Heintzelman. Indeed, he emerged from the campaign with a promotion to major general. He missed Second Bull Run, but his division spearheaded Franklin's drive through Crampton's Gap. After Couch took over the Second Corps, Slocum became the Army of the Potomac's senior division commander. These factors, along with his pro-McClellan inclinations, made him an obvious choice for the Twelfth Corps. Slocum was a small, spare man with considerable poise. Although both ambitious and opinionated, no one could deny his honesty and courage. He lacked Hooker's and Kearny's flamboyancy, but his calm demeanor under fire was just as reassuring. Slocum did not think much of the Twelfth Corps when he took over, despite its laudatory performance at Antietam, but he managed to whip it into shape while simultaneously earning the friendship and trust of its officers, including even the displaced Williams.[97]

A few weeks after Slocum's appointment, the Army of the Potomac permanently lost Samuel Heintzelman's services. Heintzelman's Third Corps had sustained heavy casualties on the peninsula and in northern Virginia, so Halleck kept it in Washington during the Maryland campaign to rest and refit, and he assigned Heintzelman to command the city's defenses south of the Potomac. After Antietam, McClellan believed as usual that the Confederates heavily outnumbered him, so he pressured Halleck for as many reinforcements as possible. In mid-October, Halleck ordered two of the three Third Corps divisions—Hooker's old one, now under Brigadier General George Stoneman, and a newly created one led by Brigadier General Amiel Whipple—to join the Army of the Potomac. McClellan did not keep the two divisions together but rather doled them out to other corps. As for Heintzelman, he was initially unsure whether he would accompany those divisions or remain in Washington. On 27 October, however, Lincoln ordered Nathaniel Banks to supplant Major General Benjamin Butler as head of the Department of the Gulf in New Orleans. To take his place as commander of Washington's defenses, Halleck chose Heintzelman. As Heintzelman later noted, he never received any orders relieving him from the Third Corps; instead, Halleck and McClellan simply took the corps away from him, piece by piece. Heintzelman stayed in Washington until October 1863. Thereafter he commanded the Department of the North and then sat on various courts martial. After the conflict he served in Texas until he retired in 1869. He moved to Washington and lived there until his death in 1890.[98]

Despite his victory at Antietam, McClellan was an unhappy man that autumn for several reasons. For one thing, he was disappointed with many of his high-ranking subordinates. It was not surprising that he complained about Sumner, whom Lincoln had forced upon him the previous March, but he also found fault with some of his closest friends and supporters. With unconscious irony, he criticized even Porter for his lack of aggressiveness at

Antietam. Porter's alleged flaws, however, paled in comparison with Burnside's. McClellan had been dissatisfied with Burnside ever since the Army of the Potomac marched out of Washington in pursuit of Lee, and Antietam only exacerbated his feelings. Indeed, McClellan considered Burnside a downright hindrance, even though he put him in charge of operations in and around Harper's Ferry. In late September, he grumbled to his wife, "I *ought* to rap Burnside *very* severely and probably will—yet I hate to do it. He is very slow and is not fit to command more than a regiment. If I rap him as he deserves he will be my mortal enemy hereafter—if I do not praise him as he thinks he deserves and as I know he does *not*, he will be at least a very lukewarm friend."[99] Unfortunately, McClellan could not relieve his corps commanders without Lincoln's approval, and in the past the president had not been sympathetic to such drastic measures. He asked Halleck for the authority to reassign ineffective generals to Washington, but nothing came of his request. Instead, he had to make do with the corps commanders he had and hope that, as with Heintzelman, circumstances would remove some of them from his army.[100]

In addition, McClellan's own position was by no means secure. Lincoln visited the Army of the Potomac in early October, and although he pledged to protect McClellan from his domestic political enemies, there were plenty of signs in the following weeks that the president's continued support depended upon McClellan's aggressive prosecution of the war. A few days later, Lincoln peremptorily ordered the Army of the Potomac to advance, but McClellan responded with his usual litany of excuses. On 13 October, Lincoln admonished McClellan for his excessive timidity in a private letter designed to spur him on, but this tactic proved no more fruitful than his more direct approach the previous week. Instead, McClellan continued to demand more equipment, supplies, and men. When Lincoln learned that McClellan had requisitioned more horses to replace the army's worn-out nags, he telegraphed sarcastically, "Will you pardon me for asking what the horses of your army have done since the battle of Antietam that fatigues anything?"[101] Such mockery was not a good sign. In fact, McClellan already suspected that Lincoln's patience was just about exhausted. Two days after he received Lincoln's private letter, McClellan paid Darius Couch a visit. The two men sat together on some rocks on a ledge and talked, which Couch found odd because McClellan had never confided in him before. McClellan showed him Lincoln's letter and commented, "But I may not have command of the army much longer. Lincoln is down on me."[102]

McClellan was right about that. Indeed, he was becoming both a military and political liability to the Lincoln administration. On 23 September, the president issued his Preliminary Emancipation Proclamation, which turned the conflict into a war both to reunite the country and to end slavery. Mc-Clellan personally opposed slavery, but he did not believe the Constitution prohibited it. As he saw things, the pressures of war were already destroying the slave system, so Lincoln's actions were unnecessary and premature. Moreover, the proclamation changed the character of the conflict from a simple political imbroglio to suppress the rebellion to a revolutionary struggle to alter the very fabric of U.S. society. McClellan had already gone on record against such a war in his Harrison's Landing letter to Lincoln the previous July, and now some of his officers urged him to speak out against Lincoln's new policy. Two days after the president issued his proclamation, McClellan invited Brigadier Generals Jacob Cox and John Cochrane to dinner in his tent. Both men were political generals with connections to the Lincoln administration, so McClellan sounded them out. Cox and Cochrane recommended against condemning the proclamation, but McClellan was not sure. Less than a week later, McClellan summoned Baldy Smith to his headquarters. When Smith arrived he found the reception tent full of generals. McClellan beckoned him over and showed him a letter he was drafting to the president opposing the proclamation. Smith was puzzled as to why McClellan chose to confide in him, but in a low voice he beseeched him to pigeonhole the letter because opposing his commander in chief could ruin his career. McClellan did so, but it was no secret in either the Army of the Potomac or in Washington that he disliked the proclamation.[103]

As evidence began to accumulate that his days as Army of the Potomac commander were numbered, McClellan sought to cut a deal with the Lincoln administration that would enable him to retain some role in the war. On 7 October, McClellan asked Cochrane to sound out Salmon Chase to see if he would support a campaign to promote him to general in chief. McClellan wanted Cochrane to inform Chase that they were really not that far apart on the slavery issue and that as general in chief he could rally War Democrats to Lincoln's banner. Cochrane traveled to Washington and consulted with Chase. The secretary of the treasury did not inquire how McClellan could simultaneously agree with him about slavery *and* appeal to Democrats, but he did express interest in the proposed arrangement. With this endorsement, Cochrane hurried to the Soldiers' Home to speak with Lincoln. As things turned out, Lincoln was already toying with the idea of bumping McClellan upstairs, and he said that he was sure he could find Halleck a new job somewhere. In the end, however, nothing came of these indirect negotiations. Chase later explained to Cochrane that he had been too ill to present the scheme to the cabinet, but in all likelihood Cochrane was closer to the truth when he speculated that Stanton killed the concept. Cochrane had alluded to Stanton about McClellan's idea, but the secretary of war, who hated McClellan just about as much as McClellan hated him, abruptly rejected it.[104]

McClellan was not the only high-ranking Army of the Potomac officer politicking and stringpulling that autumn. Joe Hooker was too, but his efforts were designed to advance his career at McClellan's expense. In fact, Hooker had set his sights on nothing less than command of the Army of the Potomac. McClellan did not know this; he was as blind to Hooker's ambition now as he had been on the peninsula. Indeed, he not only thanked Hooker for his performance at Antietam but also recommended his promotion to brigadier general in the Regular Army to Lincoln and Halleck. Such gratitude, however, did not deter Hooker's soaring ambition. Hooker was convalescing at Washington's insane asylum—no one seems to have commented on this irony, though—and this provided him with plenty of opportunities to lobby personally those in a position to help him advance his career. He was the biggest hero the Army of the Potomac had yet produced, so innumerable powerful and connected well-wishers were eager to talk with him. Chief among them was Salmon Chase. Chase visited Hooker several times that fall, and he liked what he saw and heard. Although Hooker was neither a Radical Republican nor an abolitionist, he tailored his remarks to appeal to Chase, who was both. Hooker stated that McClellan was militarily incompetent, and he denied that the Army of the Potomac officer corps felt any particular loyalty to the man. Chase nodded his agreement and said, "General, if my advice had been followed you would have commanded after the retreat to James River if not before." Hooker replied solemnly, "If I had commanded, Richmond would have been ours." From that point on, Chase viewed Hooker as the man who could win the war, and he devoted his efforts to making his vision a reality.[105]

Gaining Chase's support was a significant accomplishment, but Hooker did not stop there. He took his political allies where he could find them. The governor of Massachusetts, John Andrews, pledged his support, as did Vice President Hannibal Hamlin. Hooker also worked hard to nurture his brother officers. For example, he won George Meade's thanks by recommending him to McClellan as First Corps commander, though Meade worried that Radical Republicans might try to use Hooker as a weapon against McClellan. Hooker also kept in touch with his old Third Corps comrades such as Hiram Berry and David Birney. Those new to Hooker's self-laudatory and self-assured monologues were impressed, but others more familiar with him had their doubts. Heintzelman, for instance, scoffed in his diary, "Gen[eral] Hooker has said that he felt that he is the only general in the country competent to lead the armies of the Republic. What vanity!"[106] As for rumors that Hooker was slated to replace McClellan, Heintzelman commented, "What a mistake and what an outrage."[107] Heintzelman had commanded Hooker on the peninsula and in northern Virginia, so he was familiar with his modus operandi. He dismissed Hooker's bluster for what it was. Unfortunately for the Army of the Potomac and the Union cause, others were not as astute.[108]

McClellan was alone in his tent near midnight on 7 November, writing a letter to his wife, when Ambrose Burnside and Brigadier General Catharinus Buckingham knocked on the tent pole. Buckingham was the army's assistant adjutant general, and Halleck had sent him from Washington to the Shenandoah Valley with orders from the president relieving McClellan from his command and putting Burnside in his place. McClellan had predicted this event weeks earlier, so he was hardly surprised by the news. Lincoln had bided his time, though, waiting until circumstances were right, but by early November he had concluded that McClellan's political and military usefulness was at an end. The midterm elections had just concluded, so Lincoln no longer needed McClellan to attract War Democrats. McClellan's support in the cabinet had long since evaporated. In fact, Stanton and McClellan were on such bad terms that McClellan bypassed him—and Halleck too, for that matter—and communicated directly with Lincoln, which the secretary of war resented. Finally, Lincoln had concluded that McClellan lacked sufficient drive and determination to crowd the rebel army into the climactic and decisive battles necessary to successfully end the war. The president had hoped that McClellan could interpose the Army of the Potomac between Lee's army and Richmond, but McClellan did not move fast enough. As Lincoln explained to elder statesman Francis Blair, "He [McClellan] has got the slows, Mr. Blair."[109]

No one in the know should have been surprised at McClellan's relief, but the Army of the Potomac's rank and file was shocked and dismayed by the news. McClellan had made them soldiers, cared for them, and led them from the peninsula to Antietam. As McClellan put it, they had grown up together and should not be separated. Many officers saw McClellan in the same light, and they damned the president for removing him in the middle of a promising campaign. Indeed, some of McClellan's staffers were so furious that they suggested that the army march on Washington and impose McClellan on the government. Nothing came of such foolish talk, but it was indicative of the anger so many felt toward the Lincoln administration for its seemingly unappreciative and cavalier treatment of their commander. McClellan agreed to remain with the army for a few days to help Burnside get acclimated to his new responsibilities, and this permitted the troops to express their gratitude in healthier ways. Before McClellan left, he, his staff, and many high-ranking officers rode down a road lined for miles with soldiers from the Second and Fifth Corps drawn up to say their goodbyes. The men cheered and hollered and waved their banners in appreciation and affection for McClellan's efforts on their behalf. He got a similar reception from the First and Sixth Corps a bit later. Soldiers swarmed his train as he prepared to leave and refused to let him go, but McClellan admonished them to obey Burnside's directives, and all would be well. Before he left he issued a farewell order:

> In parting from you, I cannot express the love and gratitude I bear to you. As an army, you have grown up under my care. In you I have never found doubt or coldness. The battles you have fought under my command will proudly live in our nation's history. The glory you have achieved, our mutual perils and fatigues, the graves of our comrades fallen in battle and by disease, the broken forms of those whom wounds and sickness have disabled—the strongest associations which can exist among men—unite us still by an indissoluble tie. We shall ever be comrades in supporting the Constitution of our country and the nationality of its people.[110]

All this was true enough, but the clear-headed George Meade supplied a better epitaph for McClellan's military career when he wrote his wife, "We must encounter risks if we fight, and we cannot carry on war without fighting. That was McClellan's vice. He was always waiting to have everything just as he wanted before he would attack, and before he could get things arranged as he wanted them, the enemy pounced on him and thwarted all his plans."[111]

In the months that followed, rumors occasionally swept the Army of the Potomac that McClellan was back in command, but they never became reality. McClellan's military days were over, but he remained in the public eye. He gravitated to politics, and the Democrats nominated him for the presidency in 1864 against Lincoln, but he lost in a bitterly divisive election. Although the Army of the Potomac's affection for him remained, most of the soldiers were unwilling to vote for a man whose party platform called for a negotiated end to the war. By then too many bluecoats had been killed or wounded to accept anything other than complete victory. McClellan resigned his commission on election day and went on a three-year European tour. After the war he served as chief engineer of New York City's Department of Docks from 1870 to 1872 and as New Jersey's governor from 1878 to 1881. He died of heart failure in 1885.

McClellan was not the only victim of Lincoln's 5 November directive. The same order removed Fitz John Porter as well. Although Lincoln had agreed to McClellan's request to reinstate Porter during the Maryland campaign, Pope's charges against him remained unresolved. With McClellan gone, the path was open to determine Porter's fate, and he was court-martialed in December for disobeying Pope's orders at Second Bull Run. Stanton handpicked the judges, some of whom were hostile to Porter. Most Army of the Potomac officers saw the trial as politically motivated, but they still expected Porter's acquittal. It shocked everyone, therefore, when the court found Porter guilty on 10 January 1863 of the most serious charges. Lincoln approved the verdict eleven days later and ordered Porter cashiered and dismissed from the army. The president did not believe that Porter was guilty of treason, but he felt that the general had not given Pope sufficient assistance and cooperation. It was a severe sentence—on the other hand, Radical Republican Zachariah Chandler thought that Porter should be shot—but Lincoln wanted to set an example for an officer corps that seemed to place personal loyalties above duty to country. Porter left for the mining business in Colorado and missed the rest of the war. Afterward he worked as receiver of a New Jersey railroad and later as New York City commissioner of public works. At the same time, he waged a dogged and determined campaign to get his verdict reversed. His efforts, however, became entangled in postwar politics, so his progress was glacial. Finally, in 1886, Democratic president Grover Cleveland signed a bill restoring Porter to his Regular Army rank, and he returned triumphantly to Washington. He died in 1901.[112]

Conclusions

McClellan commanded the Army of the Potomac for less than sixteen months, but he cast his shadow over its command structure long after Lincoln relieved him. When McClellan organized the army after First Bull Run, he seeded many of its divisions and brigades with his friends. These men were therefore well positioned to gain the necessary rank, experience, connections, and seniority to attain corps command. By the time Lincoln replaced McClellan, some of them—Porter, Franklin, Reynolds, Couch, and Slocum—had already become corps commanders. They were just the tip of the iceberg; as the war continued more McClellanites climbed to corps command and played crucial roles in subsequent campaigns and battles. Some of them performed credibly enough, but others exhibited the same cautiousness and lack of initiative McClellan had repeatedly displayed. Either way, though, they were McClellan's progeny.

McClellan exhibited considerable favoritism in advancing his allies to corps command. Indeed, he was willing to do so even at the expense of seniority. As his adjutant explained to an officer who asked for a command based on his seniority, "The Commanding General cannot consent to withdraw General French from the command of a division, which he has had charge of since its formation and which he has gallantly led in action, simply on the ground of seniority."[113] McClellan's willingness to disregard seniority was laudable, but he generally elevated his favorites because of their loyalty to him, not because of their record on the battlefield. In doing so, he helped foster in the Army of the Potomac a sense of cliquishness that never went away. McClellan often ignored and denigrated corps commanders in whose selection he did not have a hand, which antagonized officers who were not part of his informal family. Those who did not agree with him or benefit from his partiality—most notably Kearny, Hooker, and their allies in the Third Corps—formed their own disgruntled faction that denounced McClellan, his allies, and his ideas. This undermined unity in the officer corps and hindered its performance on the battlefield. McClellan also helped politicize the army by opposing the Lincoln administration's policies such as the Preliminary Emancipation Proclamation, making the army a battleground for Radical Republicans, War Democrats, and others. In short, by his actions McClellan constructed an almost Byzantine culture in which high-ranking officers operated for the remainder of the conflict. Officers who understood and manipulated this culture had a much better chance at gaining and maintaining a corps command than those who did not.

CHAPTER TWO

Burnside's Unhappy and Insecure Tenure
November 1862 to January 1863

Burnside Restructures the Army of the Potomac

In retrospect—that is, after the rebels had shot down thousands of Yankees at the Battle of Fredericksburg—Lincoln's decision to appoint Ambrose Burnside to command the Army of the Potomac seemed unwise indeed. At the time, however, it made perfect sense; Burnside possessed positive qualities no other available high-ranking Union officer enjoyed. For one thing, in early 1862 he had successfully led an expedition to the North Carolina coast that resulted in the Union occupation of Roanoke Island and New Bern. No one else in the Army of the Potomac—not Hooker or Sumner or Franklin—had held such an important independent command. Burnside was therefore familiar with the awesome responsibilities that leading large numbers of soldiers far from higher authority entailed. In addition, Burnside was a McClellan man, despite his deteriorating relationship with Little Mac. If John Pope's experience proved anything, it proved that an army commander needed cooperative subordinates, and Lincoln undoubtedly recognized that the fractious Army of the Potomac officer corps was more likely to back one of its own than an outsider. Finally, Burnside's personality certainly commended him. His modesty, friendliness, and openness toward the Lincoln administration and everyone else stood in stark and refreshing contrast to the truculent McClellan.

Choosing Burnside as the Army of the Potomac's new commander was one thing, but persuading him to accept the job was something else. Indeed, Lincoln had twice before offered Burnside the position, but each time he had declined because he did not feel qualified for it. When Catharinus Buckingham appeared outside his tent on 7 November with Lincoln's latest orders, a shocked and surprised Burnside was inclined to refuse yet again. Lincoln, however, had a good understanding of human nature, and he tailored his directive to bend Burnside to his will. Buckingham was accompanied by Brigadier General James Wadsworth, a prominent Republican politician-turned-soldier close to the president. Wadsworth carried verbal instructions from Lincoln informing Burnside that if he again rejected the command, it would go to Joe Hooker instead. Burnside did not like Hooker much to begin with, and the idea of serving under him was even more distasteful. Burnside asked for time to consult his conscience and a couple of his staff officers, which took an hour and a half. Burnside's staffers insisted that orders were orders, so saying no was out of the question. In that light, Burnside's duty was clear. Even so, he was not happy about the sudden turn of events. He explained to Brigadier General Orlando Willcox, one of his division commanders, "Under the present circumstances, I don't feel equal to [the command]. I cannot expect the hearty cooperation of the McClellan element, but the worst of it is that I cannot decline it, according to Wadsworth."[1] Five days later, he met with Halleck at Warrenton, Virginia, and reiterated his reluctance to take charge, stating, "I am not fit for it. There are many more men in the army better fitted than I am; but if you and the President insist, I will take it and do the best I can."[2]

Despite his misgivings, most of the Army of the Potomac's high-ranking officers were initially willing to give Burnside the benefit of the doubt. McClellan's public support before he left helped, but Burnside's personality played an equally important role. Almost everyone liked Burnside. Even as a West Point cadet he had had a reputation as a fun-loving, amiable, sincere, and jovial man. This was true enough, but Burnside also possessed traits that hindered his ability to effectively lead an army. He depended on fortune as much as on thorough preparation and planning, so much so that "trust to luck" was one of his favorite expressions. He leaned on his staff excessively, was easily swayed by the opinions of others, and was not very efficient. Although he was normally easygoing, he became bullheaded and obstinate under pressure. Burnside's biggest problem, however, was his firm, candid, and well-known conviction that he was unsuited to command the Army of the Potomac. It was easy to attribute his assertions to his natural humility, but more perceptive observers recognized it as honest self-assessment. One division commander later wrote:

> Burnside in his hearty way expressed his thanks for our friendly greeting and then, with that transparent sincerity of his nature which made everyone believe what he said, he added that he knew he was not fit for so big a command; but since it was imposed upon him, he would do his

best, and he confidently hoped we all would faithfully stand by him. There was something very touching in that confession of unfitness, which was evidently quite honest, and one could not help feeling a certain tenderness for the man. But when a moment later the generals talked among themselves, it was no wonder that several shook their heads and asked how we could have confidence in the fitness of our leader if he had no such confidence in himself?[3]

Burnside may have lacked self-confidence, but the Lincoln administration initially had faith in him. Several days after he assumed command, Halleck authorized Burnside to organize the army as he saw fit and to submit the names of any officers he wanted transferred out. Halleck also noted that only Lincoln could permanently change corps commanders, but he strongly implied that the president would be receptive to Burnside's recommendations. Unfortunately, Burnside was an easygoing man, so he did not seize the opportunity to purge the army of ineffective and unsupportive officers, assuming he even recognized that such men existed in his high command. He did, however, restructure his force. Burnside believed that the Army of the Potomac contained too many corps for one person to manage efficiently, so he decided to create a new level of command to reduce the number of units for which he was directly responsible. Burnside divided the army into three grand divisions and placed them under his three senior officers. He assigned the Second and Ninth Corps to Sumner's Right Grand Division, the Third and Fifth Corps to Hooker's Central Grand Division, and the First and Sixth Corps to Franklin's Left Grand Division. He planned to leave Slocum's Twelfth Corps behind in the Shenandoah Valley for the time being, and he made Franz Sigel's Eleventh Corps the army's reserve.[4]

Burnside undoubtedly hoped that putting grand divisions in his organizational tables would simplify his tasks, but it did not make the Army of the Potomac more effective. Instead, it added another layer to the army's already cumbersome command structure, and it did nothing to reduce the number of understrength corps. Nor did Burnside take sufficient advantage of the leeway Lincoln had given him in personnel matters. He used seniority instead of performance to determine the grand division commanders, so he did not get the best men available for the jobs. Sumner was brave, loyal, and indomitable, but he was also a tired old soldier with limited imagination who was still coming to grips with the horror he had witnessed at Antietam. Although everyone acknowledged Franklin's intelligence, he had yet to display much flair in battle. Indeed, at Crampton's Gap he had showed himself to be timid, cautious, and slow. Finally, in appointing the recently returned Hooker to his new position, Burnside increased the potency of his chief rival, a man of insatiable ambition who saw superiors as obstacles to be removed. Hooker had little respect for Burnside—the feeling was mutual—and even predicted to Meade that it was just a matter of time before he supplanted him. Hooker was undoubtedly a hard fighter, but chances were slim that Burnside could count on his wholehearted cooperation.[5]

The elevation of Burnside, Sumner, Franklin, and Hooker created additional holes in the Army of the Potomac's high command. Here, too, Burnside had the opportunity to select the most qualified officers and make them corps commanders, but he did not do so. Instead, he again relied on seniority by promoting the highest-ranking officer in each corps to lead it. It was an orderly, safe, and predictable way of doing things, but it did not marry the best men available to the most important positions. Although the new corps commanders were familiar with their units, some of them were hardly equal to their responsibilities.

Sumner's Right Grand Division was least affected by these changes in command. Darius Couch had temporarily led the Second Corps during Sumner's leave of absence, so it was a simple matter for him to take over the corps on a permanent basis. As for Burnside's Ninth Corps, Lincoln had originally assigned it to Major General David Hunter, an old Regular Army soldier and staunch Lincoln administration ally. In the end, however, nothing came of it. Instead, Stanton ordered Hunter to sit on Fitz John Porter's court martial, no doubt believing that Hunter would be more useful combating the administration's domestic enemies than in exercising his limited military abilities in the field.

Ultimately, the Ninth Corps went to Brigadier General Orlando Willcox, Burnside's old friend. Willcox was the Ninth Corps' senior officer after Halleck transferred Jacob Cox and his division back to western Virginia in early October. Willcox had acted as the Ninth Corps' temporary commander when McClellan put Burnside in overall charge of operations around Harper's Ferry, so he was familiar with the job. The Michigan-born Willcox had graduated eighth in his West Point class of 1847, and then he had served in Mexico and Florida. He had resigned his commission in 1857 to join his brother's law practice in Detroit, but returned to the Army when the war broke out. He was wounded and captured at the head of a brigade at First Bull Run, and he spent more than a year as a prisoner of war before he was finally exchanged in August 1862. His friend McClellan offered him Isaac Stevens' Ninth Corps division after Stevens's death at the Battle of Chantilly, and Willcox led it well enough during the Maryland campaign. Willcox was a kind, dispassionate, ambitious, and religious man with minimal respect for Washington and its politicians. He was anxious to hang on to the Ninth Corps, but he believed that his position was tenuous. John

Sedgwick was on the mend from the wounds he had sustained at Antietam, and Willcox knew that Burnside would have to find a new post for Sedgwick commensurate with his rank once he returned to the army. As a mere brigadier, Willcox was an obvious choice for demotion. To forestall the unhappy scenario he envisioned, Willcox exerted considerable time and energy lobbying for a major generalship. McClellan and Burnside promised to do what they could to help, and Willcox even wrote to Zachariah Chandler, one of Michigan's senators, to plead his case. Unfortunately for him, his efforts came to naught. This was all the more discouraging to him because hitherto junior officers such as John Reynolds, George Sykes, and Winfield Scott Hancock managed to secure major generalships that autumn. Even so, Willcox had the corps for now, and he retained Burnside's friendship and support, so he tried to look at his future philosophically and keep things in perspective. He wrote his wife, "But if God will only let me *live* and spare you and the children, how really insignificant all else [is] in comparison."[6]

In the Left Grand Division, Reynolds retained command of the First Corps, but now as its permanent commander. Franklin's elevation, however, placed the Sixth Corps in Baldy Smith's hands. Smith was born in Vermont, had graduated fourth in his West Point class of 1845 and had spent the years before the war as a topographical engineer conducting surveys, teaching mathematics at the Military Academy, and sitting on the Lighthouse Board. In 1855, he had contracted a severe case of malaria in Florida from which he never completely recovered. He fought at First Bull Run and later commanded a division on the Peninsula and during the Maryland campaign. He got along very well with Meade, Reynolds, and especially Franklin. In fact, he and Franklin shared a tent, mess, and headquarters whenever they worked together. They also brought out the worst in each other by reinforcing their mutual inclination toward discord and conspiracy. Everyone acknowledged Smith's cleverness and ability, but unfortunately less admirable traits overshadowed his positive qualities. Smith was a carping, acrimonious, critical, and spiteful man completely blind to his own limitations and weaknesses. He had a knack for ascribing noble motives to his most selfish actions. During the Civil War he eventually fell out, often in spectacular fashion, with practically every commander with whom he served. Indeed, one observer called him "a perfect Ishmaelite to his superior officers."[7] Even Franklin later admitted, "I have a very soft spot in my heart for Baldy, but one has to excuse him for a great many curious hitches."[8] It was McClellan, however, who best summed up Smith's deficiencies:

WF Smith was undoubtedly a man of a high order of ability; he possessed great personal courage and a wonderfully quick eye for ground and for handling troops. On the other hand he was indolent, not a good administrator, was not well versed in the details of service. He was also too quick tempered towards those under him, very selfish, and had a most bitter tongue which often ran away with him and got him into trouble. Smith was one of those personalities who must always intrigue the acts of all above him. He did much harm in that way. His faults incapacitated him from ever being more than a [commander] of a Corps.[9]

Hooker's Central Grand Division included two new corps commanders. Burnside reconstituted the fragmented Third Corps and gave it to Brigadier General George Stoneman. Stoneman was a career soldier, West Point class of 1846, who had been stationed mostly in the southwest before the war. He had refused to surrender Fort Brown to state authorities when Texas seceded from the Union, but he instead made his way back north. He served on McClellan's staff in western Virginia, and Little Mac thought enough of him to bring him to Washington after First Bull Run. In fact, it was Stoneman who suggested designating the forces around the capital the "Army of the Potomac." Stoneman led most of the Army of the Potomac's cavalry on the peninsula to McClellan's and Porter's satisfaction, but illness forced him to give up his position and return to Washington. He counted Halleck among his patrons, and Old Brains assigned him Kearny's old division, from where he ascended to command of the Third Corps. Stoneman was a polite, reserved, severe, and gristly-looking man with little initiative or aggressiveness. His record upon taking over the Third Corps was satisfactory but hardly distinguished. Indeed, there were other available officers who deserved the job more, such as Winfield Scott Hancock, Alpheus Williams, and George Meade. Here, as elsewhere, however, Burnside's commitment to seniority trumped performance.[10]

Brigadier General Daniel Butterfield assumed command of the Fifth Corps. The handsome and well-dressed New York–born businessman had had minimal prewar military experience, but he turned out to be a superb disciplinarian. Butterfield was an energetic, ambitious, and charming man with extensive political connections that included Radical Republicans such as Chandler and Chase. Unfortunately, his penchant for intrigue, his imperious attitude, and his willingness to ally himself with those who shared these traits would eventually undermine his promising military career. He had commanded a Fifth Corps brigade on the peninsula and at Second Bull Run, and his performance there had won Porter's effusive praise. While at Harrison's Landing, he and his bugler composed the military call "Taps" as a way of informing his brigade that it was time to bed down for the night. He took over George Morrell's division on 1 November when McClellan put

Morrell in charge of the upper Potomac's defenses, and now, scarcely two weeks later, he had a corps by virtue of his seniority. Some commented negatively on his meteoric rise through the ranks, but it was difficult to find anyone in the Army of the Potomac who had fought harder.[11]

The Eleventh Corps constituted the Army of the Potomac's reserve, and it remained under the command of Major General Franz Sigel. Sigel was one of Lincoln's political generals, appointed on the recommendation of powerful politicians such as Massachusetts senator Charles Sumner to help secure German-American support for the war. Sigel was born in Baden and had graduated from a German military academy. He had fought on the losing side of the Revolution of 1848 and emigrated to the United States four years later. By the time the Civil War began, he was director of St. Louis's schools and a leader in the German-American community. He played an important role in keeping Missouri in the Union, and he went on to take part in the Battle of Pea Ridge in northern Arkansas. His German soldiers loved him so much that "I fights mit Sigel" became one of the war's catchphrases. He was transferred east in June 1862 to take charge of the heavily German Eleventh Corps, and he participated in Second Bull Run. The Eleventh was so badly decimated by illness and casualties that Halleck kept it in Washington during the Maryland campaign to rest and refit.

Unfortunately, Sigel was not very popular among the Army of the Potomac's cliquish officer corps. It was bad enough that he was a foreigner from a western theater who had never attended West Point, but his personality did little to compensate for these shortcomings. No one doubted his commitment to nineteenth-century liberalism and the Union, but Sigel was an unfriendly, touchy, reserved man without a sense of humor. He alienated most of his superiors at one time or another, and Halleck in particular could not stand him. Sigel had recently submitted his resignation when Halleck refused to explain why he put the more junior Heintzelman in charge of Washington's defenses, but Stanton had smoothed things over—this time.[12]

Burnside's decision to promote by seniority was motivated primarily by his desire to avoid favoritism and conflict among the officer corps over relative merit, but his flawed application of the principle generated some discontentment. In particular, it angered George Meade. Although Meade was not in the Fifth Corps, he ranked Butterfield. He did not believe it was fair that a junior officer should have a corps while he was stuck with a division. Meade asked his friends Baldy Smith and William Franklin for advice. They urged him to appeal to Burnside because they felt that in all likelihood he was unaware of Meade's seniority. Meade hesitated because he feared that such overt politicking might backfire, but after a few days of thought he decided to go ahead. On his way to Burnside's headquarters he stopped to see

Hooker. The Fifth Corps was in Hooker's Central Grand Division, so Meade believed it would be best to inform Fighting Joe about his mission. Hooker was noncommittal because he liked Butterfield. He did, however, state that Meade deserved to be a major general, and he castigated McClellan for giving Reynolds the First Corps. Meade continued on to the Army of the Potomac's headquarters and managed to secure a few minutes alone with Burnside to plead his case. Burnside said that he did not know that Meade ranked Butterfield, and he agreed that his complaint was justified. Besides, continued Burnside, Meade was more qualified for the position than Butterfield anyway. Burnside promised to ask Halleck if he planned to send any officers senior to Meade to the army—meaning John Sedgwick, who was still recovering from his Antietam wounds—and if not, then he would give the Fifth Corps to Meade. For now, however, Meade could do little but return to his division and await events.[13]

The Battle of Fredericksburg

Burnside was no doubt sincere in his desire to placate Meade, but he had more important things on his mind just then. Lincoln had fired McClellan in part because of his lack of initiative, and Burnside did not intend to make the same mistake. He conceived a bold strategic plan to march the Army of the Potomac rapidly from the Blue Ridge Mountains to Fredericksburg on the Rappahannock River in central Virginia. Once there, Burnside believed that he could beat Lee's army to Richmond and seize the Confederate capital. Lincoln went along with the proposal, but he warned Burnside that it would only succeed if he moved fast.[14] Burnside did just that—at least at first. Leaving Sigel's Eleventh Corps at Manassas, Burnside marched his remaining 113,000 troops from the Warrenton area on 15 November, and his army reached the Rappahannock two days later. Unfortunately, the pontoon trains the soldiers needed to cross the river were not there to meet them, owing to one of those innumerable slipups that plagued the Army of the Potomac throughout its existence. The trains did not begin to arrive until 25 November, giving the rebels plenty of time to position themselves on the Rappahannock's south bank.

While the Army of the Potomac cooled its heels on the Rappahannock's north bank, Burnside pondered his options. He ultimately decided on the simplest and most direct approach—an all-out assault on the rebel defenses around Fredericksburg. He hoped that his plan's very boldness and audacity would catch the Confederates by surprise. Burnside chose to cross the river on two sets of pontoon bridges he would build, one at Fredericksburg and the other approximately a mile downstream. On 11 December, the army lurched into motion, but it immediately ran into trouble. A pesky Confederate brigade dug into the buildings of Fredericksburg shot a good many of the engineers struggling to construct the pontoon bridges there, bringing progress to a halt. Shelling the town did no good, and in the end three Union regiments had to mount a small-scale amphibious attack to clear Fredericksburg and open the way for the rest of the army to cross. This cost Burnside a day, and he presently burned away another one deploying his troops on the west bank—the Rappahannock ran north to south for a short distance at this point—which gave Lee plenty of time to concentrate all his forces around the town. Burnside's plan called for a two-pronged assault on the rebel line. To the south, Franklin's Left Grand Division would assail the Confederate right and crumble its flank. At the same time, Sumner's Right Grand Division—but not Sumner himself; Burnside ordered him to remain on the opposite bank because he feared Old Bull might heedlessly expose himself—would punch its way through the rebel defenses outside of Fredericksburg. Finally, Hooker's Central Grand Division would reinforce whichever grand division required its assistance.[15]

A good many Union general officers had serious reservations about Burnside's plan. Some, such as Orlando Willcox, kept their opinions to themselves, but others became increasingly vocal in their opposition. On the evening of 9 December, Sumner called a meeting of his corps, division, and brigade commanders. The more they talked, the unhappier they became, and eventually most reached the conclusion that the attack could not possibly succeed. Couch suspected that Sumner agreed, but the old soldier was more disturbed by his subordinates' lack of confidence in their commanding general. As it was, Burnside heard the rumblings of discontent—in fact, two colonels told him point-blank that the offensive would fail—so on 10 December he summoned the Right Grand Division generals to his headquarters. There he castigated the assembled group for their doubts, focusing his anger in particular on Winfield Scott Hancock, a Second Corps divisional commander. Burnside insisted that his subordinates' first and foremost responsibility was to obey their commander's orders. Couch felt guilty because he had been more outspoken than anyone in his opposition at the meeting the previous day, so he rose and assured Burnside that everyone would do his best. The fact was, however, that bluff Major General William French was the only one present who showed much enthusiasm. Opposition was more muted in the Left Grand Division, in part because its mission seemed less daunting and because Franklin and Smith and Reynolds wanted to give Burnside's plan the benefit of the doubt.[16]

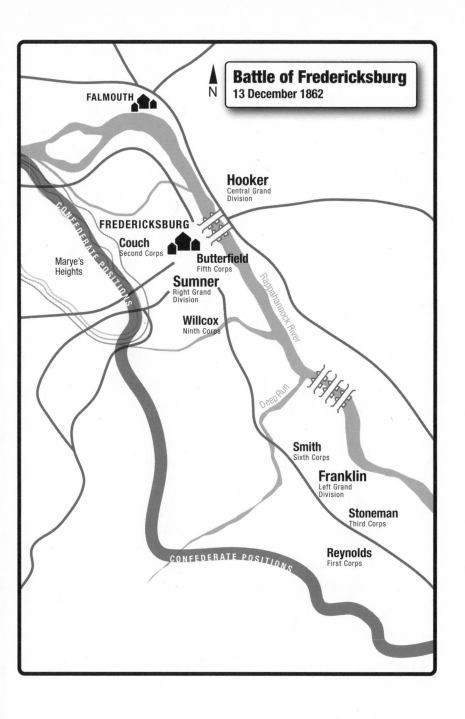

Joseph Hooker was unwilling to cut Burnside any such slack. He had small use for Burnside's military abilities to begin with, and he disliked his strategy as much as almost everyone else. Unlike the others, however, Hooker perceived an upside to the disaster he and his brother officers predicted. He recognized that the defeat he foresaw would discredit Burnside and make his position as Army of the Potomac commander vulnerable, if not untenable. Hooker understood that he needed to place his opposition to Burnside's scheme squarely on the record if he hoped to become the Army of the Potomac's next leader. Therefore, in the weeks before Fredericksburg, Hooker vigorously denounced Burnside's strategic and tactical ideas to both his fellow officers and visiting journalists. In addition, he wrote several letters to Stanton critical of Burnside. His actions violated military regulations and etiquette, but Hooker gambled that the Lincoln administration would be more interested in the prescience he had demonstrated.[17]

Attention to detail was not Burnside's strong suit, and the Army of the Potomac paid a steep price for this weakness on 13 December in front of Fredericksburg. Burnside wanted Franklin's Left Grand Division to launch a full-scale assault on the Confederate right, or southern, flank. Unhappily, he did not issue clear-cut orders for Franklin to do so. He directed Franklin to attack with at least one division, and he gave him discretion in carrying out his orders. Franklin was an intelligent man, but he had not demonstrated much initiative or aggressiveness in the war so far. Although he would follow orders to the letter, he would not go much beyond that. Instead of a massive attack on the rebel line with his entire grand division, he sent in Reynolds's First Corps only. The First Corps had seen plenty of action at Second Bull Run, Turner's Gap, and at the infamous Cornfield at Antietam, but it could not overcome rebel opposition. Brigadier Generals John Gibbon and Abner Doubleday made little headway with their divisions, and in fact Gibbon was seriously wounded. Only George Meade's division managed to get within slugging range of the enemy, but he accomplished all that could be expected with his limited forces. Meade led his men across some swampy ground, found a gap in the Confederate line, and plunged through. Unfortunately, they received no support, and Confederate reinforcements rushed forward to plug the hole in the line and drive the bluecoats back. Meade survived unhurt even though he received two bullet holes through the top of his hat, and his division lost a third of its men. The remainder of the Left Grand Division—specifically, Smith's Sixth Corps, the Army of the Potomac's largest—as well as one of the two Third Corps divisions Burnside sent over to help, scarcely engaged the Confederates at all, although Franklin insisted for the rest of the day that he needed every soldier he could get to resist the enemy attack he feared might develop.

Meanwhile, to the north, the second part of Burnside's disjointed offensive opened up late in the morning. Sumner's Right Grand Division, reinforced by some of Hooker's troops, had the difficult task of assailing Confederate soldiers dug in along Marye's Heights just above Fredericksburg. Here, too, Burnside's directives lacked detail and specificity; he merely called for a general attack. Because Burnside had ordered Sumner to remain on the opposite side of the Rappahannock, it was difficult for Old Bull to manage his units, so they assaulted in an uncoordinated fashion. French's and Hancock's Second Corps divisions crossed the open plain and drove toward the enemy's fieldworks, but withering Confederate fire stopped their attacks cold. Oliver Otis Howard then attempted to outflank the rebel left flank with his division, but swampy ground there channeled his unit into the same route that had brought French's and Hancock's divisions to grief, with similar results. After the Second Corps' operations ground to a halt, Willcox tried his hand with his Ninth Corps. He sent Brigadier Generals Samuel Sturgis and George Getty forward with their divisions, but they were repulsed one after the other.

At about this time, Burnside dispatched Hooker across the Rappahannock for a firsthand look at the situation. Burnside had dissipated most of Hooker's Central Grand Division, so Fighting Joe had comparatively few men under his command. Even so, Couch was relieved to see someone of higher authority capable of providing assistance and reassurance. He briefed Hooker on the situation and told him candidly he did not think that his troops could carry the enemy line. Hooker consulted Willcox, Hancock, and French and found them of the same mind. Hooker was not surprised, and he recommended to Burnside that he suspend the offensive. Burnside, however, believed that Franklin might break through over on the Union left at any minute, and he wanted corresponding pressure exerted on the other end of the line. He ordered the assaults resumed, even after Hooker galloped across the river to plead his case in person. In response, Hooker threw a Third Corps brigade and a Fifth Corps brigade into the Confederate buzzsaw to be chewed up. Finally, near dusk, Couch rode up to Brigadier General Andrew Humphreys and, with tears streaming down his cheeks, implored him to commit his untried Fifth Corps division into action to relieve the pressure on his beleaguered men. Hooker gave the necessary orders through Butterfield, and Humphreys bravely led his men right up to the rebel lines. Although a wounded soldier from a previous assault propped himself up on his elbow and yelled at Humphreys, "Give it to them, General! Give it to them!" the attack, like all the others, broke in blood.[18]

By the end of the day, some 12,300 Union soldiers were killed, wounded, or captured in front of Fredericksburg. Confederate losses were less than half that. Burnside had done his worst, but he refused to acknowledge defeat.

Although he was outwardly cheerful and upbeat during the battle, observers recognized the facade for what it was. In fact, Burnside was deeply distressed by the disaster he had authored, and his anguish made him increasingly irrational and stubborn. In desperation, Burnside decided to personally lead his old Ninth Corps in an all-out assault on the rebel lines the next morning. Talking among themselves, some of the general officers—Willcox, Humphreys, Butterfield, and others—concluded that such an attack was bound to fail. Willcox went to Sumner to express his concerns. Sumner believed that soldiers should obey orders, but he too had misgivings about Burnside's latest plan. Although he would not publicly challenge his superior officer, Sumner agreed to suggest to Burnside that he summon a council of war of senior commanders to examine the situation.[19]

Sumner was as good as his word. Meeting privately with Burnside, he not only asked for a council of war, but he also recommended against renewing the offensive. Old Bull said, "General, I hope you will desist from this attack; I do not know of any general officer who approves of it, and I think it will prove disastrous to the army."[20] Such strong language from the stouthearted veteran gave Burnside pause. Willcox also talked with Burnside in confidence, and he seconded Sumner. Sometime after midnight, Burnside convened a meeting of senior commanders. No one endorsed his plan, and in fact almost everyone there came out against it. Hooker was lying on a bed in the corner of the room, and he rose to bluntly condemn the idea of continuing the battle under these circumstances. He was careful, however, to preserve his reputation for aggressiveness by stating that the army needed to engage the enemy at some point. Burnside crossed the Rappahannock and spoke with Couch and some of the other officers there, and then he sought out Franklin for his opinion. Once again, he found no support. Confronted with a phalanx of doubters, Burnside reluctantly cancelled his proposed attack and ended the battle. He had originally intended to occupy Fredericksburg to maintain a foothold on the other side of the Rappahannock, but on 15 December he pulled his men back across the river. The Army of the Potomac withdrew so secretly that the rebels did not even know it was gone until morning. The campaign was over, but not its impact. Watching the Union corpses stiffen on the plain in front of Fredericksburg, Burnside exclaimed to Baldy Smith, "Oh! Those men! Oh! Those men! Those men over there! I am thinking of them all the time!"[21]

Burnside Relieved

Fredericksburg was merely the first of several setbacks and disappointments that plagued the Union that winter. In Mississippi, the Confederates foiled

Grant's offensive against Vicksburg by raiding his supply base at Holly
Springs on 20 December and repelling Major General William Sherman's
unwise assault on Chickasaw Bluffs nine days later. Although Major General
William Rosecrans's Army of the Cumberland fought off Braxton Bragg's attack at the Battle of Stone's River southeast of Nashville the day before and
after the new year, the casualty figures—over 13,000 Union killed,
wounded, and missing—hardly justified the results. Lincoln was more than
willing to label the engagement a victory, but it did not bring the Union any
closer to crushing the rebellion.

No one ever questioned Ambrose Burnside's sincerity, and no doubt his
anguish about the Union dead decomposing across the Rappahannock was
genuine. Indeed, he readily accepted responsibility for the defeat at Fredericksburg. Whatever his faults, Burnside was no quitter, so within a couple
weeks after the battle he decided to recross the Rappahannock for another
go at the Confederate army. This time, though, he chose to cross at Skinker's
Neck, downstream from Fredericksburg. Just as the Army of the Potomac
was getting underway, however, on 30 December Burnside received a cryptic
telegram from Lincoln ordering him to suspend any operations he had
planned.[22]

Lincoln's orders were not coincidental. Although the Army of the Potomac's officer corps had initially been supportive when Burnside assumed
command, their confidence in his leadership and strategy had rapidly evaporated after Fredericksburg. This discontent extended all the way up to the
grand division commanders, all of whom opposed Burnside's latest plan.
William Franklin and Baldy Smith were among the army's biggest doubters.
As far as they were concerned, Fredericksburg demonstrated among other
things the futility of waging war along the Rappahannock. They believed
that the Army of the Potomac should instead transfer its operations back to
the James River. In fact, on 20 December they sent a letter to Lincoln arguing their case. Lincoln responded two days later. He did not question the
propriety of two subordinates communicating with the president on strategy
without their commander's knowledge, but he instead promised to refer the
letter to the experts—meaning Halleck. The president did, however, dryly
note that the previous July at Harrison's Landing Franklin had argued in favor of abandoning the peninsula in order to conduct operations in northern
Virginia.[23]

Franklin's and Smith's doubts about strategy were symptomatic of their
growing belief that Burnside was not fit to command the Army of the Potomac. Their concern took on an increased urgency when they learned that
Burnside was preparing to resume operations across the Rappahannock. As
they saw things, the soldiers' declining confidence in their leadership, combined with the lessons of Fredericksburg, both pointed to imminent disaster

if Burnside again led the army into battle. Clearly, someone had to alert the Lincoln administration. Franklin and Smith were not the only officers who had these sentiments. So did Brigadier General John Newton, who commanded a division in Smith's Sixth Corps. Newton planned to travel home to Delaware for medical treatment, and he confided in Franklin and Smith that he intended to stop in Washington to seek out some influential policymakers and inform them of the army's plight. Newton later testified that although Franklin and Smith knew of his mission, he acted on his own accord. This may or may not have been true, but neither general made any effort to dissuade him, and in fact Franklin authorized his leave of absence.[24]

On his way to Washington, Newton encountered Brigadier General John Cochrane, the same officer who with Jacob Cox had the previous September advised McClellan to accept the Preliminary Emancipation Proclamation. In the course of their conversation, Newton learned that Cochrane shared his concerns about the Army of the Potomac's current status and leadership. In fact, Cochrane intended to talk to some of his political allies on the Committee on the Conduct of the War about the army's situation. Since Cochrane had political connections and Newton possessed military credibility, the two men decided to join forces to increase their effectiveness. When they reached Washington, however, they discovered to their dismay that Congress had recessed for the Christmas holiday, so the committee members were gone. Luckily, Cochrane managed to secure an interview with Lincoln, so the two men hustled over to the White House. Although they believed that the army had lost all confidence in Burnside, they were reluctant to say this bluntly to the president. Instead, they hemmed and hawed around the subject, talking in allusions and innuendos. Lincoln listened in silence, and when they were through he suggested that they were simply two troublemakers trying to undermine their commanding officer. Newton and Cochrane assured him that this was not the case; they simply wanted to inform him of the army's dismal condition. They noted that another offensive might destroy the army, and they urged him to look into the matter personally. Lincoln had already heard rumors to this effect, and he responded that he would do so, which prompted his 30 December telegram to Burnside. Newton continued home to Delaware, but Cochrane returned to the army. On his way to back, he met Smith and told him about his mission. The next day Franklin and Smith summoned him to their headquarters so Franklin could also hear the details firsthand.[25]

Burnside was stunned by Lincoln's order. He was already disheartened by his defeat at Fredericksburg, but the president's obvious lack of confidence in him deepened his depression. He hurried to Washington to learn the details behind this latest directive, and there he huddled with Lincoln, Stanton, and Halleck. Lincoln informed Burnside that some generals had visited him and claimed that a new offensive would ruin the army, so he hesitated to au- thorize one until he consulted Stanton and Halleck. Burnside was angered by this breach of military regulations, and he demanded to know the officers' identities so he could punish them. Lincoln, however, declined to divulge their names, even though Halleck weighed in on Burnside's side. As far as Lincoln was concerned, they had bigger problems right then than a couple of renegade generals. Burnside stated that he believed the army should recross the Rappahannock, but some of his subordinates clearly disagreed. Under these circumstances, Burnside thought it was best for the public good for him to resign as the Army of the Potomac's commander. He later claimed that he recommended that Stanton and Halleck step down as well, but Old Brains denied that this happened in his presence. Lincoln refused to accept Burn- side's resignation, even when the general resubmitted it on 5 January after he had returned to Falmouth. Lincoln wrote to Burnside that he regretted that his subordinates' lacked confidence in him, but he did not think that chang- ing commanders right then was the solution. The president wanted Halleck to resolve this impasse, but Old Brains as usual refused to commit himself. As a result, Burnside received no guidance from Washington.[26]

Personnel problems also kept Burnside busy, but in this case the Lincoln administration was more helpful. On 23 December, Burnside fulfilled his promise to George Meade by appointing him Fifth Corps commander. Meade had fought well at Fredericksburg—in fact, he was the only Union general who had achieved any success at all on that unhappy occasion—and he had recently been promoted to major general. Burnside would have as- signed him the corps sooner, but Hooker had objected. Although Fighting Joe shared the general consensus that Meade was a capable officer, he felt that Butterfield deserved to keep his corps because he had done a fine job too. Moreover, Hooker did not like the idea of changing commanders in the middle of a campaign. Burnside, however, believed that Meade was more qualified for the post, and Stanton and Halleck agreed. After celebrating the good news with old friends Franklin, Smith, Reynolds, Brigadier General William Brooks, and others, Meade rode over to Fifth Corps' headquarters to claim his prize. Butterfield was gracious, and he insisted that Meade stay for Christmas dinner with him and the unit's division and brigade leaders. After the meal the two men talked alone. Butterfield confessed that he was unhappy with his sudden demotion to division command because Burnside had assured him that his promotion was permanent, but Meade went away convinced that Butterfield understood the changed circumstances.[27]

Meade was sorely mistaken if he expected Butterfield to meekly accept his demotion. Whatever his military accomplishments, Butterfield was first and foremost a political animal thoroughly familiar with wire-pulling and arm-twisting. As soon as he learned of Meade's promotion, Butterfield penned letters to, among others, Republican senators Zachariah Chandler and Henry Wilson. Both were powerful politicians; the former was a member of the Committee on the Conduct of the War, and the latter chaired the Senate Military Affairs Committee. Butterfield justified his military record, inquired about the circumstances of Meade's promotion to major general, and asked them to lobby Lincoln to put him back in his rightful command. Butterfield was a formidable force on his own, but he also had Hooker's assistance. Although Hooker may have appreciated Meade's combat abilities, he recognized that Butterfield was a useful man both on and off the battlefield. Hooker wrote directly to Stanton to plead Butterfield's case. In the end, Butterfield's efforts accomplished nothing, so he had to be satisfied with Burnside's promise to find him a corps at a future date. The incident did, however, help to cement an alliance between Hooker and Butterfield that would be very important to both men.[28]

Unfortunately for the Army of the Potomac, Burnside possessed a stubborn streak that often overruled his common sense and intelligence. He was determined to recross the Rappahannock and engage Lee's army, despite the opposition of his leading generals, Halleck's refusal to provide substantive guidance, and the Lincoln administration's obvious doubts in his military ability. This time, however, Burnside decided to cross the river at Banks Ford, upstream from Fredericksburg, in an operation that became known as the Mud March. On 20 January, the Army of the Potomac rolled into motion, but it quickly ran into trouble. The good weather that had prevailed since Fredericksburg suddenly soured. It began to rain; a heavy, cold, sleety rain that turned the roads into troughs of mud. Wagons mired in the muck up to their axles, marching columns ground to a halt, tempers ran short, and the rebels mocked the floundering army from the south side of the river.

Burnside tried to remain cheerful and upbeat, but this was hard to do when the luck upon which he had always relied so dramatically deserted him. To make things worse, he received little support from his high-ranking officers, almost all of whom opposed the operation. Sumner at least tried to execute his orders and keep the marching columns on schedule, despite his doubts. The same could not be said of the other grand division commanders. Hooker did little but publicly criticize Burnside, his ideas, and the Lincoln administration. He stated that only a military dictatorship could save the Union now. Fighting Joe had told Burnside that his plan had only a 5 percent chance of succeeding, but these were better odds than Franklin offered. He and Smith lobbied Burnside hard to cancel an operation they believed was bound to fail, but without luck. Although Smith later claimed that he told his staff to loyally do their best to carry out Burnside's orders regardless of their personal feelings, his actions belied his words. Once the Mud March got underway, Franklin, Smith, and their staffs abdicated their responsibilities and spent their time in comfort at their headquarters disparaging Burnside. Burnside persevered for two days, but he finally admitted defeat and ordered the army back to camp. The Mud March was over, and although battle casualties were almost nonexistent, the humiliation the army felt stung almost as much as defeat.[29]

Burnside tried to be philosophical about the setback, telling Meade that perhaps it was just as well that the operation had failed because so many officers opposed it. The truth was, however, that he was increasingly demoralized, exhausted, and angry. Indeed, Burnside's pleasant disposition was wilting under the heat of constant disappointment and animosity. On 17 January, for example, he reviewed the Second Corps and received such a cold reception that Couch and Sumner were both embarrassed. Nor was the disenchantment limited to the rank and file. He had already ordered the arrest of Smith's and Franklin's friend Brigadier General William Brooks, an outspoken pro-McClellan Sixth Corps brigade commander, for insubordination because he complained so much about the army's current mess. Although Burnside had initially accepted responsibility for Fredericksburg, the more he thought about it, the more inclined he was to blame others for the defeat. In particular, he believed that Franklin should have been more aggressive in his assaults on the rebel right flank. Burnside kept his views to himself and his staff, biding his time and letting his resentment fester. Reports that Hooker and others were openly denigrating his leadership stoked his growing rage. Defeat at Fredericksburg exposed him to criticism from McClellanites such as Franklin and Smith on the one side and Hooker on the other. It was becoming obvious to him that he could not exercise his authority with such a recalcitrant high command. Shortly after the Mud March, Franklin and Smith stopped at Burnside's headquarters for dinner. The two men found their commander in an odd mood, alternately talkative and reticent. At one point he blurted out, "In a day or two you will hear of something that will surprise you all."[30]

Burnside's surprise was General Orders Number Eight, dated 23 January. In drawing up this directive, Burnside attempted to purge the Army of the Potomac's officer corps of those who had hindered his efforts to prosecute the war as he saw fit. Not surprisingly, Hooker was the primary target. Burnside relieved him from his Central Grand Division command and dismissed him from the United States Army for his unjust criticisms of his superiors, his proclivity for sowing dissent and mistrust among his fellow officers, and his tendency to distort the truth. Hooker was not the only thorn Burnside pulled from his side. Franklin and Smith had repeatedly condemned and obstructed his plans, so he removed them too. Sacking these three prominent men was dramatic enough, but Burnside, demonstrating a predilection for all-out measures that characterized his tactics at Fredericksburg, was not through. He had uncovered Cochrane's and Newton's identities—it was an open secret in the army that they were the men who had complained to Lincoln, and anyway it was a simple matter for Burnside to check and see who was on leave around the turn of the year—so he fired them from their posts and from the service. Burnside doled out a similar punishment to William Brooks. Brooks had a bad attitude toward superior officers like Burnside, whom he considered incompetent, and he was not the type of man to keep his opinions to himself. Burnside had already arrested Brooks for insubordination, and now he sought to expel him from the United States Army permanently. Finally, Burnside took the opportunity to rid the Ninth Corps of two of its division commanders, Brigadier Generals Edward Ferrero and Samuel Sturgis. Sturgis was a heavy-drinking malcontent who had complained that he deserved to command the Ninth Corps more than Willcox, and it is possible that this motivated Burnside to take action against him. As for Ferrero, he had angered Burnside by recently overstaying his leave of absence.[31]

Although Burnside had drawn up his directive, he hesitated to publish it, and in fact he initially showed it to only a few people at his headquarters. The more he thought about it, though, the more he realized that his authority over the army was at stake, so he prepared to issue his orders. His chief of staff, John Parke, suggested that Burnside should obtain Lincoln's approval before he took such drastic action. Burnside agreed, and the next day he traveled to Washington with both General Orders Number Eight and his resignation in hand. Burnside claimed that he did not want to dictate to the government, but he was in effect giving the president an ultimatum to choose between him and his opponents in the officer corps. He was confident he could persuade Lincoln to see things his way, so he was probably surprised when the president hesitated. Although Lincoln had been willing to let Burnside reshape the army's high command the previous November—an opportunity of which he had not taken advantage—circumstances were different now. Fredericksburg had exposed Burnside's shortcomings and stripped away the aura of success he had possessed when Lincoln had put him in charge of the Army of the Potomac. Lincoln acknowledged that Burnside's grievances against Hooker, Franklin, and others had merit, but he was reluctant to bless the proposed remedy. Instead, he said that he needed time to consult his advisers, so Burnside returned to his army.[32]

While Burnside pondered his future, Lincoln met with Halleck and the cabinet. Halleck supported Burnside and his General Orders Number Eight, but Lincoln was unwilling to wreck the Army of the Potomac's high command for one man's sake, especially when that one man, however likable, had recently suffered a staggering defeat. In this light, it was clear to Lincoln that Burnside, not the others, had to go. Having determined Burnside's fate, Lincoln, Halleck, and the cabinet focused on finding his replacement. There was some discussion about summoning William Rosecrans from out west to take the job. Rosecrans commanded the Army of the Cumberland, and he had recently won—"survived" was perhaps the better word—the Battle of Stone's River, so he had a successful record. However, everyone remembered John Pope's dismal experience with the Army of the Potomac's cliquish officer corps when Lincoln and Halleck brought him in from out west, and no one wanted to go through that again. This limited the selection pool to the Army of the Potomac. Everyone valued and respected Bull Sumner for his straightforward courage, but it was no secret that he was increasingly enfeebled. Although Franklin was next in seniority behind Burnside and Sumner, he was under a cloud for his lackluster performance at Fredericksburg, and anyway he was a McClellan man who had conspired against Burnside. Couch aroused no enthusiasm, and Reynolds had told Halleck that although he would obey orders, he only wanted the position if he could have more freedom of action than previous commanders had enjoyed, a condition Lincoln was unwilling to grant.[33]

All this culling left only two prominent high-ranking officers under consideration: George Meade and Joe Hooker. Despite Meade's admirable performance at Fredericksburg, he was a mostly unknown quantity who did not possess any of Hooker's advantages. Hooker was a senior officer in an army that valued rank and precedence. In addition, Hooker was the biggest war hero the Army of the Potomac had, and as such he was very popular among the public. He had been actively lobbying for the job for some time, and in fact he had been to Washington earlier in the month for that purpose, so he had plenty of politically powerful supporters who would be pleased with his ascension. Salmon Chase and many Radical Republicans were especially enamored with Hooker, apparently believing that his hatred of McClellan was synonymous with support for their political agenda. On the other hand, Halleck and Stanton had serious reservations about entrusting Hooker with the Union's foremost army. They had both been in prewar California with Hooker, and they knew all about his significant character flaws that included heavy drinking and excessive womanizing. Moreover, it was no secret that Hooker had worked hard to undermine Burnside, and promoting him might seem like a reward for such unethical actions. Halleck and the cabinet could advise, but the decision was Lincoln's. He carefully weighed the pros and cons, and he ultimately concluded that there was only one viable option. On 25 January, he issued orders relieving Burnside and giving Hooker command of the Army of the Potomac.[34]

Lincoln's decision required some shuffling of the Army of the Potomac's high command, although nothing as dramatic or vindictive as Burnside's General Orders Number Eight demanded. The same directive that entrusted the army to Hooker also removed Sumner and Franklin from their positions. Neither officer liked Fighting Joe much, and Sumner was senior to Hooker, so Lincoln understood that keeping them in their current posts would be begging for trouble. Sumner had asked to be relieved the previous autumn, and now Lincoln granted his request. The president, however, still valued Old Bull enough to appoint him commander of the Department of Missouri two months later. Unfortunately, the war had sapped Sumner's strength, and he died in Syracuse, New York, en route to his new post, on 21 March 1863. As for Franklin, in August 1863, Lincoln assigned him to lead the Nineteenth Corps in Louisiana. He participated in Nathaniel Banks's disastrous Red River campaign the following spring and was wounded in the shin. He resigned his command in May 1864 and played no further active part in the conflict. After the war, he was general manager of the Colt Fire Arms Manufacturing Company in Connecticut and later the American commissioner general at the Paris Exposition. He died in 1903.

As for Burnside, he wanted to resign both his command and his commission, but Lincoln refused to accept the latter. Like almost everyone else, Lincoln was fond of Burnside, and he thought the general could still be of use to the Union war effort. Unfortunately, there were only a limited number of slots available for a man of Burnside's high rank, so finding a place for him was not easy. Lincoln, Stanton, and Halleck considered sending him back to North Carolina, but Burnside noted that the current commander, Major General John Foster, was already doing a fine job there. In the end, Lincoln decided to give Burnside a thirty-day leave of absence while he pondered his future. When Burnside got official word that he had been relieved as Army of the Potomac commander, he literally broke out the champagne and threw a party for his headquarters. Burnside was not an especially astute man, but he had some uncharacteristic words of wisdom for a young officer who inquired about the celebration: "Why, I am relieved of the Army of the Potomac, and the orders are being circulated now, that Hooker is to be my successor. . . . They will find out before many days, that it is not every man who can command an army of one hundred and fifty thousand men."[35]

Conclusions

Burnside failed as Army of the Potomac commander in all sorts of often spectacular ways, but surely one of his biggest faults was his inability to uti-

lize his subordinates effectively. The Lincoln administration showed its confidence in Burnside by giving him considerable leeway in the selection and
retention of his corps commanders, but he fumbled the opportunity. Burnside relied exclusively on seniority in assigning his corps and grand division
commanders. He did so partly because he was committed to the old Army
emphasis on rank and partly because he was a good-natured man unwilling
to antagonize his friends by judging them according to the ruthless standards
of war. As a result, Burnside merely rewarded longevity and pushed inade-
quate officers such as Stoneman and Franklin higher up the chain of command and beyond their talents. Thus, Burnside missed the chance to build
an officer corps committed to him and his ideas. Instead, he got intractable
subordinates who failed him on the battlefield and worked against him in
camp. No doubt Burnside bore primary responsibility for his defeats at Fredericksburg and elsewhere, but the efforts of some of his subordinates, such as
Hooker and Franklin, to undermine him certainly did not make his job any
easier.

It is important, however, to keep things in perspective. For one thing,
Burnside's system did result in some capable men such as Meade and Couch
attaining corps command. For another, it is not altogether certain that
Burnside could have located enough qualified and loyal generals to fill the
available corps even if he wanted or had been able to. The Army of the Potomac had precious few victories to its credit so far, and there simply were
not that many brigade and division commanders who had demonstrated sufficient tactical skill—as opposed to courage, which they almost all had—to
effectively lead a corps. Moreover, doing so would have alienated innumerable officers wedded to the concept of promotion through seniority, further
poisoning an officer corps already rent with dissension. All these difficulties
could have been overcome through strong leadership and force of will, but
these were not among Burnside's attributes. The problem, then, was not so
much that Burnside failed to take advantage of the opportunity the Lincoln
administration presented him, but rather that the president chose the wrong
man for the position in the first place.

CHAPTER THREE

Fighting Joe's Big Opportunity
January to June 1863

The Finest Army on the Planet

Unlike Ambrose Burnside, Joseph Hooker brimmed with self-confidence. He combined this breezy self-assurance with the cavalier, combative, and outspoken attitude of a man who was accustomed to success and expected more of it in the future. Indeed, Hooker had reasons for his positive disposition. His record on the battlefield, although not as stellar as he often claimed, had been on the whole praiseworthy. Indeed, he had seen as much action as any officer in the army, having fought at Williamsburg, Fair Oaks, the Seven Days Battles, Second Bull Run, Antietam, and Fredericksburg. He had lobbied hard for command of the Army of the Potomac, and his efforts had gained him numerous powerful allies in Washington, including Radical Republicans such as Salmon Chase and Zachariah Chandler. Finally, the Union public idolized him as a war hero for his actions on the peninsula and at Antietam. Unfortunately, Hooker did not recognize his own numerous weaknesses and limitations. Lincoln appointed Hooker head of the Army of the Potomac knowing full well that he was entrusting the Union's preeminent army to a deeply flawed officer, but Lincoln was convinced that Fighting Joe was the only viable option among the available candidates. The president's reluctance compelled him to write a candid and heartfelt letter to Hooker that summed up his concerns:

> I have placed you at the head of the Army of the Potomac. Of course I have done this upon what appears to me to be sufficient reasons, and yet I think it best for you to know that there are some things in regard to which I am not quite satisfied with you. I believe you to be a brave and

skillful soldier, which, of course, I like. I also believe you do not mix politics with your profession, in which you are right. You have confidence in yourself, which is a valuable, if not an indispensable, quality. You are ambitious, which, within reasonable bounds, does good rather than harm; but I think that during General Burnside's command of the army you have taken counsel of your ambition, and thwarted him as much as you could, in which you did a great wrong to the country and to a most meritorious and honorable brother officer. I have heard, in such a way as to believe it, of your recently saying that both the Army and the Government needed a dictator. Of course, it was not for this, but in spite of it, that I have given you the command. Only those generals who gain successes can set up dictators. What I now ask of you is military success, and I will risk the dictatorship. The Government will support you to the utmost of its ability, which is neither more nor less than it has done and will do for all commanders. I much fear that the spirit which you have aided to infuse into the army, of criticising [sic] their commander and withholding confidence from him, will now turn upon you. I shall assist you as far as I can to put it down. Neither you nor Napoleon, if he were alive again, could get any good out of an army while such a spirit prevails in it. And now beware of rashness. Beware of rashness, but with energy and sleepless vigilance go forward and give us victories.[1]

Lincoln undoubtedly hoped that once Hooker was made aware of his deficiencies, he would undertake efforts to overcome them. As it was, Hooker's character contained other significant flaws that Lincoln knew about but chose not to put in his letter. These included persistent rumors of excessive drinking and womanizing dating back to his dissolute California days. In addition, Hooker had never held an important independent command, so he was unfamiliar with the loneliness and isolation this entailed. Moreover, in his cold-blooded climb to the top of the military hierarchy he had made plenty of enemies who would not be unhappy to see him fail, Halleck being among the most significant. In fact, Hooker was so concerned about Old Brains's hostility that he insisted on communicating directly with Lincoln, short-circuiting the general in chief right out of the chain of command. It was George Stoneman, however, who best articulated Hooker's biggest and least-recognized flaw. Stoneman had served with Hooker in the old army, and he later said of him, "He [Hooker] could play the best game of poker I ever saw until it came to the point when he should go a thousand better, and then he would flunk."[2]

Stoneman's misgivings about Hooker were indicative of those of the rest of the Army of the Potomac's officer corps. Most of the senior officers knew

Hooker personally, and many were uncomfortable with his cocky, faultfind-ing, underhanded, and hyperbolic nature. Others questioned his moral char-acter. One colonel later wrote, "I can say from personal knowledge and experience, that the Headquarters of the Army of the Potomac was a place to which no self-respecting man liked to go, and no decent women could go. It was a combination of barroom and brothel."[3] Even so, the consensus among men such as Meade and Slocum was that anyone was better than Burnside, so they were prepared to give Fighting Joe the benefit of the doubt for now. The fact that these men, normally so sensitive to honor and dignity, were willing to support Hooker showed their desperate desire for a com-mander who could finally lead them to victory. In Hooker's old Third Corps there was genuine enthusiasm among high-ranking officers such as David Birney, Daniel Sickles, and Hiram Berry for their friend's ascension to the top spot. As for the enlisted men, they were on the whole pleased with Hooker's promotion because they knew him by his reputation as a hard-fighting and charismatic officer who had demonstrated concern for their well-being by speaking out against the futile assaults at Fredericksburg.[4]

Others questioned the people with whom Hooker chose to associate. When Hooker assumed command of the Army of the Potomac, he proposed making Brigadier General Charles Stone, the disgraced and persecuted scapegoat from the Battle of Ball's Bluff in October 1861, his chief of staff, but the Lincoln administration vetoed that idea. Instead, Hooker asked Daniel Butterfield if he wanted the job. Butterfield hesitated because he still hoped for a corps, but he ultimately agreed. Although Butterfield ran Hooker's headquarters efficiently enough, he generated considerable resent-ment. Officers such as Meade took offense at his imperious and conceited at-titude that was all the more galling because he was not a professional soldier. Butterfield's arrogance drove the provost marshal, Brigadier General Marsena Patrick, almost to distraction until he secured a private interview with Hooker to explain his problems with the chief of staff. Small wonder that antagonized officers dredged up and circulated rumors that Butterfield's prewar Utica, New York, fire company intentionally set a church ablaze so it could make money extinguishing it.[5]

As a matter of fact, Hooker and Butterfield did good work that winter. Burnside had been as careless in administration as in strategy and tactics, so Hooker inherited an army in terrible condition. Defeat and humiliation at Fredericksburg and the Mud March were bad enough, but other factors also contributed to a dramatic decline in morale and efficiency. The troops had not been paid for months, and poor sanitary conditions had led to the spread of diseases such as typhoid and dysentery. Predictably, the desertion rate had skyrocketed. To everyone's surprise, Hooker turned out to be a first-rate administrator and organizer, one of whom even McClellan would have been proud. He and Butterfield resorted to commonsense remedies for the army's innumerable problems. They improved sanitary conditions by ensuring that the troops kept clean, received fresh fruits and vegetables, and regularly aired out their quarters. They established hospitals that were not pestholes, and they clamped down on the unchecked distribution of liquor. These actions in and of themselves went a long way toward restoring the army, but Hooker and Butterfield went further. They raised morale by developing badges for each corps, making sure the soldiers got paid, creating a furlough system for each company, and holding numerous grand reviews. They also established an effective intelligence system to gather and analyze information on the enemy, thus putting an end to the days of exaggerated Confederate troop strength. By spring, Hooker could and did boast that the Army of the Potomac was the finest army on the planet.

In his efforts to revitalize the Army of the Potomac, Hooker did not neglect its organizational structure. On 5 February, he abolished the unwieldy grand divisions, leaving him with seven infantry corps under his direct command. He also focused his attention on its deficient cavalry. Hitherto, the army's cavalry had been scattered among its various corps and divisions and used mostly for picket and escort duty. Its divisions never worked together, so it was no wonder its Confederate counterpart frequently ran rings around it. Hooker wanted to create a cavalry corps capable of operating as an independent unit. To command it, he transferred George Stoneman in from the Third Corps. It was a logical, if uninspired, choice, as some officers recognized. Stoneman had led the Army of the Potomac's cavalry on the peninsula to McClellan's satisfaction until illness removed him from the saddle. Moreover, he was an old acquaintance of Hooker's, and he understood what Fighting Joe wanted to accomplish. He was not, however, an inspiring or brilliant officer. Stoneman's only real competition for the job was Brigadier General Alfred Pleasonton, who commanded a cavalry division. Hooker, however, did not yet think much of Pleasonton, who was in any case junior to Stoneman and a McClellan man, so it was easy for Fighting Joe to pass him over.[6]

Lincoln as usual reserved the right to approve any changes in corps commanders, but he was willing to go along with the few adjustments Hooker wanted to make. Stoneman's transfer to the cavalry left the Third Corps leaderless, so Hooker filled the vacancy with Brigadier General Daniel Sickles, one of the Civil War's most controversial and colorful officers. Sickles was an ambitious, determined, unscrupulous, and charismatic man who provoked strong reactions in everyone he met. Born in New York City in 1819, Sickles had had a turbulent and depraved youth. He was not without intellect, though, and he eventually studied law with Benjamin Butler before opening his own practice. Although allegations of wrongdoing had swirled around him from the very start of his professional career, he managed to get elected to the New York legislature in 1847. He became active in Tammany Hall, and he played a major role in establishing Central Park. In 1853, he accepted a position as secretary to the American legation in London, and while overseas he helped formulate the infamous Ostend Manifesto that sought to pry Cuba from Spanish rule. His personal behavior was even more disreputable. He had married a sixteen-year-old girl in 1852, but he did not take her to Europe with him. Instead, he squired around in public his mistress, a well-known New York City prostitute. Sickles returned to the States in 1855 and won election to Congress as a Democrat the following year. While in Washington, his wife embarked on a surreptitious affair with Philip Barton Key, son of Francis Scott Key, author of the "Star Spangled Banner." When Sickles found out, he killed the unarmed Key in broad daylight in Lafayette Square on 27 February 1859. Sickles was tried for murder, but a legal team that included Edwin Stanton used a temporary insanity defense to secure his acquittal. Despite this vindication, Sickles's career was in ruins—not so much for slaying his wife's lover but rather because he publicly forgave her.

The Civil War offered Sickles an opportunity for redemption. He immersed himself in the Union cause, raised a brigade of New Yorkers, and got himself commissioned a brigadier general. He was widely disliked by the Army of the Potomac's officer corps for his scandalous past, but he worked hard to overcome this antipathy and win public approval. He threw elaborate parties for officers that rivaled even Kearny's, cultivated the press to inflate his military reputation, and ingratiated himself with politicians all the way up to his friend the president. Although he was part of the anti-McClellan Third Corps, he was careful not to criticize Little Mac until after Lincoln removed him as Army of the Potomac commander. His actions won the grudging respect of some, and the friendship of others. Joseph Hooker was among the latter category. Hooker initially disliked Sickles, but the two men were kindred spirits, and they eventually formed a strong bond. Hooker praised Sickles's performance on the peninsula in his battle reports, but Sickles's military talent was more apparent than real. In fact, after the Army of the Potomac reached Harrison's Landing, Sickles secured a leave of absence to recruit in New York, and he did not return to the army until after Second Bull Run and Antietam. Sickles then assumed command of a Third Corps division by virtue of his seniority. When Hooker took over the Army of the Potomac, he assigned the Third Corps to Sickles even though many other eligible officers outranked him, including Major Generals Winfield Scott Hancock, George Sykes, William French, Abner Doubleday, and fellow

Third Corps divisional commander Hiram Berry. Sickles, however, managed to procure a major generalship in mid-March 1863, and he persuaded the Lincoln administration to backdate it so that he became senior to Berry and most of his competitors.[7]

There was at first only one corps commander Hooker wanted removed: Baldy Smith. Smith was a chronic complainer and intriguer who was never happy with any superior officer. Hooker was cut from the same cloth, so he recognized Smith for what he was. Smith had worked hard to undermine Burnside, and Hooker did not intend to give Baldy the opportunity to employ his talent for discord against him. It was a reasonable precaution; Smith had even less respect for Hooker than he had for Burnside. Fortunately for Hooker, on this issue he had Lincoln's and Halleck's sympathy and support. A week after he assumed command, Hooker transferred Smith to command the Ninth Corps, which Halleck had just ordered to Fortress Monroe. The only problem was that Hooker had already assured Orlando Willcox that he would remain Ninth Corps commander. Promises could be broken, though, and Hooker was not the kind of man to keep his word when it contradicted his immediate best interests. As a result, Willcox lost his corps and his respect for Hooker. Fighting Joe was willing to pay that price, however, to rid himself of the troublesome Smith. Indeed, he wrote, "This change, I am satisfied, will conduce to the good feeling and efficiency of this army."[8] Unfortunately for the Army of the Potomac's officers and men, they had not seen the last of Baldy Smith.[9]

To replace Smith, Hooker gave the Sixth Corps to John Sedgwick, the army's senior major general without a corps. Sedgwick was a career soldier—West Point class of 1837—who had seen extensive service in the Seminole War, along the Canadian border, with Zachary Taylor and Winfield Scott in Mexico, and in the Utah Expedition. He had led a Second Corps division on the peninsula and had been injured at the Battle of Glendale. McClellan had thought enough of Sedgwick to choose him to command the Twelfth Corps over other officers who had been promoted to major general on the same day—men such as Darius Couch, Israel Richardson, Henry Slocum, George Morrell, and Baldy Smith—but Sedgwick, whose modesty and diffidence were well known, had apparently declined the offer. Sedgwick was seriously wounded at Antietam when Sumner led his division into the horrific ambush at the West Woods, and he had only recently returned to duty. He was a humble, phlegmatic, unobtrusive, and unglamorous bachelor admired for his sturdy common sense and reliability. Although a known McClellan booster, Sedgwick avoided the politicking and backbiting that so characterized the Army of the Potomac's officer corps, preferring to spend his time horseback riding and playing endless games of solitaire in his tent. His staff loved him, and his men affectionately called him "Uncle John." He was not a brilliant officer, but he was still a steady and brave man to have in a fight.[10]

Military units, like people, develop distinct identities based on their composition and performance, and this was true of each of the Army of the Potomac's corps. Unfortunately, the Eleventh Corps had the worst reputation in the army. It possessed a large number of German-Americans with bizarre-sounding names such as von Gilsa, Buschbeck, Soest, and Schimmelfennig. Many native-born Americans viewed them with suspicion. The nativist Know-Nothing movement had peaked scarcely a decade earlier, and xenophobia lurked just beneath the surface of U.S. society. In addition, the Eleventh had not served with the Army of the Potomac very long or very well. While the Army of the Potomac was on the peninsula, the rebels were outfighting and outmaneuvering the Eleventh in the Shenandoah Valley. The corps participated in the Second Bull Run campaign as part of Pope's Army of Virginia, but it missed both Antietam and Fredericksburg. As a result, the Army of the Potomac's officer corps treated the unit like a much-abused stepchild. This disrespect extended all the way to the Eleventh's commander, Major General Franz Sigel. Sigel was a sincere and patriotic man, but his brittle and staid personality made it difficult for him to accept the contempt heaped upon him and his outfit. Moreover, he resented the fact that his corps was the army's smallest. On 12 February, he asked to be relieved of his command. Hooker was reluctant to accept it, perhaps because Radical Republicans had embraced Sigel, but he eventually agreed and forwarded his request to the War Department. Lincoln, however, initially refused to approve it, even though Sigel was among his most troublesome and needy political generals, because he saw the German officer through both a political and military lens. Sigel was a hero to German-Americans, and Lincoln did not want to jeopardize their support for the war by separating him from his conspicuous command. Besides, it would not be easy to find a new slot for such a high-ranking officer. Sigel twisted in the wind for a month, but on 11 March he resubmitted his resignation. This time Lincoln gave in, and he eventually transferred Sigel to head the Department of the Susquehanna. The following year the president put him in charge of the Shenandoah Valley, where the rebels defeated him at the Battle of New Market. Sigel was relieved of his command and played no further part in the war. After the conflict he remained active in politics, although he switched his loyalties to the Democratic party; he died in 1902.[11]

To add to Lincoln's woes, he found himself involved in a squabble over who should succeed Sigel. Eleventh Corps officers Brigadier Generals Carl Schurz, Julius Stahel, and Adolph von Steinwehr all wanted the job. All three men were European immigrants—Schurz and von Steinwehr from

Germany; Stahel from Hungary—and the first two were veterans of and refugees from the Revolutions of 1848. Schurz's advantages were his political connections and his promotion to major general in mid-March. He was a prominent Republican gadfly and Lincoln intimate, but his ambition was greater than his military talent. Although in January he publicly stated that he did not want to command the Eleventh Corps, he changed his mind when he learned of Sigel's resignation. Like Schurz, von Steinwehr also wrote directly to Lincoln to plead his case. He based his claims on his seniority and his professional military training. Sigel recommended Stahel as his successor, but he added that he was really best suited for the cavalry. Lincoln seized upon this to transfer Stahel to command the cavalry in Washington's defenses, but this still left Schurz and von Steinwehr in competition. In the end the president dumped the whole problem onto Hooker's lap.[12]

Hooker had no intention of turning the Eleventh Corps over to either Schurz or von Steinwehr. Indeed, he wrote to Stanton, "I would consider the services of an entire corps as entirely lost to this army were it to fall into the hands of Maj. Gen. Schurz."[13] Instead, Hooker's solution was to assign the Eleventh Corps to Major General Oliver Otis Howard, the Army of the Potomac's senior divisional commander. Howard was unhappy with Hooker's decision to appoint the more junior Sickles to head the Third Corps, and he had asked for a new command commensurate with his rank. Hooker saw the opportunity to kill two birds with one stone, so he immediately dispatched Howard to the Eleventh Corps. Born in Maine in 1830, Howard had attended Bowdoin College before going off to West Point, where he graduated fourth in his class in 1854. Thereafter he had served in Florida before returning to the Military Academy as a math instructor. When the war broke out, he accepted the colonelcy of a Maine regiment and fought at First Bull Run and on the Peninsula. He lost his right arm at the head of a brigade at Fair Oaks, which prompted Kearny to tell him, "General, I am sorry for you; but you must not mind it; the ladies will not think the less of you!" Howard laughed and responded, "There is one thing that we can do, general, we can buy our gloves together!"[14] Despite the seriousness of his wound, he had returned to duty in time to participate at Antietam. After the battle, McClellan gave him Sedgwick's division in the Second Corps, which Howard led bravely at Fredericksburg. Although he possessed plenty of courage, Howard was not a typical West Pointer. He was an abolitionist and a devout Christian without the martinet mannerisms that characterized so many Regular Army officers. He frequently visited hospital wards to talk to the sick and injured about religion, and he demonstrated a sincere concern for the growing number of freedmen. Although Howard admired and respected McClellan, he also believed that the war should terminate slavery. Howard had a good military record, but his reception by the Germans in the Eleventh Corps was not very enthusiastic. The Germans had liked Sigel, and they resented his replacement. Moreover, Howard's obvious piety rubbed many people the wrong way. On the other hand, many of the native-born Americans in the corps welcomed his leadership and hoped he would turn around the outfit's fortunes.[15]

Battle of Chancellorsville

Hooker's confidence in himself and his army soared as winter came to an end. He had plenty of reasons for feeling this way. The Army of the Potomac contained 130,000 soldiers, and Hooker knew this was twice as many men as the hungry rebels across the Rappahannock could muster. Moreover, due to Hooker's and Butterfield's reforms, their men were well fed and well equipped, with high morale and faith in their leadership. Hooker expected success, and he said as much in the course of his conversations throughout that spring. Indeed, he referred to victory as a done deal and prefaced his sentences by saying, "When I get to Richmond" and "After we have taken Richmond." Such optimism was perhaps refreshing after Burnside, but his brazenness raised more than a few eyebrows. Lincoln visited the army early in April to consult on military matters and review the troops. Lincoln liked Hooker, but he too was taken aback by Fighting Joe's brash self-assurance. The president sighed to a friend, "That is the most depressing thing about Hooker. It seems to me that he is overconfident."[16] Even so, Lincoln tried to be helpful and supportive. Although he lacked military experience, few would gainsay his common sense. Shortly before he left, he talked privately with Hooker and Couch, who by virtue of his seniority was the army's second in command. No doubt thinking of Franklin's performance at Fredericksburg, Lincoln admonished the two officers, "Gentlemen, in your next fight *put in all your men*."[17] It was good advice that, as things turned out, Hooker chose not to take to heart.[18]

One last reason for Hooker's sublime confidence was that he had developed a plan that he believed would beat Lee's vaunted Confederate army. The rebel lines extended 25 miles along the Rappahannock River, and they had had plenty of time to make them impenetrable to any kind of frontal assault. Hooker had no intention of repeating Burnside's mistakes from the previous December; instead, he proposed to go around the Confederate defense system. Hooker planned to divide his army and send part of it upstream across the Rappahannock and Rapidan rivers, through the aptly named Wilderness, and toward Lee's left flank and rear. At the same time, the balance of his force would fix the rebels in place and divert their attention by crossing the Rappahannock at Fredericksburg. To complete the scheme, Hooker intended to dispatch Stoneman and his cavalry around the rebel left flank to attack Lee's supply lines back to Richmond. If all went as expected, Hooker would cut Lee's army off and destroy it. At worst, he would force the Confederates back to Richmond for a siege that he believed would ultimately lead to their surrender.

The Army of the Potomac began its campaign on 27 April, when Henry Slocum led the Fifth, Eleventh, and Twelfth Corps upstream to outflank the rebels. Slocum's column made good progress, fording both the Rappahannock and Rapidan rivers on 28 and 29 April, and it reached the tiny crossroads of Chancellorsville on the 30th. Despite its name, Chancellorsville was not a village, but rather a big brick manor located in one of the Wilderness's rare clearings. Slocum and Howard arrived at around noon and found Meade already there. Meade was in an uncharacteristically jubilant mood. He praised Hooker's generalship and then suggested that Slocum continue eastward to get out of the Wilderness and into the open ground that would enable the Army of the Potomac to better maneuver. Hooker, however, had directed Slocum to halt at Chancellorsville, and neither Slocum nor Howard thought it best to disobey orders. Meade was disappointed, but the campaign still seemed to be unfolding well. By evening, most of Couch's Second Corps arrived to reinforce them. Hooker was in a confident mood as he established his headquarters at Chancellorsville that day. He ate dinner with Slocum, but instead of praising his Twelfth Corps commander for a job well done, he spent most of the meal predicting Lee's imminent defeat.[19]

Next day, 1 May, Meade's Fifth and Slocum's Twelfth Corps, supported by Howard's and Couch's men, pushed eastward along three roughly parallel roads to get to the open ground near Fredericksburg. Once there, Hooker could best use his superiority in men and artillery to grind the Confederate army to powder between the two Army of the Potomac millstones. The Yankees trudging along the northernmost and southernmost roads met almost no opposition, but the center column did. A few miles from its starting point, Major General George Sykes's Fifth Corps division of mostly tough Regular Army soldiers ran into enemy fire. As Confederate resistance stiffened, Couch rushed forward with Winfield Scott Hancock's Second Corps division to stabilize the Union lines and jumpstart the advance. Before it could make its weight felt, however, Hooker directed everyone to fall back to Chancellorsville. Couch, Hancock, and Sykes were stunned. Although Couch sent word back that the situation was under control, he ultimately obeyed orders and retreated. As his men pulled back, Couch got further instructions from Hooker telling him to hold on until five o'clock. A disgusted

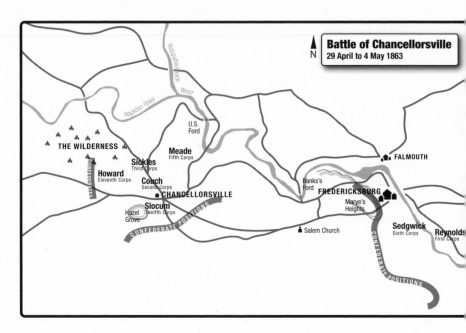

Couch responded, "Tell General Hooker he is too late, the enemy are already on my right and rear. I am in full retreat." To the north and south, the bluecoats also withdrew. When Brigadier General Charles Griffin, now one of Meade's division commanders, learned that he had to retreat to Chancellorsville in the Wilderness, he said with disgust, "Call that a position? Here I can defy any force the enemy can bring against me."[20] By evening all the Yankees were back at Chancellorsville, right where they started. Couch went to see Hooker for an explanation, and Fighting Joe said, "It's all right, Couch, I have got Lee just where I want him; he must fight me on my own ground." Hooker, it seemed, had decided to surrender the initiative to Lee in the hope of repulsing a Confederate attack on the Union positions around Chancellorsville. If the Army of the Potomac's past experiences had shown anything, they had shown the danger of remaining passive in the face of Robert E. Lee. Hooker may not have grasped this lesson, but Couch did. He wrote years later, "I retired from his presence with the belief that my commanding general was a whipped man."[21]

On 2 May, Union scouts spotted heavy rebel columns moving southward, which Hooker interpreted incorrectly as evidence that Lee was retreating in that direction. In response, he dispatched Sickles's recently arrived Third Corps to pursue the supposedly backpedaling Confederates and inflict as much damage as possible on them. Sickles's departure, though, left Howard's Eleventh Corps isolated from the rest of the army on the far right of the Union line. Throughout the day, Howard received innumerable reports from various subordinates, such as Schurz, that the rebels were not withdrawing but were instead massing for an attack on his exposed right flank. Hooker also advised him to keep on his toes. For whatever reason, however, Howard did not take the warnings seriously, although some of his lieutenants took matters into their own hands and made what preparations they could. Late in the afternoon, Stonewall Jackson's entire Confederate corps launched an all-out assault on Howard's vulnerable right flank. Some bluecoats put up strong resistance, but the rebel wave rolled over the corps and washed it from the field. Hooker learned of the disaster only when Howard's refugees streamed past his headquarters, but he immediately mounted his horse to rally the men. Fortunately, it was too late in the day for the Confederates to follow up on their success. Throughout the night, bewildered and tired Union and rebel soldiers floundered in the darkness in search of safety. In the confusion, Jackson's own men accidentally shot him from the saddle, and he died eight days later. Nearby, Sickles and his Third Corps suffered heavy losses—including many from friendly fire—in their efforts to reach the safety of the main Union line.[22]

By 3 May, all of the Army of the Potomac's infantry, except for Sedgwick's Sixth Corps and Brigadier General John Gibbon's division of the Second Corps, was deployed around Chancellorsville. Lee renewed the battle that morning, and Couch's Second, Sickles's Third, and Slocum's Twelfth Corps bore the brunt of the ferocious rebel attacks. Hiram Berry, commander of a Third Corps division, was among the Union casualties, shot dead through the heart as he crossed a road to rally a regiment. The bluecoats fought valiantly as usual, but they labored under big disadvantages that nullified their courage and numerical superiority. For one thing, early that morning the Confederates had seized Hazel Grove from the retreating Third Corps. Hazel Grove overlooked the surrounding area, and the rebels soon stuffed it with artillery that gradually exerted its power over Union movements. The fact that Hooker had before the campaign removed the artillery from Brigadier General Henry Hunt's centralized control made it difficult for Union cannoneers to respond effectively.

To make things worse, the Union soldiers received precious little leadership from Hooker, for whom the war was about to become a very personal matter. He issued very few orders that morning, but he instead watched the battle develop from his headquarters at the Chancellor house. He was standing on the veranda, anxious and careworn, when a Confederate round shot hit the stone steps and split the wooden pillar on which he was leaning. Half of it ricocheted off the right side of Hooker's body, knocking him down and stunning him for half an hour. He eventually got up and insisted on mounting his horse to stop any rumors that he had been killed. He and his staff headed for a nearby white house to establish a new headquarters there, but before they reached it Hooker was overcome by pain, so he dismounted, vomited, and rested on a blanket. Someone brought him some brandy that revived him, and he got back on his horse. No sooner was he back in the saddle than a rebel shell tore through the blanket. Eventually his staff put him in a tent, and he dozed on and off, seemingly in a daze, as aides brought him information. Couch found him there about forty-five minutes after his injury. He went inside, and Hooker raised himself and, to his staff's consternation, said, "Couch, I turn command of the army over to you." He did not mean that he was abdicating his authority though, because he continued, "You will withdraw it and place it in the position designated on this map." Couch was crestfallen that Hooker did not intend to fight it out from the present position, and when he emerged from the tent he saw Meade standing there. Meade had several times beseeched Hooker for permission to take his hitherto unengaged corps into the battle, but Fighting Joe refused because he feared that the Confederates might take advantage of the Fifth Corps' departure to attack the denuded Union line there. Meade looked at Couch inquiringly, but Couch could only shake his head. Couch and Meade, soon accompanied by Sickles, rode off to implement Hooker's orders. Although Hooker later joined them, he made no effort to interfere with Couch's redeployment or to provide any guidance whatsoever. The Union army fell back to a bridgehead around United States Ford, and Hancock's Second Corps division fought a skillful rear guard battle that kept the surging Confederates at bay.[23]

While Hooker slipped in and out of semiconsciousness at Chancellorsville, Uncle John Sedgwick and his Sixth Corps were locked in combat with the Confederates on the slopes leading up to Marye's Heights. The Sixth Corps had been in existence since the previous May, but it had seen comparatively little action. It had played a minor role in the Seven Days Battle, had missed Second Bull Run, and had taken no part in Antietam and Fredericksburg. As a whole, therefore, it was less experienced than other Army of the Potomac units. Sedgwick had crossed the Rappahannock on 29 April as part of Hooker's plan to fix Lee in place and deceive him as to Union operations upriver. Soon after Jackson had mauled Howard's Eleventh Corps, Hooker had ordered Sedgwick to march his corps to Chancellorsville to reinforce the beleaguered Union forces there. To do so, Sedgwick had to overcome the same rebel defenses that had brought Burnside to grief the previous December. Sedgwick had not participated in the Battle of Fredericksburg due to the wounds he sustained at Antietam, but he had heard plenty of stories about the army's nightmarish experience in front of Marye's Heights. Although the Confederate lines were even more formidable now, by 3 May most of the rebels had marched westward to confront Hooker. Lee had left behind only a skeleton force to keep the Sixth Corps at bay, but it was sufficient to repel Sedgwick's first two assaults. Finally, Sedgwick directed his troops to rush straight for Marye's Heights without pausing to load and fire. This tactic worked; Major General John Newton's division seized the position and scattered the rebels hither and yon.

The Union soldiers paused to catch their breath after their exhausting but triumphant morning, but Sedgwick knew that there was little time for celebrating. Overcoming the rebel defenses, although an impressive accomplishment, was merely preliminary to the ultimate goal of reaching Hooker at Chancellorsville. Sedgwick hurriedly reorganized his men and put them into column, but this took time, and they did not get under way until two o'clock. He left Gibbon's Second Corps division behind to garrison Fredericksburg, and he pushed his men westward. At Salem Church, about a half dozen miles from Chancellorsville, the Sixth Corps ran into substantial opposition when the rebels ambushed Brigadier General William Brooks's division. Darkness ended the fighting, but Sedgwick guessed correctly that the Confederates were concentrating against him, so he placed his men into defensive positions and prepared for the worst. Lee had by now taken Hooker's measure sufficiently enough to gamble that Fighting Joe would not venture out of his entrenchments around United States Ford, so he left a screening force there to keep an eye on him and took the balance of his men to assault Sedgwick. Deploying all those troops took time, though, and Lee was unable to launch his attack until near dusk on 4 May. The fighting went on after dark, but Sedgwick managed to hold out. Late that night Hooker directed Sedgwick to withdraw across the Rappahannock, which the Sixth Corps did via a pontoon bridge established a mile downstream from Banks Ford. At Fredericksburg, Gibbon also pulled back across the river.

Unfortunately for Hooker, he got very little help from his new cavalry corps. On 29 April, Stoneman's troopers splashed across a shallow crossing on the Rappahannock and plunged into central Virginia. Because Stoneman took as many men with him as possible, he deprived Hooker of sufficient cavalry to collect information on the rebel army. Lee, on the other hand, ignored Stoneman and used his cavalry to gather intelligence on the Army of the Potomac and to control the road network. Although Stoneman eventually reached the Virginia Central Railroad, he did not use his power to truly cripple it. Instead, he dissipated his force by ordering his units to scatter and destroy various targets of opportunity. They inflicted damage on the Virginia economy, but they had little impact on the Chancellorsville campaign. Stoneman returned to Union lines on 8 May with his cavalry corps more or less intact, but with little to show for his efforts.

While Sedgwick was fighting for his life, Hooker and the rest of the Army of the Potomac remained quiescent within the entrenchments around United States Ford. Indeed, Fighting Joe's self-confidence seemed to have dissolved under the pressure of combat and responsibility, replaced by paralyzing irresolution. Around midnight on 4–5 May, Hooker called a meeting at his headquarters tent for his corps commanders, Butterfield, and Brigadier General Gouverneur Warren, his chief engineer. Sedgwick of course could not be there, and Slocum arrived too late to take part, but the other five officers showed up. Hooker updated them on the military situation and reviewed his instructions. He stated that his primary missions were to defend Washington and preserve his army, and he expressed concern about the unsteadiness of some of the Union soldiers. Couch later claimed that it was obvious that Hooker had already made up his mind to withdraw the army across the Rappahannock, so he was clearly using the war council to generate support for a predetermined decision. When Hooker finished his briefing, he, Butterfield, and Warren left the corps commanders to talk among themselves.

Sickles for one had clearly lost heart. He said he was surprised that Hooker would place the army's fate in their hands, but he defended his superior and friend. He added that although he was not a professional soldier, he did not believe that withdrawing the army would be catastrophic for the Union cause. On the other hand, remaining south of the Rappahannock could lead to the destruction of the army, which would expose Washington to Confederate attack. Reynolds had fallen asleep, but before he nodded off he had told Meade to vote his proxy in favor of resuming the battle. Meade agreed with Reynolds, if for no other reason than he doubted that the army could salvage all its artillery if it retreated. Later Sickles and Hooker claimed that Meade came around in favor of falling back after Hooker assured him that he could save the guns without any difficulty, but Meade and others denied this. Howard felt that the bad conduct of his corps had contributed to the army's present predicament, so he wanted to stay and fight to make things right. Couch was reluctant to voice an opinion, but he agreed with Meade's concerns about the artillery. Whatever confidence he had had in Hooker had now vanished, and he did not want to continue the battle under his leadership. The vote, therefore, was three to two for fighting on. Sickles presented the results to Hooker when he returned, but, as Couch suspected, Hooker had already made up his mind. He stated that the army would withdraw across the Rappahannock, and he would accept responsibility for the decision. As the officers filed out, Reynolds exclaimed, "What was the use of calling us together at this time of night when he intended to retreat anyhow?"[24]

The day after the council of war broke up, the Army of the Potomac began its dreary retreat in the rain across the Rappahannock River at United States Ford. Meade's Fifth Corps served as rear guard, and by the end of the morning on 6 May the entire army was back on the north side of the river. The Chancellorsville campaign was over a little more than a week after it had begun, and it had ended in a stunning Confederate victory. Union losses totaled 17,300 men, well over the 12,700 casualties the Confederates sustained. Although the Army of the Potomac outnumbered its opponent two to one, the rebels outmaneuvered and outfought the Yankees and sent them scurrying back across the Rappahannock. The Union rank and file performed well, even in Howard's Eleventh Corps. The problem, as usual, was one of consistent leadership. On the positive side, Slocum did a good job getting Hooker's flanking column to Chancellorsville, and his corps helped bear the brunt of the vicious rebel assaults on 3 May without breaking. Sedgwick successfully stormed Marye's Heights, fought off the bulk of the rebel army at Salem Church, and got away with his corps more or less intact, all without much guidance from Hooker. Despite Couch's profound inner doubts, it was hard to criticize him for his actions. Through no fault of their own, Reynolds and Meade had almost no opportunity to prove themselves. On the other hand, Sickles did little to promote Union victory, and Howard's inexplicable refusal to take seriously warnings of a Confederate flank assault did the Army of the Potomac great damage.

In the final analysis, however, Fighting Joe Hooker bore primary responsibility for the Army of the Potomac's defeat at Chancellorsville. Hooker had organized the army well, planned his campaign well, and maneuvered his soldiers into position well, but when the time came to engage in battle—to, as Stoneman put it, go a thousand better—he folded. He did not use the resources available to him, exercise firm control over his command, or act with the aggressiveness his plan required. Instead, he readily surrendered the initiative to Lee and awaited his fate. There was no end to the theories people presented to explain Hooker's peculiar behavior. Some blamed his excessive drinking, but others argued that his decision to abstain from alcoholic beverages was the problem. Some pointed to the injuries he sustained on 3 May. Finally, some stated that his humiliation was divine retribution for his blasphemous statements and immoral lifestyle. Whatever the cause, the fact was that when the time came for Hooker to step up to the plate, he lost his nerve.[25]

Fighting Joe's Demise

The Union defeat at Chancellorsville reverberated all the way back to Washington. The battle's results brought to the surface all the doubts observers had had about Hooker but had been willing to suppress in the hope that he could deliver victory. This was as true in the cabinet as elsewhere.

Secretary of the Navy Welles, for example, had always had reservations about Hooker, and in his mind Chancellorsville confirmed them. Postmaster General Blair had opposed Hooker's selection from the beginning, and in fact after Chancellorsville Blair's influential father wrote to Lincoln to recommend McClellan's reappointment as Army of the Potomac commander. On the other hand, Secretary of the Treasury Chase remained loyal to Fighting Joe, as did powerful Radical Republicans such as Zachariah Chandler and Benjamin Wade. They had adopted Hooker as one of their own because of his vehement opposition to McClellan, and they did not intend to abandon him as long as he remained politically useful. Secretary of War Stanton was no Hooker fan, but he promised Chase that he would continue to back Fighting Joe for now.[26]

The cabinet could influence policy, but Lincoln's opinion was the one that mattered most. When he learned that Hooker had retreated across the Rappahannock, his face turned ashen and he exclaimed, "My God! My God! What will the country say! What will the country say!"[27] He and Halleck rushed to Falmouth on 7 May to learn the details of the defeat. The president was understanding and supportive, but the battle and comments from the corps commanders reinforced the doubts he had always harbored about Hooker. Moreover, grumbling from high-ranking officers about Hooker's insufficient leadership continued to reach his ears even after he returned to Washington. When he informed Hooker of this, Fighting Joe invited the president to talk with any general about his performance. In doing so, Hooker foolishly provided a venue for disgruntled generals to visit the capital, see the commander in chief, and air their grievances without fear of retribution. Despite this mounting evidence against Hooker, Lincoln did not remove him from his command. For one thing, Lincoln liked Hooker and wanted to give him every reasonable chance to redeem himself. He commented later that he was not disposed to throw away a gun simply because it misfired once, but he would instead pick the lock and try it again. In addition, the Radical Republicans had embraced Hooker, and Lincoln did not want to start a fight with some of the Union's most determined and hard-nosed men, whose support he needed to win the war. Finally, there was no obvious replacement for Hooker. As a result, he stayed in charge for the time being.[28]

Hooker may have been beaten, but he was not about to admit it publicly. After he returned to Falmouth, he telegraphed Lincoln that he had only withdrawn across the Rappahannock because "I saw no way of giving the enemy a general battle with the prospect of success which I desire." Moreover, he continued, "Not to exceed three corps, all told, of my troops have been engaged."[29] The reality, of course, was much different, and Hooker knew it. After he issued the orders to retreat, he confessed to Meade that he wished he had never been born and that he was tempted to turn command over to him and be done with all things military. Lincoln's encouragement and sympathy, however, helped him regain his bluster. Within a few days, he was more willing to acknowledge Chancellorsville as a defeat, but he refused to accept responsibility for it. Instead, he sought to deflect criticism of his performance by finding scapegoats. Unfortunately, doing so effectively required a degree of circumspection and acumen that the outspoken and cocky Hooker did not possess. Rather than blame one person for Chancellorsville, Hooker and his allies targeted several, thus needlessly alienating officers whose support for him was already shaky.[30]

Oliver Otis Howard and his Eleventh Corps were among Hooker's most obvious culprits. The Eleventh was the only unit of any size that broke and ran at Chancellorsville, and its rout marked the beginning of the end of Hooker's campaign. Hooker had criticized Howard for his loose marching discipline even before the army crossed the Rapidan, and Howard did little afterward to redeem himself in Hooker's eyes. Hooker rarely specified Howard by name, but he instead castigated the corps' officers for failing to prepare adequately for the rebel attack he had warned them against. Criticism of the Eleventh resonated throughout the army. The unit had a bad reputation to begin with among an officer corps prejudiced against German-Americans, and Chancellorsville merely confirmed the prevailing view that it was a third-rate outfit. To make things worse, Howard sought to distance himself from his corps by blaming his soldiers for the disaster, which did not endear him to his men. It may, however, have helped him maintain his command. Most officers respected Howard for his courage, and they saw him as a fine officer in a bad unit, an interpretation Howard did nothing to discourage. The Eleventh Corps' officers, on the other hand, knew good and well that this was not the case. They quite rightly believed that Howard was the person most responsible for the debacle on 2 May, so they protested the unfair accusations leveled against the Eleventh. Schurz even wrote directly to Lincoln to recommend Howard's removal. None of these efforts did much to restore the Eleventh's tarnished reputation, and it remained the Army of the Potomac's pariah.[31]

Hooker also took aim at George Stoneman for his role in the campaign. In fact, Hooker had been unhappy with Stoneman even before he began his offensive across the Rappahannock. Hooker's original design had called for Union cavalry to conduct the upstream outflanking maneuver, but heavy rains had forced its cancellation before Stoneman could get under way. Although Hooker thereupon developed a better plan, he was still unhappy with Stoneman's dilatory performance. To make matters worse, Stoneman did nothing to redeem himself during the Chancellorsville campaign. Instead of severing Lee's supply and communication lines back to Richmond, he had diluted his forces in inconsequential raids that inflicted little substantive damage. Hooker seized upon this failure to make Stoneman one of his scapegoats. He complained to Stanton, "My instructions appear to have been entirely disregarded by General Stoneman."[32] Although Hooker's criticism convinced both Lincoln and the secretary of war of Stoneman's culpability, Fighting Joe did not remove Stoneman from his command. Instead, in the weeks following the battle, Hooker repeatedly badgered and criticized him. Unlike Howard, the officer corps had little respect for Stoneman's abilities, so very few people rushed to his defense. Finally, frustrated and beleaguered, Stoneman requested an indefinite sick leave, which Hooker was more than happy to grant. Stoneman's old patron Halleck made him Cavalry Bureau chief, but he did not fulfill this new role to Stanton's satisfaction. In the winter of 1863–1864, he was transferred to the western theater, and he commanded the Army of the Ohio's cavalry during the Atlanta campaign. He was captured in a raid, was eventually exchanged, and was operating in the Appalachian Mountains when the war ended. He retired from the Army in 1871, moved to California, and was elected that state's governor in 1873. He died in 1894.[33]

On 22 May, Hooker replaced Stoneman with Alfred Pleasonton. Pleasonton had been born in 1824 in Washington, D.C., had graduated seventh from his West Point class in 1844, and had been brevetted for heroism in the Mexican War for his actions at the Battles of Palo Alto and Resaca de la Palma. Afterwards he had served in Florida and out on the frontier. He had emerged as McClellan's favorite cavalry commander during the Peninsula and Maryland campaigns, even though he provided Little Mac with little usable or accurate information, and had been promoted to brigadier general along the way. Hooker initially distrusted and disliked him, but the Chancellorsville campaign changed his mind. Pleasonton commanded what little cavalry Stoneman left behind with the Army of the Potomac, and he performed well enough to win Slocum's, Sickles's, and Hooker's praise. Others, however, had their doubts about Pleasonton, and many believed that Brigadier General John Buford deserved the post more. Although Pleasonton was a fiery, peppery, and courageous man, he was never as good as advertised. He was, in fact, a notorious publicity hound who exaggerated his accomplishments, and his dandified mannerisms annoyed many people. He was not the ideal cavalry commander, but he was an improvement over Stoneman.[34]

Finally, Hooker took John Sedgwick to task for his actions at Chancellorsville. Hooker and his supporters gradually developed the theory that the Army of the Potomac could have recrossed the Rappahannock at Banks

Ford and resumed the campaign if Sedgwick had not retreated after his fight at Salem Church. As early as 5 May, Butterfield wrote Lincoln, "Sedgwick failed in the execution of his orders, and was compelled to retire."[35] When a Sixth Corps staff officer visited Hooker after the battle, Fighting Joe snidely noted that Sedgwick had encountered very few rebels in the course of his adventure from Marye's Heights to Salem Church. Here, as elsewhere, Hooker erred. Sedgwick had done well during the campaign under adverse circumstances and with little direction, and everyone knew it. He was also one of the army's best-loved generals, a man who always looked after his men's welfare. As a result, the officer corps rallied around him and rejected Hooker's accusations. Sedgwick himself, unflappable as ever, expected nothing less, and in fact he predicted accurately that Hooker's charges would boomerang against him.[36]

Hooker's character, his lack of success on the battlefield, and his clumsy efforts to scapegoat others for his failures at Chancellorsville all undermined his remaining support among the Army of the Potomac's high-ranking officers. His attempts to blame Howard, Stoneman, and Sedgwick of course turned them into enemies, but Reynolds, Couch, Meade, Slocum, and many others had also lost confidence in him. For example, William Brooks, one of Sedgwick's division commanders, was so disgusted with Hooker that he resigned his commission, though he reconsidered after Stanton promised to transfer him out of the Army of the Potomac. Indeed, after Chancellorsville, Butterfield and Sickles were just about all of Hooker's remaining powerful allies. Sickles, however, went on sick leave until late June because he had received a painful contusion from a rebel shell at Chancellorsville, so he was not around to back up Hooker. As the magnitude of the Union defeat at Chancellorsville sank in, more and more of the corps commanders were willing to voice their lack of confidence in Hooker. Butterfield later claimed that there was a conspiracy among them to remove Hooker, but this was an exaggeration. Although none of them wanted to go into battle under Hooker's command again, no one wanted to supplant him either. This collective sense of modesty probably enabled Hooker to maintain control of the army longer than would have otherwise been the case because there was no obvious and willing replacement for him. Instead of working aggressively together to topple Hooker, the various corps commanders reacted according to their own individual inclinations.[37]

No doubt Henry Slocum was the corps commander most hostile to Hooker, and most willing to move against him. Slocum had had his reservations about Hooker from the start, and Fighting Joe's performance at Chancellorsville had confirmed his worst fears about the man. Slocum was frequently sick in the weeks after the battle, but he still mustered enough energy to denounce Hooker vehemently. In a letter to a friend, Slocum wrote, "Our movements up to and arrival at Chancellorsville were very successful and well planned. Everything after that went wrong, and Fighting Joe sunk into a poor driveling cur. The fact is whiskey, boasting, and vilification have been his stock in trade. . . . I have no faith whatever in Hooker's ability as a military man, in his integrity or honor."[38] Slocum made no secret of the contempt with which he held his commanding officer, and soon everyone in the army, including Hooker, knew of it. This might explain the angry tongue-lashing to which Hooker subjected Slocum in mid-May when he found that the Twelfth Corps was not sufficiently closed up during a march. Although Slocum thought seriously about resigning his commission so he would not have to participate in another Hooker-authored defeat, he instead decided to take action. He approached Meade about a cooperative effort to get Hooker removed, but Meade turned him down. Slocum also traveled to Washington and persuaded Secretary of State Seward to secure an interview with Lincoln for him. At the White House, Slocum bitterly denounced Hooker's abilities and character, but he left without any commitment from the president.[39]

Slocum was not the only corps commander who journeyed to Washington to condemn Hooker to the president. Reynolds did too. Reynolds's First Corps was scarcely engaged at Chancellorsville, and he was very unhappy with Hooker's management of the battle. John Gibbon later remembered, "He was the picture of woe and disgust and said plainly that we had been badly outgeneraled and whipped by half our number. He expressed himself as intensely dissatisfied with the result of the campaign and did not hesitate to say that we should not have recrossed the river."[40] Reynolds was normally a reticent man, a trait that had served him well in his climb up through the Army of the Potomac's hierarchy. Now, however, he felt compelled to take action when he heard rumors that the Lincoln administration was considering him as Hooker's replacement. Reynolds did not want the job because he had no desire to clean up the mess Burnside and Hooker had left behind, so he immediately went to the capital to tell Lincoln personally. Hooker's name naturally came up, and Reynolds spoke his mind. He recommended his good friend Meade as Army of the Potomac commander.[41]

Chancellorsville prompted plenty of speculation in the officer corps as to Hooker's future. The emerging consensus was that Fighting Joe had choked under pressure and that Reynolds or Meade would be his best replacement. Meade was well aware of this talk. Slocum, Howard, Sedgwick, and Couch had all sent word to him that they would willingly serve under his command, even though he was junior to all but Howard. Indeed, Couch and Slocum each individually asked Meade to join them in undermining

Hooker. Meade, however, rejected all such overtures and said little publicly about the swirling controversy, even though he too doubted that Hooker would do any better if he again led the Army of the Potomac in battle. For one thing, Meade liked Hooker more than most, and Fighting Joe had on the whole been good to him. For another, Meade had no desire to lead the army, and he did not believe the Lincoln administration would ever give him the opportunity to do so anyway. Meade knew he had as much combat experience as any high-ranking officer, but he had never held an important independent command. Besides, he thought it was ridiculous for the army to change leadership after every unsuccessful campaign. Summing up his thoughts, he wrote his wife, "Having no political influence, being no intriguer, and indeed unambitious of the distinction, it is hardly probable I shall be called on to accept or decline."[42]

Despite his claims to the contrary, Meade had already done his bit to undercut Hooker. Shortly after Chancellorsville, Governor Andrew Curtin of Pennsylvania visited the army. After talking with Hooker, Curtin called on Meade before he returned to Washington. Curtin later told Lincoln that Meade and Reynolds had lost confidence in Hooker, which prompted the president's message to Fighting Joe that high-ranking officers were questioning his leadership. Lincoln also revealed the source of his information, so it was relatively easy for Hooker to deduce Curtin's contact. When confronted by Hooker, Meade said he had merely mentioned that he and Hooker disagreed over tactics at Chancellorsville. Even so, the rumor spread that Hooker and Meade were at odds, which was hardly conducive to Fighting Joe's efforts to maintain control over the army.[43]

Darius Couch's discontent with Hooker ran as deep as anyone's, and his continuing bad health did little to alleviate his unhappiness. Couch had seen Hooker up close more than any other corps commander during the Battle of Chancellorsville, so he understood full well that Fighting Joe—not Howard and his men, Stoneman, or Sedgwick—was most responsible for the Union defeat there. He felt strongly that Hooker was not fit for command, but he did not let his staff and subordinates in on his thoughts. Even so, it was common knowledge among higher-ranking officers. Couch was not about to sit idly by while Hooker ran the Union military effort right into the ground. When Lincoln visited the army right after Chancellorsville, Couch not only informed the president of his concerns with Hooker's leadership, but he also unsuccessfully urged Meade to join him in protesting Fighting Joe's continued leadership in the army. Indeed, Couch was so discouraged that he asked Lincoln for a transfer, but Hooker refused it when it crossed his desk. Like Slocum and Reynolds, Couch went to Washington and met with Lincoln and Stanton. There he again criticized Hooker's military abilities and suggested that the president give the army to Meade. Couch was Meade's senior, but he knew he lacked the temperament and constitution to run the army. Nothing seemed to come from his efforts, though, and as the weeks went on, Couch grew increasingly depressed at the thought of taking his men again into battle under Hooker. Finally, he again asked to be relieved, and this time Lincoln and Hooker complied. On 10 June, Couch left the Army of the Potomac for good to assume command of the Department of the Susquehanna. The following year he ably directed a division at the Battle of Nashville and then oversaw the transfer of the Twenty-Third Corps to North Carolina. After the war he left the army, ran unsuccessfully for governor of Massachusetts in 1865 as a Democrat, and held various state jobs in Connecticut. He never shook his chronic illness, though he lived until 1897.[44]

Couch's resignation left the Second Corps leaderless. Lincoln waited a couple of weeks until he had the opportunity to consult personally with Hooker, and then he replaced Couch with the man who would become the most famous Union corps commander of the war: Major General Winfield Scott Hancock. It was an easy decision; Hancock was the Army of the Potomac's senior and most distinguished division commander. He was a Pennsylvania-born twin who had graduated near the bottom of his West Point class of 1844. Afterward he had served out west and in Mexico, earning a brevet along the way. He directed a brigade on the peninsula, and he won the sobriquet "Hancock the Superb" for his actions at Williamsburg, even though he did not do nearly as much fighting there as did Kearny and Hooker. McClellan thought a lot of him and gave him Israel Richardson's old Second Corps division after Antietam. Hancock was promoted to major general in late November 1862, along with Reynolds, Meade, Howard, Butterfield, George Sykes, and William French. Hancock subsequently led his division through some of the thickest fighting at Fredericksburg and Chancellorsville, and he gained innumerable accolades along the way. There was talk of making him head of the cavalry corps after the Chancellorsville campaign discredited Stoneman, but in the end he remained with the infantry.[45]

Hancock's personality and character matched his illustrious record. He was a tall, soldierly, and handsome man; a born leader who took responsibility for granted. He inspired everyone with his decisiveness, sound judgment, courage, and initiative. He possessed an aggressive streak that so many Union officers lacked, but he was also charming, generous, and friendly. He used profanity like artists use color, and his men admired him for it. He cultivated journalists, so he almost always enjoyed good press. A stickler for detail, he often rousted brigade adjutants out of their beds in the middle of the night when he discovered a spelling error in their paperwork. One person noticed that even in the grime and smoke of battle he always wore a spotless white shirt. Hancock was basically a McClellan man, and he agreed with the majority of officers that Hooker had mishandled the army at Chancellorsville. All in all, Hancock was just the type of officer the lackluster Army of the Potomac required.[46]

Indeed, the Army of the Potomac needed all the help it could get. While Hooker quarreled with his subordinates, Robert E. Lee decided to seize the strategic initiative and invade the North for a second time. On 3 June, the Confederate army began to move westward to the Shenandoah Valley. To figure out exactly what the enemy was up to, Hooker sent Pleasonton's cavalry corps across the Rappahannock to investigate. Rebel and Union horsemen clashed at the Battle of Brandy Station on 9 June in the biggest cavalry engagement of the war. The Confederates beat off the Union assault, but the troopers fought well enough to convince Hooker to recommend Pleasonton's promotion to major general, and they confirmed that Lee's army was in fact on the march.[47] Hooker considered taking advantage of the new situation to attack Richmond, but Lincoln nixed the idea, noting that Lee's army, not the Confederate capital, should be the objective. In response, on 13 June the Union army headed northward to the Potomac, taking the chord of the Confederate arc. As the two armies plodded along roughly parallel routes, cavalry units skirmished in the Blue Ridge Mountain passes, but neither Lee nor Hooker was able to gain much information on the other. Lee's soldiers routed the Union forces in the Shenandoah Valley at the Battle of Winchester on 15 June and began crossing the Potomac the next day. By the time the Army of the Potomac got over the river, the rebels were already deep in Pennsylvania.

The Army of the Potomac's corps commanders were not the only men of importance who lacked confidence in Hooker and dreaded the consequences of another battle with him at the helm. Stanton and Halleck shared these feelings. Both men had questioned Hooker's abilities even before Chancellorsville, and their misgivings had blossomed since the engagement. Getting rid of Hooker, however, was more easily said than done. Hooker was closely allied with Radical Republicans who provided the moral backbone for the Union war effort, and alienating them was never wise. Moreover, only the president could remove Hooker from his command. Lincoln was also concerned about Hooker, but he liked the man and wanted to give him a chance to redeem himself for the military sins he had committed at Chancellorsville. He was well aware of the hostility between Hooker and Halleck, and he did his best to smooth over the differences between them. Although Lincoln terminated Hooker's right to communicate directly with him in mid-June, he did so to facilitate communications between Fighting Joe and Halleck. To circumvent these obstacles, it is likely that Stanton and Halleck colluded to force Hooker to quit, thus placing on him the onus for his removal.[48]

To pressure Hooker to resign, Stanton and Halleck made use of the Union garrison at Harper's Ferry. There were approximately 10,000 bluecoats there, but Hooker believed that they served no strategic purpose. Lee had easily seized the place and captured its defenders during his last invasion, and Hooker foresaw a similar outcome this time. He asked Halleck for authority to evacuate the garrison and incorporate it into his army, but Old Brains refused. To Hooker, this was more evidence that the Lincoln administration was burdening him with too many incompatible instructions. He did not believe that he could maintain Harper's Ferry, cover Washington, and engage Lee's army with the resources available to him. Frustrated with this lack of cooperation from his superiors, and perhaps fearing another test of wills with Lee, Hooker submitted his resignation on 27 June. Although Lincoln was probably aware of Stanton's and Halleck's machinations, he made no effort to impede them. Indeed, as June wore on Lincoln was increasingly concerned with Hooker's behavior. Hooker's incessant demands for reinforcements and his unwillingness to accept responsibility reminded Lincoln more and more of McClellan. Hooker's resignation neither surprised not disappointed Lincoln, and he accepted it that day.[49]

Lincoln, Stanton, and Halleck quickly decided to appoint George Meade the new Army of the Potomac commander. Meade had been runner-up for the post the previous January, and now he won the prize mostly by default. Halleck had sounded out Reynolds and Sedgwick, but neither one was interested in the job. Even so, Meade possessed certain assets that appealed to the president. His combat record was extensive and solid. Of equal importance, Reynolds and others had recommended him, so he would have the support of the officer corps. Next day Lincoln met with most of his cabinet to seek their blessing. He informed them of Hooker's resignation and offered Meade's, Couch's, and Sedgwick's names as possible replacements. It was clear to Welles, however, that the president had made up his mind, and when asked, Lincoln admitted that Halleck had already issued the orders putting Meade in charge. Chase was outraged by this empty ritual and even more so by the events that prompted it. He knew nothing of Hooker's troubles, even though the two men corresponded frequently. By forcing Hooker's resignation through Stanton and Halleck, though, Lincoln made it difficult for the Radical Republicans to blame him for something Fighting Joe did of his own volition. Now, out of the blue, Lincoln had entrusted the Army of the Potomac to an officer whose qualities—political and otherwise—were comparatively unknown.[50]

Conclusions

Despite his poor track record on the battlefield, Hooker left the Army of the Potomac high command in better shape than he had found it. During the Peninsula campaign Hooker emerged as the leader of those who for whatever reason opposed McClellan, his philosophy, his supporters, and their dominance of the army. He waged a prolonged campaign to gain control of the army, and along the way he forged alliances and exchanged promises with innumerable politicians, generals, and journalists. Once Lincoln appointed him to command the Army of the Potomac, however, Hooker was in personnel matters surprisingly moderate, and his actions are more noteworthy for what he did *not* do. With a few exceptions like Baldy Smith and Daniel Sickles, Hooker did not purge the officer corps or resort to blanket favoritism. To be sure, Hooker's personnel options were limited. Although the president pledged to help Hooker exert his authority, he had no desire to rock the officer corps with wholesale removals. Moreover, Hooker had comparatively few allies with sufficient rank and seniority to qualify as corps commanders. In the end, Hooker perpetuated that status quo by relying primarily on seniority in recommending corps commanders to the president. Most of these men were McClellanites who continued to climb up the army's hierarchy even though Lincoln had long since relieved Little Mac. As it was, Hooker inherited some good corps commanders from Burnside, men such as Reynolds, Couch, Meade, and Slocum. By the time Fighting Joe submitted his resignation, the Army of the Potomac had the best batch of corps commanders it had so far possessed. There were some weak links in the chain of command, but as a group they were a marked improvement over those McClellan and Burnside had taken into combat. Hooker's problems on the battlefield lay not in the quality of his chief subordinates but in the fact that he did not use them wisely.

Hooker also forged his corps commanders into a more tightly knit unit than ever before, but this was more by accident than design. Except for Sickles, none of them harbored any burning ambition to lead the Army of the Potomac. As a result, they were less likely to see each other as rivals and more likely to cooperate with each other and with their commander. The fact that most of them were friends and McClellan men reinforced this tendency. In the end, however, the one thing that bound most of them—beyond their common devotion to the Union, of course—was their mistrust and resentment of Hooker. From this perspective, their unity caused Fighting Joe considerable grief, but it paid big immediate dividends for his successor.

CHAPTER FOUR

Meade Marks Time
June 1863 to March 1864

An Inopportune Time to Change Army Commanders

The streets of Frederick, Maryland, were full of drunken and boisterous Union soldiers on the night of 27–28 June 1863. This in and of itself was enough to pain Colonel James Hardie's Regular Army soul, but he had additional reasons for his unhappiness. Hardie was Stanton's chief of staff, and the secretary of war had dispatched him from Washington to hand deliver the orders giving Meade command of the Army of the Potomac. Hardie did not want the job because he was friends with both Hooker and Meade, but Stanton said that that was exactly why he had drawn the assignment. To get past roving rebel cavalry, Stanton told Hardie to dress in civilian clothes and memorize the directive. Hardie took a train to Frederick, asked around for the location of Meade's headquarters, and then spent his last dollar to hire a buggy and a driver familiar with the region. Although Meade's headquarters was only a few miles outside of the town, it was slow going through the soldier-clogged roads. It was past 3:00 A.M. when Hardie reached Meade's headquarters, and he had to talk his way past the guards to get access to the general.[1]

Meade was asleep in his tent, so Hardie woke him up. Hardie told him that he had come to give him trouble, which Meade interpreted to mean that Hooker had ordered his arrest as part of his power struggle with his chief subordinates. Hardie assured him otherwise, however, and handed him his orders. This did not make Meade any happier because he did not want the job. He said that Reynolds deserved it more, and at any rate he was totally ignorant of the army's current dispositions. Indeed, Meade wanted to telegraph Stanton and decline the offer, but Hardie said that the orders were final. Meade dressed, and the two men rode over to Hooker's headquarters. There Hardie broke the news to Hooker, though Fighting Joe probably guessed it when he saw the two men together. Hooker was gracious enough to brief Meade on the military situation, but it was obvious that he was not very pleased that Lincoln had accepted his resignation. That evening, after Hooker's staff officers said their goodbyes, Hooker and Hardie left for the train station on a spring wagon. Before they departed, Meade approached and exchanged a few final low-toned words with Hooker. Meade watched the wagon bounce off, and then he walked silently into the tent just vacated by his predecessor and assumed his new responsibilities as the Army of the Potomac's last commander. As for Hooker, he detrained in Baltimore and awaited further instructions for about a week, as directed. None were forthcoming, so he traveled to Washington to see Stanton and Lincoln. When Halleck learned that Hooker had come to the capital without his permission, he ordered his arrest. Although Lincoln had him released, the incident further poisoned the relationship between Hooker and Old Brains.[2]

While Hooker cooled his heels in Baltimore, Meade struggled to get a grip on the army that Lincoln had so unexpectedly entrusted to him. There was little in Meade's biography that marked him as a man of destiny. He was born in Cadiz, Spain, the son of a wealthy American merchant. He had attended Mount Hope Institution in Baltimore before entering West Point, from which he had graduated in the middle of his class in 1831. He had seen some service in Florida and Massachusetts, but he had resigned in 1836 to try his hand in civil engineering. Civilian life was not to his liking though, and he returned to the army in 1842. He spent most of his time up to the Civil War as an engineer surveying coastlines and building lighthouses and breakwaters. He fought in the Mexican War along the way, and saw action at Palo Alto, Resaca de la Palma, and Monterrey. Despite his battle record, however, Meade had had almost no experience commanding troops until the Civil War. He led a Fifth Corps brigade on the peninsula and participated in the battles of Mechanicsville, Gaines's Mill, and Glendale. He was seriously wounded at Glendale—shot through the lung—but recovered in time to take part in Second Bull Run and then Turner's Gap as a First Corps brigade commander. He directed a division at Antietam and Fredericksburg and a corps at Chancellorsville. Meade had as much combat experience as any high-ranking officer, but he had displayed little in the way of tactical brilliance.

Nor did Meade's personality and character mark him for greatness. He was a dour-looking, tall, gaunt, plain-dressed, bespectacled man with a Roman nose and dark bags under his sad eyes. He wrote long thoughtful letters to his wife, to whom he was deeply devoted. He spoke French fluently and was by old army standards an intellectual. He possessed ample dignity, reserve, and modesty, but he had almost no charisma and was incapable of inspiring the rank and file. Although he treated his subordinates like the friends they often were, he could be hurtfully blunt. In combat he was clearheaded, careful, and full of good judgment and common sense. On the other hand, he was excessively cautious and displayed limited imagination. His worst and most pronounced trait, however, was a violent hair-trigger temper that manifested itself when he was under stress. His angry outbursts had cost him the friendship and respect of more than one officer during the war. His staff officers called him a "damned old goggle-eyed snapping turtle." Indeed, his rage could be so fierce that, as Ulysses Grant later remarked, it was unwise to approach him even with information. Although no one argued that Meade was a military genius, everyone agreed he was unlikely to make big mistakes, crumble under pressure, or be intimidated by Lee and his veterans.[3]

The average soldier did not think much of Meade one way or another, but the Army of the Potomac's senior officers were on the whole pleased with his appointment. Most respected his ability, and they were confident that he would be more reliable than Hooker. In addition, Meade was close friends with many of them, including Reynolds, Hancock, Andrew Humphreys, and John Gibbon. Although Reynolds and Sedgwick both were senior to Meade and might have resented his advancement, neither wanted the responsibility of command. Instead, they both heartily approved of Lincoln's decision. There were, however, pockets of opposition. Hooker may have resigned, but his allies remained in the army. Meade recognized McClellan's flaws and was never slavishly devoted to Little Mac, but he was still a McClellanite more than anything else. High-ranking officers such as Sickles, Butterfield, and David Birney had allied themselves with Hooker because they disapproved of McClellan's generalship, and they had prospered under Fighting Joe's leadership. These men believed that the same West Point clique that had embraced McClellan and his unprofitable limited war philosophy had secured Meade's elevation at Hooker's expense. Moreover, Sickles in particular had ambitions of leading the Army of the Potomac someday, but he could not do so as long as Meade stood in his way. They were a minority, but as events turned out, an exceedingly troublesome one for Meade.[4]

Assuming command of a 90,000-man nineteenth-century army would have been difficult under the best of circumstances, but Meade had to do so in the middle of a campaign, with battle only days away. Although he did not have time to make any dramatic changes, Meade wanted to remove Butterfield as the army's chief of staff. Meade did not like Butterfield much, having witnessed his overbearing and arrogant ways as Hooker's right-hand man. Before Meade and Hardie traveled to Hooker's headquarters to relieve Fighting Joe of his command, Meade had stopped to see his friend, Brigadier General Gouverneur Warren, the army's chief engineer. Meade woke Warren up and invited him to be his chief of staff. Warren's sights were set on a divisional command, so he did not want the post. He urged Meade to retain Butterfield for now because he was familiar with the army's disposition, and Meade would need his expertise while he learned his new responsibilities. The next day Meade talked with Butterfield. Butterfield said that he preferred to lead troops, and he had only become chief of staff at Hooker's request. Obviously Butterfield had no desire to continue in his position. Meade then asked Andrew Humphreys, now a Third Corps divisional commander, if he was interested in the job. Humphreys said he was, but he agreed with Warren that Meade needed Butterfield to remain as chief of staff until after the upcoming battle with Lee's army. Meade thought it over and concurred. Besides, he wanted a tough regular like Humphreys in the Third Corps to keep an eye on Sickles, in whom Meade had little confidence. As a result, Butterfield remained as Meade's chief of staff for the time being.[5]

Halleck's orders to Meade gave him the authority to select or remove any officer he wanted, but Meade was too busy just then to reorganize the army's high command. His elevation meant that the Fifth Corps needed a new leader, however. Meade gave the outfit to its senior officer, Major General George Sykes. The appointment was temporary; that is, without the president's explicit consent. The Delaware-born Sykes had graduated from West Point in 1842 and had been sent to Florida for the tail end of the Seminole War. He had later seen action in Winfield Scott's campaign against Mexico City and then had spent most of the years before the Civil War in the southwest. He commanded a Regular Army battalion at First Bull Run, winning fame for covering the Union retreat back to Washington. The following year he led a brigade of regulars in Porter's Fifth Corps on the Peninsula. He was in the thick of the fighting at Gaines's Mill and Malvern Hill, and his unit served as the Union rear guard at Second Bull Run. Porter extolled him in his reports, and in return Sykes branded himself a McClellanite by testifying in Porter's defense at his court martial. Fortunately for Sykes, he took the stand after his promotion to major general. He directed a division at Fredericksburg and Chancellorsville, but he saw little combat in either engagement. Even so, Meade approved of him. There was nothing spectacular about Sykes. He was a small, thin, well-dressed man who always seemed weary and ill natured, though outwardly courteous. In battle he demonstrated ample steadiness and courage—in fact, he was famous for not moving a muscle in combat—but never displayed much initiative or dash. Indeed, his nickname was "Tardy George." He was not, in short, the man to fill Meade's shoes as a corps commander.[6]

Meade inherited an army that was scattered widely across central Maryland. After examining the available intelligence, Meade decided to assemble his troops along Pipe Creek in northern Maryland. He reasoned that doing so would force Lee to abandon his invasion of Pennsylvania and respond in a similar manner. Hooker had divided his army into two wings for the hard hike north from the Rappahannock by giving Reynolds authority over the First, Third, and Eleventh Corps. Reynolds's wing was on the left of the Union advance, closest to the enemy. Ahead, Union cavalry probed in search of the rebel army. As part of this effort, Pleasonton ordered Brigadier General John Buford's cavalry division to Gettysburg, Pennsylvania, the hub of the surrounding road network. Buford reached the town on 30 June, and he quickly deduced that the Confederates were heading his way. In response, he dismounted his troopers, deployed them on a ridge northwest of town, and sent word back to Reynolds of his suspicions. Reynolds had not yet received Meade's directive to concentrate at Pipe Creek—an omission for which Meade later roundly damned Butterfield—so he told Buford to hold the town and wait for him to arrive with reinforcements.[7]

The Battle of Gettysburg

John Reynolds was one of the Army of the Potomac's most respected and admired generals, but oddly enough, he had never had the opportunity to distinguish himself in battle. He had been captured on the peninsula, had missed Antietam, had accomplished little at Fredericksburg, and had been denied a role at Chancellorsville. Despite his mediocre record, Meade had great faith in him. The two men were very close, and scarcely a day went by when the army was in camp in which one did not visit the other. On the last day of June, Reynolds was in an uncharacteristically downbeat mood, probably because he was worried about the scattered condition of the three corps under his general command. Even so, he was determined to rid his home state of the invading Confederate army. He did not, however, anticipate a big fight at Gettysburg the next day as he roused his staff and got the First Corps on the road for its 10-mile trek to the town. On the way there, he received word from Buford that he was under attack from large numbers of rebel infantry, so Reynolds galloped ahead to confer with the cavalry general. Reynolds did not want the Confederates to seize the high ground around Gettysburg, so he chose to make his stand there. He ordered Howard

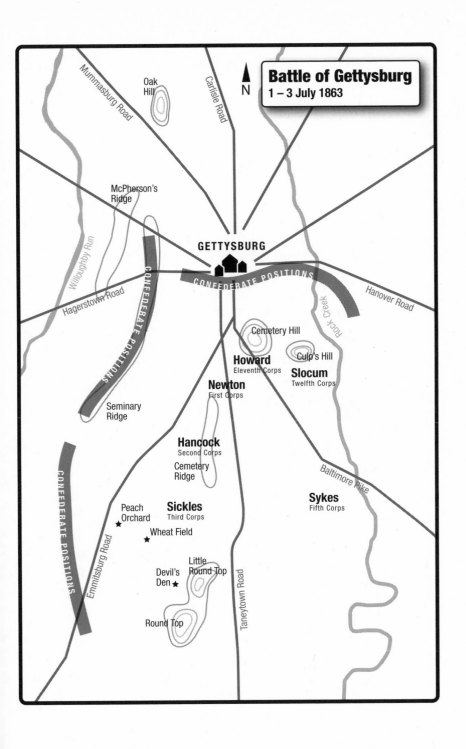

Battle of Gettysburg
1 – 3 July 1863

N

Mummasburg Road

Oak Hill

Carlisle Road

McPherson's Ridge

Willoughby Run

GETTYSBURG

CONFEDERATE POSITIONS

Hagerstown Road

Hanover Road

Rock Creek

Cemetery Hill

Howard
Eleventh Corps

Culp's Hill

Slocum
Twelfth Corps

Newton
First Corps

Seminary Ridge

CONFEDERATE POSITIONS

Hancock
Second Corps

Cemetery Ridge

Baltimore Pike

Peach Orchard ★

Sickles
Third Corps

Wheat Field ★

Sykes
Fifth Corps

Emmitsburg Road

CONFEDERATE POSITIONS

Devil's Den ★

Little Round Top

Taneytown Road

Round Top

and Sickles to join him with their corps, and he dispatched an aide to Taneytown to inform Meade of his decision. He hurried the First Corps forward, but as he deployed it along McPherson's Ridge, northwest of the town, a rebel sharpshooter shot him dead off his horse. An aide lugged his body off the field despite calls from the nearby rebels to drop it. His staff accompanied his corpse to Lancaster with two of his siblings, and although the train did not arrive until midnight several days later, an immense and solemn crowd was there to greet his remains with a prayer service. His fiancée was so heartbroken that she entered a convent, and the entire army shared her grief. As one officer put it, "His death at this time affected us much, for he was one of the *soldier* generals of the army—a man whose soul was his country's work, which he did with a soldier's high honor and fidelity."[8]

Although the First Corps barely had time to brace itself for the Confederate onslaught, it had the advantage of surprise. The rebels expected to encounter exhausted Union cavalry, but they instead ran into fresh Union infantry that handled them roughly at first. Moreover, Union reinforcements were arriving in the form of Howard's Eleventh Corps. Howard assumed command of the field by virtue of his seniority and placed his men to the right of the First Corps. Unfortunately, the Confederates heavily outnumbered the bluecoats, and they soon made their strength felt. The rebels assaulted both the exposed Eleventh's right flank and the vulnerable hinge connecting it with the First Corps. Once again, as at Chancellorsville, the Eleventh Corps was swept from the field, its soldiers fleeing through the streets of Gettysburg. To the west, the First Corps fought a valiant and stubborn rear guard action from which it never completely recovered, but it too was forced to retreat. The two corps—what was left of them, that is; their losses had been enormous—fell back to Cemetery Hill, south of the town.

Reynolds's decision to commit his three corps to Gettysburg's defense upset Meade's plan to concentrate the Army of the Potomac at Pipe Creek. Meade, however, was loath to second-guess the man on the spot, especially someone whose instincts and judgment he trusted as much as Reynolds's. Indeed, when he got Reynolds's initial message, Meade exclaimed, "Good! That is just like Reynolds."[9] Reports of Reynolds's death or injury, though, planted doubts in Meade's mind. Although he clearly needed to select between Gettysburg and Pipe Creek, he lacked enough information to make an informed choice. He did not want to leave centrally located Taneytown just yet, but someone on the scene obviously needed to make the call—or at least make a recommendation to Meade. With Reynolds out of the picture, there was no one at Gettysburg in whom Meade had sufficient confidence. After Reynolds fell, command of the First Corps devolved upon Major General Abner Doubleday, the outfit's senior divisional commander and the supposed founder of baseball. Doubleday was actually a professional soldier who had graduated from West Point in 1842, fought in Mexico, and been stationed at Fort Sumter at the war's outbreak. He was not very popular among his fellow officers; he was a stiff, proud, and somewhat obtuse man whose abolitionist and anti-McClellan leanings alienated many. Moreover, he resented Meade's decision to give the Fifth Corps to Sykes because he felt he deserved the position more. There was never much chance of that; Meade had little use for Doubleday either personally or professionally, and he was not about to let him choose the site of the battle that might well determine the war's outcome. Although the Third Corps was on its way to Gettysburg, Meade did not want to give the nonprofessional Sickles any more authority than he had to. That left Howard, but his recent record was also suspect.[10]

Thinking things over, Meade ultimately decided to dispatch Winfield Scott Hancock to Gettysburg. Hancock was an old friend in whom Meade had complete confidence, and he and his Second Corps were conveniently located at Taneytown. Meade ordered Hancock to turn his corps over to John Gibbon, one of his division commanders, and ride to Gettysburg as fast as possible. Gibbon was just getting over a bout with dysentery and his young son's death, but Meade and Hancock had no qualms in entrusting him with the Second Corps. Once Hancock arrived at Gettysburg, Meade told him to assume command of the First, Third, and Eleventh Corps—of Doubleday, Sickles, and Howard—survey the situation, and submit a recommendation as to whether the army should fight it out there or fall back to Pipe Creek. Hancock noted that Sickles and Howard ranked him and might not be happy with his taking charge, but Meade showed him Halleck's orders authorizing him to make any changes in command he saw fit. That was good enough for Hancock, who at any rate needed little incentive to boss people around.[11]

Hancock traveled part of the 13 miles to Gettysburg in an ambulance so he would have the opportunity to examine some maps of the area, but as he approached Union lines he mounted his horse and rode forward. There he found the scattered and broken remnants of the First and Eleventh Corps. Hancock picked his way through the wounded and blown bluecoats and headed for Cemetery Hill, south of the town. Howard was there doing his best to bring about a semblance of order out of the prevailing chaos. His corps had been routed twice in two months, and it must have appeared to him that his career and cause were crashing around him at the same time. Even so, he was hardly the type of man to give up the fight. Hancock galloped up to him, saluted, and stated that Meade had sent him to take charge. For all his misfortune, Howard's pride remained intact, and he said *he* was the senior officer present. Hancock admitted that this was the case, but he had orders from Meade giving him command if Howard cared to see them. "No," replied Howard, "I do not doubt your word, General Hancock, but you can give no orders here while I am here." Hancock paused, unwilling to engage in a public squabble with Howard while the army was in such a precarious state. He said he would support any decision Howard made, but he had to provide Meade with a recommendation. Howard commented that they were on strong ground, so Hancock, who had probably already made up his mind, replied, "Very well, sir, I select this as the battlefield." Although later there was controversy as to who was most responsible for the Union stand on the low hills south of Gettysburg, there was no doubt that it was Hancock who put the heart back into the demoralized Yankees. He and Howard got to work sorting out and deploying the survivors and reinforcements. At one point Hancock rose in his stirrups and roared at a recalcitrant Doubleday, "Sir, *I* am in command on this field; send every man you have got."[12] Writing years later, one officer remembered about Hancock, "His person was well known; his presence inspired confidence, and it implied also the near approach of his army corps."[13]

Hancock remained at Gettysburg until around 5:30 P.M., when Slocum finally showed up at the tail end of his corps. Hancock turned the command over to him and galloped back to Taneytown to talk with Meade. As it was, Meade had already acted on Hancock's recommendations by ordering the rest of the army to march to Gettysburg. Part of Sickles's Third Corps reached the battlefield just as Hancock left, and the Second and Fifth Corps arrived in the vicinity late in the night and moved into position the next morning. Sedgwick's Sixth Corps, however, was more than 30 miles away at Manchester, Maryland. Sedgwick put his men on the road that night, and after a long trek they got to Gettysburg the following afternoon. By 10:00 P.M. Meade had finished all the necessary paperwork, so he and his staff mounted their horses and trotted for Gettysburg. Three hours later a collection of high-ranking officers—Howard, Sickles, Slocum, Sykes, and Hancock—greeted him at a hospital tent. Slocum and Howard assured him that the army was well posted, to which Meade responded gruffly, "I am glad to hear you say so, gentlemen, for it is too late to leave it."[14]

Among the innumerable details that delayed Meade's departure from Taneytown was designating Reynolds's successor. Butterfield and Doubleday were the army's senior major generals without corps, but Meade did not care for either man. Instead, he gave the First Corps to Major General John Newton, the same officer who had with John Cochrane gone to Washington in January 1863 to talk with Lincoln about Burnside's deficiencies. Newton currently led a division in the Sixth Corps, so Meade ordered him to hurry ahead of Sedgwick's marching men and assume his new command. As with

Sykes, the appointment was a temporary one made without Lincoln's explicit consent. Newton was a Virginian who had remained loyal to the Union, the son of a longtime congressman. He had graduated second in his West Point class of 1842 and had spent most of his prewar years as an engineer overseeing various construction projects. In fact, he was one of his few contemporaries who had missed service in Mexico. After the war began, he helped design Washington's defenses, but he eventually transferred to line duty with the Sixth Corps. He fought well enough as a brigade commander on the peninsula and at Crampton's Gap to earn Franklin's praise and recommendation for promotion to major general. Lincoln complied, but the Senate refused to go along. In all likelihood, his machinations against Burnside, combined with rumors of his pro-McClellan leanings, persuaded Radical Republicans in the Senate to eventually block his confirmation in the spring of 1864. For now, however, Newton was a major general while Congress was in recess. His division had played the key role in the successful storming of Marye's Heights during the Chancellorsville campaign, winning him kudos from Sedgwick. Like many old army officers, Meade thought a lot of Newton; he was an affable, fidgety, good-natured man admired for his ability to size up the terrain. Those who worked closely with him, on the other hand, quickly recognized that he was overrated. He squandered his talents with his laziness, self-indulgence, and heavy drinking. Indeed, he possessed one of the army's best-stocked liquor caches. He was not, in short, the best man available for the position, and Meade would have done better to give the corps to someone else. His elevation did, however, convince a disgruntled Doubleday to put in for a transfer, and he left the Army of the Potomac right after the Battle of Gettysburg.[15]

On the morning of 2 July, Meade surveyed the battlefield he had chosen but not yet seen. The Union line resembled a fishhook. Sickles's Third Corps was at the far left, or south, of the Union line, next to the Little Round Top. Northward, on the shank, was Hancock's Second Corps deployed along Cemetery Ridge. The remnants of the First and Eleventh Corps were stationed on Cemetery Hill, and Slocum's Twelfth Corps held the far right, or barb, of the line on Culp's Hill. Finally, Meade placed Sykes's Fifth Corps in reserve behind Cemetery Hill.

All things considered, Meade had chosen a good position. In fact, many Union officers welcomed an enemy attack as an opportunity to repay the Confederates for debts incurred at Fredericksburg. Dan Sickles, however, did not share this optimism. According to the maps, Sickles's Third Corps was posted on high ground on the southern part of Cemetery Ridge, but in reality the terrain there was pretty flat. As a result, Sickles felt exposed. To make things worse, he received reports of rebel infantry on the march out beyond his left flank. To Sickles, it appeared that the Confederates were preparing to do to him what Jackson had done to Howard and his Germans at Chancellorsville. He received little guidance from Meade, who did not think much of Sickles or his warnings. Finally, unwilling to sit idly by while Lee engaged in his predilection for mischief, Sickles on his own authority ordered his entire corps to advance westward by about a half mile into a wheat field and peach orchard. He hoped this would render his corps less vulnerable, but it did not. Instead, the Third Corps was now isolated in a salient ahead of the rest of the Army of the Potomac, and its new line was too long for its two divisions to defend adequately. Up at the other end of Cemetery Ridge, Hancock recognized the problem immediately. He watched the Third Corps move out, smiled darkly, and said, "Wait a moment. You'll see them tumbling back."[16] Meade was inclined to agree when he rode up and saw Sickles's handiwork. Sickles offered to pull his troops back to their original position, but before Meade could agree the Confederates began their long-awaited assault—right at the Third Corps. Meade told Sickles to stay put and hold on, and he galloped off to hurry reinforcements forward.

As Meade had feared and Hancock had predicted, rebel fire soon ripped the vulnerable Third Corps apart. Sickles may have lacked tactical acumen, but there was nothing wrong with his courage. He mounted his horse and rode behind the fraying Union lines, rallying and encouraging his men. Unfortunately, a round shot or shell struck his right leg just below the knee and shattered it. Despite the shock, Sickles had enough sense to direct an aide to improvise a tourniquet to staunch the blood flow and to inform Birney that he was now in command of the corps. He was removed from the field, and surgeons amputated his leg just above the knee. Next day he was carried on a stretcher 20 miles to the nearest railroad. The long and painful trek included a twelve-hour stopover at a farmhouse to hide from roaming Confederate cavalry supposedly in the area. By 5 July, however, Sickles was safely ensconced in a private house on F Street in Washington. Lincoln and his son Tad were among the few visitors granted access to the general. The two men shook hands warmly and talked about the battle for a long time. Sickles kept a cigar clenched between his teeth, and he occasionally winced in pain and barked at his orderly to wet his raw stump with water. Notwithstanding his agony, Sickles was careful to answer Lincoln's questions in ways that put his actions in the best possible light. He remained upbeat and looked forward to returning to duty.[17]

While Sickles was losing his leg, Meade scrambled to salvage a worsening situation. The rebels overran Birney's and Humphrey's Third Corps divisions and drove for the Union rear. Birney's horse was shot out from under him, and he was so disheartened by the deteriorating situation that he confessed to one of his brigade commanders that he wished he could share his steed's fate. Even so, the Third Corps was a tough outfit that had seen plenty of action at Fair Oaks, the Seven Days Battle, Second Bull Run, Fredericksburg, and Chancellorsville, and Birney and Humphreys were not the type of men to give ground unless they absolutely had to. Meade rushed reinforcements from the Second, Fifth, and Twelfth Corps to confront the escalating Confederate attacks that rippled along Cemetery Ridge. Fortunately for Meade, he received valuable service from several of his subordinates. Chief engineer Gouverneur Warren recognized the importance of undefended Little Round Top and without orders hustled a brigade from the Fifth Corps there just in time to repulse a rebel assault. To the north, Meade placed Hancock in command of the remnants of the Third Corps, and Hancock used his expanded authority to skillfully plug whatever gaps appeared in the Union lines. In the evening, the Confederates tried to storm Culp's and Cemetery Hills, but here too they failed.[18]

Late in the evening, Meade summoned his leading generals to a council of war at his headquarters behind Cemetery Ridge. The officers—Meade, Butterfield, Newton, Hancock, Birney, Sykes, Sedgwick, Howard, Slocum, Gibbon, and Alpheus Williams—crowded into the tiny room, the latecomers standing after everyone else filled the chairs and the solitary bed. Gibbon and Williams were there as temporary corps commanders while Hancock and Slocum assumed larger duties that Meade had assigned them. In fact, Gibbon was unsure if he belonged at the meeting, but his friend Meade told him afterward, "That is all right. I wanted you here."[19] Meade asked the assemblage whether the army should assume the offensive or stick to the defensive, stay put or retreat, and, if it remained, for how long. The consensus was that the army should fight on the defensive for at least another day, although Hancock and Howard were willing to attack under certain conditions. Meade agreed with the recommendations and sent the generals back to their outfits. As the meeting broke up, Meade exchanged sharp words with Birney, who complained about Meade's decision to place Hancock in temporary command of the Third Corps. Meade also took Gibbon aside to warn him that Lee might assail his position on Cemetery Ridge because he had tried unsuccessfully to storm both Union flanks. Gibbon found Meade's logic odd, but he was even more perplexed when Butterfield asked him to review orders for the army's withdrawal. Butterfield, however, explained that Meade wanted to be ready for all contingencies, a reasonable precaution that would eventually come back to haunt him.[20]

On the morning of 3 July, fighting resumed at Culp's Hill on the Union right flank, but the Twelfth Corps gradually gained the upper hand and threw the rebels back. Indeed, Slocum informed Meade that he had surplus troops available for employment elsewhere. In the afternoon, the Confederates initiated the biggest artillery duel in U.S. history up to that point in preparation for the massive assault on Cemetery Ridge that Lee wanted. Although the barrage disrupted Meade's headquarters operations, it did little damage to the Union soldiers dug in along Cemetery Ridge. Even so, Hancock still aroused plenty of admiration from the men there by riding slowly along the line in defiance of rebel fire. After the preliminary bombardment lifted, more than 12,000 Confederate soldiers centered on Major General George Pickett's division assaulted the Second Corps lines along Cemetery Ridge. They reached the Union position, but in vicious hand-to-hand combat the Yankees repulsed them and inflicted heavy casualties. In the confused melee, Gibbon was shot in the shoulder, and Hancock received a serious wound on his inner thigh. The failed attack convinced Lee that he had lost the battle, and the Confederate army retreated the next day.

Meade did not put his troops in motion until 7 July, but it was slow going. The Army of the Potomac had suffered staggering casualties at Gettysburg—about 23,000 in all—and the confusion and chaos of battle had blown thousands more temporarily from their outfits. The Sixth Corps had seen little action, so it spearheaded the advance. Meade moved cautiously and indirectly, marching his army to the Potomac via Frederick, Maryland, to avoid any Confederate ambushes or roadblocks. Lee's army had lost approximately 28,000 men, but defeat spurred them back to Virginia. They reached the Potomac River at Williamsport, Maryland, on 10 July. Unfortunately, heavy rains had raised the river, making it too high to cross. Lee could do little but dig in, wait anxiously, and hope that the river fell before the Union army arrived and attacked. Sure enough, the Army of the Potomac appeared a couple days later, but Meade did not like the look of things. He had been in charge of the army for scarcely two weeks, hardly enough time to become accustomed to the awesome responsibilities of command. Gettysburg had been trying enough, but now Meade had to deal with the celebrity that came with victory, and he was not the man for such a role. For example, at Frederick a collection of local ladies insisted on giving him bouquets and kisses, an incident which he somehow neglected to mention in his numerous letters to his wife. Moreover, he was learning the hard way the pressure that the Lincoln administration was capable of exerting on its field commanders. Halleck's constant henpecking undoubtedly gave Meade a new appreciation for Hooker's woes when he had led the army. The rebels were strongly positioned at Williamsport, and Meade did not want to throw away his hard-won gains from Gettysburg by launching a foolhardy assault that might replicate Fredericksburg. On the evening of 12 July, he called a council of war to discuss his options. Only Brigadier General James Wadsworth, substituting for the ailing Newton as the First Corps' commander, enthusiastically favored an all-out assault, though Pleasonton and Howard were willing to go along with one. Meade mulled things over the next day, examined the ground, and finally determined to attack the following morning, despite his generals' misgivings. When his forces moved forward at dawn, however, they discovered that the Potomac had fallen enough to permit Lee to ford the river overnight and make his escape. The Gettysburg campaign was over.[21]

The campaign may have been over, but not the recriminations stemming from it. Lee's crossing of the Potomac capped two increasingly maddening weeks for Lincoln. He believed that Meade had had a golden opportunity to destroy the isolated Confederate army and end the war, and he was frustrated by the slow pace of the Union army's pursuit. Watching events from Washington, Lincoln did not understand the difficulties under which Meade labored or the stout defenses at Williamsport he confronted. When Lincoln learned that Lee had made good his escape, he was more upset than Chase had ever seen him. Indeed, the president groaned to his secretary, "We had them within our grasp. We had only to stretch forth our hands and they were ours. And nothing I could say could make the Army move."[22] It was of course much more complicated than that, but Lincoln did not see it that way. Halleck informed Meade of Lincoln's dissatisfaction as part of his running harangue for more aggressive action, and in response, Meade promptly asked to be relieved. Halleck hurried to explain rather lamely that his pestering was meant as encouragement, and he rejected Meade's resignation. Lincoln, too, telegraphed Meade to tell him that although he was unhappy that the rebels got away, he remained grateful for the victory at Gettysburg. Meade let the matter drop, but he noted wearily to his wife, "I took the command from a sense of duty. I shall continue to exercise it, to the best of my humble capacity, in the same spirit. I have no ambition or ulterior views, and whatever be my fate, I shall try to preserve a clear conscience."[23]

Whatever happened, no one could take away from Meade his victory at Gettysburg, although both contemporaries and historians would do their best in subsequent months and years. The Battle of Gettysburg exemplified the growth and development of the Army of the Potomac's high command. For once, the army commander's chief subordinates were united behind him. Although a few of the army's corps and division commanders disliked Meade, no one actively worked to undermine him before or during Gettysburg, in part because there was no time to do so. This in and of itself gave Meade a big advantage over Hooker, Burnside, and even McClellan. Moreover, unlike Hooker or McClellan, Meade had confidence in most of his corps commanders, and this paid him big dividends at Gettysburg. For example, he gave Reynolds and Hancock considerable autonomy to use their best judgment. Had he done otherwise, the rebels might well have driven the bluecoats right out of Gettysburg and inflicted heavy losses on them. Finally, Gettysburg demonstrated the wisdom behind the Lincoln administration's decision to give Meade authority to choose and place his subordinates as he saw fit. Meade used this power to entrust the most capable men with the biggest responsibilities and to prevent unqualified officers from undertaking important assignments simply on the basis of their seniority. Meade assigned Hancock to take charge on the first day even though he was junior to Howard and Sickles, and he prevented Doubleday from assuming command of the First Corps despite his seniority. Unhappily, Gettysburg also cost the Army of the Potomac many of the very advantages that so marked its performance there. The battle removed both Reynolds and Hancock from the army—the former permanently; the latter for months—and deprived Meade of his two most capable and closest subordinates. Moreover, the wisdom Meade had displayed in choosing subordinates during the campaign disappeared afterward, which contributed to the army's problems in the months that followed.

Military and Political Skirmishing

Despite its enormous casualties, Gettysburg was not the biggest or most decisive Union victory that summer. On Independence Day, as Lee's tired soldiers began their long retreat back to Virginia, Vicksburg and its 30,000 defenders surrendered to Ulysses Grant's besieging army. Two hundred winding miles downstream, Port Hudson, Louisiana, succumbed five days later, opening the entire Mississippi River to Union shipping and severing the Confederacy in two. Moreover, minor successes accompanied the major ones. Union soldiers repulsed a rebel assault on Helena, Arkansas, the same day that Grant's men marched into Vicksburg. In Ohio, Confederate General John Hunt Morgan was captured with the remnants of his force on 26 July after a three-week-long raid. Finally, William Rosecrans's Army of the Cumberland maneuvered the rebels right out of Tennessee in an almost bloodless campaign that cumulated in the occupation of Chattanooga on 9 September.

In the months after Gettysburg, the Union and Confederate armies maneuvered skittishly and indecisively across northern and central Virginia without the dignity of a full-scale battle. There were plenty of reasons for the vacillation that seemed to characterize the Army of the Potomac's activities. It had suffered enormous casualties at Gettysburg that could hardly be rectified overnight. Moreover, the Lincoln administration had raided the army for troops to use in operations in New York City, Charleston harbor, and Chattanooga, depriving Meade of additional manpower. Finally, Meade got little guidance from his superiors. He was a man of limited imagination, and he wanted Halleck to give him more strategic direction. Meade believed he could probably drive Lee's army back to Richmond, but he did not see that this would accomplish much because it would merely force the rebels into the impenetrable fortifications surrounding the city. Halleck, however, was as usual unwilling to do more than offer vague suggestions and talk in generalities. Lincoln was more forthcoming. He insisted that Lee's army, not Richmond, should be Meade's objective. This was clear enough, but as with much in life, more easily said than done because Lee could hardly be counted on to cooperate in such a venture. As a result, the two armies spent the late summer and autumn searching for opportunities to inflict substantial damage on the other, but without much success. Instead, there was a series of sharp skirmishes in which the Army of the Potomac did surprisingly well. These minor victories—Bristoe, Rappahannock Station, and Kelly's Ford—did not, however, bring the Union any closer to winning the war.[24]

Gettysburg had been as hard on the Army of the Potomac's high command as on its rank and file, presenting Meade with both the burden and opportunity of filling the holes the Confederates had punched in the army's leadership. Daniel Butterfield was among the battle's many casualties. He was hit in the back by a spent piece of shell on the third day of the battle, a painful wound that forced him to go home to recuperate. Butterfield's performance as his chief of staff had not changed Meade's negative opinion of him, and in fact he had all along planned to replace him at the first opportunity. Butterfield's injury made it much simpler to ease him out, which Meade did on 8 July. Everyone expected Meade to assign Gouverneur Warren as his new chief of staff, but instead he gave the post to Major General Andrew Humphreys. Six days later, Butterfield wrote to Meade to inquire about his future. Meade replied that since Butterfield would be convalescing for some time, and since he had never really wanted to be chief of staff anyway, he thought it best to bring in Humphreys. After Butterfield recovered a few months later, he wrote to Meade again and asked about his role in the army. Meade responded that Humphreys's appointment was permanent, but he added, "If you come here I will do the best I can for you, but it is impossible to say in advance what that will be as changes may take place before you arrive."[25] Butterfield knew better than to entrust his fate to Meade, who might well give him a brigade. Instead, he accompanied Hooker out west as his chief of staff when Lincoln dispatched Fighting Joe and two corps to Chattanooga. Unfortunately for Meade, it was not the last time he had to deal with Daniel Butterfield.[26]

It would be an exaggeration to call Andrew Humphreys Meade's alter ego, but the two men had much in common. They were both Pennsylvanians, West Point graduates, and engineers who had left the army for a short time and had spent most of their prewar careers working on projects in and around water. In fact, Humphreys—the grandson of the famous shipwright who had helped design the USS *Constitution*—was one of the country's foremost experts on flood control, having spent considerable time managing projects on the Mississippi River. Humphreys and Meade also shared intellectual bents, immense courage, and ferocious tempers. Although Humphreys had started the war on McClellan's staff, he was an ambitious man who coveted a combat assignment, so in September 1862 he had secured command of a raw new Fifth Corps division. He marched the outfit 23 miles overnight to reach Antietam on the morning of 18 September, and he later courageously led it into combat for the first time at Fredericksburg. There his division came closer than any other unit to reaching the crest of Marye's Heights. In recognition of his performance, Burnside had recommended Humphreys's promotion to major general. Lincoln, Stanton, and Halleck had all supported his claim, but nothing came of it at first. Humphreys had been close to Jefferson Davis before the war, and rumors spread by men such as David Birney pegged him inaccurately as a die-hard McClellanite. In all likelihood, these factors caused Radical Republicans in the Senate to delay his confirmation until the summer. The rebuff angered Humphreys, especially because he considered himself basically nonpartisan both in and out of the army. Meade liked Humphreys but had to disband his division after Chancellorsville because its men's enlistments had expired, so Hooker transferred him to Hiram Berry's old Third Corps division, which he led through its ordeal at Gettysburg.[27]

Humphreys did not really want to become chief of staff, but he accepted the post as a favor to his friend Meade. When he thought about it, though, he realized that there were advantages to the position that could help advance his career. As he put it in a letter, "I shall gain one of my chief objects, familiarity with the handling of a great army. The Chief of Staff must form an opinion respecting everything of importance that takes place in the Army. That as a commander of a division I could not do; nor even as a corps commander; as Chief of Staff I do."[28] As things turned out, Humphreys was good at his new job. In fact, he was one of the best all-around soldiers the Union army produced during the war, excelling as a combat commander, staff officer, and engineer. He was a peppery, gentlemanly, pleasant, and boyish man who managed to charm almost everyone with his humility and enthusiasm, despite a certain eccentricity, his temper, and a predilection for profanity that rivaled even Hancock's. He was easily identifiable by his spectacles, his turned-down black felt hat, and his trademark red necktie. His only major deficiency was that he was ill much of the summer, but on the whole it is hard to see how Meade could have made a better choice.[29]

On the other hand, Meade's selection of Major General William French as his Third Corps commander was surely his worst. French was a Baltimore-born West Point graduate—class of 1837, the same year as John Sedgwick and Joe Hooker—who had seen extensive service in Mexico with Winfield Scott. He was stationed in Texas when the Confederates fired on Fort Sumter, but he managed to make his way to Key West, Florida, before returning north. He led a brigade on the peninsula, and Sumner put him in charge of a new division after Second Bull Run, which he directed at Antietam, Fredericksburg, and Chancellorsville. Along the way he was promoted to major general, saw some of the heaviest fighting of the war, and earned praise from superior officers such as Couch. After Chancellorsville, Hooker sent him to command the Union post at Harper's Ferry, but as soon as Meade took over the Army of the Potomac, he ordered French to evacuate the garrison and join the main army. Once they arrived, Meade assigned the troops to the bled-down Third Corps, and he put French in charge of the outfit. His appointment, like those of Sykes and Newton, was made without Lincoln's consent. To be sure, French was the army's senior major general without a corps, but Meade probably also wanted to keep the unit out of the hands of the nonprofessional and abolitionist David Birney.

French was a bluff, hearty man with an oversized ego that exposed him to ridicule. At Fair Oaks, for example, he fell into a deep mudhole and could not get out until a captain shouted at the guffawing soldiers around him, "The general will be drowned; come and pull him out!"[30] He had a good combat record, despite a tendency to exaggerate his battlefield accomplishments. By the summer of 1863, however, he was past his prime and skittering rapidly downhill. French was an alcoholic who was obviously losing his battle with his affliction. One officer described him, "He is so repulsive in appearance as to invite nausea at the sight of his bloated and discolored visage. He looks a perfect old soaker, a devotee of lust and appetite. One eye has a habit of blinking, which makes it seem drunker than the rest of him. He is the meanest looking general I have ever seen."[31] In fact, the troops nicknamed him "Old Blinky" for his noticeable facial twitch. He punctuated his monologues by saying, "Do you see the point? Do you understand the point?" Everyone in the corps recognized the danger he presented, so they resented and disliked him. Indeed, that summer he frequently disappeared into his tent and gave orders not to be disturbed while he drank whiskey, which so outraged Birney that he finally barged in on him to conduct army business. French was, in short, not the man to command an army corps.[32]

Neither was Daniel Sickles, at least as far as Meade was concerned. Sickles of course thought otherwise. Despite his injury, his ambition remained intact, and he understood as well as ever that military service was a stepping-stone for bigger and better things. On 7 August, a little more than a month after he had lost his leg at Gettysburg, he wrote to Stanton that he would be ready for duty soon. Sickles wanted an independent command, so he suggested that Stanton dispatch him and his Third Corps to Texas to conquer the state. Stanton sent his warmest regards, but he stated that it was premature to discuss Sickles's future until he had fully recovered from his wound. By mid-October, however, Sickles claimed that his convalescence was complete, so he boarded a train and traveled to rejoin the Army of the Potomac in northern Virginia. Although French sent his carriage to the train station to fetch Sickles, he deeply resented his appearance. French complained that political generals like Sickles monopolized the spotlight while hardworking career officers labored unrecognized in the shadows. He spent most of Sickles's visit in his tent, undoubtedly drowning his sorrows in liquor. As for Sickles, he received a warm welcome from officers who preferred him to French. Birney hosted a party in his tent in his honor, and then Sickles mounted his horse to review the troops. Despite the damage he had inadvertently inflicted on them at Chancellorsville and Gettysburg, the rank and file had always liked Sickles, so they cheered him with unbridled enthusiasm. Unfortunately for Sickles, he received a different reception from Meade. Meade had no intention of letting Sickles take command of the Third Corps, and he seized on Sickles's wound to deny him the opportunity. In fact, Sickles was in no physical condition to resume active service; his unhealed stump was not yet capable of supporting an artificial limb, so he had to hobble about on a crutch. Even if he did recover, astute observers recognized that Sickles's days in the Army of the Potomac were over as long as Meade remained the commander. Others, blinded by Sickles's charisma and the heroic welcome his former corps accorded him, continued to view him as the man of the future. Birney, for one, wrote, "Sickles will I think command this army and in time be President. I have great confidence in him and in his management."[33]

Finally, Meade had to find a temporary substitute for the all-but-irreplaceable Winfield Scott Hancock. He initially assigned the Second Corps to the undistinguished Brigadier General William Hays, even though divisional commanders Brigadier Generals John Caldwell and Alexander Hays both had seniority. Although Meade probably bypassed Caldwell because he was not a career soldier, it is not clear why he failed to give the post to the capable Alexander Hays. William Hays was a Virginia-born Regular Army officer who had graduated from West Point in 1840. He had seen action in Mexico and then had spent the prewar years in routine garrison duty. He served in the artillery on the peninsula and at Fredericksburg before taking over a brigade in the Second Corps. He was wounded and captured at Chancellorsville, but he was back with the Army of the Potomac by Gettysburg. Meade probably gave Hays the Second Corps because he was available and unemployed. Soon enough, however, he regretted his decision. Hays was not very popular among his fellow officers in the corps, and Meade was unimpressed with his leadership. In August, the War Department transferred Hays to a noncombat post in New York City, but he returned to the Army of the Potomac as a division commander during the Siege of Petersburg. Three days before Lee's army surrendered at Appomattox, Second Corps commander Humphreys relieved Hays from his duties after he discovered Hays and his entire staff asleep at 6:30 A.M. He remained in the army after the war, and died in 1875.[34]

The more Meade thought about it, the more convinced he became that Gouverneur Warren was best suited to run the Second Corps until Hancock returned to duty, and on 12 August he issued the orders making it so. The New York–born Warren had graduated second in his West Point class of 1850 and had then worked as an engineer on Mississippi River flood control projects—where he befriended Humphreys—surveying possible transcontinental railroad routes, mapping the Dakota and Nebraska territories, and teaching mathematics at the Military Academy. Along the way he had seen action against the Sioux Indians in 1855 at the Battle of Blue Water. He commanded a Fifth Corps brigade on the peninsula and was wounded at Gaines's Mill. Even so, he remained with his unit and led it through Malvern Hill and Second Bull Run. Hooker appointed him the army's chief engineer in February 1863, and in that capacity he participated in the battles of Chancellorsville and Gettysburg. At Gettysburg he recognized Little Round Top's importance to the federal position and took quick action to help secure the hill. He was praised by almost everyone he served under, including McClellan, Burnside, Hooker, and his friend Meade. Indeed, Meade lobbied hard to get Warren his major generalship, which came through on 8 August. It was probably at Meade's instigation that the Lincoln administration backdated Warren's promotion to 8 May so that he would rank Birney, who might otherwise have made a claim on the Second Corps.[35]

Gouverneur Warren was perhaps the Army of the Potomac's most controversial corps commander. He was a small and sallow man with a dark complexion, black eyes, and long straight black hair. He had simple tastes, enjoying card playing and, oddly enough, limericks. He disliked secessionists and abolitionists about equally, though he only took up his sword against the former. He initially impressed almost everyone with his intelligence, perception, courage, and sensitivity. He seemed like an excellent choice to run the Second Corps, and in fact he did a solid job that late summer and autumn. The following year, however, the burdens and pressures of command revealed a dark side of his character that ultimately ruined his career. He was tightly wound and possessed a temper that dwarfed even Meade's and Humphreys's. His growing ego made it difficult for him to take orders, and he often seemed to believe that he knew what was best for the entire army. Indeed, second guessing his superiors became part of his modus operandi. He was also unable to delegate authority because he generally thought as little of his subordinates as he did of his commanding officers. Finally, he was subject to morbid depression that occasionally sucked the life and energy out of him. It was Ulysses Grant, however, who best summed up Warren's military deficiencies: "He could see every danger at a glance before he had encountered it. He would not only make preparations to meet the danger which might occur, but he would inform his commanding officer what others should do while he was executing his move."[36] In 1863, however, all this was in the future. For now he was the army's rising young star, a designation strengthened when he improvised an ambush that mauled a Confederate corps at the Battle of Bristoe on 14 October. His future looked bright, so it was no wonder he wrote his new bride that summer "how elated I feel at commanding a Corps d'Armee with its Generals, Divisions, Brigades, Regiments and artillery knowing that I know the duties of each by fruitful study and dangerous experience in the great battles of the world."[37]

Meade toiled under innumerable disadvantages that summer and autumn as he marched his troops back and forth across the northern Virginia countryside, but he believed that one of his biggest difficulties was the overall low quality of his corps commanders. Although they had continued confidence in him, he could not say the same of most of them. As he wrote his wife, "Another great trouble with me is the want of active and energetic subordinate officers, men upon whom I can depend and rely upon taking care of themselves and commands."[38] He missed Reynolds and Hancock keenly, old friends who had served him well during their short but intense time under his command. The remainder were not all bad. Warren won his bright little victory at Bristoe, and in early November, Sedgwick organized and implemented a surprise nighttime assault on the Confederate post at Rappahannock Station that netted him a thousand prisoners, disrupted Lee's plans, and forced the rebels to retreat southward. Meade was also so impressed with Pleasonton's performance during the Gettysburg campaign that he asked Halleck to officially designate him the cavalry corps commander. Unfortunately for Pleasonton, Stanton refused. Stanton had recently learned that Pleasonton had denigrated the War Department's efforts to maintain the Army of the Potomac's cavalry, so the secretary of war was not inclined to do him any favors. On the other hand, Stanton did not want to inconvenience Meade. By way of compromise, Stanton assured Meade via Old Brains that there were no plans to remove Pleasonton, but he declined to prevail upon Lincoln to make his appointment permanent.[39]

On the whole, though, Meade saw little but routine mediocrity and blinding incompetence around him. Newton, Hays, French, and Sykes in particular failed to display much initiative that summer and autumn. In one respect, Meade had no one to blame but himself for their positions in the chain of command, though he did not admit this. On the other hand, however, he was hamstrung by some factors beyond his control. With a few minor exceptions, Army of the Potomac corps commanders had almost always been major generals, but Meade was running out of such officers. In the weeks after Gettysburg, the only major generals in the army available to lead corps were French, Birney, Newton, Schurz, and Humphreys. Meade had already tapped Humphreys for chief of staff, and he had small use for Birney and Schurz. This left French and Newton. Although Meade had some capable brigadiers, getting them promoted was difficult because Congress had limited by law the number of major generals allowed in the army. As a result, there was no longer a plethora of major generals ready to be appointed to corps command. Meade managed to secure Warren's major generalship, but he had no luck in persuading the Lincoln administration to advance others such as John Gibbon. To put it another way, Meade's bench was much thinner than Hooker's, Burnside's, and even McClellan's had been. Under these circumstances, it was hardly surprising that his new corps commanders left much to be desired.

In the meantime, Meade made do with the material at hand, but it was not easy. Sykes and Warren got into a semipublic squabble over whether or not the Fifth Corps had provided the Second Corps with sufficient support at Bristoe, showing that unadulterated victory could be as divisive as the defeats to which the Army of the Potomac was accustomed. Warren, on the other hand, interpreted the row as more evidence that all his fellow corps commanders were incompetent. People in and out of the army continued to criticize the unlucky Eleventh Corps for its misfortunes at Chancellorsville and Gettysburg, so in late July Meade proposed breaking up the unit and sending Howard over to command the Second Corps. Nothing came of the suggestion, probably because divisional commander and Lincoln intimate Carl Schurz lobbied the president against it. Moreover, some of the outfit's division and brigade commanders went on record in support of Howard's continued leadership, apparently preferring the devil they knew to the denigration to which they would be subjected in some other corps. Taken together, it was small wonder that Meade was leery of engaging the rebels in another all-out engagement.[40]

Lincoln tried to help Meade. The president had always liked Joe Hooker personally, and he continued to believe Fighting Joe could contribute to the Union war effort despite his defeat at Chancellorsville. As Lincoln saw things, Hooker excelled as a combat commander in a subordinate role, without the burden of overall responsibility to weigh him down and unnerve him. Lincoln decided that securing Hooker a corps in the Army of the Potomac would not only provide him with gainful employment but would also improve Meade's lackluster army. On 27 July, Lincoln wrote to Meade to inquire if he would be willing to accept Hooker as a corps commander. If so, then the president promised to approach Hooker about it. Meade had always gotten along with Hooker more than most Regular Army officers, so he replied positively. Shortly thereafter, however, Meade received an indirect warning from Halleck that Hooker would undoubtedly cause him as much trouble as he had caused McClellan and Burnside, which was substantial indeed. This jolted Meade out of the selective amnesia that had apparently overcome his mind. On 11 August, Lincoln wrote that he had talked to Hooker, who said he was grateful for the offer and the kindness behind it. Although he was busy compiling his report on the Chancellorsville campaign, Hooker said he would be happy to take over a corps in September unless Meade wanted him sooner. Meade hurried to Washington to explain rather disingenuously to the president in writing and in person that he had assumed that Lincoln's original offer of Hooker's services was an order, not a request. In all honesty, he stated, he did not want Hooker in his army.[41]

As things turned out, about five weeks later Lincoln found a way to employ Hooker without foisting him on Meade. Meade no doubt appreciated this, except that he had to pay a big price for Fighting Joe's removal from the scene. On 19–20 September, the Confederates inflicted on William Rosecrans's Army of the Cumberland a staggering defeat at the Battle of Chickamauga in northern Georgia, driving the shattered bluecoats into Chattanooga and placing them under siege there. In response, the Lincoln administration decided to take advantage of the relatively quiescent Army of the Potomac by depriving it of two corps—Howard's Eleventh and Slocum's Twelfth, the army's two smallest and least popular—and shipping them to Chattanooga. Hooker possessed the necessary rank, experience, and availability for the mission, so Lincoln put him in charge. It was a bold proposal, but its biggest flaw lay in the personalities involved. Hooker blamed his defeat at Chancellorsville on Howard, and he despised Slocum—a feeling that Slocum reciprocated in spades. Indeed, when Slocum learned of the plan, he immediately wrote to the president and threatened to resign rather than serve under Hooker again. Lincoln respected Slocum, so he appeased him by promising to ask Rosecrans to remove the Twelfth Corps from Hooker's command as soon as possible and to compensate Fighting Joe with an equal number of troops. As for Hooker, less than two weeks after the two corps reached Tennessee, he asked Lincoln to banish Slocum to Missouri or anyplace else and to give the Twelfth Corps to Butterfield, who had accompanied him westward as his chief of staff. Slocum, Hooker explained with unconscious irony, was too discontented, ambitious, and incompetent for his present job. In the end, Rosecrans was relieved of his command before he had a chance to act on the matter, and Ulysses Grant took overall charge of operations in and around Chattanooga. Grant had little patience with Hooker's and Slocum's squabble, so he wanted to strip both men of their commands, consolidate the Eleventh and Twelfth Corps, and give the new unit to Howard as a reward for the Christian forbearance he had demonstrated throughout this quarrel, despite his adverse feelings toward Hooker. Grant, however, asked the War Department to issue the orders because it had created the row in the first place, but Stanton and Halleck did not act.[42]

Hooker's, Slocum's, and Howard's days with the Army of the Potomac were over, but they continued to play active roles in the war. Hooker participated in the Battle of Chattanooga in late November, winning laurels for seizing lightly defended but formidable-appearing Lookout Mountain. The following year he commanded the combined Eleventh and Twelfth Corps—denominated the Twentieth Corps—in the Army of the Cumberland in the Atlanta campaign, but his primadonna ways alienated his superiors, Major Generals George Thomas and William Sherman. When Major General James McPherson was killed at the head of his Army of the Tennessee outside of Atlanta, Sherman refused to appoint Hooker his successor, even though Fighting Joe was the senior officer available. Instead, Sherman gave the job to Howard, who had led the Fourth Corps to Atlanta's outskirts. Hooker was outraged at Howard's elevation over his head, so he submitted his resignation, which Sherman and Thomas were happy to accept. Lincoln sent Hooker to replace Samuel Heintzelman as chief of the Northern Department, and he spent the remainder of the war there. After the conflict, he suffered from partial paralysis on his right side as a result of the injuries he sustained at Chancellorsville, so he retired from the army in 1868. He married in 1865, but his wife died three years later. Hooker followed her to the grave in 1879.

Howard capably commanded the Army of the Tennessee during the fighting around Atlanta, Sherman's March to the Sea, and the push through the Carolinas. After the war he gained renown as commissioner of the Freedmen's Bureau, founder of Howard University, superintendent of West

Point, and Indian fighter. He remained active in religious and educational organizations after he retired from the Army in 1894; he died in 1909. As for Slocum, Sherman put him in charge of the Department of Vicksburg to get him away from Hooker, but after Fighting Joe quit, Sherman brought Slocum back to command the Twentieth Corps. He led Sherman's right wing—eventually titled the Army of Georgia—on the march from Atlanta to the Carolinas. Ironically enough, when Sherman took his western army through the streets of Washington in the war's big victory parade, his two chief subordinates—Howard and Slocum—were both former Army of the Potomac officers. After the war Slocum practiced law in New York and served three terms in Congress as a Democrat. He died in 1894.

At about the same time that Grant lifted the Confederate siege of Chattanooga, the Army of the Potomac was undertaking Meade's first offensive campaign. After months of indecisive maneuvering and skirmishing, in mid-November Meade decided that the time was ripe for him to cross the Rapidan River and try to destroy Lee's army. Despite the loss of the Eleventh and Twelfth Corps, Meade knew that the Army of the Potomac outnumbered its opponent by about two to one, with 85,000 Union soldiers facing 45,000 Confederates. In addition, Meade's men had finally finished repairing the Orange and Alexandria Railroad, ensuring him a relatively secure supply line to the Rapidan. His plan was to bull his way across the Rapidan at Jacob's, Germanna, and Ely's fords and hit the rebel right flank before Lee had time to concentrate his forces to resist the blow. The key, Meade knew, was speed, so he prepared carefully. After a two-day rain delay, the Army of the Potomac got moving on 26 November, and it immediately ran into trouble. The problem was not the Confederate army—not yet, at any rate—but rather William French. French's Third Corps was supposed to lead the Union drive across the river. Unfortunately, French got started late, arrived at Jacob's Ford behind schedule, and then discovered that the slopes there were too steep for his artillery. He sent his guns to nearby Germanna Ford, but this merely cluttered up the crossing there. Next day French took the wrong road, and when he finally got back on track he ran into large numbers of rebels whose skirmishing delayed him further. To make matters worse, there were persistent rumors that French was drunk. Meade observed Old Blinky's blundering with growing fury, and he sent him increasingly tart messages to hurry up. In the end, the Confederates had plenty of time to deploy their forces behind Mine Run Creek in front of the advancing Union army.[43]

Union soldiers approached Mine Run in a cold driving rain on 28 November. Meade spent the next day reconnoitering Confederate lines for an opening, but at first he had little luck. Finally, Warren discovered what appeared to him to be a chink in the enemy armor on the far right, or southern, part of the Confederate position. Meade reinforced Warren's Second Corps with two of French's divisions and ordered him to attack the following morning. To support Warren's offensive, Meade directed Sedgwick to assail the other end of the Confederate line with the Fifth and Sixth Corps. As 30 November dawned, however, Warren discovered that the rebels had spent the night strengthening their defenses, so any assault would be foolhardy. On his own authority, Warren risked Meade's wrath and canceled the attack. When Meade learned of Warren's actions, he barely had time to call off Sedgwick's assault before he rode over to the Union left wing to consult Warren. Looking things over, Meade agreed with Warren's judgment. The Yankees were thus spared another Fredericksburg, but Meade's options were rapidly narrowing. His troops were quickly consuming their rations, and the muddy roads made it impossible to properly resupply the army. As Meade saw things, he could not advance or stay where he was, so his only realistic choice was to retreat. On the night of 1–2 December, the Army of the Potomac withdrew across the Rapidan, having suffered 1,600 casualties in its fruitless six-day adventure. Confederate losses were somewhat over 600. The Mine Run operation was over, and while it could hardly be compared to the Army of the Potomac's last two disastrous forays across the Rappahannock, it brought the Union no closer to victory.[44]

Although abortive, there was still fall-out from Meade's short-lived offensive. Meade held French responsible for the campaign's failure, and he wanted an official investigation into Old Blinky's performance, but nothing ever came of it. French denied all the accusations of drunkenness and incompetence, and he told Meade that he welcomed any inquiry into his conduct. He blamed Brigadier General Henry Prince, one of his division commanders, for the innumerable snafus that plagued the Third Corps throughout its adventure across the Rapidan. Most officers sided with Meade, but French got surprising support from his old friend John Sedgwick. Sedgwick was so disgusted with the bungled offensive that his staff officers avoided the subject. Although Sedgwick was not normally one to insert himself into controversy, he wrote an open letter to French published in the *New York Times* refuting all allegations that French was inebriated during the offensive. Sedgwick stated that he had spent considerable time with French during the skirmishing on 27 November, and he had seen nothing that indicated that his old classmate had been drinking. People in and out of the army also castigated Warren for calling off the planned attack on 30 November. They were a minority though; most officers and men commended him for his moral courage in canceling a surely doomed assault. Warren himself was proud of his decision, and even Meade viewed the incident philosophically. On the other hand, afterward Warren and Meade got into the first of what would be many tiffs because Meade refused to relieve some officers Warren deemed incompetent.[45]

To some, French's and Warren's problems were merely indicative of Meade's inadequacies as Army of the Potomac commander. There had never been much enthusiasm in the Lincoln administration for Meade, and his inability or disinclination to prosecute the war more aggressively sapped whatever support remained. Welles, for example, was more impressed than he had expected to be when he met Meade for the first time, but he still believed he was better suited for a subordinate role. It was therefore hardly surprising that throughout the late summer and autumn rumors swirled that Meade's days were numbered. Meade himself had little ambition for the position, and he said to an aide that he would be happy to return to his family in Philadelphia if the Lincoln administration was dissatisfied with his performance. In fact, in mid-September, he offered to step down, but Lincoln and Halleck said no. Even so, the rumors persisted, and Meade's failure at Mine Run did nothing to dampen them. Scuttlebutt said that Sedgwick, Hancock, or even Pleasonton was in line to replace Meade. On 27 December, Meade himself told his provost marshal that there was no doubt in his mind that Hancock would take over for him as soon as he recovered from his Gettysburg wound. Next day, Hancock returned from his convalescence and talked with Meade. He too had heard that he was slated for Meade's spot, but Halleck had told him that he had persuaded Lincoln and Stanton to stick with Meade. This might or might not have been true, but the story certainly reflected Lincoln's ambivalence toward Meade. Although the president did not see Meade as the man to win the war, he did not believe that there was anyone readily available with the rank and record to supplant him. Besides, Meade had the officer corps' support, something Lincoln valued after his experiences with Pope, Burnside, and Hooker. As a result, Meade remained in command by default.[46]

There were, however, some people who believed that Joe Hooker was the man to replace Meade. Although the Lincoln administration had transferred Hooker out west, he retained support in and out of the Army of the Potomac. Secretary of Treasury Chase and fellow Radical Republicans such as Zachariah Chandler believed that Meade's badly managed and indecisive campaigning demonstrated that he was little more than a McClellan surrogate. They had embraced Hooker as one of their own, and they hoped to use him as a bulwark against the resurgent McClellanite contingent whose collective heart was not in the revolutionary war against slavery that Lincoln had proclaimed and Radical Republicans demanded. Hooker's boosters also included officers such as Butterfield, Sickles, and Birney who had climbed the military ladder with Fighting Joe. Meade's elevation had brought their ascent to a standstill, but if Hooker returned they could resume their former positions of power. Finally, men such as Doubleday were attracted to Hooker's banner because they had scores to settle with Meade. As Birney put it, "We must have Hooker back to this army and I believe he will be sent to us! I have faith in God . . . and believe Hooker will come to us."[47]

Sickles was the ringleader of this loosely organized conspiracy against Meade, but he had plenty of help from others. Sickles's plan was to so discredit Meade that the Lincoln administration would jettison him and bring Hooker back to command the Army of the Potomac. To implement his design, Sickles and his allies concentrated on Meade's performance at Gettysburg, though obviously all facets of Meade's career were fair game. Gettysburg had been a Union victory, but Meade's actions there generated plenty of controversy for his detractors to plumb. They especially focused on Meade's supposed willingness to abandon the battlefield and fall back to Pipe Creek. Sickles also took the opportunity to rebut charges that he had endangered the Union position by moving his Third Corps forward on the second day of the engagement. In short, Sickles and his associates sought to demonstrate that the Army of the Potomac won the Battle of Gettysburg in spite, not because, of George Meade.[48]

To disgrace Meade, Sickles and his allies employed a two-pronged assault. First, they initiated a smear campaign against Meade to ruin his reputation with the public. Its centerpiece was an anonymous 12 March 1864 article in the *New York Herald* under the pseudonym "Historicus." Written by either Sickles or one of his aides, the exposé glorified Sickles's role in Gettysburg at Meade's expense. Second, Sickles plotted with Chandler to hold Committee on the Conduct of the War hearings into Gettysburg in late February and March. This gave Meade's enemies the opportunity to put on the record their charges against him. On the other hand, it also exposed them to the light of day for all the world—including Meade—to see, disparage, and retaliate. Even so, Birney, Butterfield, Doubleday, former Sixth Corps divisional commander Albion Howe, Pleasonton, and Sickles all gave testimony unfavorable to Meade. They emphasized that Meade and his chief subordinates did not have the support of the rank and file and that they were McClellanites who lacked the drive and determination to win the war.[49]

Meade had on more than one occasion offered his resignation to the Lincoln administration, and indeed he viewed command of the Army of the Potomac as a thankless task that he did more out of duty than anything else. Even so, he did not plan to stand by idly while Sickles and his friends denigrated his character, generalship, and reputation. He expected no less from Birney, Butterfield, Doubleday, and Sickles, but he was surprised by Pleasonton's hostility. Pleasonton, however, had ties with Hooker and Sickles, both of whom had recommended his promotion to cavalry chief the previous summer. Like everyone else, Meade assumed that Sickles was behind the "Historicus" article, and he felt obligated to respond. To do so, he asked the War Department for a court of inquiry into his conduct at Gettysburg. Lincoln, Stanton, and Halleck all counseled against this, however, arguing that such a forum would play right into Sickles's hands by generating all sorts of publicity that he could spin and manipulate to his advantage. They advised Meade to ignore the attacks and let his victory at Gettysburg speak for itself. Although Meade accepted this sensible advice, he longed for the chance to tell his side of the story. Fortunately for him, he got his opportunity when the Committee on the Conduct of the War called him and some of his subordinates to testify. There Meade and his allies—Gibbon, Hancock, Army of the Potomac artillery chief Brigadier General Henry Hunt, and Warren— all spoke out in Meade's defense. Moreover, they brought along plenty of documentary evidence to bolster their case and show that Meade had played a vital role in the Union victory at Gettysburg.[50]

In the end, Sickles's campaign against Meade fizzled for several reasons. For one thing, although the men in charge of the Union war effort—Lincoln, Stanton, and Halleck—had scant enthusiasm for Meade, they were not about to put Hooker back in command of the Army of the Potomac. Moreover, Sickles and his allies lacked the necessary political firepower to generate the kind of public and political pressure required to compel the Lincoln administration to replace Meade with Hooker. Indeed, some Radical Republicans on the Committee on the Conduct of the War, such as Benjamin Wade, were friendly toward Meade, gave him a fair hearing, and were satisfied with his answers. Finally, Ulysses Grant's promotion to lieutenant general and elevation to general in chief diverted the public's attention away from the Meade/Sickles imbroglio. Grant disliked Hooker, Sickles, and Butterfield; and he was not about to use his new power to advance their agenda. By early April, it was clear to Meade that he had won his battle with Sickles.[51]

Ultimately, most of those associated with Sickles's plot suffered professionally for their poor judgment. Hooker remained out west and never commanded another field army. Butterfield went on to lead a division in Hooker's corps during the Atlanta campaign, but illness then forced him out of active service for the rest of the war. After the conflict he maintained a high profile in business and, ironically enough, as a Grant booster; he died in 1901. As for Sickles, Lincoln eventually dispatched him first on an inspection tour of southern territory under Union control and then on a diplomatic mission to Colombia. After the war Sickles served as military governor of South Carolina, minister to Spain (where he attracted notoriety for a romantic liaison with the former queen), congressman, and chairman of the New York State Monuments Commission. He died in 1914.

David Birney managed to survive his role in Sickles's cabal, though at the cost of his pride. Birney had small use for Meade, whom he rightly believed had obstructed his efforts to gain a corps command. In mid-March, he responded to Meade's request for elaboration on his comments before the Committee on the Conduct of the War by claiming that he only answered direct questions and that he saw no reason to expound on his testimony now. By early April, however, Birney saw the writing on the wall and admitted defeat. He visited Meade and declared that he was not a Sickles partisan, that he had always entertained the warmest feelings toward Meade, and that he hoped to continue to serve under him. Meade knew better, but he matched Birney's lies by blandly commenting that he was unaware of any rumors that Birney disliked him. Birney also submitted his resignation, but Meade, generous to a defeated foe, refused to accept it. As a result of his supplication, Birney held onto his division.[52]

Conclusions

Unhappily for Meade, some of the events that helped him maintain command over the Army of the Potomac also eventually drastically curtailed much of the autonomy the Lincoln administration had initially bestowed on him in personnel matters. Grant's elevation to general in chief helped protect Meade from Sickles and his cronies, but Grant eventually curtailed the freedom Meade had in choosing corps commanders. As it was, Meade's record in this area was mixed at best and at worst a good deal less than that. Lincoln initially gave him considerable leeway in picking corps commanders, so much so that Meade never asked the president to formally approve his choices, probably because he did not think it was necessary. Unfortunately, whereas Meade used the corps commanders he inherited from Hooker well, he did a poor job of selecting their replacements. Newton, Hays, French, and Sykes all proved disappointing, and even Warren ultimately caused more problems than he was worth. In Meade's defense, Congress's decision to limit the number of major generals severely restricted his options, so it is perhaps hardly surprising that the quality of the Army of the Potomac's corps commanders declined so precipitously in the last half of 1863.

On the other hand, much of the dissension that wracked the Army of the Potomac's high command under McClellan's, Burnside's, and Hooker's leadership disappeared during Meade's watch. Meade had to contend with Sickles's efforts to displace him, but this assault came primarily from outside of the Army of the Potomac and had little impact on Meade's day-to-day operations. Meade owed his good fortune to several factors. For one thing, some of the biggest troublemakers—men such as Kearny, Hooker, Sickles, Franklin, and Smith—were no longer with the Army of the Potomac. Moreover, except for Pleasonton, the remaining corps commanders all respected Meade. After all, Meade had seen as much combat as anyone in the army, and he shared their McClellanite prejudices. Finally, none of the corps commanders had much ambition to supplant Meade, and even if they did, none had the political connections and combat record to persuade Lincoln to appoint them. By quieting these troubled waters, Meade performed a service for the Union war effort second only to his victory at Gettysburg.

Irvin McDowell

Edwin Sumner

Samuel Heintzelman

Erasmus Keyes

Ambrose Burnside

Joseph Hooker

George Meade

Fitz John Porter

William Franklin

William Smith

Gouverneur Warren

Daniel Butterfield

Daniel Sickles

David Birney

Alfred Pleasonton

Oliver Otis Howard

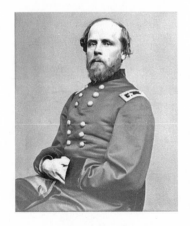

Darius Couch

John Sedgwick

Henry Slocum

George Stoneman

John Gibbon

Winfield Scott Hancock

Andrew Humphreys

Horatio Wright

CHAPTER FIVE

Grant as General in Chief
March 1864 to April 1865

Clearing the Decks

He was an unlikely war hero—in fact, he did not even look much like a soldier—but by March 1864 Major General Ulysses Grant had led Union
armies to more battlefield victories than anyone else. He was a stumpy,
slouchy, round-shouldered man who ambled about with a cigar in his mouth,
his head down, and his hands thrust deep into his pockets. He usually dressed
like a common soldier, and at first glance there was nothing remarkable about
him. Indeed, people frequently commented on his overwhelming ordinari-
ness. His taciturnity, modesty, and shyness disguised deeper qualities, however, that less astute observers often overlooked. He possessed a rough dignity
and a lack of pretentiousness perfectly in keeping with his Midwestern up-
bringing. Despite a history laced with personal failure and disappointment,
he had enough confidence in his judgment to escape the self-doubt that
plagued so many other Union officers with more impressive pedigrees. He
brought clarity of mind and purpose to his tasks that enabled him to cut right
to the heart of military problems. This, combined with his single-minded determination and relentlessness, allowed him to overcome the most intractable obstacles and stubborn opponents time and again. Although his
tactical abilities were limited, he grasped grand strategy like few other high-
ranking Union officers. He formulated simple, straightforward, and practica-
ble plans whatever the geographical, logistical, and personnel constraints. He
was not much for office work or petty details, so he relied heavily on his staff
and subordinates to implement his decisions. He believed in letting a man
find his own way to achieve his objectives, and he refused to scapegoat those
who tried their best and failed. Similarly, he never sought to escape authority

and responsibility or to undermine his superiors. Most important, he recognized that the Union's manpower and matériel superiority could, if properly applied, grind the Confederacy into powder.[1]

The Ohio-born Grant had graduated from West Point in 1843, twenty-first in his class of thirty-nine. As his class standing indicated, there was little in his record that marked him for future greatness. He had served capably under both Zachary Taylor and Winfield Scott in the Mexican War, but after the conflict his career had skidded downhill. Posted in the isolated Pacific Northwest far away from his family and bored by the stifling routine of the peacetime army, he had turned to the bottle for comfort. He had resigned his commission under a cloud in 1854, and the following years had brought him little but hardship and poverty. He had failed as a farmer and real estate salesman, and when the war broke out he was clerking at his brothers' leather goods store in Galena, Illinois. Fortunately, local congressman Elihu Washburne secured him a brigadier generalship, and he eventually found himself under Halleck's command along the Mississippi River. He gained instant fame and the sobriquet "Unconditional Surrender Grant" by seizing Fort Donelson and its 15,000-man Confederate garrison in February 1862. Two months later, however, the rebels surprised Grant and his army at Pittsburg Landing along the Tennessee River at the Battle of Shiloh. Although the bluecoats repelled the ferocious Confederate assault, the huge casualty list—13,000 Union and 10,700 rebel killed, wounded, and missing—shocked a nation as yet unaccustomed to the horrors of total war. Lincoln stood by Grant despite calls for his relief because he sensed in him a grittiness and resolve lacking in so many other Union generals. Halleck, on the other hand, had been suspicious and jealous of Grant since Fort Donelson, and he relegated him to the sidelines during the Union army's glacial march on Corinth, Mississippi. Grant was so demoralized that he considered quitting the war, but Halleck's fortuitous elevation to general in chief cleared the way for Grant to regain army command. For five months Grant campaigned doggedly against the Confederate citadel of Vicksburg, Mississippi, without success. In April 1863, however, he crossed the Mississippi River, outmaneuvered and outfought the scattered rebel forces, and placed the city under siege until its 30,000 defenders surrendered on 4 July. Vicksburg's fall severed the Confederacy in two and opened the Mississippi River to Union shipping. Five months later, Grant solidified his reputation by driving the rebel army outside of Chattanooga headlong into Georgia.

On 1 March 1864, Lincoln appointed Grant a lieutenant general. Congress had recently resurrected the rank with Grant in mind, despite some reservations about placing one soldier in such a lofty position, and the Senate quickly confirmed him. Not only did Grant get a third star, but Lincoln also chose him to replace Halleck as general in chief, thus putting all the Union's armies under his control. Grant had spent the entire conflict out west, and he hoped to direct the Union war effort from that familiar theater. A mid-March visit to Washington, however, convinced him that no deputy he left there to look after his interests could resist the pressure politicians and officers were capable of exerting. Even so, Grant had no intention of running the war from a stuffy Washington office; he wanted to be in the field. Mulling things over, he decided that he would personally accompany the beleaguered Army of the Potomac on its next campaign. Doing so would enable him to oversee the Union's most troublesome army, and he would remain close enough to the capital to keep an eye on events there. To supervise the army's day-to-day operations and liaison with the Lincoln administration, Grant asked Halleck to stay in the capital as his chief of staff. Although unconventional, the arrangement suited everyone involved. Grant escaped the tedious day-to-day operations that running the army entailed so he could concentrate on plotting strategy, Lincoln and Stanton retained access to a military man for consultation and advice, and Old Brains could indulge in his proclivity for military routine and paperwork without the accountability he so abhorred.[2]

Grant originally assumed from newspaper reports that the Lincoln administration intended to relieve Meade as Army of the Potomac commander, so he brought Baldy Smith to Washington with him to take Meade's place. Smith had fallen a long way since Hooker had ousted him from the Army of the Potomac, but his relationship with Grant put him back to the center of the Union war effort. When Grant met Smith, Smith was the Department of the Cumberland's chief engineer. He impressed Grant by devising the plan that opened up the supply lines to the besieged Union army in Chattanooga, and thereafter Grant saw Smith as some sort of deus ex machina. Once in Washington, however, Grant discovered that the Lincoln administration had no intention of supplanting Meade, so he temporarily put Smith on the back burner. On 10 March, Grant and a small entourage that included Smith traveled to Culpeper, Virginia, to have a firsthand look at Meade and his army. Although Meade and Grant knew each other from their Mexican War days, they had not spoken since. When Grant arrived, Meade greeted him warmly. The two officers retired to Meade's headquarters, sat down, lit cigars, and talked. Meade said that he realized that big changes were in the works, so he offered to step aside if Grant wanted to assign the Army of the Potomac to Halleck, William Sherman, or some other western general. The Union cause, Meade intoned, was more important than any one person. Grant replied that he needed Sherman out west, and he later noted that Meade's selflessness impressed him even more than his victory at Gettysburg. Grant assured Meade that he had no intention of removing him from his command, despite Smith's presence, and in fact in the following weeks he denounced Hooker's, Sickles's, and Butterfield's efforts to pressure the Lincoln administration to do so. Grant did, however, inform Meade that he expected to accompany the Army of the Potomac on its next campaign. Grant returned to Washington the next day, and that evening he boarded a train for Nashville to consult with his western generals. There he pronounced the Army of the Potomac in fine shape, but he noted that a good many of its officers cautioned him, "You have not yet met Bobby Lee."[3]

This was true enough—although, conversely, Bobby Lee had not yet met Ulysses Grant either. Grant's decision to accompany the Army of the Potomac was an indication of the respect he already held for Lee and his Army of Northern Virginia, but it also presented the Union Army with innumerable potential problems. By Grant's superimposing himself on the Army of the Potomac's command structure, he and Meade would in effect share authority over the army, a recipe for confusion and possible disaster. Indeed, some of Grant's staff officers urged him to simply return Meade to a corps and assume direct control of the Army of the Potomac. Grant, however, argued that he lacked the time to run the Army of the Potomac, oversee the Union's other forces, and formulate strategy. Grant believed that Meade was thoroughly familiar with the army's organization and officers, so he was the best man to manage its day-to-day administration. Besides, continued Grant, foisting himself on the army would arouse the jealousy and resentment of its notoriously touchy officer corps.[4]

Grant realized that his relationship with Meade was the key to making this peculiar arrangement successful. Meade understood from the start that Grant's presence would overshadow him and crimp his authority. He did not believe that Grant was a military genius, but he recognized his merits. Although he sometimes grumbled about Grant's judgment and complained that he was being slighted, he accepted his plight with enough grace to make their relationship work. For his part, Grant recognized the awkward circumstances in which he placed Meade, and he tried to be sensitive to his feelings because he thought Meade was a good and capable soldier. The two men never became intimate friends, but they respected each other and learned to cooperate. When the Army of the Potomac campaigned, they kept their headquarters in close proximity, and they consulted with each other before either man issued orders affecting the army's tactical and personnel dispositions. Indeed, Grant had little contact with Meade's corps commanders. Although Grant rarely interfered with Meade's administrative decisions, as time went on he increasingly intruded on tactical and personnel matters, reducing Meade to a glorified chief of staff. Grant, however, promised those who commented unfavorably on Meade's anomalous position that he would make sure Meade received proper credit. In the trying months that followed—months that stretched friendships in the Army of the Potomac's officer corps to and beyond the breaking point—it was a promise Grant kept.[5]

Grant's ascension was not the only change the Army of the Potomac underwent that late winter. As Grant was familiarizing himself with his new responsibilities, Meade was preparing to subject the Army of the Potomac to its biggest structural reorganization since Hooker's days. Despite the departure of the Eleventh and Twelfth Corps, Meade believed that the army still contained too many corps for its numbers. To rectify this, he asked Halleck and Stanton to consolidate the five remaining corps into three. This would not only create bigger corps with more combat power, but it would also give Meade the opportunity to rid the army of a couple of his substandard corps commanders. Halleck and Stanton agreed, and Meade issued the necessary orders on 24 March. Meade's victims were the First and Third Corps. The two units had never fully recovered from their ordeals at Gettysburg, and their temporary commanders, John Newton and William French, had hardly sparkled in their positions. Meade combined two of the Third Corps' divisions into one under David Birney and sent it to the Second Corps. Its remaining division—the one French had brought to the army from Harper's Ferry after Gettysburg—went to the Sixth Corps. As for the First Corps, Meade merged its three divisions into two and grafted them onto the Fifth Corps. Needless to say, the members of the First and Third Corps were shocked, even though the changes had been rumored for months. It especially worried staff officers who now had to look for new posts. Both corps had long and distinguished combat records dating back to the Army of the Potomac's infancy, and by now their men had developed deep attachments to them. Meade tried to assuage their consternation by permitting the troops to retain their corps badges, and he pledged to reconstitute the units if sufficient reinforcements arrived. In the end, however, the Army of the Potomac never had enough manpower to make good on Meade's promise, so the two corps went out of existence. On the other hand, many outside observers welcomed the restructuring. In fact, some Radical Republican politicians and officers incorrectly interpreted it as a purge of McClellanite officers such as Newton and French because the orders came from Stanton's office.[6]

Amazingly enough, Meade lobbied Stanton and Halleck to give both Newton and French divisions in the army's new organizational structure. Fortunately, Stanton and Halleck did not let sentimentality blind them to both men's faults, so they refused. They ordered French to report to

Philadelphia for orders, and he played no further active role in the war. He remained in the army though; he died in 1881. Newton feared that he would share French's fate, and he denounced Meade for removing him from his corps. To add insult to injury, the Lincoln administration also revoked his nomination to major general. On Grant's recommendation, however, Stanton and Halleck sent Newton out west to George Thomas's Army of the Cumberland. Newton led a division in Oliver Otis Howard's Fourth Corps during the Atlanta campaign and later commanded the District of West Florida until the end of the war. After the conflict, he eventually became the army's chief engineer. He retired in 1886 and died nine years later.[7]

Meade did not stop there. He still considered Gouverneur Warren the army's golden boy, but Hancock's imminent return would displace Warren as the Second Corps' temporary commander. Meade wanted to find a slot appropriate to Warren's abilities, so he persuaded Lincoln, Stanton, and Halleck to assign him to the Fifth Corps in place of George Sykes. As with Newton and French, Meade tried hard to secure a divisional command for Sykes, but Stanton and Halleck refused. Some speculated that Stanton and Halleck disliked Sykes's brusque manner, others said his pro-McClellan sympathies did him in, and still others blamed the severe rheumatism he suffered from all winter. Whatever the reason for his relief, at Grant's suggestion the War Department transferred Sykes to the remote Department of Kansas. Unlike Newton and French, many officers lamented Sykes's departure. He had never been an outstanding soldier, but he had built a dependable record during his long tenure with the Army of the Potomac. Sykes passed the remainder of the conflict in Kansas, and afterwards he led a regiment out on the frontier. He died in 1880. As for Warren, he was elated to attain a corps command by presidential fiat. He spent a lot of time with Grant that spring, and he impressed the new general in chief as much as he had impressed Meade. In fact, Grant made a mental note to give the Army of the Potomac to Warren if anything happened to Meade. Small wonder Warren wrote to his wife, "We are going to have a magnificent campaign and I have a situation commensurate with it. Let me have a fair chance where I now am and I do not fear the result."[8]

Cavalry commander Alfred Pleasonton was the last major victim of the March shake-up. Grant's brief inspection of the Army of the Potomac convinced him that its cavalry needed new leadership, and he recommended Major General Philip Sheridan to Lincoln and Stanton for the job. Stanton readily agreed, mostly because he had never really liked Pleasonton. Indeed, Meade had on several occasions fended off the secretary of war's efforts to replace Pleasonton. Pleasonton's opposition to Brigadier General Judson Kilpatrick's disastrous Stanton-backed raid on Richmond in February did little to improve his standing with the War Department. Moreover, Pleasonton's unwise decision to support Sickles during the Committee on the Conduct of the War's hearings cost him Meade's loyalty. At Grant's urging, the War Department transferred Pleasonton to the Department of Missouri, where he spent the remainder of the conflict. There he played an important role at the Battle of Westport in repelling Sterling Price's raid through the state. After the war he resigned from the army in a dispute over rank, held various minor federal jobs, and died in 1897.[9]

Philip Sheridan would emerge from the Civil War as the Union's foremost combat general. It is unclear whether he was born in Ireland, on his family's transatlantic voyage to America, or in New York, but he grew up in Ohio. Although he had entered West Point in 1848, he was suspended for a year for fighting with another cadet, so he did not graduate until 1853. He had ranked near the bottom of his class, and he gave little indication of his potential in the following prewar years out on the frontier. He served as a quartermaster for Halleck in the conflict's early days, but he eventually secured a transfer and rose to command a division in the Army of the Cumberland. He fought with distinction at the Battles of Perryville and Stone's River, saw his division break and run at Chickamauga, and redeemed himself by shattering the supposedly impregnable Confederate line along Missionary Ridge at the Battle of Chattanooga. His actions at Chattanooga caught Grant's attention, and Grant became one of his biggest boosters. When Grant was brainstorming for a new Army of the Potomac cavalry corps commander, Halleck suggested Sheridan. Sheridan had little experience with that branch of the service, but Grant overlooked this and said, "The very man I want." Lincoln and Stanton, however, had their doubts. They believed that the thirty-three-year-old Sheridan was too young for such a big responsibility. Moreover, Sheridan did not make a very good impression when Halleck introduced him to first Stanton and then Lincoln. He was physically unimposing under the best of circumstances, but the rigors of recent campaigns had reduced him to a skeletal 115 pounds. He was also a squat and compact man who looked like a cross between an Irish bowery boy and a Mongol warrior, with close-cropped black hair that appeared sprayed on his scalp. In addition, meeting two of the prime architects of the Union war effort left him tongue-tied, timid, and unsure of himself. Fortunately, in this instance first impressions were false. Sheridan was actually a tough, self-reliant, energetic, and optimistic man. In battle he was fearless, impatient, pugnacious, and instinctive. He possessed the rare ability to inspire his soldiers to give that extra effort that made the difference between victory and defeat. His can-do attitude quickly won over the Army of Potomac's cliquish cavalry corps officers. Grant understood all this, and in response to Lincoln's hesitations he said, "You will find him big enough for the purpose before we get through with him."[10]

Meade's reorganization was disruptive for officers and men who suddenly lost their unit identities and found themselves thrown in with corps and divisions whose traditions and experiences were unfamiliar. Under such circumstances, anyone who could provide a sense of continuity and dependability was a welcome sight. Fortunately, the Army of the Potomac retained the services of Winfield Scott Hancock and John Sedgwick, two of its longest-serving generals. There was nothing inevitable about either man's presence, though. Hancock had resumed command of his Second Corps in late December, but his Gettysburg injury had proved so painful that he had gone home again a few weeks later. Although he returned on 24 March, he was not quite the same man who had led his troops so gallantly at Fredericksburg, Chancellorsville, and especially Gettysburg. His inner thigh wound remained unhealed, and it periodically sloughed off pieces of bone and metal. Riding on his horse was so painful that Hancock asked for and received permission to travel in an ambulance if he felt it was necessary. There was nothing wrong with his courage and determination, but in the upcoming campaign his injury eventually forced him to temporarily relinquish his command at the most inopportune and critical time. Even so, Meade was still happy to see his old friend again; if Hancock had lost some of his edge, he was still head and shoulders above most Army of the Potomac corps commanders.[11]

Unlike Hancock, Sedgwick spent the winter with the army, passing his time with endless games of solitaire and long horseback rides. Indeed, he had yet to take a leave of absence from the army during the war, and the only time he had gone home to Connecticut was to recuperate from his Antietam wounds. When Meade consulted with Stanton about the army's reorganization, he was shocked to learn that the secretary of war wanted to remove Sedgwick from the Sixth Corps and relegate him to the same fates that awaited Newton, French, and Sykes. As one observer noted, "Stanton always spoke of Sedgwick as a brave, thoroughgoing soldier, who staid [sic] in camp, gave Washington a wide berth, and did not intrigue against his superiors; but I never heard him attribute to Sedgwick such high qualities for a great command as he imputed to some officers of that army."[12] Sedgwick himself would have welcomed such a change, and in fact a few weeks before he had written his sister, "We hear that there is to be a reorganization of this army, probably for the purpose of getting rid of some obnoxious Generals. I shall not be sorry to hear that I am one of them. I feel that I have done my part of field duty, although my health is quite good. A few weeks' rest would be beneficial, and I could even leave altogether without many regrets."[13] Meade, on the other hand, argued strenuously to retain his most reliable subordinate. Stanton, however, only agreed to transfer Sedgwick to command Union forces in the Shenandoah Valley. As for his replacement, Meade suggested his close friend John Gibbon, who had by now recovered from his Gettysburg wound, and Stanton agreed. In the end, however, Lincoln upset Stanton's calculations by putting Franz Sigel in charge of the Shenandoah Valley, so Sedgwick held on to his corps and Gibbon stayed with his division in the Second Corps.[14]

Finally, in April, a familiar face from the unhappy past arrived in Virginia to take part in the upcoming campaign: Ambrose Burnside. After Burnside had left the Army of the Potomac, Lincoln had directed him to take charge of the Department of the Ohio. While he fulfilled his new duties with a heavy-handedness consistent with his past performances, the Ninth Corps embarked on an odyssey of its own. The War Department first sent it down to Newport News, off the southern Virginia coast, and then to Kentucky. From there John Parke, Burnside's old chief of staff, took the corps to Mississippi to join Grant's army in the siege of Vicksburg. Afterward the Ninth accompanied William Sherman on his march to Jackson, Mississippi, before returning to Kentucky in August. By then Burnside had begun an offensive into eastern Tennessee, and the War Department ordered his old unit to join him there. The Ninth successfully defended Knoxville from Confederate attack, but by the end of the year its exertions left its numbers depleted. The War Department sent the corps north to recruit up to strength, and in mid-March Grant had it concentrated under Burnside's command at Annapolis, Maryland. Although Burnside reorganized the corps into four divisions, including one composed of black soldiers, he did little else to prepare the unit for combat, which caused innumerable problems in subsequent months as its rookies learned their new trade the hard way. Grant intended the Ninth to go with the Army of the Potomac in its next campaign, but he put it under his direct command because Burnside ranked Meade. It was an awkward arrangement that did not last long. Most people, however, were more concerned about Burnside's competency than his place in the command structure. Earlier in the winter, one officer had summed up the army's feelings toward him by noting, "It is astonishing how a man who has shown himself so utterly unfit manages to continue getting independent commands."[15]

The Overland Campaign

Three years of war had taken its toll on the Confederacy. Union armies had overrun Missouri, Kentucky, Maryland, and Tennessee as well as large chunks of Virginia, North Carolina, Mississippi, Louisiana, and Arkansas.

Tens of thousands of rebel soldiers had succumbed to enemy fire and disease, and the Confederate manpower pool was all but dry. The Union naval blockade was gradually isolating the South from the outside world, depriving it of access to the military equipment and supplies it needed to wage the conflict. The Confederate government, never well suited for modern war anyway, was becoming increasingly dysfunctional and ineffective. Its inability to protect its citizens prompted increasing numbers of rebel soldiers to desert their units and return home in order to take care of their starving families. Despite these burdens, however, the Confederacy remained a powerful entity. If the Union had ripped away its geographical extremities, it retained its heartland and the resources there. Confederate armies possessed sufficient power to fend off Union attacks and even regain the initiative on occasion. Indeed, in early 1864 the rebels ran up a string of victories. Confederate forces repelled a Union invasion of Florida at the Battle of Olustee on 10 February, and they seized Plymouth, North Carolina, in mid-April. Most impressive of all, they routed Nathaniel Banks's large-scale offensive up the Red River in Louisiana. For all the Confederacy's weaknesses, there was no doubt that Grant had his work cut out for him.

Grant's grand strategic plan called for all the Union armies to exert maximum pressure on the Confederacy by simultaneously assuming the offensive. Out west, William Sherman would march on Atlanta, Georgia, with the Armies of the Cumberland, the Tennessee, and the Ohio. In Virginia, this meant that the Army of the Potomac's advance would be accompanied by ones undertaken by Major General Benjamin Butler's Army of the James up the James River and by Franz Sigel's army in the Shenandoah Valley. As usual, the Army of the Potomac outnumbered Lee's Army of Northern Virginia by about two to one, or 120,000 Yankees to 65,000 rebels. The two armies faced each other across the Rapidan River, but Grant hoped to use this normally unfavorable geographical fact to his advantage. He decided to cross the river at Ely's and Germanna fords and march rapidly past Lee's right flank through the all-but-impenetrable Wilderness that had brought Hooker to grief the previous year. Once the Army of the Potomac reached the clear ground to the south, it would sever Lee's supply lines back to Richmond. Lee would be forced to either backpedal and fight the Union army out in the open or order a general retreat. As far as Grant was concerned, either option would spell the end of the Confederate Army of Northern Virginia.

On 4 May, the Army of the Potomac crossed the Rapidan for the last time. There was no opposition, and Grant counted himself lucky to reach the south side of the river without sustaining any losses. He could have pushed his men all the way through the Wilderness that day, but he decided against doing so because he did not want the army's supply trains to fall too

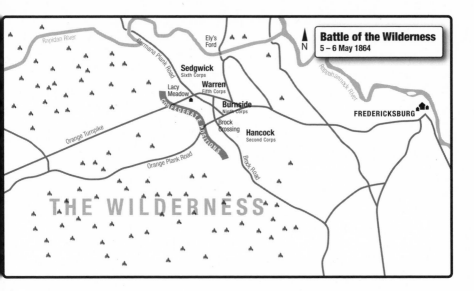

far behind. Unhappily, this gave Lee the time he needed to march his soldiers into the Wilderness to provoke a battle in which the dense underbrush
would nullify the Union army's superiority in numbers and artillery. The
next morning, Union patrols spotted a heavy column of Confederate infantry moving eastward up the Orange Turnpike. After consulting with
Meade and Warren, Grant decided that if Lee wanted a fight in the Wilderness, he would oblige him. He rapidly sent out orders to redeploy the Army
of the Potomac for battle. As part of his impromptu plan, Grant directed
Warren's Fifth Corps to assault westward down the Orange Turnpike. Under
heavy pressure from Grant and Meade to get going, Warren fed his divisions
into the smoky woods piecemeal, and as such they were badly mauled. Reinforcements from Sedgwick's Sixth Corps got lost in the woods and failed to
make contact with Warren's men in a timely fashion. Brigadier General
Charles Griffin, one of Warren's division commanders, was so infuriated
with the way his superiors mishandled his division that he mounted his
horse and galloped off to Grant's and Meade's headquarters at Lacy Meadow.
There he roundly and loudly denounced Warren and Brigadier General Horatio Wright, a Sixth Corps divisional commander, for their failure to properly support his unit. Meade managed to hear him out without losing his
famous temper, and he did his best to assuage him. Having vented his
spleen, Griffin got back on his horse and returned to the front lines. Grant
had taken up position on a stump on a knoll, and he smoked and whittled as
he issued a stream of orders. He did not interfere with Griffin's tirade, but afterwards he asked Meade, "Who is this General Gregg? You ought to arrest

him!" Meade replied, "It's Griffin, not Gregg, and it's only his way of talk-ing."[16] Although Griffin's trip may have been therapeutic for him, it did lit-tle to improve Union fortunes on that part of the confused and sprawling battlefield. For the rest of the day, Warren's and Sedgwick's men blundered about north and south of the Orange Turnpike, took heavy casualties, and made no headway against the thickening rebel defenses.

Meanwhile, at about the same time, a more desperate battle was going on at the intersection of Orange Plank and Brock roads. If the Confederates seized this crossroads, they would cut the Army of the Potomac in two by isolating Hancock's Second Corps from the rest of the army. To secure it from the advancing rebels, Grant dispatched Brigadier General George Getty's Sixth Corps division. Getty's men got there just before the rebels, but they were heavily outnumbered. Even so, they were tough and experi-enced soldiers under a capable commander, and they fought hard, but the rebels gradually pushed them back. Fortunately, Hancock and the leading el-ements of his Second Corps arrived in the nick of time. Hancock deployed his men in the tangled undergrowth and sent them crashing forward through the smoldering woods. They overtook Getty's exhausted men and drove the Confederates back in disarray. There was nothing easy about it though; no one could see more than a few feet in any direction, and it was not difficult to get lost and disoriented. Despite these problems, Hancock's men might have shattered the rebel line once and for all had darkness not put an end to the day's fighting.

Aggressive as ever, Grant wanted to renew the battle next day to capital-ize on the successes he had already achieved. He planned to reinforce Han-cock with two Ninth Corps divisions and send him westward down the Orange Plank Road early in the morning to complete the work so promis-ingly begun the previous day. At the same time, Warren and Sedgwick would continue to hammer away along the Orange Turnpike, and Burnside would bring two of his divisions into the gap separating Hancock from War-ren and Sedgwick. Burnside had the farthest to go, but he was confident his men would be in position on time. Emerging from Grant's headquarters tent after receiving his orders, he threw back his shoulders and said to the col-lected assemblage, "Well, then, my troops shall break camp at half past two." After he left, though, Meade's chief engineer sneered, "*He* won't be up. I know him well."[17]

Early next morning, Hancock launched his soldiers down the Orange Plank Road. The exhausted rebels had made no effort to entrench or even straighten out their chaotic lines, so they rapidly broke and ran. Hancock drove his men forward, repeatedly sorting out and reforming them in the thick woods. He was at his best, which prompted one officer to later write,

"At this moment he looked like a spirited portrait from the hands of a master artist, with the deep brown of the dense forest forming a fitting background. It was enough to inspire the troops he led to deeds of unmatched heroism."[18] Indeed, it looked like victory was just around the corner, and Hancock cried to a staff officer, "Tell General Meade we are driving them most beautifully!"[19] Unfortunately, problems were already developing that would doom his offensive. For one thing, Warren and Sedgwick were making no progress to the north, although at least their attacks kept the Confederates there from sending reinforcements to their beleaguered comrades facing Hancock's juggernaut. In addition, in response to unfounded rumors of Confederates massing to the south, Hancock had dispatched Brigadier General Francis Barlow's division to watch his left flank, thus reducing the number of soldiers available to exploit the gains made along the Orange Plank Road. Hancock eventually sent for the unit, but the orders never got through, so the division stayed put. Finally, as Meade's chief engineer had predicted, Burnside was not up yet. In fact, he and his two divisions had gotten lost, and they would spend much of the day wandering around in the trackless woods in search of Union lines. Hancock was hardly surprised by Burnside's absence—there was bad blood between them dating back to Fredericksburg—and when informed of Burnside's tardiness he exclaimed, "Just what I expected!"[20] In the end, Confederate reinforcements arrived just in time to stop Hancock's forces from splintering their army once and for all. Nor was that the worst of it; although Hancock did not yet know it, both of his flanks were exposed, providing the Confederates with an opportunity of which they did not fail to take advantage. The rebels launched a furious counterattack that hit Hancock's blown men on their exposed left flank, between them and Barlow's detached division, driving them back for more than a mile to their starting point. Hancock managed to stop the rout and repel the Confederate attack at the intersection of the Brock and Orange Plank roads, but it was touch and go. This was not the only crisis the Army of the Potomac faced that day. Just before dusk, another rebel assault struck Sedgwick's uncovered right flank, pushed the Yankees back more than a mile, and captured 600 of them. Although Sedgwick managed to restore the Union line, here too it was a close thing.

Both Grant and Meade remained calm and unruffled throughout the ups and downs of the battle. This was in itself important; after all, similar stresses had unhinged Joe Hooker about a year ago on practically the same ground at Chancellorsville, costing the Union victory. After dusk, for example, Grant discovered Meade consulting with Horatio Wright, whose Sixth Corps division had participated in the debacle on the Union right. "Hello Wright," Grant said matter-of-factly. "I thought you had gone to Richmond."[21] Grant abandoned his composure publicly only once. At one point, a panicky officer proclaimed that Lee was about to cut the Army of the Potomac off from the Rapidan. Grant heard him out and exclaimed, "Oh, I am heartily tired of hearing about what *Lee* is going to do. Some of you always seem to think he is suddenly going to turn a double somersault and land in our rear and on both flanks at the same time. Go back to your command and try to think what we are going to do ourselves, instead of what *Lee* is going to do."[22]

Despite his outward stoicism and defiance, Grant was actually under considerable strain. The Battle of the Wilderness had not gone especially well. Grant had fought the engagement on Lee's terms on ground that negated the Army of the Potomac's advantages in manpower and artillery. During the battle, the outnumbered Confederates had pummeled both exposed Union flanks, and Grant could count himself lucky that Lee had not taken advantage of the gaping hole that Burnside's tardiness had created in the center of the Union lines. The Army of the Potomac's losses topped 17,000, considerably more than the approximately 11,000 casualties the rebels sustained. Among the Union dead were Major General James Wadsworth and Brigadier General Alexander Hays, commanders of, respectively, a Fifth Corps division and Second Corps brigade. Finally, Union leadership left much to be desired. Grant and Meade had forgone any attempt at tactical finesse and instead had relied on brute strength to achieve their objectives. Such assaults, however, usually collapsed in the face of devastating rebel rifle fire delivered from behind increasingly intricate defenses. Hancock had fought magnificently, but Warren's and Burnside's performances were sorely lacking. All things considered, it was hardly surprising that Grant broke down and wept from the tension when he retired to his tent for the night.[23]

The fact was, Grant had lost the battle. By dawn on 7 May, Lee's veterans had constructed all-but-impenetrable fortifications, so any Union assault was bound to fail. While Grant pondered his plight, his men caught their breath, collected their wounded, improved their entrenchments, and counted noses. Despite his rude and horrific introduction to eastern theater combat, Grant was no more inclined to admit defeat now than before. Scanning his maps, Grant concluded that if he could not go through the thickening rebel defenses, then he would bypass them. He decided to march the Army of the Potomac a dozen miles southward to Spotsylvania Courthouse. If he seized the crossroads first, he would cut the Confederates off from Richmond. By refusing to retreat back across the Rapidan, Grant transformed a tactical defeat in the Wilderness into a strategic victory.

On the night of 7–8 May, the Army of the Potomac quietly evacuated its entrenchments in the Wilderness and began its march for Spotsylvania. The bluecoats had a head start over their surprised opponents, and morale was high when the men realized that they were advancing and not retreating. Unhappily, the rebels managed to occupy Spotsylvania first, in the nick of time. There were plenty of reasons for this, but Philip Sheridan deserved a good deal of the blame. Fifth Corps infantry on its way to Spotsylvania found the road clogged with Union cavalry that had no idea what to do or where to go. Meade bypassed Sheridan and gave the cavalrymen new orders to get them out of the way. By then, however, the damage had been done, so when Warren's troops approached Spotsylvania they found the rebels already entrenching in front of it. In an effort to knock them loose before they transformed their sketchy fortifications into an impenetrable defensive network, Warren ordered his divisions to attack as soon as they came up the road. As at the Wilderness, he committed them to battle piecemeal, and they were chewed up the same way. Although Sedgwick's soldiers arrived later and joined the disjointed assaults, they too failed, and the rebels held on to Spotsylvania. By the end of the day, Warren was exhausted, demoralized, and close to incoherence.[24]

At about the same time the rebels were mangling Warren's corps, Sheridan and Meade were engaged in a profanity-laced shouting match at Meade's headquarters. As far as Sheridan was concerned, Meade had improperly interfered with his cavalry, and he was not about to let that happen without registering his objections. Meade, for his part, believed that Sheridan was not handling the cavalry effectively. Eventually, Meade calmed down first and said, "No, I didn't mean that," and put his hand on Sheridan's shoulder in a friendly fashion. Sheridan, however, pulled away and exclaimed, "If I am permitted to cut loose from this army I'll draw [Confederate cavalry commander Jeb] Stuart after me, and whip him, too."[25] Meade appealed to Grant, who commented blandly, "Did he say so? Then let him go out and do it."[26] Meade returned to his tent and drew up the necessary orders. Next day, Sheridan and his cavalry corps left on a sixteen-day raid behind enemy lines, during which they engaged, defeated, and killed Stuart at the Battle of Yellow Tavern. Although this was quite an accomplishment, it did not obviate the painful fact that thousands of Union soldiers suffered as a consequence of Sheridan's bungling on the road to Spotsylvania.[27]

Confederate and Union soldiers poured into the Spotsylvania area, and they quickly began constructing intricate entrenchments that soon snaked across the Virginia countryside. These were usually invulnerable to all except the strongest and best-planned assault, which of course benefited the rebels most because they were generally on the defensive. The fortifications provided some protection to the troops working, resting, or fighting behind them, but they were not foolproof, as Uncle John Sedgwick discovered on 9

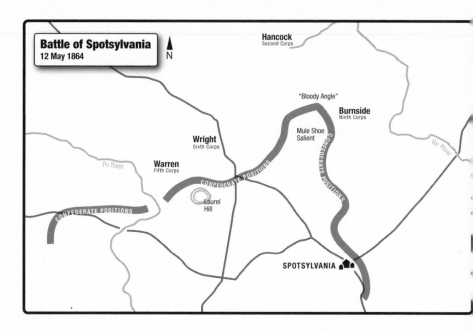

May. Sedgwick was the Army of the Potomac's steadiest corps commander, so he had been perhaps least affected by the tribulations over the past few days. Indeed, he was in an optimistic and buoyant mood that morning as he joked with Colonel Martin McMahon, his chief of staff, about which one of them really ran the Sixth Corps. The two men rode to a section of the front lines, and McMahon warned Sedgwick to be careful because rebel sharpshooters had shot every officer who had exposed himself there the previous day. When Sedgwick saw his jittery men flinch with every rifle crack, however, he laughed and said, "What! What! Dodging this way for single bullets! What will you do when they open fire along the whole line? I am ashamed of you. They couldn't hit an elephant at this distance." Unfortunately, he underestimated rebel marksmanship. A few moments later, a Confederate sniper put a bullet through his left cheek, just below his eye. A medic rushed up and poured water into the wound, but that did little to staunch the spurting fountain of blood. He had a quiet smile on his face, as if to acknowledge the grim irony of what turned out to be his last words. An ambulance, trailed by his grief-stricken staff, took his body back to Meade's headquarters, where it was laid out on an improvised bower of evergreens until it was shipped back to his home in Connecticut. Soldiers throughout the army mourned Sedgwick's death. Grant was stunned when he heard the news, and he twice asked, "Is he really dead?" He compared Sedgwick's loss to that of an entire division. Another officer explained the prevailing sorrow, "'Uncle John' was loved by his men as no corps commander ever was in this army."[28]

Shortly after the rebels removed Sedgwick from the Union army for good, Brigadier General James Ricketts arrived on the scene. Ricketts had transferred out of the Army of the Potomac after Antietam because McClellan had refused to give him command of the First Corps. He had subsequently served on Fitz John Porter's court martial, but he had returned to the Army of the Potomac the previous winter to take charge of a Sixth Corps division. He was the corps' senior officer, so McMahon informed him that he was now in charge. For the second time in his career, Ricketts had a chance to lead a corps. Ricketts, however, declined to accept the job. He said that he knew that Sedgwick had designated Brigadier General Horatio Wright, a fellow division commander, as his successor, and he wanted to respect his fallen chief's wishes. He may or may not have realized that Meade had criticized him as slow and phlegmatic, so there was little chance that his seniority would propel him to corps command anyway. Ricketts suggested that McMahon ride to the Army of the Potomac's headquarters and get Meade to issue the appropriate orders. McMahon did so, but by the time he got there he discovered that Meade had already anticipated Ricketts and directed Wright to take over the Sixth Corps. Despite Wright's lackluster performance in the Wilderness, Grant had no objection, and a week later Lincoln made the appointment official.[29]

Horatio Wright had had an interesting war. The Connecticut-born West Pointer—he had graduated second in his class of 1841, the same year as John Reynolds—had spent much of his prewar career as an engineer in Florida building fortifications. He was captured while aiding in the destruction of the Norfolk Naval Yard, but he was released in enough time to participate in First Bull Run as chief engineer in Heintzelman's division. He then served in the same capacity in the Port Royal expedition on the South Carolina coast. He was promoted to brigadier general in September 1861 and led a division in the Union defeat at the Battle of Secessionville near Charleston. In August 1862, he took over the politically sensitive Department of the Ohio, where he alienated some politicians with his lack of aggressiveness. Indeed, this almost certainly explained the Senate's refusal to confirm his appointment to major general. To make way for Burnside, Lincoln transferred Wright to the Army of the Potomac, where he took command of Bully Brooks's old division in the Sixth Corps. Wright participated in all the army's battles from Gettysburg on, and by the Overland campaign his division was the best in the Sixth Corps. Almost everyone liked Wright, including Meade and Sedgwick. Indeed, he was a big, strong, and kind man, with smiling eyes and a pleasant nature. Earlier in the war, Meade had called

Wright the ideal soldier and expected great things of him. Wright was an outstanding engineer and a thoughtful officer, but some observers worried that he was too cautious for a corps commander. Although this was true up to a point, Wright also demonstrated the ability to learn and grow, so that by the end of the war he had successfully carried out some of the Army of the Potomac's most difficult assignments and earned the praise of even the exacting Phil Sheridan.[30]

The Battle of Spotsylvania lasted until 19 May. For twelve days Grant tried repeatedly and unsuccessfully to break through Lee's lines. In the end, the engagement claimed about 18,300 Union and more than 10,000 Confederate casualties. The battle's climax occurred on 12 May, when some 6,800 bluecoats and about an equal number of rebels fell. At first light, Grant sent Hancock's entire Second Corps against an exposed Confederate salient called the Mule Shoe. Applying tactics developed and used on a smaller scale two days previously by Colonel Emory Upton and his Sixth Corps brigade, the Union troops charged the rebel fortifications at a rush, without stopping to fire. The careful preparation Upton had called for was lacking, but Hancock's troops had the advantage of surprise and numbers. Approximately 20,000 bluecoats flooded over and through the network of enemy trenches, seized several thousand prisoners, and practically annihilated an entire rebel division. Unfortunately, there were too many Union soldiers crammed in too small a space, so maneuvering or even sorting them out became impossible. A Confederate counterattack pushed the Yankees back into the maze of rebel trenches they had seized in their initial rush, where they stopped and held their ground. Nearby, on Hancock's right, Wright brought his entire Sixth Corps into a part of the rebel line subsequently dubbed the Bloody Angle, with similar results. All day long Hancock's and Wright's men slugged it out with the enemy at close quarters in the labyrinth of trenches while the rebels struggled to complete a new line at the base of the salient. Rifle fire destroyed trees and pulverized bodies beyond recognition. Cannon fire ripped huge holes in the opposing ranks until the artillerymen were killed or wounded. Wright was wounded by a piece of shell in the leg, but he dismounted and directed his corps—to the extent that it could be directed, that is—seated on the ground. A steady rain turned the acreage into a muddy mess that drowned some wounded soldiers. At nightfall the Confederates withdrew to their new line, leaving the Yankees in possession of the blood-soaked field. Writing years later, one veteran commented, "I never expect to be fully believed when I tell what I saw of the horrors of Spotsylvania, because I should be loath to believe it myself were the case reversed."[31]

Just the day before, Grant had written Halleck that Lee's army was on its last legs, so he was undoubtedly disturbed and surprised by the fierce resistance the bluecoats had encountered on 12 May. Any frustration Grant felt toward the rebels, however, paled compared to his frustration with some of his ranking subordinates. Although Hancock and Wright had gotten all their men into sustained action—indeed, that was part of the problem, as things turned out—Burnside and Warren had not. Burnside had assailed the far right of the rebel line at about the same time Hancock had sent his men forward, but the rebels had easily repulsed the attack. The Ninth Corps was composed of a far greater percentage of green troops than the other three, and this contributed to its difficulties. Grant, however, wanted Burnside to renew his assaults to keep Lee from sending reinforcements against Hancock and Wright. He sent Burnside order after order, but the Ninth Corps contributed little to the battle.[32]

Considering Burnside's record, his failure was hardly surprising. On the other hand, both Grant and Meade had expected a lot more from Warren than he had so far delivered in the campaign, and the events of 12 May did little to restore their confidence in him. There was nothing wrong with Warren's courage or sense of style; he was conspicuous in his full uniform, sash and all, as he rode on his big white horse. Warren was aware of his poor showing so far, and he had become increasingly snappish and irritable toward both his staff officers and Meade. Although Hancock, Wright, and Burnside all attacked as directed on the morning of 12 May, Warren held his soldiers back. He and his division commanders feared that Confederate enfilade fire would rip their corps apart before their men reached well-defended Laurel Hill. Grant and Meade, however, wanted the added weight a Fifth Corps assault would provide. Meade sent Warren repeated and increasingly strident orders to engage the enemy, but Warren still delayed. In response, Meade dispatched Humphreys over to get Warren moving. Warren finally sent his troops forward, but the attack failed just as he and his division commanders had expected. Meade and Grant wanted the assaults renewed, and in fact Grant told Meade to put Humphreys in charge of the Fifth Corps if Warren failed to act. In the end, it became clear to everyone that the Fifth Corps had shot its bolt, so Warren kept his corps. Even so, Grant later wrote, "If the Fifth Corps, or rather if Warren, had been as prompt as Wright was with the Sixth Corps, better results might have been obtained."[33] Grant and Meade subsequently showed their displeasure with Warren by sending two of his divisions to Wright temporarily and by ordering Humphreys to remain with Warren to keep an eye on him. As for Warren, he was thoroughly disgusted with the day's events, which he attributed to Grant and Meade's miserable generalship.[34]

After a week of intense combat—first at the Wilderness and now at Spotsylvania—Grant was beginning to form some opinions about his subordinates. The day after the horrific fight at the Mule Shoe and the Bloody Angle, Grant asked Stanton to nominate for promotion Meade and Hancock in the Regular Army and to make Wright, Humphreys, and John Gibbon major generals. All five men had impressed Grant with their aggressiveness, but he was especially effusive in his praise of Meade. Grant wrote, "General Meade has more than met my most sanguine expectations. He and Sherman are the fittest officers for large commands I have come in contact with."[35] On the other hand, Grant made no mention of Warren and Burnside. Stanton responded the next day that the Senate had already confirmed Wright and Humphreys as major generals. There were now no vacancies currently available for Gibbon, but Stanton promised to muster out some inactive major general to make room for him. As for Meade and Hancock, Stanton agreed to do what he could to fulfill Grant's wishes. A week later, however, Halleck wrote that Meade's and Hancock's promotions would have to wait for now. Halleck explained that some politicians wanted to reduce West Point influence in the Army by giving nonprofessionals such as Benjamin Butler and Sickles the limited number of slots for generals permitted by law.[36]

After unsuccessfully pounding away at the Confederate lines around Spotsylvania for more than a week, Grant decided to again move the Army of the Potomac around Lee's right flank in yet another attempt to cut the rebels off from Richmond. Lee conformed, and the two armies met along the North Anna River on 26 May. There was considerable skirmishing, but nothing like the ghastly fighting in the Wilderness and at Spotsylvania. Stymied there, Grant continued to probe around Lee's right, down the Pamunkey River to Totopotomoy Creek. At the end of the month, Grant had reached Cold Harbor near the Chickahominy, but he had also run out of room to maneuver. Hoping that even a limited breakthrough might shatter Lee's army, on 3 June Grant ordered Hancock's Second, Wright's Sixth, and Baldy Smith's newly arrived Eighteenth Corps to assail the rebel lines. The attack was a disastrous failure, with thousands of bluecoats falling in little more than an hour. These losses, combined with those suffered getting into position around Cold Harbor in the days leading up to the doomed assault, raised the Union butcher's bill to 12,000 men. Confederate casualties were only half that. Worse yet, Grant's options were now very limited. Although he had reached the gates of Richmond, he did not want to mount a time-consuming siege against the well-fortified city. Moreover, Cold Harbor again demonstrated the futility of direct attack against entrenched infantry. As a result, after a month of almost continuous marching and fighting, the Army of the Potomac finally paused to take a breather while Grant took stock, although the hot, dangerous, and dusty trenches around Cold Harbor made the respite anything but idyllic.

Indeed, the Army of the Potomac sorely needed the rest. Its losses had been astronomical. Almost 55,000 Union soldiers had been killed, wounded, or gone missing during the Army of the Potomac's trek from the Rapidan to Cold Harbor. Although Halleck had sent almost 50,000 reinforcements, these new soldiers were not of the same quality as Meade's veterans. In fact, by early June Meade's veterans were not the same men they had been a month earlier either. A good many had fallen, and it was usually the bravest who became casualties because they were most likely to expose themselves to danger. Others had gone home when their enlistments expired. The remainder were exhausted and demoralized, having realized long before Grant the senselessness of storming the invulnerable rebel lines. To take an extreme example, at the beginning of the campaign, John Gibbon's tough Second Corps division contained 6,799 officers and men. By 31 May—even before Cold Harbor—it had sustained 3,562 casualties. Of its original membership, nearly half had been shot or captured.[37] The Yankees could take some comfort in the knowledge that they had inflicted nearly 30,000 casualties on the rebel army, which had suffered greater proportional losses than its Union counterpart. The Confederates had also received reinforcements, but not enough to replace all those who had fallen. Even so, the fact remained that Lee's troops, although bloodied, remained unbowed.

The Overland campaign was as hard on many of the generals as on the rank and file. Generals certainly had their privileges, but the danger and the stress of responsibility took their toll. This was especially true for Gouverneur Warren. Warren's generalship had been at best uneven and at worst a good deal short of that. His tendency to micromanage and question his superiors was bad enough, but there was more to it. Warren did not believe that direct attacks could break the rebel lines. Therefore, he was torn between his duty to obey orders and his knowledge that many of those orders would lead to the deaths of his soldiers for no purpose. Warren's high-strung and sensitive nature made it difficult for him to overcome this cognitive dissonance he faced every day. After Cold Harbor he exclaimed, "For thirty days now, it has been one funeral procession, past me; and it is too much!"[38] He took his frustrations out on his staff. An officer who witnessed one of his temper tantrums wrote, "I have heard Meade in one of his towering passions. But I never heard anything which could begin to equal the awful oaths poured out tonight [by Warren]; they fairly made my hair stand on end with their profaneness, while I was filled with wonder at the ingenuity of invention and desperate blackguardism they displayed."[39] While the army rested at Cold Harbor, Warren became increasingly lethargic, spending much of the day alone in his tent sleeping. He himself admitted to his wife that he was exhausted. Grant was aware of the problem and kept an eye on Warren, but his erratic behavior did little to inspire confidence.[40]

Like Warren, Burnside had done little to distinguish himself in the course of the campaign. Because Burnside was senior to Meade, Grant initially kept the Ninth Corps separate from the Army of the Potomac and issued orders directly to Burnside, but this proved awkward and cumbersome. Therefore, on 24 May, Grant officially put Burnside and his Ninth Corps under Meade's command. Grant was by now accustomed to the touchy egos that infected the Army of the Potomac, so he was undoubtedly surprised when Burnside heartily approved the decision. "The order is excellent. I am happy it has been made," Burnside told Grant.[41] Regrettably, this did not lead to the collegiality Burnside implied. Within days, Meade tartly criticized Burnside for mishandling his corps, and Burnside responded in kind. The exchange was symptomatic of the disrespect many officers in the Army of the Potomac felt toward Burnside, and it did not bode well for the future.[42]

Warren and Burnside were not the only uninspired and uninspiring generals. Although Wright had initially impressed Grant by getting all his men into action at the Bloody Angle at Spotsylvania, his performance since then had been lackluster. He was slow and inflexible and had demonstrated little tactical imagination, though he knew enough to question the wisdom of assailing rebel fortifications. Hancock's injury continued to bother him, and this reduced his effectiveness. Only Sheridan demonstrated a consistently aggressive attitude. As for Meade, he was increasingly irritable and short-tempered and quick to resent any criticism of himself or the Army of the Potomac. He was very disappointed with his corps commanders, especially Warren and Wright, and at one point he contemplated relieving one or both of them. He continued to get along with Grant, but he had growing doubts about Grant's tactics that called for headlong charges against invulnerable rebel entrenchments. Meade was not much of a publicity seeker, but he confided in friends like Hancock and Gibbon that even he resented the fact that the press and public gave Grant all the credit for the Army of the Potomac's accomplishments.[43]

Grant held up better than his chief subordinates, but even he was deeply affected by the carnage and bloodshed around him. He freely admitted that the campaign was worse than anything he had experienced out west. He maintained his faith in Meade, but like Meade he too questioned some of his corps commanders, especially Warren and Wright. Individuals could be replaced, but Grant was also increasingly convinced that the Army of the Potomac's problems were systemic and institutional. After Cold Harbor, Grant talked with Brigadier General James Wilson, one of Sheridan's division commanders. "Wilson," Grant asked, "what is the matter with this army?" Wilson had plenty of explanations—a flawed organizational structure, defective communications, a confused chain of command, an inferiority complex among the officers toward Robert Lee, and declining élan due to the heavy casualties the rank and file had sustained—but he had a ready solution. One of Grant's staff officers was Colonel Ely Parker, who was an Iroquois Indian. Wilson recommended that Grant ply Parker with liquor until he was roaring drunk, give him a tomahawk and knife, and send him to collect the scalps of the first major generals he came across. Grant chuckled, but his question indicated his concern with the instrument with which he sought to destroy the main Confederate army.[44]

Whatever Grant's worries, he had to work with the materials at hand, and in the days following Cold Harbor he devised a new plan to free the Army of the Potomac from its cul-de-sac along the Chickahominy. Scanning his maps, Grant focused on Petersburg, south of Richmond, as the solution to his strategic problems. Located on the Appomattox River, Petersburg served as a conduit through which ran most of Richmond's railroads. If Grant could seize the city, Lee's army would have to starve in its fortifications protecting the Confederate capital, disperse into the surrounding countryside, or emerge from its entrenchments to engage in a battle out in the open that the numerically superior Union army could scarcely lose. To be sure, marching on Petersburg was not risk free. The Army of the Potomac would have to turn its back on Lee's army, making it vulnerable to a sudden assault. Moreover, in transferring Union operations south of the James River, Grant would expose Washington to Confederate attack. Grant, however, believed that the benefits outweighed the potential dangers. Once he made up his mind, he moved fast. On the night of 12–13 June, the Army of the Potomac quietly departed from its trenches around Cold Harbor. Baldy Smith's recently arrived Eighteenth Corps embarked from White House on 13 June for a long boat ride down the York River, around Fortress Monroe on the tip of the Peninsula, and up the James River to Bermuda Hundred. The rest of the army plodded south through the old Seven Days battlefields to Windmill Point. There engineers constructed a long pontoon bridge that the Union troops used to cross the James River. The movement went like clockwork, and Lee initially had no idea where the Union host had gone.

Once over the James, though, the Army of the Potomac's high command suffered a collective failure of nerve that rivaled even McClellan's performance at Antietam. Smith's Eighteenth Corps disembarked on 15 June and marched 8 miles to the outskirts of Petersburg. The city's defenses looked impressive, but Smith did not know that there were almost no rebels there to man them. Although reconnoitering and various snafus delayed a Union assault until near dusk, the bluecoats—spearheaded by Brigadier General Edward Hincks's division of black soldiers—made good progress against minimal opposition. Smith, however, worried that Confederate reinforcements

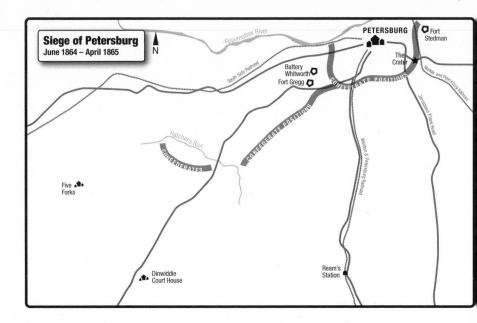

might arrive at any time and launch a counterattack against his tired troops, so he ordered a halt. Besides, most of Hancock's Second Corps had just arrived, providing Smith with twice as many men to throw into the fight the next day. Hancock himself was in a bad mood. After crossing the James that morning, he had waited around for several hours for rations he did not need, and then he and his corps had taken the wrong road and marched twice as far as necessary to get to Petersburg. Moreover, his wound was hurting him so much that a few days later he temporarily turned the Second Corps over to David Birney, its senior division commander. Smith could sympathize with Hancock; his malaria was acting up, making it difficult for him to sit on his horse. Despite these problems, the effort was going well. Lee's troops remained north of the James, trying to figure out where the enemy was going. Over the next two days, Warren's Fifth and Burnside's Ninth Corps both arrived, giving Meade some 80,000 troops to pit against the 15,000 rebels now defending Petersburg. Unfortunately, Meade was never able to effectively coordinate the army for the sustained assault necessary to overwhelm the rebel defenses because of communication breakdowns, the men's reluctance to assail enemy entrenchments, lack of intelligence on the rebel positions, and, finally, a timely Confederate withdrawal to an inner defensive line. Indeed, malaise seemed to infect the entire high command. Warren was especially recalcitrant. The Fifth Corps was on the left of the Union line, and Meade directed Warren to flank the Confederates and drive them out of their positions. There were almost no rebels there, but Warren was too cautious to press his advantage, so the opening went unexploited. Although Grant might have provided the necessary drive, he chose not to impose himself on Meade. As for Meade, he became so frustrated with his inability to synchronize his attacks that on 18 June he practically abdicated all responsibility, writing, "Finding it impossible to effect co-operation by appointing an hour for attack, I have sent an order to each corps commander to each attack at once at all hazards and without reference to each other."[45] By that time, however, it was too late; Lee's veterans had arrived, slamming the door into Petersburg shut. The Army of the Potomac suffered another 11,400 casualties in its most heartbreaking setback.[46]

There was no doubt plenty of blame to go around for the botched assault on Petersburg, but Meade felt that Warren deserved a disproportionate share of it. As far as Meade was concerned, Warren's timidity and refusal to promptly obey orders prevented the Fifth Corps from taking advantage of the exposed rebel right flank. On 19 June, Meade rode over to the Fifth Corps and angrily rebuked Warren in his tent in front of one of his divisional commanders for his dismal performance. Warren was hardly the type to meekly accept such treatment, so he responded in kind, and the entire camp heard the ensuing row. Warren insisted that Meade should support his decisions, or else relieve him of his command. Meade stomped off to see Grant, determined to take Warren up on his offer. As Meade interpreted things, it was Warren's job to obey *his* orders and defer to *his* judgment, not the other way around. Grant's patience with Warren was also just about exhausted, so he agreed with Meade. Meade prepared a letter to Warren demanding his resignation and threatening a court martial if he refused to submit it. Grant's headquarters staff debated names to replace Warren, and the consensus was that Sheridan was the best candidate. Grant, however, did not think that Sheridan could be spared from the cavalry corps. In the meantime, Meade had second thoughts now that his temper had cooled. In the end, he decided against relieving Warren. As he explained later, he did not want to ruin Warren's career, and he hoped that such disagreements would not occur again.[47]

A few days later, Grant received conclusive evidence that the Army of the Potomac had indeed reached a state of exhaustion. Grant ordered Wright's Sixth and Birney's Second Corps to move around the Confederate right flank and sever the Weldon Railroad into Petersburg. Unfortunately, the rebels drove the Yankees back at the Jerusalem Plank Road, mauling the Second Corps in particular and capturing 1,700 of its men. Hancock listened to the battle from his sickbed, and he became so anxious and restless that he finally ordered his horse brought up so he could ride to the front. His doctors insisted that he return to bed, and he reluctantly agreed. "I am afraid something will happen to the Corps," he said over and over.[48] Although Birney did his best and impressed observers with his courage and diligence, he was no Hancock. Of perhaps equal import, the Second Corps was no longer the same unit that had fought so well at the Wilderness and Spotsylvania. It had lost approximately 20,000 men, and the rest were all used up. Indeed, most of its regiments had been reduced to shadows of their former selves. Hancock's wound finally discharged a big piece of bone, and he improved so rapidly that he was able to resume command of his corps on 27 June. Whether his corps would recover as quickly was another question. What was clear to everyone, however, was that the assault on Petersburg had now become a siege.[49]

The Army of the James

To the public, the Army of the Potomac as usual occupied center stage in Union operations that spring, but this did not negate the importance of other, more subsidiary, armies to the strategic drama Grant had authored to bring the Confederacy to its knees. At the same time that Grant and Meade were grinding their way from the Wilderness to Spotsylvania, the 30,000-man Army of the James was undergoing its own trial by fire that was every bit as frustrating and divisive as that experienced by the Army of the Potomac. Grant expected the newly organized Army of the James, scraped together from static Union garrisons scattered up and down the southern coastline from Virginia to Florida, to advance up the James River against Richmond via its back door while the Army of the Potomac was pounding on the front gate. At best, Grant hoped the Army of the James could occupy the rebel capital. At worst, he believed it could sever Richmond's supply and communications lines southward, forcing Lee's army to backtrack to confront this threat. Unfortunately, neither gambit worked; instead, the outnumbered rebels effectively neutralized the Army of the James. Later, the Army of the Potomac crossed the James River and besieged Petersburg. From that point on, the Armies of the Potomac and James remained in close proximity, and Army of the Potomac officers frequently took charge of units in the Army of the James. As a result, it is impossible to understand the Army of the Potomac's high command in the last year of the war without taking into account its smaller companion army.

Grant's plan for the Army of the James was sound enough, but as with all plans, it was only as good as the people assigned to implement it. Unfortunately, this meant that the plan was really no good at all. The Army of the

James was commanded by Major General Benjamin Butler, perhaps the Union's most controversial officer. Butler was a classic political general, with all the baggage that went with the concept. Raised in Massachusetts, Butler had graduated from Waterbury—later Colby—College in 1838, joined the bar two years later, and prospered. He had eventually moved into politics and served in both houses of the Massachusetts legislature. Butler was originally a staunch advocate of states rights, and he vigorously supported first Jefferson Davis and then John Breckinridge at the 1860 Democratic national convention. After the Confederates fired on Fort Sumter, however, he executed a complete political turnabout and embraced the war as one to destroy slavery and restore the Union. Doing so put him in the best of all political worlds; the Lincoln administration valued and promoted him as a War Democrat, but he also possessed the strong support of Radical Republicans. He made a name for himself early in the war by administering rebel-infested Baltimore and then as commander of Fortress Monroe on the peninsula. He lost one of the conflict's first battles at Big Bethel, but he also resolved the thorny dilemma presented by the thousands of runaway slaves escaping to Union lines by designating them as war contraband liable for government seizure. In May 1862, he led the army that occupied New Orleans after the navy forced the city's surrender. His tenure there was contentious and divisive. He had a man tried and executed for hauling down the Union flag, and rumors of corruption and graft swirled around him. He was most famous for issuing Order Number 28, which implied that local women insulting Union soldiers could be arrested as prostitutes. All the negative publicity compelled Lincoln to recall Butler in December 1862, but he was too politically important for the president to sideline for long. In October 1863, Lincoln put him in charge of the Department of Virginia and North Carolina, which gave him claim to the Army of the James.

Physically, the rotund, balding, and puffy Butler was hard to miss. One officer described him, "He *is* the strangest sight on a horse you ever saw; it is hard to keep your eyes off him. With his head set immediately on a stout shapeless body, his very squinting eyes, and a set of legs and arms that look as if made for somebody else, and hastily glued to him by mistake."[50] Behind his dumpy appearance, however, Butler wielded a shrewd, cunning, and powerful mind. He was intensely ambitious, and he hoped to parlay battlefield success into a prominent postwar political career. Unfortunately, he lacked military talent, and his war record was one long string of defeats and setbacks after another. Normally, this would have ruined him, but Butler was no typical general. For one thing, he was a War Democrat allied to Radical Republicans with a large following in New England. Although his lack of military aptitude was no secret—Stanton, Welles, Halleck, and others recognized and commented on it—he was too politically valuable to depose, a fact he well understood and of which took full advantage. The president himself thought Butler was a dangerous fool and a scoundrel, but this did not prevent Lincoln from indirectly asking Butler to join his ticket as the Republican party's vice presidential candidate in 1864. Butler declined because he saw the vice presidency as a dead-end job. In fact, he joked that he would only take the position if Lincoln promised to die within three months of his inauguration. Moreover, he was not lacking in ability; he was a skilled administrator and would have served the Union well if confined to that activity. Finally, as an accomplished attorney, he was a genius at using and manipulating facts to obscure obvious truths, permitting him to shift blame for his defeats onto less articulate generals. His complete lack of scruples and conscience gave him an edge over those hampered by integrity and honor. He projected total confidence in himself and his authority and had a reputation for being mean-spirited, curt, and condescending.[51]

Grant was aware of some of Butler's problems, but he did not want to upset delicate political calculations made at the presidential level by removing him as the Army of the James's commander. Besides, Butler had seemed energetic and competent enough when Grant had visited him at Fortress Monroe in April to explain his part of the upcoming spring campaign. Just to be sure, though, Grant decided that Butler needed a competent professional at his side to keep an eye on him and provide good advice. To that end, Grant assigned Baldy Smith to lead the Army of the James's newly created Eighteenth Corps. Smith was conveniently unemployed, and Grant thought a lot of him from their service together in Tennessee the previous year. In fact, Grant had lobbied the Lincoln administration hard to secure Smith's promotion to major general. The Senate had complied, even though some senators had had doubts about Smith because of his actions against Burnside during his tenure as head of the Army of the Potomac. Years later, Grant himself acknowledged that these reservations were legitimate and justified. Although it made sense to place a trained officer near Butler, Smith was just about the worst possible choice. Such a job required deference, tact, and the ability to suggest ideas in ways to make Butler think they were his own. Smith possessed none of these qualities; indeed, he was a critical, carping, and sarcastic man who found fault in almost everyone with authority, and he had quarreled with just about all of his superiors. Moreover, he had serious doubts about Butler and his campaign before the Army of the James even engaged the rebels. It was wishful thinking to expect him to display any tolerance and understanding toward an egotistical amateur like Butler.[52]

Major General Quincy Gillmore led Butler's other corps—the Tenth. The Ohio-born Gillmore had taught school for several years before obtaining an appointment to West Point, from which he had graduated first in his class of 1841. He had spent his prewar years mostly as an instructor at the Military Academy, and he had missed the Mexican War. After hostilities began, Gillmore participated in the Port Royal expedition in South Carolina and then commanded the force that reduced Fort Pulaski outside of Savannah, Georgia, in April 1862. His success there earned him a brigadier generalship as well as valuable experience in coastal operations. After that he served credibly in Kentucky, and in June 1863 the War Department sent him back to the Atlantic coast to command the Tenth Corps and the Department of the South that contained it. He doggedly prosecuted the siege of Fort Wagner on Morris Island in Charleston harbor for two months until the rebels evacuated it on 6 September. The victory earned him Lincoln's nomination for a second star, but it also aroused the jealousy of some naval officers who had had no success in their own operations against nearby Fort Sumter.

When Grant ordered the Tenth Corps transferred to Butler's command, he expected Gillmore to remain behind in his department. Gillmore, however, lobbied to accompany his men. He stated that he wanted to participate in a campaign that did not require much cooperation with the navy. Although Grant may or may not have sympathized with Gillmore's desire to avoid further interservice collaboration, he acceded to his request. Gillmore was an intelligent and careful man, but like Smith he lacked the patience, tact, and forbearance to work under Butler. Before Grant's spring offensive began, Brigadier General John Turner, Gillmore's chief of staff, wrote to Butler to ask him to use his influence to secure Senate confirmation for Gillmore's appointment to major general. Otherwise, Turner warned, Brigadier General Alfred Terry would assume command of the Tenth Corps by virtue of his seniority. Turner noted that morale would suffer if Gillmore was superceded, and he added that Terry himself believed that Gillmore was most qualified for the job. Butler did not like the idea of switching corps commanders at the onset of a big campaign, so he asked Senator Henry Wilson, chair of the Senate Military Affairs Committee, to push Gillmore's confirmation through. Unfortunately, the issue was still undecided when Butler assembled his 30,000 troops on transports off Hampton Roads for their trip up the James River.[53]

On 5 May, the Army of the James disembarked at Bermuda Hundred at the confluence of the Appomattox and James rivers, some 20 miles from Richmond. After fortifying the 3-mile neck between the two rivers, Butler pushed his army southward along the vital railroad between Richmond and Petersburg. Just north of Petersburg, however, the Union troops encountered rebels drawn up behind Swift Creek. Gillmore and Smith informed Butler that if he really wanted to seize Petersburg, he should return to

Bermuda Hundred, throw a bridge across the Appomattox, and then march on the city along the river's south bank. Such advice would have been more helpful if rendered several days earlier, before Butler had set out to attack Petersburg from the north. Butler scornfully responded that he did not intend to build a bridge for a couple of West Pointers like Gillmore and Smith to retreat over, which dissuaded the two officers from offering any more unsolicited counsel. Mulling things over, Butler decided that he had no choice but to withdraw back to Bermuda Hundred and rethink his strategy. After doing so on 11 May, he opted to disregard secondary targets such as Petersburg and instead go after the main prize: Richmond. On 12 May, Butler marched northward toward the Confederate capital until he ran into a rebel line anchored on Drewry's Bluff. Before Butler could do little more than probe the enemy defenses, the rebels launched a vicious counterattack on 16 May. Heavy fighting raged for several hours, until Butler chose to retreat back to Bermuda Hundred. His two forays cost the Army of the James some 6,000 casualties, twice as many as their opponents. To make things worse, the rebels quickly constructed their own set of entrenchments across Bermuda Hundred, trapping Butler there, in Grant's colorful phrasing, as in a bottle tightly corked.[54]

Butler's ill-fated offensive generated plenty of disappointment and controversy. Not surprisingly, Baldy Smith was among the castigators. Phil Sheridan and his cavalry passed through the Army of the James's lines after their successful raid, and Smith and Sheridan had a long talk about recent events. Smith asked Sheridan to tell Grant that, under the circumstances, he should order Butler to remain on the defensive and transfer the bulk of his force to the Army of the Potomac. Smith was clearly disgruntled, but Butler did not immediately notice because his ire was focused on Quincy Gillmore. As far as Butler was concerned, Gillmore deserved most of the blame for the campaign's failure, though of course Butler did not call it that. It was bad enough that transportation shortages and snafus had prevented Gillmore and the Tenth Corps from reaching Hampton Roads until 3 May, the day before Butler commenced operations. This had deprived Butler of the opportunity to familiarize himself with half his army. Moreover, Gillmore did nothing to redeem himself in subsequent operations. Gillmore of course saw things somewhat differently, and he refuted Butler's accusations by noting that he never retreated except on Butler's orders. Butler was so disgusted with Gillmore's performance that on 7 May—only three days into the campaign—he wrote to Henry Wilson and asked him to use his influence to forestall, not facilitate, Senate confirmation of Gillmore's promotion to major general. Gillmore, Butler stated, might be a good engineer, but he was a terrible combat officer, and many of his men disliked him. "I am convinced," Butler explained to Wilson, "and I think it in the judgment of any well judging officer, that General Gillmore is not fit for the command he exercises."[55] Wilson showed Butler's letter to his Radical Republican colleagues, and they tried hard to kill his confirmation. In the end, though, the Senate approved Gillmore's promotion, probably because Halleck intervened on his behalf.[56]

While Butler was attempting to ruin Gillmore, Grant was taking a hard look at Butler. Even before Sheridan returned to the Army of the Potomac with Smith's tale of incompetence and mismanagement, Grant suspected that there were problems with the Army of the James. On 21 May, he shared his concerns with Halleck. Old Brains responded by dispatching Major General Montgomery Meigs and Brigadier General John Barnard—the army's chief quartermaster and chief engineer, respectively—to Bermuda Hundred to investigate. Meigs and Barnard worked fast, and by 24 May they had completed their task. Butler recognized their "smelling mission" at once, but after they left he smugly noted that he had allayed their concerns and concluded that he had nothing to fear from them. This was not exactly the case. Although Meigs and Barnard stated that reports of dissension among the high-ranking officers were exaggerated, at least as far as Smith was concerned, they noted that Butler was dissatisfied with Gillmore. The military situation was obviously unpromising, so they recommended that Grant either withdraw 20,000 of Butler's troops for use elsewhere or put someone with military ability like Smith in command to resume the offensive. The problem, they noted, was that although Butler had plenty of administrative skills, he was ineffective in combat operations. Unfortunately, Butler did not recognize this, and he wanted to retain his field command. If Grant did not wish to remove Butler, then Meigs and Barnard suggested that he fire Gillmore, put Smith in charge of both corps, and relegate Butler to the Department of Virginia and North Carolina's administrative duties at Fortress Monroe. Grant clearly did not want to tangle with the politically powerful Butler by redefining his responsibilities, but he also recognized that the Army of the James needed to be reorganized somehow. His solution was to order Smith and his Eighteenth Corps to report to the Army of the Potomac to reinforce its depleted ranks. This put Smith and his men to better use than twiddling their thumbs in their Bermuda Hundred bottle, but it also condemned them to participate in the terrible Cold Harbor assault and the heartbreakingly unsuccessful effort to storm Petersburg.[57]

Butler may have failed to block Gillmore's Senate confirmation, but he did not abandon his efforts to divest himself of his supposedly troublesome subordinate. On 26 May, Butler increased the pressure on Gillmore by accusing him of leaking derogatory and untrue information to the *New York*

Herald about him and his conduct during the recent campaign. Gillmore denied the charges, but this did little to assuage Butler. Butler also denigrated Gillmore's engineering abilities, and when Gillmore objected to Butler's use of the word "incompetent" to describe them, Butler lamely responded that there were multiple definitions for the word. By now Gillmore wanted out of Butler's command as much as Butler wanted to be rid of him. He wrote to Halleck to suggest that since Butler was not accomplishing anything, the Tenth Corps should be transferred elsewhere, and he implied that he would be more than happy to accompany it. Gillmore also penned a report defending his actions, which Butler devoted considerable time to tearing apart point by point with lawyer-like precision. By now, Butler's patience had run out, and on 14 June he relieved Gillmore as Tenth Corps commander. Gillmore was in Washington within a week, denouncing his former superior. Although Grant sympathized with Gillmore's plight, he did not want to impose a corps commander on Butler. Instead, he asked Butler to let Gillmore resign so his record would not be permanently stained, and Butler agreed. Gillmore demanded a court of inquiry into this performance, but nothing ever came of it. He later led two divisions in the Nineteenth Corps during Jubal Early's raid on Washington in August, during which he was injured in a fall from his horse. After he recovered, Grant put Gillmore back in charge of the Department of the South for the remainder of the war. Afterward he remained in the army and gained renown for his engineering exploits and theories; he died in 1888.[58]

To replace Gillmore, Grant turned to Brigadier General William "Bully" Brooks. There is no record of Lincoln's approving the appointment, but in all likelihood Grant cleared it with him during the president's mid-June visit to the Petersburg lines. Brooks had been born in Ohio, had graduated near the bottom of his West Point class in 1841, and had then served in Florida, Mexico, and on the frontier in the years before the Civil War. He commanded a brigade on the peninsula and in the Maryland campaign, sustaining a slight wound at Crampton's Gap. McClellan gave him Slocum's division in the Sixth Corps when Slocum took over the Twelfth Corps, and Brooks led the unit at Fredericksburg and Chancellorsville. Both McClellan and Sedgwick praised him in their reports, even though he pushed his division into an ambush at Salem Church on its march to Chancellorsville to rescue Hooker, and he was well respected by many officers, including Hooker. After Chancellorsville, Brooks directed the Department of the Monongahela until April 1864, when Grant dispatched him to lead a division in the Army of the James.[59]

On the surface, Brooks possessed a solid record, but the truth was more complicated. In fact, Brooks's Civil War career was astonishingly turbulent, and perhaps the most impressive thing about it was that he avoided outright dismissal. He was an outspoken, sickly, thin-skinned man, and this, combined with his pro-McClellan and anti-Lincoln inclinations, caused him considerable grief. Early in the war he had made no secret of his hatred of the Lincoln administration, and indeed in his letters to his father he had denounced the president as a knave and dictator. He was hardly alone in these views, but McClellan's removal made officers like him vulnerable to vindictive Radical Republicans keen on punishing those who did not seem to support the war wholeheartedly. He was among Burnside's biggest critics, which prompted Burnside to order his arrest for insubordination and then cashier him as part of his General Orders Number Eight in January 1863. Brooks denied the charges, and fortunately for him Burnside's relief rendered the decree null and void. Although Stanton assured Brooks that Burnside's directive would not affect his career, Brooks began to have doubts when the secretary of war's promised promotion failed to materialize. Brooks compared General Orders Number Eight to a sting he could not remove. He questioned Hooker's abilities long before Chancellorsville, but he seems to have done a better job at keeping his opinions to himself. Frustrated with his stalled career and disillusioned with the Army of the Potomac's prospects, he asked for a transfer after Chancellorsville, despite Sedgwick's best efforts to dissuade him. Sedgwick even wrote directly to Lincoln to extol Brooks and recommend his promotion. This may have contributed to Stanton's decision to appoint him a major general and put him in charge of the Department of the Monongahela in June 1863. Unhappily, the following spring Brooks quarreled with Stanton over his administrative responsibilities, a quarrel that cost him both his department and his promotion. Thoroughly disgusted with what he believed was unfair treatment, Brooks again contemplated resigning from the army.[60]

Fortunately for Brooks, his old friend Baldy Smith prevailed upon Grant to send him to the Army of the James to command an Eighteenth Corps division. Brooks led the division throughout the spring and early summer to everyone's satisfaction. In their report to Halleck, Meigs and Barnard recommended Brooks as Gillmore's replacement, should it become necessary. After Butler finally fired Gillmore, Grant decided on 17 June to give Brooks the Tenth Corps because he was the Army of the James's senior division commander and because he wanted Brooks to have the opportunity to regain his major generalship. Oddly enough, Brooks and Butler got along well, despite their different backgrounds and politics. Unfortunately, Brooks resented the fact that he did not possess the rank commensurate with his new responsibilities. He complained to Grant and threatened to resign his commission, but Grant responded that it would be useless to recommend him for promotion because there were currently no vacancies for new major generals. Although Butler persuaded Grant to change his mind, it was too late to appease Brooks. He insisted on quitting, much to Butler's regret. He gave up his command on 18 July, just over a month after assuming it, moved to Alabama of all places, and became a farmer. He died in 1870.[61]

Baldy Smith was every bit as disgruntled as Brooks that summer. People criticized him for his failure to seize Petersburg on 15 June, a disconcerting experience for a man accustomed to denigrating others for *their* setbacks and inadequacies. Moreover, Smith was thoroughly disgusted with the Army of the Potomac's high command after his short sojourn with it. He was especially appalled with the purposeless bloodshed, lack of coordination, and incompetence he saw all around him at Cold Harbor and Petersburg. For this he blamed Meade, with whom he had become disenchanted even before the campaign began. In fact, he recommended to Grant that he fire Meade and replace him with William Franklin. Although Smith was as usual indiscreet, Meade was unaware of Baldy's backbiting and continued to claim him as a friend. Finally, Smith's woes were compounded by his ill health. His malaria had flared up, subjecting him to dysentery and making it impossible for him to stay in the sun for more than a few minutes without suffering debilitating headaches.[62]

Smith directed most of his abundant scorn, however, at Butler. The two men initially got along reasonably well, but their relationship gradually declined with the Army of the James's fortunes. On 21 June, after the Eighteenth Corps returned to Butler's command, the two men had a falling out. That day Butler criticized Smith's inability to keep his men marching on schedule. The rebuke was mild enough, but Smith responded by stating that he knew more about marching troops than Butler and that he did not fear a court martial. Butler replied placidly that Smith misunderstood him; he did not mean to blame him for the slowness of the march and had never even mentioned a court martial. Despite Butler's conciliatory rejoinder, Smith was furious. In all likelihood, Smith's taut nerves finally snapped. He forwarded all his relevant correspondence with Butler to Grant's headquarters and asked to be reassigned. Grant did not want to let him go, but he instead agreed to give him a ten-day leave of absence. Before Smith left, he wrote to Grant to summarize his problems with Butler: "I want simply to call your attention to the fact that no man since the Revolution has had the tithe of the responsibility which now rests on your shoulders, and to ask you how you can place a man in command of two army corps, who is as helpless as a child on the field of battle and as visionary as an opium eater in council."[63] Before Smith departed for New York on 9 July, Grant assured him that he would make the necessary changes.[64]

Smith's denunciations reinforced Grant's growing doubts about Butler. Like almost everyone, Grant admitted that Butler was a sound administrator, but he had also concluded that the squint-eyed general's military inexperience made him a liability on the battlefield. Moreover, Butler had quarreled not only with Gillmore and Smith but also with mild-mannered Horatio Wright during the Sixth Corps' short stint at Bermuda Hundred in mid-June. Although Gillmore and Smith were flinty men with whom a superior officer might reasonably expect to have trouble, no one could gainsay Wright's good-natured disposition. On 1 July, Grant telegraphed Halleck that perhaps the best solution was to transfer Butler to a noncombat command where he could exercise his administrative talents without jeopardizing the lives of any bluecoats. Halleck had had plenty of experience with Butler over the last two years, so he was hardly surprised by Grant's disenchantment with him. He stated that although the War Department could send Butler to Kentucky or Missouri, it would probably spark an insurrection in whichever state was saddled with him. Or, Old Brains suggested, they could create a new department for Butler in New England. Halleck, however, believed Meigs and Barnard had come up with the best solution during their inspection trip to the Army of the James in late May: assign Butler to administer the Department of Virginia and North Carolina from Fortress Monroe and put Smith in charge of the Army of the James at Bermuda Hundred. Grant had rejected this idea a month earlier, but Smith's condemnation apparently helped change his mind, so on 6 July he told Halleck to draw up the necessary orders. Old Brains did so, but like the good bureaucrat he was, he made sure he secured Lincoln's and Stanton's approval for such a sensitive directive. Next day, General Orders Number 225 reached Grant's desk at City Point.[65]

Two days later, on 9 July, one of Butler's allies in the War Department sent him a copy of General Orders Number 225. Butler was hardly surprised by this effort to kick him upstairs. Less than a week earlier he had written to his wife, "I am in much trouble."[66] He was convinced that West Pointers were persecuting him because he was a nonprofessional Democrat. Specifically, he believed that Smith and Halleck had concocted this latest salvo against him. Whatever Butler's deficiencies on the battlefield, he was still a shrewd political operator, and he had no intention of surrendering his position without a fight. As soon as he had digested General Orders Number 225, he boarded a steamer that took him to see Grant at City Point. Grant received him cordially, and as soon as they were alone, Butler produced his copy of the directive. According to Butler, a surprised Grant said, "Oh—I did not mean you should have seen that order. It is a mistake. I suppressed all the copies that were transmitted through me. How did you get this? Well,

I don't want this at all. I want Smith to report to you—you shall have the full command."[67] In all likelihood, Grant realized that he did not have the stomach to fight the kind of bureaucratic battle reducing Butler's status would require, especially during that long desultory pre-election summer when Union fortunes were at a low point and Lincoln's reelection uncertain. Confronted by Butler, Grant immediately chose to cut his losses and back down. For his part, Butler was triumphant and vengeful. To his wife he wrote ominously, "He [Grant] has vindicated me and my military operations in a way it would not have been done but for these people—whom God and his humble instrument will take care of before we get through."[68] At the same time, however, Butler was sobered by the knowledge that Lincoln had okayed the order and that only Grant's intervention had prevented its implementation. Butler sent his chief of staff to Washington to sound out the president. Lincoln had no desire to anger the politically powerful Butler three months before the election, so he assured him of his continued support. Even so, Butler's correspondence with Grant thereafter took on a more supplicated tone. Butler was a thick-skinned man, but the recent ordeal had taken a toll on him. "I am pretty sick of struggling with these people," he wrote to his wife. "In the view of . . . the attacks made upon me; the spies and others set over me by this abortion of a government, I am sometimes about to give up the contest, and leave all to go home and be quiet. But I must struggle on. . . . You will see that I am dispirited."[69]

Butler was not the only unhappy general. Rescinding General Orders Number 225 did not of course solve all of Grant's problems. Neither Smith nor Butler was willing to work with the other. Since Butler was staying, that meant that Smith had to go. As it was, Grant's estimation of Baldy's value had declined markedly since Smith went on leave. In particular, Grant resented Smith's criticisms of Meade. When Smith returned from New York, he was shocked to learn that Grant had relieved him from command of the Eighteenth Corps. According to Smith, he confronted Grant about his decision, and Grant pointed to Smith's constant grousing to justify his actions. As evidence, Grant later accused Smith of planting a story hostile to Hancock in the *New York Tribune* about the failed assault on Petersburg. Smith denied undermining Hancock, but there was no doubt that he had disparaged pretty much everyone who outranked him. When Smith continued to argue his case, Grant responded, succinctly and accurately enough, "You talk too much," and walked away."[70] Smith later claimed that there were more sinister reasons behind Grant's order. As Smith explained it, in late June Grant had in Smith's presence gotten drunk at Butler's headquarters. Throughout the war, there had been concerns about Grant's sobriety, so any hint that he had been drinking would have irrevocably damaged his standing with the public and the Lincoln administration. Smith believed that Butler seized upon this incident to blackmail his commander into canceling General Orders Number 225. Although there was in fact evidence from Smith and others that Grant had consumed alcohol that summer, there was nothing to indicate that Butler had used this to his advantage. Indeed, the tone of Butler's subsequent correspondence with Grant suggested otherwise. Major General John Rawlins, Grant's personal chief of staff, offered the simplest and most plausible explanation for Smith's removal in a letter to his wife: "General Grant today relieved Major General William F. Smith from command and duty in this army because of his spirit of criticism of all military movements and men, and his failure to get along with any one he is placed under, and his disposition to scatter the seeds of discontent throughout the army."[71] Smith played no further active role in the war, and he resigned from the army in 1867. He later served as president of a cable telegraph company, head of the New York City police commissioners' board, and a civil engineer. His bitterness toward those he felt had wronged him never dissipated, and he expressed it in his numerous postwar writings. He died in 1903.[72]

Smith's and Brooks's departures left the Army of the James without any permanent corps commanders. The Tenth Corps' slot opened first, and Grant planned to offer the unit to Major General Andrew Humphreys. In so doing, Grant again passed over David Birney, who ranked all other division commanders in the Army of the Potomac and the Army of the James. Humphreys had earned Grant's respect by his skillful performance as Meade's chief of staff. Indeed, Grant had recommended Humphreys's promotion less than two weeks after the Overland campaign began. After Brooks resigned, Grant asked Meade if he could spare Humphreys and, if so, to then sound him out and see if he wanted the post. Grant told Meade to warn Humphreys, however, that the Tenth Corps was a small outfit, and it might be necessary to incorporate into it substantial numbers of black soldiers. Humphreys was initially tempted to accept the assignment. He was an ambitious and capable man, and he believed that his career had stagnated as chief of staff. A corps command was a step up, and Humphreys welcomed the opportunity to lead troops again. After thinking it over, however, he decided to decline the offer. As he put it in a letter to Grant,

I confess that while I have the kindliest feelings for the Negro race and gladly see anything done that promises to ameliorate their condition, yet as they are not my own people, nor my own race, I could not feel towards the Negro troops as I have always felt towards the troops I have commanded, that their character, their reputation, their honor was a part of mine, that the two were so intimately connected that they could not be separated. Feeling thus I would prefer not to command such troops, although I trust that my preferences could never interfere with the performance of duty.[73]

Moreover, Humphreys had no desire to command the Eighteenth Corps either, probably because of recent rumors that Hancock might replace Meade, thus opening the way for Humphreys to take charge of the Second Corps and remain in the Army of the Potomac. Before he could send the letter, though, Grant had changed his mind.[74]

In early July, Major General Edward Ord had visited Grant at City Point. Born in Maryland and raised in Washington, D.C., Ord had graduated from West Point in 1839 and then served in Florida. He had fought in California during the Mexican War and afterwards had been stationed in the Pacific Northwest. Early in the war, he had commanded an Army of the Potomac brigade, which he led to victory at the Battle of Dranesville in northern Virginia in October 1861. He was rewarded with a promotion to major general, and in the spring he was transferred out west. He was so seriously wounded in the Battle of Corinth in November that he did not return to duty until the following summer, when Grant gave him a corps at the Siege of Vicksburg. After a stint in Louisiana, Grant assigned him to assist Franz Sigel in his offensive up the Shenandoah Valley, but Ord resigned before the campaign began because he distrusted Sigel. Surprisingly, Grant did not hold this against him. In fact, Grant had a lot of faith in Ord, even though he had seen comparatively little action. He believed Ord was brave, a skillful manager of troops, a good administrator, and prompt in obedience of orders. Since Ord had both seniority and a proven record at the corps level, Grant felt that he would be the best candidate for the Tenth Corps. Before he could make the assignment, however, Confederate General Jubal Early crossed the Potomac River and launched his raid on Washington. Grant lacked confidence in the gaggle of Union generals preparing to resist Early's attack—indeed, Grant had sent many of them to the capital precisely to keep them out of trouble—so he dispatched Ord there to help. Once Ord arrived, Halleck assigned him to command the Eighth Corps. After Early retreated on 12 July, Grant brought Ord back south. By now Grant had relieved Smith, so on 22 July he put Ord in charge of the Eighteenth Corps instead of the Tenth, and Lincoln made it official six days later. Ord was a grim, restless, eccentric, and steady officer full of common sense who enjoyed debating fellow officers in long rambling discussions. He dressed like a common soldier, possessed a quiet sense of humor, and looked older than he was. He did not make a good initial impression, but he had a first-rate reputation among the prewar officer corps.[75]

As for the Tenth Corps commander, Grant asked Butler to choose between the Army of the Potomac's two major generals still leading divisions, David Birney and John Gibbon. Butler responded by lobbying for Brigadier General John Martindale, a friend of his who commanded an Eighteenth Corps division. Martindale was a West Pointer—though not a career soldier—with combat experience dating back to the peninsula. Butler withdrew his recommendation, however, when he realized that Martindale was so ill that he would have to go home. Instead, Butler opted for Birney. The two men were both close to Radical Republicans, whereas Gibbon was a McClellanite, so Butler's selection was hardly unexpected. Grant agreed, secured the president's approval, and on 21 July a surprised and pleased Birney finally got his own corps.[76]

By the summer of 1864, Birney had become an Army of the Potomac fixture. Son of a famous abolitionist, Birney had been born in Alabama and had moved to Cincinnati with his family when he was young. He had graduated from Andover, studied law, and become a successful businessman and lawyer in Philadelphia. He secured command of a brigade in the winter of 1861–1862, and in the next three years he compiled an exemplary combat record in practically every one of the Army of the Potomac's campaigns and battles: Williamsburg, Fair Oaks, the Seven Days Battle, Second Bull Run, Chantilly, Fredericksburg, Chancellorsville, Gettysburg, Mine Run, Wilderness, Spotsylvania, and Petersburg. Along the way, he won the praise of almost everyone under whom he served, including Phil Kearny, Ambrose Burnside, George Stoneman, William French, and Winfield Scott Hancock. Although uninspiring, there was no doubt about his courage and dedication to the Union cause. He was promoted to major general in May 1863 for his performance at Chancellorsville and should have rightly assumed command of a corps long since. Unfortunately, Birney's advancement was hindered by several factors. As an abolitionist, he had early on allied himself to officers such as Kearny, Hooker, and Sickles, who were opposed to McClellan's conduct and ideas. Although Radical Republicans supported these men, the McClellanites dominated the Army of the Potomac's officer corps, and they looked after their own first and foremost. Indeed, Birney's allegiance to Sickles and Hooker had nearly cost him his military career when he had unwisely testified against Meade in Committee on the Conduct of the War hearings in March 1864. In addition, Birney's intense ambition was well known and occasionally off-putting. He frequently asked his friends and supporters to lobby the Lincoln administration on his behalf, and he had been tenacious in pursuing his promotion to major general. Finally, Birney did not possess a warm and endearing personality. One of Meade's aides best summed him up:

Birney was one who had many enemies, but, in my belief, we had few officers who could command 10,000 men as well as he. He was a pale, Puritanical figure, with a demeanor of unmovable coldness; only he would smile politely when you spoke to him. He was spare in person, with a thin face, light blue eye, and sandy hair. As a General he took very good care of his Staff and saw they got due promotion. He was a man, too, who looked out for his own interests sharply and knew the mainsprings of military advancement. His unpopularity among some persons arose partly from his promotion, which, however, he deserved; and partly from his cold covert manner. I always felt safe when he had the division; it was always well put in and safely handled.[77]

By the time the Army of the Potomac had dug in before Petersburg, Birney had just about given up hope that he would ever receive a corps. He had been passed over several times, and he did not believe that he had done well temporarily commanding the Second Corps during Hancock's recuperation in June, although Meade, Humphreys, and Hancock thought otherwise. Then, from out of the blue, Grant assigned him to the Tenth Corps.[78]

Birney led the Tenth Corps for less than three months. Among his division commanders was his older brother, Brigadier General William Birney. Except for some fighting around Deep Bottom in August and an unsuccessful assault on Fort Gilmer on 29 September, his corps saw comparatively little action, though his new troops sustained their notorious reputation for straggling. No one recognized it at first, but Birney was actually an increasingly ill man. He had contracted dysentery sometime in the summer, and the disease gradually weakened him. He should have gone on furlough, but he kept putting it off because he did not want to leave the army. Finally, in early October, Butler ordered him home to Philadelphia because he feared Birney would not survive otherwise. Unfortunately, Birney died in his house on the evening of 18 October. The officer corps lamented his loss, including Meade, who had grown to respect Birney's military abilities. Birney may have been cold and overly ambitious, but no one could deny his devotion to the Union—a devotion that cost him his life.[79]

After Birney departed, Butler assigned the Tenth Corps to its senior division commander, Brigadier General Alfred Terry. Butler, however, did not recommend Terry's permanent appointment. Instead, Butler hoped to completely reorganize the Army of the James. On 30 November, he officially asked Grant for permission to abolish both the Tenth and the Eighteenth Corps and to replace them with two new ones: the Twenty-Fourth and Twenty-Fifth. He planned to place all his army's white soldiers in the Twenty-Fourth, and its black soldiers in the Twenty-Fifth. Butler believed that the black soldiers had performed well, and he wanted to reward them by giving them their own corps. Moreover, he intended to actively employ the unit. Butler's proposal would cement his alliance with Radical Republicans, and he also felt it would improve his army. Ord would take over the Twenty-Fourth as soon as he recovered from the wound he had sustained at Fort Harrison during the Battle of Chaffin's Farm in late September, and Butler asked Grant to give the Twenty-Fifth to Major General Godfrey Weitzel. Grant raised no objections, and the War Department issued the necessary orders on 3 December.[80]

Weitzel had started the conflict as a twenty-six-year-old lieutenant, so his rise through the Union army's ranks had been remarkable. He had graduated second in his West Point class of 1855 and had spent most of his prewar years in the army working on New Orleans's defenses and teaching at the Military Academy. He returned to Louisiana as Butler's chief engineer in 1862 and was promoted directly to brigadier general in late August. Weitzel was a skilled engineer who impressed almost everyone under whom he served. He led a division under Nathaniel Banks at the Siege of Port Hudson in 1863, and at Butler's request Stanton transferred Weitzel east in April 1864 to serve as chief engineer for the Army of the James. Weitzel was conspicuous because of his big head, long neck, and lanky body. He held a variety of official and unofficial positions in the summer of 1864, including Butler's de facto chief of staff and temporary commander of the Eighteenth Corps while Ord recuperated from his Fort Harrison wound. Weitzel fielded these various duties even though he suffered a bout of sunstroke in July and an illness so severe in early September that he had to go home to recover. Although Weitzel was no doubt a good engineer and a capable officer, his close relationship with Butler played a big role his appointment to corps command. In fact, Alfred Terry outranked him until several weeks before Butler reorganized his army, but Butler wanted his protégé for the position. Despite his poor health and youth, Grant recommended to Stanton both Weitzel's appointment to major general and command of the Twenty-Fifth Corps. In all likelihood, the fact that the Twenty-Fifth Corps would consist of freedmen eliminated much of the competition to command the unit, smoothing the way to Weitzel's ascension.[81]

The Siege of Petersburg

By the summer of 1864, the Union war effort had slowed to a crawl. Although the Union armies had sustained enormous casualties, they had thus far achieved none of their objectives. Richmond remained in Confederate hands, and Lee's army continued to defend it despite sustaining heavy losses in the Overland campaign. To the west, Sherman was advancing steadily toward Atlanta without the frightful losses Meade had suffered, but he had neither seized the city nor destroyed its defending rebel army. This lack of progress posed a direct threat to the Lincoln administration's survival. The presidential elections were in the fall, and it was clear to everyone that Lincoln's fate was tied to Union success on the battlefield. To be sure, the Democratic candidate, George McClellan, eventually pledged to continue the war if elected, but the Democratic party's official platform called for reunion at any price, including the preservation of slavery. Considering the depressing circumstances, it was small wonder that at the end of the summer Lincoln had his cabinet members blind sign a letter in which they unknowingly promised to do all they could to preserve the union before he left office on the assumption that his successor would be unable to do so.

On 9 July, Meade ordered the Army of the Potomac to commence siege operations against Petersburg. In doing so, Meade merely acknowledged the army's present circumstances. Throughout the long hot summer the Yankees and rebels constructed elaborate entrenchments that ultimately stretched 35 miles and were all but impervious to frontal assaults. Union engineers developed an enormous supply base at nearby City Point and connected it to the front lines with a rickety railroad. Generally speaking, the Army of the James manned the lines from White Oak Swamp opposite Richmond down to Bermuda Hundred, and the Army of the Potomac covered the region south of the Appomattox River around Petersburg. Large-scale engagements became comparatively rare, but there was still plenty of danger. Random artillery fire blew apart parapets and the soldiers peering over them, and sharpshooters forced men to keep their heads down and crawl to and from their positions. It was all part and parcel of nineteenth-century siege warfare but with one crucial difference—the Confederates were not surrounded. Initially two railroads into Petersburg remained in rebel hands, succoring Richmond and its defenders. Although Union forces overran the Weldon Railroad in August, the rebels clung tenaciously to the more distant Southside Railroad. For the next eight months, various elements of the Army of the Potomac periodically lunged at the Southside Railroad, but the Confederates beat off all the attacks. After each such offensive, however, the Union forces extended their lines a bit farther southward and westward, compelling the rebels to conform and stretch their limited manpower a little more.

At the same time as Union soldiers were digging in before Petersburg, Washington itself was under attack. On 13 June, Lee dispatched General Jubal Early's corps to the Shenandoah Valley to counter Union efforts to seize the Confederacy's granary. Early routed Union forces there, crossed the

Potomac on 5 July, and descended on Washington. To confront the growing threat to his rear, Grant gradually dispatched most of Sheridan's cavalry and Wright's Sixth Corps. Grant had limited use for Sheridan's troopers now that the Army of the Potomac's offensive had degenerated into siege, and Wright's men were the freshest available, having seen little heavy fighting since Spotsylvania. The bulk of the Sixth Corps arrived just in time. Although the rebels tapped Washington's formidable defenses, Early quickly recognized that they were too strong to assail, so he withdrew on 12 July. Unfortunately, he settled in the lower Shenandoah Valley and continued to menace Washington. There were plenty of Union soldiers in the region available to deal with him—Sheridan's cavalry, Wright's Sixth Corps, Brigadier General George Crook's Eighth Corps (Army of the Kanawha), and Brigadier General William Emory's recently arrived Nineteenth Corps from Louisiana—but no one was really in overall command. As a result, Union operations there ground to a halt.

Grant understood the need for unity of command as well as anyone. He wanted to consolidate the various regional departments into one military division, and at first he planned to put William Franklin in charge of it. Like so many people, Grant respected Franklin as a smart, capable, and trustworthy officer, and he was inclined to attribute Franklin's losing record to bad luck. Moreover, Franklin was currently unemployed and available after his unfortunate stint in Louisiana. Grant had initially short-listed Franklin for command of the Army of the James when Butler's head was on the chopping block. After he had rescinded General Orders Number 225, Grant then had hoped to assign Franklin to lead the Eighteenth Corps. In the end, however, Franklin failed to get any job at all. The Lincoln administration had not forgotten the problems Franklin had caused during his tenure with the Army of the Potomac, so Halleck asked Grant to choose someone else for the Shenandoah. Grant telegraphed the president that he would not insist on Franklin's appointment because he wanted someone whom both he and Lincoln could trust. Grant next considered George Meade. Grant had a lot of faith in Meade, who had plenty of experience leading large armies, and Lincoln was willing to accept him. When Grant consulted Meade, Meade stated merely that he would obey any orders Grant would give him. In reality, Meade was of two minds about the assignment. On the one hand, he liked the idea of getting out from under Grant's shadow to again hold a truly independent command. On the other hand, he recognized that he would have to deal not only with some truculent subordinates but also with the often heavy-handed Lincoln, Stanton, and Halleck. In the end, however, Grant decided against Meade. He worried that the public might interpret Meade's transfer as a demotion, which could lower morale. Instead, he turned to Philip Sheridan, in whose aggressive instincts Grant had considerable respect. Stanton argued that Sheridan was too young for such an important post, but Grant carried the day. On 7 August, Grant directed Sheridan to report to Harper's Ferry as head of the newly formed Middle Division. After a period of vacillation and self-doubt, Sheridan led his Army of the Shenandoah to a series of victories at Winchester on 19 September, Fisher's Hill three days later, and Cedar Creek on 19 October. In the process he all but destroyed both Early's army and the Shenandoah Valley.[82]

While Sheridan was winning laurels in the Shenandoah Valley, the Army of the Potomac spent the remainder of 1864 in front of Petersburg. Despite several efforts to sever the Southside Railroad, on the whole the Union forces remained relatively quiescent. No doubt the army needed time to recuperate from the horrific casualties it had sustained during the Overland campaign, but the comparative inactivity gave the high-ranking officers time to dwell on and articulate their dissatisfaction. Everyone had grievances, and this discontent extended all the way up the chain of command to George Meade. Indeed, Meade was a deeply unhappy man that summer and autumn, and he expressed his despondency through his famous hair-trigger temper. One observer reported, "No man, no matter what his business or his service, approaches him without being insulted in one way or another, and his own staff officers do not dare to speak to him, unless first spoken to, for fear of either sneers or curses."[83] As a result, Meade rapidly drained the deep pool of goodwill he had built up during his long tenure with the army.

Meade's frustrations extended back to the Overland campaign. For one thing, he felt unappreciated. Although he ordinarily shunned publicity, even his modesty had limits. He complained to his confidants that he did all the Army of the Potomac's planning and Grant received all the credit. There was some truth to this, but Meade himself contributed to his anonymity. After Cold Harbor, he had expelled from the army a journalist who inaccurately claimed in an article that Meade had advised Grant to withdraw north of the Rapidan after the Wilderness. Before doing so, however, Meade ordered the reporter paraded though the lines with a placard inscribed "Libeler of the press." Other journalists considered this unfair and degrading, so they conspired to omit Meade from their dispatches. In addition, Meade increasingly chafed at his lack of autonomy. He led the Army of the Potomac, but Grant directed its actions. He was tempted to lobby for command of Union forces in the Shenandoah and was deeply offended when Grant did not offer the job to him. Although he wanted to trust Grant, he suspected that there were forces in the Lincoln administration and Congress plotting to replace him with Hancock. Meade could not even take comfort in Grant's promise to recommend his appointment to major general in the Regular Army. Lincoln quickly advanced William Sherman, Sheridan, Hancock, and others, but he failed to act on Meade's promotion. When Meade inquired about the delay, Grant admitted that he had not submitted the necessary paperwork because he wanted Sherman promoted first. Grant finally secured Meade's Regular Army major generalship in late November, and he even persuaded Lincoln to backdate it so that Meade would continue to outrank Sheridan, who had been advanced earlier in November for his success in the Shenandoah Valley. This did not assuage Meade much, especially since the Senate did not get around to confirming the appointment until the following February. Moreover, Meade was not getting along with most of his corps commanders, all of whom he yelled at and insulted at one time or another. Some of his chief subordinates, for their part, increasingly questioned Meade's judgment and leadership. Finally, throughout the campaign Meade's son was seriously ill; he would eventually die during the winter. The knowledge that his son was slowly wasting away back home weighed heavily on Meade's mind.[84]

Fortunately for Meade, he did not antagonize everyone that summer and fall. He lost his temper with Hancock and Gibbon, but neither officer took it personally. Both men had known Meade for a long time, and with friendship came patience and empathy. Meade enjoyed talking with Hancock in particular—their staffers called them "the Grannies" because of the way they gabbed when together—and the two men joked about rumors that Hancock would take over the Army of the Potomac. Indeed, Meade confided in his wife that he was perfectly willing to give way to Hancock and serve under his command. More important, Grant continued to give Meade his support. Grant understood Meade's awkward position, and he did his best to encourage Meade and give him the credit he deserved. Even so, by early July, Meade had alienated so many officers that Grant questioned his usefulness to the Army of the Potomac, which was one reason why he considered sending Meade to the Shenandoah. In the end, however, Grant opted to keep Meade where he was. Grant recognized Meade's flaws, but no one else had his stature, experience, and ability to command the fractious Army of the Potomac. Whatever his shortcomings, Grant stood by Meade. In late October, for example, Grant wrote to Meade, "I have felt as much pained as you at the constant stabs made at you by a portion of the public press. I know nothing better to give you to use in answer to these charges than copies of every dispatch sent to Washington by me, in which your name is used. These will show at least that I have never expressed dissatisfaction at any portion of your services."[85]

Gouverneur Warren was among the many officers who quarreled with Meade that summer. Unlike Hancock and Gibbon, Warren lacked the understanding and patience to take Meade's tantrums in stride. The irony was that Warren's behavior was somewhat similar to Meade's. He continued to berate his subordinates so frequently and vehemently that at least one officer questioned his sanity. Oddly enough, however, he also recommended all his division commanders for promotion. Although Warren had heard rumors that Meade had considered removing him after the failed assaults on Petersburg, he discounted them until he read an article in the *Pittsburgh Commercial* on 14 July detailing the incident. Warren wrote to Meade to demand an explanation, and Meade responded that the article's contents were accurate. Meade explained that he considered Warren a friend, but he was tired of Warren's substituting his judgment for that of his superiors. Ever since Meade and Grant had decided to retain Warren as Fifth Corps commander, they had done their best to encourage and praise him whenever he acted aggressively and obeyed orders. Unfortunately, Warren did not respond to this conciliatory approach. He felt unappreciated, and he longed for an independent command. Despite recent events, he did not think that Grant and Meade would dare relieve him. He was now more convinced than ever that Grant was a bad general who had needlessly sacrificed thousands of Union soldiers for no good results. As for Meade, he wrote his wife, "I believe Gen[era]l Meade is an unjust and unfeeling man and I dislike his personal character so much now that it is impossible we shall ever have again any friendly social relations. I have also lost all confidence in his ability as a general."[86]

Burnside's relationship with Meade was about as bad as Warren's. Meade treated Burnside as poorly as he treated his other subordinates, and Burnside found it difficult to accept such abuse from a former subordinate, especially because he had never shown Meade such disrespect when he led the Army of the Potomac. As a result, there was already plenty of tension between the two men even before the controversial Battle of the Crater. One of Burnside's regimental colonels—former mining engineer Lieutenant Colonel Henry Pleasants of the Forty-Eighth Pennsylvania—proposed that the Ninth Corps build a tunnel under the rebel lines near the Norfolk and Petersburg Railroad southeast of Petersburg, fill it with black powder, blow a hole in the heart of the Confederate defense network, and then charge through it into Petersburg. Burnside and Meade signed off on the idea, and Pleasants got to work with his men on 25 June. Despite innumerable engineering and bureaucratic obstacles, they finished the tunnel on 28 July. It ran more than 500 feet, with a 75-foot-long perpendicular shaft at the far end. Pleasants filled the perpendicular shaft with 320 kegs of black powder, for a total of 8,000 pounds of explosive power. All that remained was to light the fuse and watch the resulting eruption.[87]

Burnside's plan called for Brigadier General Edward Ferrero's division of black soldiers to spearhead the assault. Ferrero's division was the Ninth Corps' largest and freshest, and it had been training for the mission for a month, so militarily its employment made perfect sense. In addition, Grant and Meade dispatched Hancock's Second Corps to demonstrate north of the James River to draw off rebel strength in that direction, and they placed Warren's Fifth and Ord's Eighteenth Corps in support of the Ninth. The day before the assault, Meade and Gibbon visited Burnside's headquarters and found him full of enthusiasm. Afterwards Gibbon commented to Meade that whatever Burnside's zeal, it was unwise to entrust him with so much responsibility. Meade responded that Gibbon was too cynical, but in fact Meade was not terribly optimistic either. Indeed, Meade himself went a long way toward dooming the attack. Meade did not want to risk the wrath of Radical Republicans by exposing untried black soldiers to such a risky assignment, so he ordered Burnside to substitute one of his white divisions to lead the charge. Shocked by this last minute Meade-mandated change in plans, Burnside appealed to Grant, but Grant sustained Meade. Burnside's confidence thereupon collapsed like a deflated balloon, and from that point on he lost his grip on Union operations. He directed the commanders of his three white divisions to draw lots to determine which unit would replace Ferrero's, and the chore fell to Brigadier General James Ledlie. Ledlie was a well-known coward and drunkard, and it is difficult to imagine a worse choice, especially when Brigadier Generals Orlando Willcox's and Robert Potter's divisions were available for the job. Burnside, however, was apparently unaware of Ledlie's faults, so he did not interfere with fate's selection.[88]

At 4:45 A.M. on 30 July, the hill in front of the Ninth Corps rumbled and then erupted with awe-inspiring force, throwing earth and debris into the air, and obliterating the defending Confederates. The mushroom cloud–shaped explosion tore a huge hole in the rebel lines 170 feet wide, 60 feet long, and up to 30 feet deep. After some initial confusion, Ledlie's division advanced, but then the serious trouble began. Burnside had neglected to make sure that someone removed the obstacles in front of the Union trenches, so the bluecoats had to hack gaps and funnel through them a few at a time. Instead of a wave of soldiers rolling over the remaining rebels, the men filtered into the crater in driblets. Once there, they busied themselves gawking like tourists and rescuing half-buried rebels. Ledlie should have sorted them out and pushed them ahead toward Petersburg, but he was secreted in a dugout behind the lines, swigging rum. Back at his headquarters, Burnside ordered the other two white divisions to move up, and they too joined Ledlie's men in the crater. Soon the Yankees were packed in so tightly that they could scarcely maneuver. The vast conglomeration blocked

Ord's men from going forward, and Warren's men accomplished just as little. In desperation, Burnside sent Ferrero's division into the melee, but they too eventually got stuck in the crater. Ferrero joined Ledlie in his dugout and saw little of the battle. By now the rebels had recovered, and they managed to gain the crater's lip. From that point on, it was like shooting at 10,000 fish in a giant rain barrel. Grant made his way to the front lines and soon recognized that the operation could not succeed. At 9:30 A.M., he directed Meade to put an end to it, and Meade sent word to Burnside. Burnside, however, apparently hoped that the luck upon which he relied would somehow turn in his favor, so he delayed issuing the necessary orders. By the time he finally brought the men back through the gauntlet of rebel fire to their own lines, nearly 4,000 had been killed, wounded, or captured.

The Battle of the Crater was over, but not the repercussions flowing from it. Burnside sent Ledlie on sick leave on 4 August, and when he returned in December, Grant at Meade's request ordered Ledlie back home and informed him that he could not have another command. As things turned out, however, Burnside was the engagement's biggest casualty. During the battle, Burnside put the best face on things in his dispatches to Meade's headquarters, but Meade's other sources indicated the battle was not going as well as Burnside claimed. Meade telegraphed Burnside, "I understand not a man has advanced beyond the enemy's line which you occupied immediately after exploding the mine. Do you mean to say your officers and men will not obey your orders to advance? If not, what is the obstacle? I wish to know the truth, and desire an immediate answer."[89] Burnside interpreted this as an attack on his integrity, and he responded angrily, "Were it not insubordinate I would say that the latter remark of your note was unofficerlike and ungentlemanly."[90] At 10:30 A.M., Burnside and Ord showed up at Meade's headquarters, and Burnside immediately laid into Meade. Meade quickly lost his famous temper and responded in kind, and the ensuing exchange, according to one observer, "went far toward confirming one's belief in the wealth and flexibility of the English language as a medium of personal dispute."[91] Although both men later expressed regret for their behavior, Orlando Willcox failed in his efforts to reconcile them. After the argument and the battle, Meade demanded that Grant remove Burnside and order a court of inquiry into his conduct. Meade made it plain to Grant that either he or Burnside had to go. Like most people, Grant agreed that Burnside was mostly to blame for the fiasco, so the choice was obvious. Burnside offered to resign, but Grant without informing Meade opted to send him on a leave of absence for twenty days, and Burnside left for Providence, Rhode Island, on 13 August. When his leave was up, Grant told him to remain there for the time being. It was clear to knowledgeable officers, however, that Burnside's reign of incompetence with the Army of the Potomac was finally at an end.[92]

Whatever reservations Grant may have had regarding Burnside's removal were undoubtedly put to rest when the court of inquiry Meade demanded issued its ruling on the Battle of the Crater on 9 September. Hancock presided, which just about guaranteed a verdict hostile to Burnside, as there was no love lost between the two men. The court condemned Burnside's actions that day from beginning to end. On the other hand, the Committee on the Conduct of the War also investigated the battle and issued a report hostile to Meade, although Grant did not put much stock in its findings. The judgment, however, did not help Burnside much. On 17 October, Grant wrote Burnside that, considering his sour relationship with Meade, he did not think it was feasible to bring him back to the Army of the Potomac. Instead, Grant claimed he wanted to find Burnside a more agreeable assignment. Nothing ever came of that, though. Next spring, Burnside, humble as ever, wrote to Stanton, "If I can be of any service to General Grant or General Sherman as a subordinate commander or aide-de-camp, or as a bearer of dispatches from you to either of them, I am quite ready."[93] When he received no response, Burnside finally submitted his resignation from the army to the president, in which he thanked Lincoln for the kindness and encouragement he had always shown. After the war, Burnside prospered in both business and politics. He served on several boards of directors, was elected governor of Rhode Island three times, and was into his second term as the state's senator when he died in 1881.[94]

Grant did not waste time or look far for Burnside's replacement as Ninth Corps' commander. He temporarily—meaning without Lincoln's explicit consent—gave the outfit to Burnside's longtime chief of staff, Major General John Parke. No doubt Grant did not want to ask the president for a permanent appointment when Burnside's fate was still officially up in the air. It was an obvious choice, although in making it Grant passed over Orlando Willcox, a former Ninth Corps commander who still led one of its divisions. Parke was the Army of the Potomac's senior major general without a corps, but there was more to it than that. He had been closely associated with the Ninth Corps since its origins, and in fulfilling his various responsibilities he had won the respect of almost everyone under whom he had served, including Burnside, McClellan, Sherman, and Grant. Parke was a bachelor, born and raised in Pennsylvania, and he had graduated second in his West Point class of 1849. He had spent his prewar years as an engineer surveying along the Canadian border, and he was one of Secretary of War Jefferson Davis's favorite officers. After the conflict began, Parke commanded a brigade and then a division under Burnside in the North Carolina expedition and subsequently worked as Burnside's chief of staff during the Maryland and Fredericksburg campaigns. Burnside had considerable faith in Parke and gave him a free hand in running the administrative side of the Ninth Corps. After Lincoln put Burnside in charge of the Department of the Ohio, Parke capably led the Ninth Corps under Grant and Sherman at the Siege of Vicksburg and the march on Jackson, Mississippi. Parke rejoined Burnside as his chief of staff during the fighting around Knoxville and served in the same capacity during the Overland campaign. He was enough of a McClellanite to testify for the defense at Fitz John Porter's court martial, but he also blamed Franklin for the Union defeat at Fredericksburg. Parke was a pleasant, well-liked, cautious, and able man whose modesty and humility differentiated him from so many of his fellow Army of the Potomac generals. He preferred staff positions and had limited experience in leading troops in combat. His biggest deficiency, however, was his poor health. In fact, he missed the Battle of the Crater—and therefore escaped the odium attached to it—because he was home recuperating from a bout with malaria. When he returned to the army in mid-August and received his new assignment, he was still sick and demoralized. Whatever his personal feelings, he got to work repairing the Ninth Corps and readying it for combat.[95]

Winfield Scott Hancock had won the sobriquet "Hancock the Superb" for his actions on the peninsula, and since then he had been an indomitable presence on almost every Army of the Potomac battlefield. The serious injuries he had sustained at Gettysburg had not prevented him from serving as Meade's most dependable corps commander throughout the Overland campaign. Indeed, his Second Corps carried the Army of the Potomac's heaviest loads at Wilderness, Spotsylvania, and Cold Harbor. Hancock's health finally broke down during the assaults on Petersburg, forcing him to temporarily relinquish his command to David Birney. When he returned to duty on 27 June, he was unhappy with the events that had occurred in his absence. He resented newspaper charges that the Second Corps had not performed well during its initial approach on Petersburg, so he asked Meade for an official investigation. Grant turned him down by stating that the Second Corps' reputation was its best defense. Unhappily, that reputation took a beating during the long hot summer. The Second Corps fought so poorly at the Jerusalem Plank Road on 22 June that Hancock felt it necessary to officially admonish his men. The outfit's problems, however, required a far stronger remedy than a threatening memo. In mid-August, Grant ordered another lunge around the rebel right flank at Petersburg's supply lines. Warren's Fifth Corps succeeded in severing the Weldon Railroad, and Grant sent Hancock over to help out. On 23 August, though, the Confederates mauled the Second Corps at Ream's Station and inflicted more than 2,700 casualties on the unit. Although this in and of itself was disconcerting enough, the details were even more alarming and humiliating. A good many of the casualties were men who surrendered without offering much resistance, and the Second Corps lost nine cannons and a dozen battle flags. Hancock quite accurately traced his corps' woes to the large number of inexperienced and tired troops that filled its ranks, but this did little to heal his wounded pride. Nor did a supportive and sympathetic note from the normally irascible Meade. The fact was, Hancock was tired, demoralized, and testy. He was even quarreling with divisional commander John Gibbon, one of his closest friends. Hancock disapproved of Gibbon's leadership and criticized him for the way he handled his division. Gibbon, for his part, believed that Hancock was lashing out at him for no good reason, so he submitted his resignation. Hancock persuaded him to withdraw it, but the bitterness between the two men remained.[96]

As the months passed, neither Hancock's health nor his spirits improved much. On 25 October, Stanton proposed to Grant that the War Department send Hancock north to recruit a corps of 20,000 veterans for a one-year tour of duty. Stanton had always liked Hancock, and he hoped that his celebrated record would attract veterans unlikely to reenlist unless they knew a competent and skilled commander would lead them. Grant endorsed the idea, but it got put on the backburner as the presidential election approached. In mid-November, however, Grant urged Stanton to issue the necessary orders. By then Hancock was ready to go home. His wound had reopened, and he wanted to attend to personal business. He asked for and received a twenty-day leave, after which he planned to recruit his corps of veterans. He departed on 26 November, much to the sorrow of the officers and men of the Second Corps with whom he had shared and endured so much. In the end, he had little luck signing up his new corps, so the following February Stanton and Grant assigned him to command the Department of West Virginia. He finished the war there and remained in the army until he died in 1886. He stayed in the public eye, and in 1880 the Democrats nominated him to run for president, but James Garfield defeated him.[97]

Hancock was perhaps the Army of the Potomac's finest corps commander, so finding someone to fill his large shoes would not be easy. Grant, however, came very close by replacing him with Andrew Humphreys. Humphreys had grown increasingly unhappy as Meade's chief of staff because he saw the position as a dead-end job, and he had given serious thought to transferring out of the Army of the Potomac altogether. He predicted early and accurately that Grant's ascension would relegate Meade to a glorified chief of staff, which in effect reduced Humphreys into a deputy chief of staff. He continued to fulfill his duties capably, despite some laughter at his expense in the summer when the provost marshal discovered that Meade's steward was illegally selling whisky to the soldiers from Humphreys's tent. Humphreys had asked for a corps command in June, and Grant and Meade had assured him that he was in line for one. He was by autumn the army's senior major general without a corps, and many felt that he deserved one. Hancock's imminent departure opened the door for Humphreys's advancement. Grant did not seek Lincoln's approval, however, but instead appointed Humphreys the Second Corps' temporary commander in case Hancock's mission did not pan out and the Lincoln administration chose to send him back to the Army of the Potomac. Grant himself had no doubts about Humphreys, and he predicted quite correctly that Humphreys would perform superbly in his new post. The officer corps as a whole agreed. Humphreys was a popular man, so Meade's headquarters staff turned out en masse to escort him out of camp when he left to assume his new duties. Meade eventually assigned Brigadier General Alexander Webb as Humphreys's replacement as his chief of staff. Although Second Corps officers and men lamented Hancock's departure, they welcomed Humphreys's arrival. As it was, Humphreys was already familiar with many of them. Humphreys was wise enough to understand and accept the Second Corps' attachment to Hancock, so he made sure to praise him in his introductory orders. Like John Parke, Humphreys got to work bringing his new command back up to par. In March, he boasted that although the Fifth Corps division and brigade commanders were superior to his own, man for man the Second Corps was the more battleworthy outfit.[98]

John Gibbon was probably the only person unhappy with Humphreys' elevation. Gibbon had nothing against Humphreys personally or professionally, but he was insulted that Grant made Humphreys *temporary* commander of the corps. Gibbon claimed he would have had no problem if Grant had appointed Humphreys *permanent* leader, but as senior division officer he thought he deserved any provisional assignment. The truth was, Gibbon was an unhappy man who wanted a corps of his own. He had filled in as Eighteenth Corps commander while Ord was on sick leave, and he enjoyed the independence that came with the position. Like Hancock, he too was angry and embarrassed with the Second Corps' recent performance in battle. To make things worse, he was not getting along with Hancock. Gibbon was so unhappy that he again tendered his resignation just before Hancock departed. Perhaps puzzled by Gibbon's peculiar logic, Hancock sent his request up the chain of command without comment, but Meade did not want to lose the services of such a good friend and officer. Although Meade believed that Gibbon was arguing semantics, he asked Humphreys to speak with him as soon as he took over the Second Corps. Humphreys did so, but he could not persuade Gibbon to change his mind. Fortunately, Grant valued Gibbon too, and he intervened to keep him in the Army of the Potomac. He wrote to Gibbon through Meade to explain that Humphreys's promotion was not meant to reflect badly on Gibbon and that only the president could make Humphreys's position permanent. Besides, he had promised Humphreys a corps long ago. Grant concluded, "I have full confidence in General Gibbon as commander of troops, and believe him entirely capable of commanding a corps. I should not like to spare his services from this army; but if after this explanation he continues dissatisfied he will, on his application, be relieved."[99] Gibbon interpreted this to mean that Grant planned to give him a corps at some point, so he withdrew his resignation and remained with the Army of the Potomac.[100]

Endgame

As 1864 drew to a close, Grant could look back with satisfaction on the Union's progress since he had become general in chief. In Virginia, the Army of the Potomac had suffered enormous casualties in the Overland campaign, but it had also driven Lee's army southward, inflicted heavy losses on it, pinned it within its defensive network around Richmond and Petersburg, and deprived it of its offensive power. With each passing week, Meade's and Butler's veterans tightened their grip a little more on the weakening Confederate army. To the northwest, Sheridan had cleared the Shenandoah Valley of rebels and stripped it of its resources. Union forces had been as successful elsewhere. In early August, the Union navy had stormed into Mobile Bay, destroyed the defending Confederate fleet there, and shut the port down. William Sherman had seized Atlanta in September, marched through Georgia against minimal opposition, and occupied Savannah on 21 December. In doing so, the Union had again divided the Confederacy in two. Less than a week before Savannah fell, Major General George Thomas's army had shattered the besieging rebels outside of Nashville and driven them southward in disarray. Politically, the Union situation was equally promising. Lincoln was reelected in November, demonstrating that a majority of the northern population wanted the war to continue until the Confederacy and slavery were annihilated. It was increasingly clear to everyone that the Confederacy was rapidly running out of men, matériel, territory, and time.

Even so, there were still plenty of obstacles the Union had to overcome to secure final victory. After the Union navy seized Mobile Bay, Wilmington, North Carolina, was one of two remaining Confederate ports open to the outside world. Once operations around Petersburg and Richmond had ended for the season, Grant decided to use some of his idle forces to launch an amphibious assault on Fort Fisher, which protected Wilmington. On 6 December, Grant ordered two of the Army of the James's divisions to undertake the operation, and he put Godfrey Weitzel in charge. Grant believed that Weitzel's engineering background and experience in amphibious operations made him uniquely qualified to lead the expedition.[101]

Like most prewar politicians who received army commissions, Benjamin Butler was motivated as much by political ambition as by patriotism. Political generals served a valuable purpose in cementing their constituencies to the Lincoln administration and its war, but the military ineptitude of some of them cost many Union lives. Militarily, Butler represented the worst of his breed, and he proved it in December. Butler was an innovative man if nothing else, and he concocted a plan to take an old hulk, stuff it with 215 tons of gunpowder, and explode it off of the coast of Fort Fisher. Butler hoped that this would destroy the fort and everyone in it, permitting his soldiers to march in with minimal opposition. Although both Grant and Navy Secretary Welles doubted the idea, they permitted it to go forward because they did not see any harm in trying—at least not until outfitting the ship delayed the entire operation. A more serious problem was that Butler chose to accompany and lead the expedition against Fort Fisher. Indeed, Butler pocketed Grant's orders placing Weitzel in charge, so Weitzel did not know of Grant's intentions. Butler later claimed that he assumed command to protect Weitzel's young career in case he had to make any unpopular decisions, but Butler was hardly the type to do anything so charitable or selfless for anyone, protégé or not. Grant himself only learned of Butler's decision when Butler's transport fleet steamed by City Point on its way to Fort Fisher. Grant later explained that he did not direct Butler to stay behind because Fort Fisher was within Butler's Department of Virginia and North Carolina boundaries, so by military protocol he had every right to go along. The expedition arrived off of Fort Fisher on 23 December. After midnight, the navy detonated Butler's gunpowder-laden boat, but the explosion inflicted no damage on Fort Fisher or its garrison. The next day, Rear Admiral David Porter's warships began their preliminary bombardment, and on Christmas Weitzel landed north of the fort with some of his troops. Reconnoitering, Weitzel concluded that he lacked the strength to successfully storm the fort. Butler agreed, blaming the navy's ineffective preliminary bombardment. On 27 December, Butler and Weitzel evacuated the last of their men with minimal casualties and headed back to Fortress Monroe.[102]

In light of the recent wave of Union victories, Butler had picked a bad time to suffer another defeat. To make things worse, now that the November elections were safely over, Lincoln no longer required Butler's political support as much as he had previously. Finally, Lincoln had received various reports that questioned Butler's administrative integrity, which reflected poorly on his hitherto commendable managerial skills. On 28 December, Lincoln telegraphed Grant to inquire about the botched Fort Fisher expedition, a clear hint that he wanted Grant to take action. Grant responded that he hoped to assign blame soon. Grant had long since branded Butler militarily incompetent, and he disliked the fact that, as senior officer, Butler commanded both the Armies of the Potomac and James when Grant was away. On 4 January, Grant wrote to Stanton to ask for Butler's relief: "I am constrained to request the removal of Maj. Gen. B. F. Butler from the command of the Department of Virginia and North Carolina. I do this with reluctance but the good of the service requires it. In my absence Gen. Butler necessarily commands, and there is a lack of confidence in his military ability, making him an unsafe commander for a large Army. His administration of affairs of his Department is also objectionable."[103] When Grant learned that Stanton was down the Georgia coast consulting Sherman, he appealed directly to Lincoln. Halleck relayed Lincoln's assent on 7 January, and Grant dispatched two aides to hand deliver the order to Butler. There was considerable rejoicing among high-ranking officers at Butler's removal.[104]

Not surprisingly, Butler did not accept his removal quietly or gracefully. On 8 January, he issued a defiant departing message to the Army of the James, stating, "I have refused to order the useless sacrifice of lives of such soldiers, and I am relieved from your command. The wasted blood of my men does not stain my garments. For my action I am responsible to God and my country."[105] Butler actually believed, however, that his relief had little to do with his bungled Fort Fisher expedition. Instead, he blamed a conspiracy among Regular Army officers at Grant's headquarters that turned Grant against him. Later some of Butler's army friends—Weitzel and William Birney, for example—claimed that those same Regular Army officers were persecuting them, although both men held on to their positions for the rest of the war. Butler attempted to use subsequent Committee on the Conduct of the War hearings to clear his name. Most of its members were his political allies, so Butler got a sympathetic hearing. Unfortunately for Butler, during the hearings Brigadier General Alfred Terry undermined his case by successfully storming and capturing Fort Fisher on 15 January. Although the committee exonerated Butler of any blame for his failure at Fort Fisher, his army career was over. Indeed, a mid-February rumor that Lincoln was considering appointing Butler provost marshal of Charleston, South Carolina, was enough to prompt Grant to register his objections to Stanton. Butler resigned his commission in November and was elected to Congress in 1866 as a Republican. He served for nine consecutive years and later returned in

1879 as a Greenbacker. He ran repeatedly for Massachusetts governor and finally won in 1882. He died in 1893.[106]

Grant replaced Butler as head of both the Army of the James and the Department of Virginia and North Carolina with Edward Ord. It was a logical choice. Ord was not only already a member of the Army of the James but also the Union Army's highest-ranking active major general without a field army or departmental command. There was, however, more to Ord than availability and seniority. He had led the Eighteenth and Twenty-Fourth Corps credibly, most notably in the successful assault on Fort Harrison in late September at the Battle of Chaffin's Farm, during which he had sustained a leg wound. He had also filled in for Butler during one of his absences, so he had some experience running a field army. Butler had praised his work, even though his chief of staff warned him that Ord was power hungry and incompetent. Grant gave Ord the Army of the James on a temporary basis on 7 January but asked Lincoln to make the assignment permanent a little less than a month later. In all likelihood, Grant waited because he contemplated appointing Ord to command the Department of the South, but he ultimately decided to send Gillmore there instead. Halleck sent the necessary orders on 6 February, and Ord led the Army of the James for the rest of the war. He proved to be an innovative administrator and a skillful battlefield commander. Unfortunately, he did not have the complete support of some of his subordinates. Weitzel, for example, suspected that Ord wanted to break up his Twenty-Fifth Corps, and he and William Birney never completely shed their residual loyalty to Butler. Even so, it was a wise selection.[107]

Ord's elevation left the Twenty-Fourth Corps leaderless. To fill the slot, Grant turned to John Gibbon. Gibbon had been born in Philadelphia but raised in Charlotte, North Carolina. He had graduated in the middle of his West Point class in 1847 and subsequently served in Mexico, Florida, and at the Military Academy as a quartermaster and artillery instructor. Although his three brothers had joined the Confederacy when the war began, Gibbon opted to remain loyal to the Union, and Irvin McDowell secured him a brigadier generalship despite his southern roots. As he explained to his concerned wife, "You must reconcile yourself to the idea that I am bound to go into a fight if for no other reason to give the lie to my enemies and prove my loyalty to the good old stars and stripes."[108] Gibbon was a blunt, calm, fair, and ambitious man who found no glory in war. Indeed, one person compared him to cold steel for his wintry manner and the strict discipline he maintained among his men, although he was quite engaging and personable in private. He gained renown as commander of the First Corps' famous Iron Brigade, which he led well at Groveton, Second Bull Run, Turner's Gap, and Antietam. He was wounded at the head of a division at Fredericksburg, and when he returned to duty three months later, Hooker sent him to the Second Corps to take over Howard's division even though Sedgwick had asked for him. During Gibbon's rise through the Army of the Potomac's hierarchy, he won praise from everyone from Phil Kearny to Orlando Willcox to George McClellan. His biggest and most important booster, however, was his close friend George Meade. At Gettysburg, Meade put Gibbon in charge of the Second Corps while Hancock assumed larger duties. There were other divisional commanders with more seniority, but Meade trusted Gibbon. Fortunately, Gibbon repaid Meade's confidence by repelling Pickett's charge on the last day of the battle.[109]

Gibbon received a shoulder wound at Gettysburg, and while recovering he became increasingly disenchanted with his career and the Army of the Potomac. He had accumulated a wealth of combat experience, but he was still a brigadier general at the divisional level. Meade recommended him for promotion in October, and then for corps command the following March, but nothing came of his efforts. A discouraged Gibbon returned in the spring to lead his Second Corps division with distinction through the Overland campaign. Although Grant rewarded his good work by securing his major generalship, Gibbon remained unhappy. By summer, his division was so used up that it was scarcely battleworthy, and he was bickering with his old friend Hancock over the best ways to rebuild the unit. Moreover, although he did not know it, Stanton had targeted him for removal because he believed that Gibbon was too overt in his support for McClellan's presidential campaign. Fortunately for Gibbon, Grant's backing kept the secretary of war at bay. Grant had put Gibbon on his short list for future corps commanders earlier in the summer, but he did not act until Ord's elevation. In mid-January, Grant gave Gibbon temporary command of the Twenty-Fourth Corps, much to his—and Meade's—delight. Gibbon liked the freedom of corps command, and he got along well with Ord. In addition, Stanton seems to have had a change of heart regarding Gibbon. During a mid-March inspection trip from Washington, Stanton took Gibbon aside and promised to get Lincoln to make his appointment permanent. Stanton was in this case as good as his word, and on 20 March the president officially assigned Gibbon to the Twenty-Fourth Corps.[110]

As spring approached, the Confederacy was clearly crumbling under the weight of sustained Union offensives. Sherman's armies had cut a swath of destruction through the Carolinas and were approaching the Virginia border. Charleston and Wilmington had both fallen, and Union forces had placed Mobile under siege. Union cavalry columns were sweeping through Alabama and into the Carolinas. Around Petersburg, Grant made final preparations to end the siege that had frustrated him for nearly nine months. To do so, Grant had 125,000 well-fed and -equipped troops to throw at less than 50,000 tatterdemalion rebels starving and freezing in the opposing lines. Grant planned to sever the Southside Railroad, seize Richmond and Petersburg, and drive Lee's army out into the open where Union forces could capture or destroy it. To do so, he had already brought Wright's Sixth Corps back from the Shenandoah, and now he summoned Sheridan and his cavalry. Grant also directed Ord to march three of his divisions—two from Gibbon's Twenty-Fourth Corps and one from Weitzel's Twenty-Fifth—across the James and Appomattox rivers and post them opposite of Petersburg. This freed up Sheridan's cavalry, Warren's Fifth Corps, and Humphreys' Second Corps to strike at the Southside Railroad. While Meade's and Ord's troops undertook these deployments, the Confederates struck at the Union lines at Fort Stedman on 25 March. Lee hoped that doing so would compel Grant to contract his forces, thus opening the way for the rebels to slip out of Richmond and Petersburg and join General Joseph Johnston's Confederate army in North Carolina. Although the rebels met initial success and quickly overran the fort, soon everything went wrong. Neither Grant nor Meade was present when the Confederate attack began, but Parke assumed command by virtue of his seniority. He competently moved reinforcements from the Ninth Corps forward, stopped the Confederate assault, and reoccupied Fort Stedman. Nearly 4,000 rebels were killed, wounded, or captured, as opposed to fewer than 1,500 Union casualties. Lincoln and Grant arrived later that day to review the troops and look over the battlefield. By way of tying up loose organization ends before the new campaign began, at Meade's behest Grant asked Lincoln to make Humphreys and Parke permanent commanders of their corps. Lincoln agreed, and the necessary orders arrived on 27 March.[111]

Grant's plan was simple enough. He wanted Sheridan's recently arrived cavalry, supported by Warren's Fifth and Humphreys' Second Corps, to march on the Southside Railroad via Dinwiddie Court House. Although Sheridan's troopers reached Dinwiddie on 29 March, heavy rains the next day flooded the fields and turned the roads into troughs of mud. Grant considered postponing the entire operation, but Sheridan rode to Grant's headquarters at Gravelly Run and persuaded him to stay the course. On 31 March, Sheridan's men pushed north to Five Forks, from which the bluecoats could strike at the Southside or Lee's right flank. Lee's last reserves were there to meet him, and rebel infantry and cavalry drove the outnumbered Union troopers back to Dinwiddie. Sheridan managed to stop the Confederate assault, but it was a close run. That night the rebels fell back to Five Forks. Despite the setback, Sheridan sensed an opportunity. As he saw things, the opposing rebels were isolated from the rest of Lee's army and vulnerable to a counterattack. Sheridan believed he could destroy the detachment and unlock the key to Petersburg and Richmond if he had some infantry to provide the necessary punch. With this in mind, Sheridan asked Grant for Wright's Sixth Corps. The Sixth Corps had fought under Sheridan in the Shenandoah, so he was familiar with its officers and capabilities. Besides, Sheridan and Wright were old friends. Unfortunately, the Sixth was too far away to provide assistance, so Grant sent the nearby Fifth Corps. Moreover, Grant not only put the outfit under Sheridan's command but also authorized Sheridan to remove Warren if he thought it was necessary.[112]

Grant's decision grew out of his continuing frustration with Warren. He believed that Warren had on several occasions cost the Army of the Potomac victory because of his unwillingness to promptly obey orders, and Grant was determined to prevent any reoccurrence with final victory so close. Indeed, a month earlier, Grant had suggested to Stanton that he transfer Warren to command the Department of West Virginia, but the secretary of war did not think that Warren was the right man for the job. Although Meade shared some of Grant's doubts about Warren, he retained sufficient faith in him to recommend his promotion to brigadier general in the Regular Army. Warren, on the other hand, remained supremely confident in his own abilities and was oblivious to his superiors' reservations. To make things worse, Sheridan did not like Warren; there was bad blood between the two men dating back to the march on Spotsylvania the previous May. The same day that Sheridan was fighting grimly in front of Dinwiddie, the rebels surprised Warren's corps at Hatcher's Run. Warren eventually stopped the Confederate onslaught and regained the lost ground, but doing so required Humphreys's assistance, more than 1,400 casualties, and considerable time. When Sheridan showed up at Warren's headquarters on the evening of 31 March to explain his plan to destroy the rebels around Five Forks, he found Warren asleep. After Warren woke up, Sheridan was dismayed with his negative attitude. He later wrote, "Warren did not seem to me to be at all solicitous; his manner exhibited decided apathy, and he remarked with indifference that 'Bobby Lee was always getting people into trouble.'"[113] This was not the aggressive mindset that Sheridan had worked so hard to inculcate in his officers and men. Even so, he refrained from relieving Warren because he did not want to upset the Fifth Corps' chain of command on the eve of battle. Sheridan's frustrations with Warren, however, continued to mount. Although the Fifth Corps was not far from Dinwiddie, the soldiers were exhausted from their all-day fight at Hatcher's Run. Marching at night over broken and muddy ground further slowed their progress. Sheridan expected the Fifth Corps to be ready for action at dawn, but when the sun rose the outfit's vanguard was just reaching the scene. When informed that Warren was at the rear of the column hurrying his men forward, Sheridan snidely remarked, "That is where I expected to find him."[114]

Although Sheridan worried that the Confederates might escape from Five Forks, they were still there in the late afternoon when Warren finally got his men deployed. Sheridan wanted to use his cavalry to assault the rebel line from straight ahead and pin them down while Warren's infantry hit their vulnerable left flank. The troopers got into action as planned, but two of the Fifth Corps' three divisions attacked in the wrong direction and marched off on a tangent. Warren galloped frantically after his errant men to turn them around. There was nothing subtle about his conduct. One observer remembered Warren's encounter with Brigadier General Samuel Crawford, one of his division commanders:

> While Crawford was attempting to reform and renew the fighting, Gen[eral] Warren rode up white with rage, and without waiting for explanations, commenced the most abusive tirade on Crawford that mortal ever listened to. He called him every vile name at his command, in the presence of officers and privates, and totally forgot what was due to his self-respect as an officer and gentleman. Crawford sat on his horse, stolid as a block of marble, and so far as I can remember, did not utter a syllable in reply. When he had emptied his last vial of abuse on Crawford, Warren rode away.[115]

Gradually, as more and more of Warren's men entered the fight, Union numerical superiority began to tell, and the rebel line crumbled. By nightfall, more than 5,000 Confederates had surrendered, in addition to an undetermined number killed and wounded. Union losses that day approached 900. The Battle of Five Forks opened the way for the Union to seize the Southside Railroad, making Richmond and Petersburg untenable.

Sheridan was determined to grab the Southside Railroad and fend off any Confederate counterattack as soon as possible. The day's events convinced him that Warren was an impediment to the accomplishment of both these goals. Indeed, Sheridan was furious with Warren. He believed that Warren had almost lost the battle by showing up late and then permitting two-thirds of his corps to assault in the wrong direction. When a Fifth Corps staff officer arrived with a report from Warren, Sheridan bellowed, "By God, sir, tell General Warren he wasn't in the fight!" His anger mounting, Sheridan shortly afterward dispatched orders to Warren relieving him of his command. When Warren rode over to ask Sheridan to reconsider, Sheridan shouted, "Reconsider, hell! I don't reconsider my decisions! Obey the order!"[116] Later Sheridan claimed that it pained him to dismiss Warren, but he felt it was for the good of the army. An astonished and saddened Warren traveled to Grant's and Meade's headquarters. There Grant and Meade both expressed sympathy for him, but neither reversed Sheridan's actions. Both officers told Warren that the source of his problems was his tendency to question orders. Grant put Warren in charge of City Point and Bermuda Hundred, and he sat out the last weeks of the war there with scarcely any soldiers under his command. As far as Warren was concerned, he was the victim of Grant's blatant favoritism toward western generals such as Sheridan. He never understood that his removal was not so much owing to his actions at Five Forks—in fact, he arguably did as well as anyone could have under the circumstances—but rather to the accumulated sins of the past year. As soon as Lee surrendered, Warren asked for an investigation to clear his name. Although he remained in the army as an engineer, he did not get his court of inquiry until 1879. The court not only exonerated him but criticized the way Sheridan had sacked him. Unfortunately, it did not issue its findings until November 1882, several months after Warren had died.[117]

Having relieved Warren, Sheridan turned his attention to finding his replacement. Grant's orders authorized him to give the command to one of the Fifth Corps' division commanders if he thought it necessary to jettison Warren. The senior officer was Samuel Crawford. Crawford had graduated from the University of Pennsylvania's medical school in 1850 and accepted a position in the army as an assistant surgeon the following year. Coincidentally, he was stationed at Fort Sumter when the Confederates opened fire there. He gave up his medical responsibilities and got a commission, although his men always referred to him as "Old Pills." He led a Twelfth Corps brigade in the Shenandoah Valley, saw action at Cedar Mountain, and was slightly wounded at Antietam while commanding Alpheus Williams's division after Williams took over the corps from Joseph Mansfield. When Crawford returned to duty, he got a Fifth Corps division, which he subsequently led through Gettysburg, the Overland campaign, and the Siege of Petersburg. Although on paper he was well qualified to assume command of the Fifth Corps, the reality was much different. Crawford was actually a lazy, incompetent, self-indulgent, and sycophantic man who enjoyed drinking and partying. Warren was for some reason of two minds about Crawford; at times he seemed to want rid of him, but he also recommended his promotion. Others had no such ambivalence. In fact, a week before Five Forks, the Fifth Corps' other division commanders, Brigadier Generals Charles Griffin and Romeyn Ayres, warned Warren that Crawford was a liability. When Sheridan learned of Crawford's seniority, he quickly decided to pass him over.[118]

Instead, Sheridan gave the Fifth Corps to Charles Griffin. Griffin was an Ohioan who had graduated from West Point in 1847, fought with Scott in Mexico, and then served in the southwest and as an artillery instructor at the Military Academy. He lost his battery at First Bull Run but received a star and a Fifth Corps brigade on the peninsula. Griffin's stalwart commitment to McClellan nearly cost him his career. On the first day of Second Bull Run, Griffin publicly badmouthed Pope and wished that McClellan would return to save the Union forces. In response, Pope relieved Griffin of his command and ordered a court of inquiry into his conduct. Fortunately for Griffin, McClellan got the charges dropped after he resumed control of the Army of the Potomac. Griffin received Daniel Butterfield's division after Butterfield moved up to corps command and led the unit at Fredericksburg and Chancellorsville. In the summer of 1863, however, sickness forced Griffin home to recuperate. At about the same time, his only child became so seriously ill that Griffin submitted his resignation. He quickly retracted it, though, and returned to duty in time to participate in the Overland campaign and the Siege of Petersburg. He was famous for pushing his artillery as close to the front as possible, providing his infantry with nearby support. In his climb up the chain of command, he had won praise from Porter, Butterfield, Meade, and Warren, but this did not mean that he was well liked. As his tirade toward Meade at the Wilderness indicated, Griffin was a brusque, quick-tempered, spiteful, and overbearing man. He intimidated Warren, who deferred to him in a way he did not to his other subordinates. Griffin's wife was equally redoubtable and was willing to lobby even Lincoln on her husband's behalf. Given the choice between the easy-going and ineffective Crawford and the competent and unpleasant Griffin, however, Sheridan opted for the more-qualified officer for the heavy fighting still to come.[119]

When Grant learned of Sheridan's victory at Five Forks, he ordered an all-out assault on the rebel lines at Petersburg for the next day. Although recent setbacks at Fort Stedman and Five Forks had greatly reduced Lee's strength, his remaining soldiers still possessed the benefit of fighting behind the formidable defenses they had developed and enhanced over the past months. No one believed that overcoming them would be easy, but the Army of the Potomac contained more advantages than simple numerical and materiel superiority. The most prominent was that Grant's immediate subordinates were among the most capable men the Union army had produced in the war. Meade, Ord, Sheridan, Humphreys, Griffin, Wright, Parke, and Gibbon had achieved the seniority necessary for corps command more through merit than through any other criteria. Wright, for example, had absorbed some of his friend Sheridan's can-do attitude during his time in the Shenandoah and brought back to the Petersburg lines the unaccustomed taste of victory. He assured Grant that he could break through the Confederate entrenchments in fifteen minutes. His optimism was not just wishful thinking but was instead the result of careful planning. His mindset was contagious to both subordinates and superiors, and in fact Grant noted, "I like the way Wright talks; it argues success."[120] At around 4:30 A.M. on 2 April, Parke's, Ord's, and Wright's men stormed the rebel lines, followed by Humphreys's, Griffin's, and Sheridan's troops to the southwest. The outnumbered Confederates fought bravely as usual, but the bluecoats broke through in all three places. Gibbon's two divisions overwhelmed the Confederate outworks of Fort Gregg and Battery Whitworth in the late afternoon, but the rebels fell back to Petersburg's inner line. By then it was past 3:00 P.M., and the exhausted and disorganized Yankees called it a day. Some 4,100 of them had fallen, which was a small price to pay for finally gaining an unmistakable offensive victory over Lee's vaunted veterans. That night the Confederates evacuated Petersburg and Richmond, enabling Union troops to at last occupy both cities the next day.[121]

Now that he had finally blown Lee's army out of its entrenchments and into the open, Grant was determined to run it down. Fortunately, he was in a good position to do so. To reach Joe Johnston's forces in North Carolina, Lee had to slide down the Richmond and Danville Railroad before the Army of the Potomac could get astride it. Union forces were not only a good deal farther south than the rebels but almost as far west, so they had the inside track. With the rebels so clearly in trouble, Grant took no chances; he assumed direct tactical control over the Army of the Potomac, relegating Meade to the background. As it was, Meade was sick with fever and accompanied the army in an ambulance, but his illness did not dampen his aggressive instincts. Indeed, the entire army recognized that Lee was on the run and that bringing him to bay would require the utmost exertion. Grant put Parke's Ninth Corps to work fixing and extending the Southside Railroad while the rest of the army pushed after Lee. Grant kept half of his army nipping at Lee's heels, but he swung the rest southward in an effort to get ahead of the rebels and surround them. On 5 April, Sheridan's cavalry and Griffin's Fifth Corps cut across the Richmond and Danville Railroad at Jetersville before the Confederates arrived, forcing Lee to take his depleted army westward. Next day, Sheridan found a gap in the rebel columns and poured into it with his cavalry and Wright's Sixth Corps at Sayler's Creek. In the ensuing melee, the bluecoats captured over 6,000 rebels and killed or wounded another 2,000, at the cost of only 1,200 men. While Humphreys's Second and Wright's Sixth Corps tailed the limping Confederate army, Ord's, Sheridan's, and Griffin's men marched hard on a parallel track to the south. The strategy paid off on 9 April, when Sheridan's cavalry overtook Lee's army near Appomattox

Courthouse. Before the rebels could push the troopers out of the way, Ord's and Griffin's infantry arrived to slam the escape hatch shut once and for all. Faced with the prospect of fighting a hopeless battle, Lee opted to surrender, bringing the Army of the Potomac's war to a victorious end.

Conclusions

Although Grant was not the direct commander of the Army of the Potomac or the Army of the James, he kept close tabs on each army's strategy, tactics, and personnel. His recommendations to Lincoln in the selection, removal, and transfer of corps commanders played an important role in winning the war. Grant's success was in large part due to some advantages unavailable to Meade and his predecessors. Most obviously, Grant was general in chief with authority over all the Union's armies. As such, he did not have to defer to Halleck or any other officer, which simplified the negotiating required to secure Lincoln's approval for assignments to corps command. Moreover, Grant's selection pool was not limited solely to the Army of the Potomac's or the Army of the James's officer corps. He could summon any major general he wanted from the entire Union army to lead corps. Gibbon, Gillmore, Ord, Sheridan, and Smith all owed their elevation to corps command to Grant's willingness and ability to transfer officers from one field army or department to another. This infusion of new and proven talent increased the effectiveness of the Armies of the Potomac and James and contributed to Union victory.

In addition, Grant also enjoyed Lincoln's support. The president did not scrutinize Grant's personnel recommendations as closely as he did some other generals' earlier in the war. Grant reinforced Lincoln's confidence by being sensitive to the president's political needs. Grant did not, for instance, seek to remove the tactically incompetent Butler until after the 1864 election was over because he recognized Butler's political importance to Lincoln. Nor did he press for Franklin's appointment when he learned of Lincoln's reservations. Lincoln repaid this understanding by eventually approving almost all of Grant's personnel decisions.

Finally, Grant benefited from the natural selection of three years of war. Grant valued performance over everything else when he appointed or recommended corps commanders, but he still took rank and seniority into account. Fortunately, by the time he became general in chief, the stresses of war had weeded out many, though certainly not all, of the ineffective major generals competing for leadership of corps. Those officers remaining in the pool of perspective corps commanders were far more capable men than those even a year earlier. As a result, it was no coincidence that the men Grant selected for corps command—Wright, Humphreys, and Parke, for example—were usually the senior officers available, demonstrating that the pressures of war were finally pushing the most qualified people forward.

This is not to say that Grant's record on personnel matters was unblemished. Although his selections were generally good, he kept some corps commanders in their posts after they had demonstrated their military ineffectiveness. For example, Grant permitted Warren and Burnside to hold onto their corps longer than circumstances warranted. On the other hand, his tolerance gave officers like Wright and Sheridan the time they needed to learn their new responsibilities. Both men got off to rocky starts as corps commanders, but they eventually emerged as capable officers. Indeed, Grant was more likely to remove subordinates for disrupting harmonious relations in the high command than for failing on the battlefield. Burnside's fatal sin, for example, was not his defeat at the Crater but rather his quarrel with Meade. Similarly, Grant relieved Smith of his command only when it became clear that he could not cooperate with Butler. To be sure, in some cases political realities limited Grant's options, which was why Butler retained his position as long as he did. In the end, however, Grant's forbearance in personnel matters proved both an asset and a liability.

CONCLUSIONS

Keys to Corps Command

No history of the Army of the Potomac—or the Army of the James, for that matter—is complete without some discussion of the men who led its corps. Field army commanders relied on these men to implement their orders, manage their primary organizational units, and provide advice on tactics, strategy, personnel, and administration. For the system to function properly, however, army commanders had to establish good working relationships with their corps leaders, who in turn had to cooperate with each other. The effectiveness or ineffectiveness of this system helps explain the Army of the Potomac's uneven war record. For example, Burnside's failures during and after Fredericksburg were in part due to the lack of confidence his corps commanders had in him and in each other. Similarly, the hostility Hooker's corps commanders had toward him accelerated his demise. On the other hand, Union victory at Gettysburg resulted to some extent from the faith that Meade and his corps commanders had in each other. Although corps commanders were only one of many pieces in the Army of the Potomac's military machinery, they were one of the most important.

Attaining command of a corps was an impressive addition to any officer's military résumé, but getting and staying there was not easy. Only the president could officially promote someone to lead a corps, but it was actually more complicated than that. Assignment to permanent corps command was usually the result of negotiations among the president, secretary of war, general in chief, and Army of the Potomac commander. Although some officers felt that the process was purely arbitrary, most of those who became permanent or long-term "temporary" corps commanders met several prerequisites.

Rank was the most important requirement for corps command. Although a few brigadier generals such as Alpheus Williams and Orlando Willcox led corps for a short time, almost all permanent corps commanders were major generals when they were selected. For ambitious officers, therefore, the first step to corps command was securing a major generalship. Promotion to major general, however, was subject to many of the same vagaries as appointment to corps command. In fact, it could be even more complicated because the Senate had to confirm those officers that Lincoln nominated, and in that arena murky political and personal factors often played a greater role than anything else. Indeed, on numerous occasions the Senate rejected officers that Lincoln had nominated for promotion.

Becoming a major general, however, did not guarantee a corps command because there were always more major generals than there were corps available for them. This was in part due to Congress's refusal to commission more than two grades of general, except for Grant. In fact, a number of major generals never attained corps command. Confronted with a surplus of major generals, the Lincoln administration tended to assign open corps in the Army of the Potomac to the senior available major general. Promotion by seniority had a long history in the United States Army, and before the war it was the rule up through the rank of colonel. There was a logic behind promotion by seniority. In theory, it was predictable and orderly, so every officer knew where he stood in the chain of command and where he was likely to stand in the future. In addition, it provided easy solutions for army commanders who needed to fill a corps position, but who were unfamiliar or unhappy with their subordinates' abilities. Besides, ignoring seniority could be costly. Doing so generated low morale, infighting, and backbiting among officers who saw their juniors advanced ahead of them and who resented the lack of confidence in their skills this implied. Some commanders, such as Burnside, were almost slavishly devoted to the concept, and McClellan, Halleck, Hooker, Meade, and Grant all took it into account when they recommended to Lincoln an officer's permanent appointment to corps command.

Generally speaking, seniority carried the day unless there was some compelling reason against elevating the ranking major general to corps command. Although simple in concept, it could be maddeningly confusing in practice because it was susceptible to manipulation. The Lincoln administration could and did backdate promotions to give newly minted major generals seniority over their less influential colleagues. Meade, for example, successfully lobbied the Lincoln administration to elevate Warren to major general and to backdate his promotion so that he would have seniority over Birney. Hooker did the same thing with Sickles so he would rank Berry. Seniority, in short, did not guarantee a major general the next available corps, but it certainly helped.

Awarding major generals corps commands on the basis of seniority had the advantages of predictability and order, but on the whole it did not improve the Army of the Potomac's effectiveness. Seniority all too often did not equal ability or even experience, especially early in the conflict. Although Newton, French, and Stoneman all had plenty of seniority that contributed to their rise to corps command, they were not capable officers, and the Army of the Potomac would have been better off without them. They got their corps primarily because it was their turn, not because they had earned it. Moreover, officers continued to accrue seniority even when they were nowhere near the battlefield. Sickles, for example, left the Army of the Potomac for recruiting duty in New York at the end of the Peninsula campaign and did not return until after Fredericksburg, five months later. Even so, this did not hinder his climb up the army's hierarchy. Seniority rewarded survivability more than anything, and those who had survived the longest were not necessarily the best men to lead corps.

Rank and seniority were significant, but the Lincoln administration factored in other issues before appointing corps commanders. Merit was certainly an important qualification. Unfortunately, determining meritorious conduct was subjective, especially for untutored civilians making judgments far from the front lines. Oftentimes the *perception* of an officer's record and ability carried more weight than the reality. Some Army of the Potomac officers proved adept at dodging, deflecting, and obscuring blame for battlefield setbacks. At the same time, they skillfully publicized real, exaggerated, or imagined accomplishments. Some did so through embellishing their performance on the battlefield in their official reports. Others cultivated journalists to broadcast their combat exploits and gain the attention of the Lincoln administration and its constituents. These ploys were especially common early in the war when it was easy to impress everyone. It could be effective, especially for charismatic officers such as Joe Hooker. Hooker's free opinions, magnetic personality, and proximity to combat attracted journalist looking for good stories. He parlayed the good press he received for his performance at Williamsburg into a major generalship, which put him in line for a corps. No doubt Hooker had fought bravely at Williamsburg and elsewhere, but no more so than many others less adept at manipulating the press. This strategy often alienated fellow officers who were subsequently less likely to give their full support to those elevated over their heads on the basis of such grandstanding, as Hooker eventually discovered. On the other hand, some officers let their accomplishments speak for themselves and relied on their superiors to campaign for their promotions. Doing so was less likely to antagonize brother officers, thus securing their continued assistance. For example, Gibbon and Humphreys were hardly household names in or out of Congress, but they both rose to command corps because Grant and Meade recognized their abilities and lobbied the Lincoln administration on their behalf.

Personal relationships within the army also played an important role in achieving corps command. The prewar officer corps was a close-knit group of men, most of whom had attended West Point, fought in the Mexican War, and served in numerous dreary western garrison posts. Regular Army officers knew each other's abilities by reputation and from firsthand experience, creating a network of connections of which men took full advantage. Indeed, Halleck, Grant, and all the Army of the Potomac's commanders used personal relationships to advance the careers of their favorites. There was scarcely an Army of the Potomac or Army of the James corps commander who did not have some higher-ranking patron protecting his interests. This practice enabled commanders to bring forward familiar and trusted faces that helped them solidify their control over the army. For instance, McClellan strengthened his power within the Army of the Potomac by giving his good friends Porter and Franklin the Fifth and Sixth Corps and securing their promotions to major general.

On the other hand, there were downsides to this practice. For one thing, longtime friendships occasionally blinded officers to one another's weaknesses. Warren, for instance, never would have attained and held onto his corps as long as he did without Meade's support. Despite all the problems he caused, Meade could never bring himself to demand Warren's removal. In addition, this cliquishness limited opportunities for outsiders. The Civil War saw the influx of thousands of civilians into the army, some of whom developed into capable leaders. Many Regular Army officers, however, distrusted these untutored civilians and were reluctant to entrust them with greater responsibilities. This situation penalized capable nonprofessionals such as Williams and Birney who were initially unknown to their Regular Army brethren, making their climb up the chain of command more difficult. For better or worse, however, personal relationships were part of the process.

Political connections contributed to corps commander selection too. It was impossible to divorce the Army of the Potomac from the political system that created it, and no one attempted to do so. Instead, the Lincoln administration deliberately used the army as a means to solidify backing for the war by assigning prominent civilians representing important constituencies—German Americans, Irish Americans, War Democrats, Kentuckians, and so on—to command positions. Many of these men proved to be poor generals who caused the army a good deal of grief, but Lincoln was willing to tolerate their faults—up to a point—to maintain the popular support upon which victory depended. Some officers took advantage of the pluralistic nature of Union society to ally themselves with one of Washington's political factions or constituencies. This gained them patrons who lobbied the Lincoln administration on their behalf, and in return the officers endorsed their patrons' political agendas. Political connections enabled nonprofessional officers to overcome their lack of personal ties within the army. Butler, Birney, Sigel, Sickles, Butterfield, Cox, Berry, and Williams were all very different men with very different ideologies, but they were also all prominent nonprofessionals who traded on their political connections to gain important commands.

Professional officers also established symbiotic relationships with Washington's political factions. The most famous example was Hooker's aggressive courtship of Radical Republicans whose support he coveted in order to pressure the Lincoln administration into giving him command of the Army of the Potomac. Despite Hooker's Democratic background, Radical Republicans willingly embraced him because they wanted to use him as a club with which to beat McClellan and his Democratic allies. Other Regular Army officers also looked to political friends for support, though generally to achieve more limited goals. Doing so could also supply them with political protection from other hostile elements in Washington. Meade, for instance, worked with the Lincoln administration against Radical Republicans out to discredit him in Committee on the Conduct of the War hearings in late winter 1864. Even officers who normally abhorred blatant politicking were willing to do so for the good of the army. Slocum, for instance, used his political connections with the secretary of state to secure an interview with Lincoln in order to denounce Hooker. There were, in short, good reasons to cultivate political allies.

Unhappily, there were also definite problems with trading political favors. Such alliances helped turn the Army of the Potomac into a tool that Washington's political factions sought to manipulate to their own advantage, as seen by Committee on the Conduct of the War campaigns against McClellan and later Meade. Moreover, the alliances further polarized the Army of the Potomac by dividing the officer corps along political lines, thus undermining unity. McClellan no doubt had his faults, but political differences certainly sharpened the animosity exhibited toward him by some of his subordinates. Finally, using political connections did not always work; some officers lost or failed to gain commands when the Lincoln administration decided against placating a political faction. Butterfield and Keyes, for example, both discovered this when the Lincoln administration refused to intervene on their behalf, even though both men pulled all the political strings at their disposal.

Finally, availability was an important requirement to achieve corps command in the Army of the Potomac. Almost all the men assigned to lead corps were already members of the army, usually at the head of divisions. There were practical reasons for this. Corps commands often became vacant in the middle of a campaign, so filling the open slot as quickly as possible was a military necessity. Importing an outsider unfamiliar with the army and its personnel was time consuming and uncertain. Doing so risked alienating cliquish officers passed over, thus reducing morale. Besides, the Army of the Potomac's commander had authority only over his own officers, so if he wanted to bring in an officer from another army, he would have had to ask the general in chief and secretary of war. For these reasons, transferring officers from outside the Army of the Potomac to lead its corps was rare. Until Grant's ascension to general in chief, Mansfield was the only clear example of such an occurrence, and in this case Halleck took the initiative and imposed him on McClellan. The problem was that the most available officers for corps command were not necessarily the most qualified. This was especially true by the time Meade took over the Army of the Potomac because the number of available and competent major generals had all but disappeared. After Grant became general in chief, he was more willing to move officers from one field army to another, but he had the benefit of Lincoln's confidence and authority over the entire Union Army. He brought in Sheridan from out west to command the Army of the Potomac's cavalry and Smith and Ord to lead corps in the Army of the James. Even so, these officers were exceptions to the rule, albeit important ones.

Reasons for Removal from Corps Command

During the Civil War, thirty-six officers held long term "temporary" or permanent corps commands in the Army of the Potomac, as well as another seven in the Army of the James. This number is indicative of the high attrition rate among corps commanders. In fact, only three officers—Gouverneur Warren, John Sedgwick, and Horatio Wright—led corps in the Army of the Potomac for more than a year. There were several reasons for the high turnover rate, but one of the most obvious was enemy fire. Primitive communications meant that during battle corps commanders had to station themselves at or near the firing line to direct and maneuver their men, and their position on horseback amid a throng of aides made them conspicuous targets. Consequently, corps commanders suffered heavy casualties. During the war, four of the Army of the Potomac's corps commanders were killed in battle: Reno at Turner's Gap, Mansfield at Antietam, Reynolds at Gettysburg, and Sedgwick at Spotsylvania. In addition, three others—Hooker at Antietam and Sickles and Hancock at Gettysburg—

were so seriously wounded that they had to temporarily or, in Sickles's case, permanently relinquish their positions. In addition, the demands of army life in the field—bad food and water, pressures of leadership, constant fatigue, the never-ending paperwork, difficult bosses, homesickness, and so on—also took their toll, contributing to Sumner's and Birney's demise. In all, therefore, more than one in five of the Army of the Potomac's and Army of the James's corps commanders succumbed to enemy fire, illness, or serious injury.

Although most Army of the Potomac and Army of the James corps commanders hoped to use their positions as stepping-stones to greater responsibilities, it usually did not turn out that way. A few, however, went on to lead field armies. Burnside, Hooker, and Meade all vaulted from corps command—or, in Fighting Joe's case, grand division command—directly to Army of the Potomac chief. Similarly, the Lincoln administration rewarded Ord and Sheridan for their performances at the corps level by giving them command of, respectively, the Army of the James and the Army of the Shenandoah. Others acquired field armies in a more indirect manner. Howard and Slocum both rose to lead field armies after they were transferred out west, and the Lincoln administration eventually placed Sigel in charge of what was in effect an army in the Shenandoah Valley in the spring of 1864. Thus, eight Army of the Potomac and Army of the James corps commanders went on to bigger and better things.

Most corps commanders, however, were not killed, incapacitated, or promoted. Instead, they met various fates detrimental to their careers. More senior and better-connected officers eventually supplanted temporary corps commanders Butterfield, Willcox, and Williams, forcing them to return to their divisions. Sigel, Stoneman, and Couch quit their corps in disgust, and Brooks resigned both his command and his commission. Most of the remaining corps commanders eventually alienated their superiors because of their inability to perform on the battlefield or get along with others. When this occurred, the Lincoln administration had a variety of weapons at its disposal to deal with such troublemakers. The most serious was court martial and dismissal from the service, but only Porter suffered this fate. In 1864, Grant punished Burnside and Smith by sending both men home and never giving them new assignments. McDowell and Heintzelman were kicked upstairs to run inactive departments. Although Warren was relieved of his command outright for his alleged failure at Five Forks, usually the War Department simply transferred corps commanders who did not seem to measure up out of the Army of the Potomac to secondary theaters where they could do less harm to the cause. Franklin, French, Gillmore, Hays, Newton, Pleasonton, Sykes, and Smith after Fredericksburg all met this fate. Finally, in a unique punishment, McClellan marooned Keyes on the peninsula when the Army of the Potomac returned to northern Virginia.

Categories of Corps Commanders

The corps commanders in the Armies of the Potomac and James can be divided into four overlapping groups: the McClellanites, those who owed their positions to the Lincoln administration, opportunists, and those chosen on merit. The McClellanites were most common. These officers shared McClellan's political and military views, and many considered McClellan's enemies their own. Like McClellan, most were War Democrats who initially interpreted the Civil War as a conflict solely to preserve the Union, not to end slavery. They wanted to engage in a limited war that did not disturb the country's social fabric, not a cataclysmic revolutionary struggle that would abolish slavery and remake U.S. society forever. As far as they were concerned, seizing enemy territory in an orderly and methodical way was the key to victory, not destroying the Confederacy's infrastructure and social system in a ruthless war. Although some of them eventually recognized the military need to obliterate the southern slave system and even came around to supporting Lincoln's reelection, they did so with reluctance and distaste.

About half the corps commanders fit into this category, and in fact they dominated the Army of the Potomac from start to finish. In retrospect, this was not surprising. Most prewar army officers were Democrats, and those who remained loyal to the Union gravitated to Washington after the conflict began because it was the nexus of the war effort. Moreover, when McClellan became Army of the Potomac commander, he appointed his supporters to lead many of the army's newly formed divisions and brigades. These officers got the rank commensurate with their responsibilities and were then able to accumulate the seniority necessary to put them in line for corps command. Since they were first in the pipeline, and since there were so many of them, they continued to provide corps commanders throughout the war. They included not only staunch McClellan allies such as Porter and Franklin but also people such as Meade and Hancock. As generals, their performance was uneven. Some such as Newton, Stoneman, and French proved poor corps commanders, but others such as Hancock, Slocum, and Gibbon fought with distinction. Their limited war outlook restricted their strategic vision, but except for Meade and Burnside, few of them had much opportunity to plot strategy anyway. Finally, some of them contributed to the dissension that frequently wracked the Army of the Potomac through their string-pulling and backbiting. For every Franklin and Smith, however, there were also officers such as Sedgwick who avoided political infighting. There is no doubt that some of these men contributed to the Army of the Potomac's peculiar problems, but without them the Union could not have won the war.

The Army of the Potomac also contained a number of corps commanders who were beholden first and foremost to the Lincoln administration for their appointments. These included not only political generals but also the professional officers whom Lincoln assigned to the Army of the Potomac's first four corps. Lincoln picked the original corps commanders—McDowell, Sumner, Heintzelman, and Keyes—on the basis of their seniority and without consulting McClellan. In doing so, the president inadvertently reinforced the emphasis on seniority and encouraged factionalism within the army. McClellan never trusted the four officers, and he frequently searched for ways to displace them. All four had serious weaknesses that made them ineffective at the corps level, but this was really beside the point as far as McClellan was concerned; he wanted his friends in corps command. To protect themselves professionally, McDowell and Keyes in particular aligned themselves with the Lincoln administration. In the end, McClellan succeeded in divesting himself of most of them, but his actions did little to promote officer corps unity. On the other hand, Lincoln never again imposed corps commanders on an Army of the Potomac chief.

Others, however, were political generals such as Sigel and Birney with minimal prewar military experience who were selected by Lincoln to placate some constituency. They came from all points on the Union's ideological spectrum, from abolitionists waging war to end slavery to War Democrats fighting solely to preserve the Union. The one thing they all had in common, however, was that they were indebted to Lincoln for their posts. The political generals Lincoln commissioned have gone down in history as an incompetent group of men who hindered the Union war effort with their repeated failures on the battlefield. There is some truth to this, as indicated by Sigel's, Butler's, and Banks's dismal records. These officers served a vital role in the war that went beyond their generalship, however. They all represented some important constituency, and their appointments helped glue chunks of the public to the Lincoln administration and the Union war effort. So, although Sigel cost hundreds of Union soldiers their lives through his poor generalship, he also helped bring thousands of German Americans into the Union armies. Moreover, some of them—such as Birney, Cox, and Williams—developed into first-rate generals, especially when they cut their teeth at the regimental and brigade level. Political generals engaged in extensive politicking, self-promotion, and backbiting, but so did many of the professionals. And although the Lincoln administration gave them more chances at redemption than professional soldiers, Butler's and Sigel's experiences demonstrated that they were not immune from accountability. In short, as with the McClellanites, political generals caused all sorts of trouble, but they were also indispensable to the Union war effort.

The Army of the Potomac's corps commanders also included a number of opportunists. These ambitious and often unscrupulous officers sought high command as much for their own self-aggrandizement as for any devotion to the Union. This was equally true of many political generals, but the opportunists differed in that they were willing to ally themselves with almost anyone who would advance their interests, even those whose beliefs did not coincide with their own. They were often shameless self-promoters expert at cultivating journalists, and they freely criticized and denigrated their superior officers to discredit them and get them out of their way. This strategy could work in gaining corps command or better, but, as some of these men eventually learned, it also often cost them the goodwill of their disgusted brother officers whose support they needed to succeed in their positions. Some of them were military amateurs, but others were professionals. Such men are present in any institution, but they were especially troublesome in the Army of the Potomac because some of them organized themselves into a loosely knit group. Led by Hooker and Kearny, they also included generals such as Birney, Berry, Sickles, and Butterfield. They joined forces during the Peninsula campaign to combat McClellan and his tendency to reward his favorites. They manipulated the press to publicize their battlefield achievements, projecting some of them into the spotlight. Although many of the opportunists did not care about slavery one way or another, they aligned themselves with Radical Republicans who saw McClellan as an obstacle to the vigorous prosecution of revolutionary war and were determined to bring him down.

The opportunists contributed to first McClellan's, and then Burnside's, demise by providing an alternative to their management and ideas. After Hooker took over the Army of the Potomac, he placed his allies such as Sickles and Butterfield in positions of power, but the McClellanites continued to dominate the army through their numerical strength. Indeed, after the rebels defeated Hooker at Chancellorsville, these McClellanites emerged from the woodwork to denounce Hooker, which helped persuade the president to stand aside while Stanton and Halleck hounded Fighting Joe into submitting his resignation. The opportunists saw Hooker's replacement, George Meade, as another version of McClellan, so Sickles orchestrated an ultimately unsuccessful campaign to discredit him in early 1864. By then most of the opportunists had been removed from the Army of the Potomac for one reason or another, and they ceased to exert much influence over it. The opportunists played an important role in the Army of the Potomac's history, but it is hard to see that they contributed much as a group to the Union war effort. Although they presented an alternative to McClellan's, Burnside's, and Meade's leadership, in doing so they exacerbated the dissension and backbiting that plagued the Army of the Potomac.

Finally, there were a small number of officers who reached corps command in the Armies of the Potomac and James primarily on the basis of merit. Some of them had personal or political connections, but these were secondary to their performance on the battlefield. Although by the end of the conflict the Armies of the Potomac and James were full of such men at the brigade and division levels, only a few led corps. The problem was that it took a long time for most of these officers to work their way up through the hierarchy to major general so they could accumulate sufficient seniority to achieve corps command. Ord and Sheridan were the two best examples, although Wright, Humphreys, and Howard might also fit. No doubt Ord and especially Sheridan contributed much to Union victory, but as a group the officers did not exert much influence on the Army of the Potomac's high command. Indeed, it is ironic that many of the officers who through the rigors of combat proved themselves to be the most qualified to lead corps did not get much of an opportunity to do so.

The Army of the Potomac remains one of the most famous armies in American military history. Despite its numerical and matériel advantages, it lost more battles than it won and sustained more casualties than it inflicted before it finally fulfilled its mission. Moreover, although no one can deny the courage of its officers and men, it was also beset with dissension, political intrigue, backbiting, and cliquishness. There are plenty of explanations for the Army of the Potomac's troubled history, but certainly the interrelationship among the officer corps, Congress, and the Lincoln administration was an important factor. The Union government faced the Herculean task of waging a revolutionary civil war within the confines of a democratic system. It is not surprising that civilian policymakers invariably saw the Army of the Potomac through a political lens and acted accordingly. The Army of the Potomac's officer corps, for its part, was full of recalcitrant, fractious, and egotistical men who were extraordinarily sensitive to slights real or imagined. The army's proximity to Washington and its superheated political environment often brought out the worst in generals who confused their personal interests with those of their country. Even those who attempted to shun politics and concentrate on performing their duty often found themselves sucked into the intrigue around them. Nowhere was their war within a war more evident than in the selection and retention of the Army of the Potomac's corps commanders.

BIOGRAPHICAL AFTERWORD

Those officers who ended the war as leaders of the Armies of the Potomac and the James continued to influence the United States Army after the conflict.

John Gibbon capped his distinguished wartime career by serving as one of the three officers Grant designated to officially receive the surrender of Lee's army at Appomattox. After the conflict, Gibbon performed credibly out on the frontier in a series of wars against American Indians. He led the column that rescued the remnants of Colonel George Custer's command after the Battle of Little Bighorn, campaigned successfully against the Nez Perces, and thwarted anti-Chinese violence in Seattle. He retired in 1891 to Baltimore and died five years later.

Ulysses Grant's unlikely ascent continued after the Civil War. He sided with Radical Republicans against President Andrew Johnson and then ran successfully as Republican candidate for president in 1868. Grant's military skills did not translate well into the political arena, and his two terms as president were undistinguished at best. After he retired in 1877, he entered into a series of unwise financial transactions that cost him almost everything he owned. He wrote his memoirs in collaboration with Mark Twain, finishing them shortly before his death from throat cancer in 1885. His memoirs not only provided financial security for his widow but also are considered among the best written by a president.

Charles Griffin was also designated to receive the surrender of Lee's army, a token of the respect Grant held for him. After the war, he was sent to Texas as a regimental commander. Unfortunately, he succumbed to yellow fever in Galveston in 1867.

Henry Halleck was sent to Richmond for a short time immediately after the war as commander of the Department of Virginia. Stanton later dispatched him to take charge of the newly organized Division of the Pacific. Halleck remained on the west coast until 1869, when he was ordered to take over the Division of the South. He died in January 1872.

Andrew Humphreys served as the army's chief engineer from 1866 until his retirement in 1879. He wrote two books about the war before his death in 1883.

George Meade was put in charge of the Division of the Atlantic after the war and, like so many high-ranking officers, found himself embroiled in Reconstruction controversies. He was even more distressed, however, by Grant's decision to promote Sheridan ahead of him to lieutenant general in the Regular Army. Meade never really recovered from the wound he had sustained in his lung at the Battle of Glendale, and he died of pneumonia in 1872.

Edward Ord received a brigadier generalship in the Regular Army in 1866 as a reward for his distinguished Civil War service. After the war, he commanded the Department of Arkansas, where he found himself in the thick of Reconstruction controversies. Like most Regular Army officers, he was uncomfortable with the myriad number of complicated social, political, and economic issues overseeing the defeated southern states entailed, so he lobbied hard for a more conducive assignment. The War Department put him in charge of the Department of California in 1867, and he later served in the Great Plains and in Texas. He was forced into retirement in 1881 because of his age. He died of yellow fever in Havana in 1883 en route to Veracruz, Mexico, on a business trip.

John Parke got married in 1867. After the war he reverted to colonel of engineers, and from 1887 to 1889 he was superintendent of West Point. He retired to Washington, D.C., in 1889 but remained active in business, literary, and religious affairs. He died in 1900.

Philip Sheridan was dispatched to the Texas border immediately after the war with 50,000 troops as part of Secretary of State Seward's successful strategy to pressure the French to evacuate their military forces from Mexico. Sheridan commanded the Department of Louisiana and Texas, but his heavy-handed ways angered President Andrew Johnson, who transferred him to the Department of Missouri. There Sheridan forced the Arapahoes, Cheyennes, Comanches, and Kiwas into reservations. In 1869, President Grant appointed him to lieutenant general, and in 1870–1871 Sheridan traveled to Europe to observe the Franco-Prussian War. After his return, Sheridan oversaw the Divisions of the West and Southwest. He succeeded Sherman as general in chief in 1884 and was promoted to full general four years later. He died in 1888, just days after he finished his memoirs.

Godfrey Weitzel was reduced to a captain of engineers in the army's postwar contraction. He oversaw the construction of the ship canal at the Falls of the Ohio and the lock at Sault Sainte Marie. He died in the army as a colonel in 1884 after several years of poor health.

Horatio Wright commanded the Department of Texas before he returned to his engineering duties as a lieutenant colonel. He succeeded Humphreys as the army's chief engineer in 1879 and helped to complete the Washington Monument. He retired in 1884 and died fifteen years later in Washington, D.C.

NOTES

John Bates Papers	John C. Bates Papers, United States Army Military History Institute
Samuel Bates Papers	Samuel Bates Papers, Lawrence Lee Pelletier Library, Allegheny College
Berry	Edward K. Gould, *Major-General Hiram G. Berry*
Biddle Letters	James Biddle Civil War Letters, Historical Society of Pennsylvania
Birney Papers	David Birney Papers, United States Army Military History Institute
Blake Collection	Robert Blake Collection, United States Army Military History Institute
Brooks Papers	William Brooks Papers, United States Army Military History Institute
Browning's Diary	Orville Hickman Browning, *The Diary of Orville Hickman Browning*
Burns Papers	William Wallace Burns Papers, Cushing Memorial Library, Texas A & M University
Butler's Correspondence	Benjamin Butler, *Private and Official Correspondence of Gen. Benjamin F. Butler during the Period of the Civil War*
Chandler Papers	Papers of Zachariah Chandler, Library of Congress
Chase Papers	Salmon Chase, *The Salmon P. Chase Papers*
"Cochrane's Memoir"	John Cochrane, "The War for the Union: Memoir of Gen. John Cochrane," *American Civil War: Memories of the Rebellion*
Comstock's Diary	Cyrus B. Comstock, *The Diary of Cyrus B. Comstock*
Couch Papers	Darius Couch Papers, Old Colony Historical Society
Cox Papers	Jacob Cox Papers, Oberlin College Library, Oberlin College
Franklin Papers	William Franklin Papers, Library of Congress
Garland Collection	Hamlin Garland Collection, Doheny Memorial Library, University of Southern California

Gibbon Letters   John Gibbon Letters, Historical Society of
                                              Pennsylvania
Grant Papers   Ulysses Grant, The Papers of Ulysses S. Grant
Hancock Reminiscences   Alma Hancock, Reminiscences of Winfield Scott
                                              Hancock
"Hardie Memoir"   James Hardie, "Memoir of James A. Hardie,"
                                              Western Americana: Frontier History of the
                                              Trans-Mississippi West, 1550–1900
Hay's Letters and Diaries   John Hay, Lincoln and the Civil War in the Letters
                                              and Diaries of John Hay
Hays's Life and Letters   Alexander Hays, Life and Letters of Alexander
                                              Hays
Heintzelman Papers   Papers of Samuel Heintzelman, Library of
                                              Congress
Howard's Autobiography   Oliver Otis Howard, Autobiography of Oliver
                                              Otis Howard
Howland Papers   Joseph Howland Papers, the New-York
                                              Historical Society
Hubbard Letters   Letters of Robert Hubbard, M.D., United States
                                              Army Military History Institute
Humphreys Letters   Letters of Andrew Humphreys, Historical
                                              Society of Pennsylvania
Humphreys's Biography   Henry H. Humphreys, Andrew Atkinson
                                              Humphreys: A Biography
In Times of Peace and War   James Scrymser, Personal Reminiscences of James
                                              A. Scrymser in Times of Peace and War
Life and Letters of an American Soldier   Emerson Gifford Taylor, Gouverneur Kemble
                                              Warren: The Life and Letters of an American
                                              Soldier, 1830–1882
Life of Rawlins   James Harrison Wilson, The Life of John A.
                                              Rawlins: Lawyer, Assistant-Adjutant General,
                                              Chief of Staff, Major General of Volunteers,
                                              and Secretary of War
Lincoln Papers   Abraham Lincoln Papers, Library of Congress
McAllister's Letters   Robert McAllister, Civil War Letters of General
                                              Robert McAllister
Miles Papers   Nelson Miles Papers, United States Army
                                              Military History Institute
OR   The War of the Rebellion: A Compilation of the
                                              Official Records of the Union and Confederate
                                              Armies
Own Story   George McClellan, McClellan's Own Story
Reynolds Papers   John Reynolds Papers, Reynolds Family Papers,
                                              Shadeck-Fackenthal Library, Franklin and
                                              Marshall College
Sedgwick's Correspondence   John Sedgwick, Correspondence of John Sedgwick
Selected Correspondence   George McClellan, The Civil War Papers of
                                              George B. McClellan: Selected Correspondence,
                                              1860–1865

Sheridan's Memoirs	Philip Sheridan, *Civil War Memoirs: Philip Sheridan*
Smith's Autobiography	William Farrar Smith, *Autobiography of Major General William F. Smith, 1861–1864*
Stanton Papers	Papers of Edwin M. Stanton, Historical Society of Pennsylvania
U.S. Army Generals' Reports	U.S. Army Generals' Reports of Civil War Service, 1864–1887, National Archives and Records Administration
Veil Folder	Charles Veil Folder, Civil War Miscellaneous, United States Army Military History Institute
Villard Memoirs	Henry Villard, *Memoirs of Henry Villard*
Warren Papers	Gouverneur Warren Papers, New York State Library
Welles's Diary	Gideon Welles, *Diary of Gideon Welles: Secretary of the Navy under Lincoln and Johnson*
Wilderness	Morris Schaff, *The Battle of the Wilderness*

Introduction

1. Daniel Butterfield to Henry Scudder, 20 July 1863, Julia Lorrilard Butterfield, ed., *A Biographical Memorial of General Daniel Butterfield* (New York: Grafton Press, 1904), pp. 132–33; Fitz John Porter to Seth Williams, 26 September 1862, *OR*, vol. 51, pt. 1, p. 863; Marsena Patrick, 1 February 1863, *Inside Lincoln's Army: The Diary of Marsena Rudolph Patrick, Provost Marshal General, Army of the Potomac*, ed. David Sparks (New York: Thomas Yoseloff, 1964), p. 210.

2. Butterfield to [unknown], November 1891, *Biographical Memorial*, pp. 116–18.

3. Many high-ranking Civil War officers held both Regular Army and Volunteer Army commissions, so it was possible for an officer to be simultaneously, for example, a major general in the Volunteer Army and a colonel in the Regular Army. During the war, however, an officer's Volunteer Army rank was the one that mattered in attaining corps command.

4. They were Ambrose Burnside, Daniel Butterfield, Darius Couch, Jacob Cox, William Franklin, William French, Charles Griffin, Winfield Scott Hancock, William Hays, Samuel Heintzelman, Joseph Hooker, Oliver Otis Howard, Andrew Humphreys, Erasmus Keyes, Joseph Mansfield, Irvin McDowell, George Meade, John Newton, John Parke, Alfred Pleasonton, Fitz John Porter, Jesse Reno, John Reynolds, John Sedgwick, Philip Sheridan, Daniel Sickles, Franz Sigel, Henry Slocum, William Smith, George Stoneman, Edwin Sumner, George Sykes, Gouverneur Warren, Orlando Willcox, Alpheus Williams, and Horatio Wright. In addition, during the 1864–1865 siege of Petersburg the Army of the Potomac cooperated so closely with the neighboring Army of the James that they were practically one entity. The Army of the James's corps commanders were David Birney, William Brooks, John Gibbon, Quincy Gillmore, Edward Ord, William Smith, and Godfrey Weitzel. This list does not include officers who temporarily assumed command of corps during quiet times when the regular corps commander was on an ordinary leave.

Chapter 1. "McClellan Is Not the Man": July 1861 to November 1862

1. Welles, 1 September 1862, *Welles's Diary*, vol. 1, p. 104; Salmon Chase to George McClellan, 7 July 1861, Chase, *Chase Papers*, vol. 3, pp. 74–75.

2. William Stoddard, 8 August 1861, *Dispatches from Lincoln's White House: The Anonymous Civil War Journalism of Presidential Secretary William O. Stoddard*, ed. Michael Burningame (Lincoln: University of Nebraska Press, 2002), p. 17.

3. For example, McClellan wrote to his wife shortly after he arrived in Washington, "I feel that God has placed a great work in my hands—I have not sought it—I know how weak I am—but I know that I mean to do right and I believe that God will help me and give me the wisdom I do not possess. Pray for me, darling, that I may be able to accomplish my task—the greatest, perhaps, that any poor weak mortal ever had to do." McClellan to Mary Ellen McClellan, 10 August 1861, McClellan, *Selected Correspondence*, p. 82.

4. McClellan to Mary Ellen McClellan, 11 October 1861 and 16 August 1861, McClellan, *Selected Correspondence*, pp. 106–7, 85–86.

5. McClellan most clearly stated his arguments for a limited war in his Harrison's Landing letter to the president. See McClellan to Abraham Lincoln, 7 July 1862, Lincoln Papers.

6. McClellan to Mary Ellen McClellan, 8 August 1861, McClellan, *Selected Correspondence*, p. 81.

7. Hay, November 1861, *Hay's Letters and Diaries*, pp. 32–33.

8. The quote is from McClellan to Mary Ellen McClellan, 2 November 1861, McClellan, *Selected Correspondence*, pp. 123–24. See also McClellan to Mary Ellen McClellan, 2 August 1861, 13 October 1861, and 26 October 1861, ibid., pp. 75, 107, 112; Lincoln to McClellan, 1 November 1861, Abraham Lincoln, *The Collected Works of Abraham Lincoln*, vol. 5, ed. Roy Basler (New Brunswick, NJ: Rutgers University Press, 1953), pp. 9–10; McClellan, *Own Story*, p. 113; Adam De Gurowski, 6 October 1861, *Diary*, vol. 1 (Boston: Lee and Shepard, 1862), p. 108; Irvin McDowell's testimony, 26 December 1861, U.S. Congress, *Reports of the Joint Committee on the Conduct of the War*, 37th Cong., 3d sess. (Washington, DC: Government Printing Office, 1863), pp. 143–44.

9. Chase, 6 January 1862, *Chase Papers*, vol. 1, p. 322; Hay, 26 October 1861, *Hay's Letters and Diaries*, p. 31; McClellan, *Own Story*, pp. 149–51; Benjamin Wade to Zachariah Chandler, 8 October 1861, Chandler Papers, reel 1.

10. Welles, 1 September 1862, *Welles's Diary*, vol. 1, pp. 102–4; Hay, 26 October 1861 and 13 November 1861, *Hay's Letters and Diaries*, pp. 31, 34–35; Browning, 18 January 1862, 2 April 1862, and 10 April 1862, *Browning's Diary*, vol. 1, pp. 525, 537–39, 540; George Julian, *Political Recollections, 1840 to 1872* (Chicago: Jansen, McClurg, 1884), p. 210.

11. Chase, 6 January 1862, *Chase Papers*, vol. 1, p. 322; McClellan, *Own Story*, pp. 113, 122; Julian, *Political Recollections*, pp. 204–5; McDowell's testimony, 26 December 1861, U.S. Congress, *Reports of the Joint Committee*, pp. 143–44; James Wadsworth's testimony, 26 December 1861, ibid., p. 146; Montgomery Meigs, 27 December 1861, ibid., p. 159.

12. Lincoln, 11 March 1862, "President's War Order No. 3," *Collected Works*, vol. 5, p. 155; Hay, *Hay's Letters and Diaries*, pp. 37–38; McClellan, *Own Story*, pp. 155–58; William Swinton, *Campaigns of the Army of the Potomac* (New York: Charles B. Richardson, 1866), pp. 84–85; Meigs, "General M. C. Meigs on the Conduct of the Civil War," *American Historical Review*, January 1921, vol. 26, no. 2, p. 292.

13. Chase, 5–6 January 1862, *Chase Papers*, vol. 1, pp. 321–22; Chase to William Cullen Bryant, 4 September 1862, ibid., vol. 3, pp. 259–60; John Pope, *The Military Memoirs of General John Pope*, ed. Peter Cozzens and Robert Girardi (Chapel Hill: University of North Carolina Press, 1998), pp. 213–16; George Templeton Strong, 16 March

1862, *Diary of the Civil War, 1860–1865*, ed. Allan Nevins (New York: Macmillan, 1962), p. 214; Herman Haupt, *Reminiscences of General Herman Haupt* (Milwaukee, WI: Wright and Joys, 1901), pp. 303–4; James Harrison Wilson, *Under the Old Flag: Recollections of Military Operations in the War for the Union, the Spanish War and the Boxer Rebellion, etc.*, vol. 1 (Westport, CT: Greenwood Press, 1971), p. 66; Browning, 2 April 1862, *Browning's Diary*, vol. 1, p. 539; McClellan, *Own Story*, pp. 70–71.

14. Charles Wainwright, 12 August 1862, *A Diary of Battle: The Personal Journals of Colonel Charles S. Wainwright*, ed. Allan Nevins (New York: Harcourt, Brace and World, 1962), p. 84; Erasmus Keyes to Chase, 17 June 1862, Chase, *Chase Papers*, vol. 3, p. 212; Chase to Chandler, 20 September 1862, ibid., p. 275; John Gibbon, *Personal Recollections of the Civil War* (New York: G. P. Putnam's Sons, 1928), p. 105; Howard, *Howard's Autobiography*, vol. 1, pp. 181, 190–91; McClellan, *Own Story*, p. 138; Josiah Marshall Favill, 7 December 1861, *Diary of a Young Officer* (Baltimore: Butternut and Blue, 2000), p. 59; Villard, *Villard Memoirs*, vol. 1, pp. 348–49; David Davis to Lincoln, 6 March 1861, Lincoln Papers; Horatio Nelson Taft, 6 March 1863, *The Diary of Horatio Nelson Taft, 1861–1865*, vol. 2, Library of Congress, http://memory.loc.gov/ammem/tafthtml/tafthome.html.

15. Wainwright, 14 April 1862, *Diary of Battle*, p. 38.

16. Philip Kearny to Cortlandt Parker, 10 July 1862, Philip Kearny, *Letters from the Peninsula: The Civil War Letters of General Philip Kearny*, ed. William Styple (Kearny, NJ: Belle Grove Publishing, 1988), p. 129; Keyes to Chase, 17 June 1862, Chase, *Chase Papers*, vol. 3, pp. 212–23; Howard, *Howard's Autobiography*, vol. 1, p. 142; McClellan, *Own Story*, p. 138; David Birney to George Gross, 16 March 1863, Birney Papers.

17. Kearny to Parker, 24 July 1862, Kearny, *Letters from the Peninsula*, p. 137; Keyes to Chase, 17 June 1862, Chase, *Chase Papers*, vol. 3, p. 213; Erasmus Keyes, *Fifty Years' Observations of Men and Events, Civil and Military* (New York: Charles Scribner's Sons, 1884), pp. 454, 486–88; Smith, *Smith's Autobiography*, p. 34; Regis de Trobriand, *Four Years with the Army of the Potomac*, trans. George K. Dauchy (Boston: Ticknor, 1889), pp. 121–22; William Brooks to his Dad, 26 March 1862, Brooks Papers, Civil War Letters Folder; Keyes, 1 May 1861, Memorandum of Military Service, Lincoln Papers.

18. Marsena Patrick, 15 March 1862, *Inside Lincoln's Army: The Diary of Marsena Rudolph Patrick, Provost Marshal General, Army of the Potomac*, ed. David Sparks (New York: Thomas Yoseloff, 1964), p. 53; Gibbon, *Personal Recollections*, p. 21; Alexander Webb, *The Peninsula: McClellan's Campaign of 1862* (New York: Thomas Yoseloff, 1863), p. 72; Favill, 5 May 1862, *The Diary of a Young Officer*, pp. 90–91; Samuel Heintzelman to Aldred Guernsey, 30 September 1866, Heintzelman Papers, reel 10, p. 6; Keyes to Chase, 17 June 1862, Chase, *Chase Papers*, vol. 3, pp. 212–13; George Meade to Margaret Meade, 18 March 1862, *The Life and Letters of George Gordon Meade*, vol. 1, ed. George Meade (New York: Charles Scribner's Sons, 1913), p. 253.

19. McClellan to Simon Cameron, 8 September 1861, McClellan, *Selected Correspondence*, pp. 96–97; McClelland to McClellan, 6 May 1862, ibid., p. 257; Kearny to Agnes Kearny, 18 May 1862, Kearny, *Letters from the Peninsula*, p. 81; McClellan, "The Peninsular Campaign," *Battles and Leaders of the Civil War*, vol. 2, ed. Robert Underwood Johnson and Clarence Clough Buel (New York: Thomas Yoseloff, 1956), pp. 166–67; Keyes to Chase, 17 June 1862, Chase, *Chase Papers*, vol. 3, p. 213; McClellan to Randolph Marcy, 18 March 1862, OR, vol. 14, p. 15; Keyes, *Fifty Years' Observations*, pp. 437–38, 446; Heintzelman's diary, 8 March 1862, Heintzelman Papers, reel 7; McClellan, *Own Story*, pp. 70–71, 222; Heintzelman's testimony, 24 December 1861, U.S. Congress,

Reports of the Joint Committee, pp. 117–18; McDowell's testimony, 26 December 1861, ibid., p. 131.

20. McClellan to Edwin Stanton, 11 April 1862, McClellan, *Selected Correspondence*, pp. 234–35; McClellan to Lincoln, 18 April 1862, ibid., pp. 241–42; Patrick, 28 February 1862, *Inside Lincoln's Army*, p. 45; Stanton to McClellan, 6 April 1862, OR, vol. 14, p. 73; George McClellan's report, 4 August 1863, ibid., vol. 11, pt. 1, p. 10.

21. The quotation is taken from McClellan to Stanton (telegram), 8 May 1862, OR, vol. 11, pt. 3, p. 153. See also McClellan to Stanton, 6 May 1862, OR, pt. 1, p. 449; McClellan to Mary Ellen McClellan, 6 May 1862, McClellan, *Selected Correspondence*, p. 257; Smith, *Smith's Autobiography*, p. 37.

22. Lincoln to McClellan, 9 May 1862, Lincoln, *Collected Works*, vol. 5, pp. 207–9.

23. The quote is from McClellan, *Own Story*, p. 139. See also McClellan to Mary Ellen McClellan, 6 April 1862 and 27 April 1862, McClellan, *Selected Correspondence*, pp. 230, 243; William Averell, *Ten Years in the Saddle: The Memoir of William Woods Averell*, ed. Edward Eckert and Nicholas Amato (San Rafael, CA: Presidio Press, 1978), pp. 337–38; Stephen Weld to Georgianna Weld, 8 February 1862, Stephen Minot Weld, *War Diary and Letters of Stephen Minot Weld, 1861–1865* (Boston: Massachusetts Historical Society, 1979), p. 54; Weld, ibid., pp. 76–77; Weld to Weld, 21 April 1862, ibid., p. 99.

24. McClellan to William French, 6 April 1862, McClellan, *Selected Correspondence*, p. 231; McClellan to Stanton, 8 May 1862, OR, vol. 14, p. 151; Howard, *Howard's Autobiography*, vol. 1, p. 224; McClellan, *Own Story*, p. 138; William Franklin's testimony, 26 December 1861, U.S. Congress, *Reports of the Joint Committee*, p. 122.

25. Heintzelman's diary, 10 March 1862, 28 April 1862, 29 April 1862, 11 May 1862, 19 May 1862, 20 May 1862, Heintzelman Papers, reel 7; Heintzelman's report, 7 May 1862, OR, vol. 11, pt. 1, p. 458.

26. Theodore Ayrault Dodge, *On Campaign with the Army of the Potomac: The Civil War Journal of Theodore Ayrault Dodge*, ed. Stephen Sears (New York: First Cooper Square Press, 2001), p. 20.

27. See John Pope, "The Second Battle of Bull Run," *Battles and Leaders*, vol. 2, p. 492; Strong, 4 September 1862, *Diary of the Civil War*, p. 252; Gibbon, *Personal Recollections*, pp. 20–21; Keyes, *Fifty Years' Observations*, p. 470; Smith, *Smith's Autobiography*, p. 32; Robert McAllister to Ellen McAllister, 18 May 1862, McAllister, *McAllister's Letters*, p. 158; Heintzelman's diary, 11 June 1862 and 23 July 1862, Heintzelman Papers, reel 7; McClellan, *Own Story*, p. 138; George Alfred Townsend, *Rustics in Rebellion: A Yankee Reporter on the Road to Richmond, 1861–65* (Chapel Hill: University of North Carolina Press, 1950), pp. 149–50; Birney to Gross, 28 June 1862, Birney Papers.

28. Wainwright, 31 January 1862, *Diary of Battle*, p. 12; Smith, *Smith's Autobiography*, p. 32; McClellan, *Own Story*, p. 161; Lincoln to Joseph Mansfield, 19 June 1861, Lincoln Papers.

29. Kearny to Parker, 15 May 1862, Kearny, *Letters from the Peninsula*, p. 73.

30. Kearny to Kearny, 30 March 1862, 14 April 1862, 24 April 1862, 1 May 1862, 8 May 1862, 1 May 1862, 18 May 1862, ibid., pp. 37, 45, 52, 55, 60–62, 73, 81; Kearny to [unknown], 28 May 1862, ibid., p. 86; Kearny to Parker, 31 July 1862, ibid., pp. 143–45; McClellan to Stanton, 11 May 1862, OR, vol. 14, p. 164; Smith, *Smith's Autobiography*, p. 32; Swinton, *Campaigns*, p. 64; James F. Rusling, *Men and Things I Saw in Civil War Days* (New York: Eaton and Mains, 1899), pp. 54, 62–63; Heintzelman's diary, 10 May and 13 May 1862, Heintzelman Papers, reel 7; Trobriand, *Four Years with the Army of the Potomac*,

p. 214; W. M. Tilghman to Stanton, 22 May 1862, Stanton Papers, vol. 7; Townsend, *Rustics in Rebellion*, pp. 149–50; Birney to Gross, 26 February 1863, Birney Papers.

31. Howard, *Howard's Autobiography*, vol. 1, p. 237.

32. McClellan to Heintzelman, 31 May 1862, McClellan, *Selected Correspondence*, p. 284; McClellan to Stanton, 1 June 1862 and 15 June 1862, ibid., pp. 285, 302; Wainwright, 2 June 1862, *Diary of Battle*, p. 79; Kearny to Kearny, 7 June 1862, Kearny, *Letters from the Peninsula*, p. 101; Keyes to Chase, 17 June 1862, Chase, *Chase Papers*, vol. 3, pp. 212–14; Marcy to Heintzelman, 30 May 1862, OR, vol. 14, p. 201; Keyes, *Fifty Years' Observations*, pp. 454–55; Special Orders No. 189, 23 June 1862, OR, vol. 14, p. 247.

33. McClellan to Heintzelman, 31 May 1862, McClellan, *Selected Correspondence*, p. 284; McClellan to Stanton, 1 June 1862, ibid., p. 285; Wainwright, 31 May 1862, *Diary of Battle*, p. 76; Special Orders No. 168, 2 June 1862, OR, vol. 14, p. 210; Heintzelman's diary, 11–12 June 1862, Heintzelman Papers, reel 7; Brooks to his Dad, 12 June 1862, Brooks Papers.

34. Philip Kearny's report, 6 May 1862, Kearny, *Letters from the Peninsula*, p. 67; Kearny to Parker, 10 July 1862, ibid., p. 130; Heintzelman's report, 7 June 1862, OR, vol. 11, pt. 1, p. 815; Kearny to Heintzelman, 2 June 1862, Heintzelman Papers, reel 7; Birney to Heintzelman, 3 June 1862, ibid.; Kearny to Heintzelman, 20 June 1862, ibid., reel 9; Heintzelman's diary, 31 May 1862 and 17 June 1862, ibid., reel 7; Birney to Gross, 16 June 1862, 19 June 1862, and 28 June 1862, Birney Papers.

35. McClellan to Stanton (telegram), 28 June 1862, McClellan, *Selected Correspondence*, p. 323.

36. Lincoln to McClellan, 2 July 1862, OR, vol. 14, p. 286; Lincoln, 8–9 July 1862, "Memorandum of Interviews between Lincoln and Officers of the Army of the Potomac," *Collected Works*, vol. 5, pp. 309–12; Browning, 14 July 1862, *Browning's Diary*, vol. 1, pp. 558–59; McClellan to Stanton, 3 July 1862, McClellan, *Selected Correspondence*, p. 333; McClellan to Lincoln, 7 July 1862, ibid., pp. 344–45; Chase to Kate Chase, 13 July 1862, Chase, *Chase Papers*, vol. 3, pp. 226–27.

37. Welles, 3 September 1862, *Welles's Diary*, vol. 1, pp. 108–9.

38. The quote is from Wilson, *Under the Old Flag*, vol. 1, pp. 98–99. See also Hay, 28 April 1864, *Hay's Letters and Diaries*, p. 176.

39. Ambrose Burnside testimony, *Army of the Potomac. History of Its Campaigns, the Peninsula, Maryland, Fredericksburg. Testimony of Its Three Commanders, Maj.-Gen. G. B. McClellan, Maj.-Gen. A. E. Burnside, and Maj.-Gen. Joseph Hooker before the Congressional Committee on the Conduct of the War* (New York: Tribune Association, 1863), p. 15; Henry Halleck, 27 July 1862, "Memorandum for the Secretary of War," OR, vol. 14, p. 337.

40. McClellan to Burnside, 12 February 1862 and 21 May 1862, McClellan, *Selected Correspondence*, pp. 117 and 270; McClellan to Mary Ellen McClellan, 30 July 1862 and 2 August 1862, ibid., pp. 377 and 382; Chase, 15 August 1862, *Chase Papers*, vol. 1, p. 363; Burnside to Stanton, 18 July 1862, OR, vol. 14, p. 326; McClellan to Halleck, 17 August 1862, ibid., p. 378; Meade to Margaret Meade, 16 August 1862 and 19 August 1862, Meade, *Life and Letters*, vol. 1, pp. 302 and 304; Burnside, *Army of the Potomac*, p. 18.

41. Wainwright, 12 August 1862, *Diary of Battle*, p. 84; Henry Slocum to Joseph Howland, 19 July 1862, Howland Papers; Kearny to Parker, 10 July 1862, Kearny, *Letters from the Peninsula*, p. 130; Heintzelman's diary, 11 July 1862, Heintzelman Papers, reel 7; G. W. Wilson, 1 August 1862, Gould, *Berry*, p. 200; Heintzelman's diary, 10 July 1862, Heintzelman Papers, reel 7; Israel Richardson to Chandler, 10 August 1862, Chandler Papers, reel 1.

42. Kearny to Parker, 31 July 1862, Kearny, *Letters from the Peninsula*, p. 145.

43. Wainwright, 14 August 1862, *Diary of Battle*, p. 84; Kearny to Kearny, 5 July 1862, Kearny, *Letters from the Peninsula*, p. 118; G. W. Wilson, 1 August 1862, Gould, *Berry*, p. 200; Heintzelman's diary, 3 July 1862, 22 July 1862, 1 August 1862, and 17 August 1862, Heintzelman Papers, reel 7; Joseph Hooker, *Army of the Potomac*, pp. 25–27; Birney to Gross, 30 July 1862, Birney Papers.

44. Scrymser, *In Times of Peace and War*, p. 26; Smith, *Smith's Autobiography*, pp. 33, 47; Heintzelman's diary, 22 July 1862, Heintzelman Papers, reel 7; Favill, 6 July 1862, *Diary of a Young Officer*, p. 156; Thomas Hyde, *Following the Greek Cross: Or, Memories of the Sixth Army Corps* (Boston: Houghton, Mifflin, 1894), p. 81.

45. George McClellan, *Own Story*, p. 137.

46. The quote is from McClellan to Mary Ellen McClellan, 13 July 1862, McClellan, *Selected Correspondence*, p. 354. See also ibid., 18 July 1862, p. 364; McClellan to William Aspinwall, 19 July 1862, ibid., p. 364; Heintzelman's diary, 2 August 1862, Heintzelman Papers, reel 7.

47. McClellan to Stanton, 7 July 1862, McClellan, *Selected Correspondence*, pp. 341–42.

48. McClellan to Mary Ellen McClellan, 22 August 1862, ibid., p. 399.

49. Ibid., 18 July 1862, p. 364.

50. McClellan to Marcy, 5 August 1862, ibid., p. 386.

51. Pope, *Military Memoirs*, p. 114; Welles, 10 September 1862, *Welles's Diary*, vol. 1, pp. 119–20.

52. Halleck to Stanton, 30 August 1862, *OR*, vol. 12, pt. 3, p. 739.

53. Keyes to Stanton, 13 May 1863, Stanton Papers, vol. 12; McClellan, *OR*, vol. 11, pt. 1, p. 71; Keyes to Meigs, 21 July 1862, ibid., vol. 14, p. 331; McClellan to Keyes, 22 August 1862, ibid., p. 381; Keyes to Lincoln, 25 August 1862, ibid., p. 382.

54. The quote is from McClellan to Mary Ellen McClellan, 30 August 1862, McClellan, *Selected Correspondence*, p. 419. See also McClellan, "From the Peninsula to Antietam," *Battles and Leaders*, vol. 2, p. 548; Halleck to McClellan, 7 August 1862, *OR*, vol. 14, p. 359.

55. McClellan to Mary Ellen McClellan, 10 August 1862, McClellan, *Selected Correspondence*, p. 389.

56. Fitz John Porter to Burnside (telegram), 27 August 1862, *OR*, vol. 12, pt. 3, pp. 699–700.

57. McClellan's report, 4 August 1863, ibid., vol. 11, pt. 1, p. 104; Weld, *War Diary and Letters*, pp. 80–81; Jacob Cox, *Military Reminiscences of the Civil War*, vol. 1 (New York: Charles Scribner's Sons, 1900), pp. 241–42; McClellan to Porter, 1 September 1862, *OR*, vol. 12, pt. 3, p. 787; Burnside's testimony at Porter's court martial, 31 December 1862, ibid., pt. 2, p. 1002.

58. Gibbon, *Personal Recollections*, p. 66.

59. Quoted in Shelby Foote, *The Civil War: A Narrative*, vol. 1 (New York: Vintage Books, 1986), p. 644.

60. Chase, 22 July 1862, 2 August 1862, 29 August 1862, 30 August 1862, and 1 September 1862, *Chase Papers*, vol. 1, pp. 350, 358, 366, 366–67, 367–68; Welles, 17 August 1862, 31 August 1862, and 1 September 1862, *Welles's Diary*, vol. 1, pp. 83, 93–95, 100–03; Stanton to Halleck, 28 August 1862, *OR*, vol. 12, pt. 3, p. 706; Halleck to Stanton, 30 August 1862, ibid., p. 739.

61. Hay, 5 September 1862, *Hay's Letters and Diaries*, p. 47.

62. Blair's quote is from Welles, 12 September 1862, *Welles's Diary*, vol. 1, p. 126. See also Chase, 29 August 1862 and 30 August 1862, *Chase Papers*, vol. 1, pp. 366, 366–67; Welles, 2 September 1862, 7 September 1862, and 12 September 1862, *Welles's Diary*, vol. 1, pp. 104–5, 115, 124; Hay, 1 September 1862, *Hay's Letters and Diaries*, pp. 44–46; Browning, 29 November 1862, *Browning's Diary*, vol. 1, pp. 589–90.

63. Cox, *Military Reminiscences*, pp. 242–43.

64. Weld, *War Diary and Letters*, p. 82.

65. McClellan, "From the Peninsula to Antietam," p. 551; McClellan's report, 4 August 1863, *OR*, vol. 11, pt. 1, pp. 104–5; Gibbon, *Personal Recollections*, p. 70; Smith, *Smith's Autobiography*, p. 52; Cox, *Military Reminiscences*, pp. 245–46; McClellan to Halleck, 31 August 1862, *OR*, vol. 12, pt. 3, p. 773; Henry Raymond, 23 January 1863, "Extracts from the Journal of Henry J. Raymond," *Scribner's Monthly*, November 1879 to April 1880, vol. 19, p. 423.

66. Pope's report, 3 September 1862, *OR*, vol. 12, pt. 2, pp. 12–17; McClellan to Halleck, 31 August 1862, McClellan, *Selected Correspondence*, p. 426; McClellan to Mary Ellen McClellan, 9 September 1862, ibid., p. 440; Pope to Halleck, 5 September 1862, *OR*, vol. 19, pt. 2, p. 183; Halleck to Pope, 5 September 1862, ibid., p. 183; Welles, 4 September 1862, *Welles's Diary*, vol. 1, pp. 109–10.

67. Chase, 3 September 1862, *Chase Papers*, vol. 1, p. 370; Welles, 2 September 1862, 8 September 1862, and 12 September 1862, *Welles's Diary*, vol. 1, pp. 104, 116, 126; Special Orders No. 223, 5 September 1862, *OR*, vol. 19, pt. 2, p. 188; Halleck to Pope, 5 September 1862, ibid., vol. 12, pt. 3, p. 812.

68. Chase, 6 September 1862, *Chase Papers*, vol. 1, p. 371.

69. Ibid.; James Garfield to Harry Rhodes, 26 September 1862, James Garfield, *The Wild Life of the Army: Civil War Letters of James A. Garfield* (Lansing: Michigan State University Press, 1964), p. 141; McDowell to Lincoln, 6 September 1862, *OR*, vol. 12, pt. 1, p. 39; McClellan to Mary Ellen McClellan, 7 September 1862 and 9 September 1862, McClellan, *Selected Correspondence*, pp. 437–38, 440; Alpheus Williams to Irene Williams, 8 September 1862, *From the Cannon's Mouth: The Civil War Letters of General Alpheus S. Williams*, ed. Milo M. Quaife (Detroit: Wayne State University Press and the Detroit Historical Society, 1959), p. 111; Chase, 5 September 1862 and 7 September 1862, *Chase Papers*, vol. 1, pp. 370, 373; Special Orders No. 224, 6 September 1862, *OR*, vol. 19, pt. 2, p. 197; Townsend, *Rustics in Rebellion*, p. 206; Henry Blake, *Three Years in the Army of the Potomac* (Boston: Lee and Shepard, 1865), p. 135.

70. Welles, 8 September 1862, *Welles's Diary*, vol. 1, p. 118; Hay, 5 September 1862, *Hay's Letters and Diaries*, p. 47; McClellan, "From the Peninsula to Antietam," pp. 551–52; McClellan, *Own Story*, p. 551; McClellan, *Army of the Potomac*, p. 13; Halleck's testimony, 11 March 1863, U.S. Congress, *Reports of the Joint Committee*, p. 453.

71. McClellan to Halleck, 6 September 1862, *OR*, vol. 19, pt. 2, p. 189; McClellan to Lincoln, 6 September 1862, McClellan, *Selected Correspondence*, p. 436. There is no record of Halleck and Lincoln's consenting to Porter's and Franklin's reinstatement, but they obviously did so.

72. McClellan to Lincoln, 6 September 1862, McClellan, *Selected Correspondence*, p. 436; McClellan to Mary Ellen McClellan, 12 September 1862, ibid., p. 450; Chase, 2 September 1862, *Chase Papers*, vol. 1, p. 369; Wainwright, 2 September 1862, 3 September 1862, 6 September 1862, and 15 September 1862, *Diary of Battle*, pp. 90, 91, 93, 98; Halleck to McClellan, 5 September 1862, *OR*, vol. 19, pt. 2, p. 182; Special Orders No. 3, 6 September 1862, ibid., p. 197; Trobriand, *Four Years with the Army of the Potomac*, p. 307.

73. McClellan to Mary Ellen McClellan, 27 July 1861, 25 October 1861, and 26 May 1862, McClellan, *Selected Correspondence*, pp. 70, 111, 277–78; Williams to Williams, 7 December 1861, Williams, *From the Cannon's Mouth*, p. 40; Welles, 12 September 1862, *Welles's Diary*, vol. 1, p. 126; Welles, 28 April 1864 and 9 May 1864, ibid., vol. 2, pp. 18, 26–27; Special Orders No. 4, 7 September 1862, *OR*, vol. 19, pt. 2, p. 202.

74. Special Orders No. 254, 13 September 1862, *OR*, vol. 19, pt. 2, p. 283; Gibbon, *Personal Recollections*, pp. 71–73; Williams to Irene and Mary Williams, 22 September 1862, Williams, *From the Cannon's Mouth*, pp. 123–26; Pope, *Military Memoirs*, pp. 198–99; Welles, 18 September 1862, *Welles's Diary*, vol. 1, p. 140; Special Orders No. 229, 8 September 1862, *OR*, vol. 19, pt. 2, p. 213; Special Orders No. [unknown], 15 September 1862, ibid., p. 297; Mansfield to Halleck, 5 September 1862, ibid., vol. 18, p. 385; Mansfield to Chandler, 21 January 1862, Chandler Papers, reel 1; Drake De Kay to Chandler, 17 February 1862, ibid.; Richard Elliot Winslow III, *General John Sedgwick: The Story of a Union Corps Commander* (Novato, CA: Presidio Press), p. 43.

75. McClellan to Burnside, 19 April 1862, McClellan, *Selected Correspondence*, p. 242; McClellan to Lincoln, 6 September 1862, ibid., p. 436; Williams to Irene and Mary Williams, 22 September 1862, Williams, *From the Cannon's Mouth*, p. 123; Kearny to Kearny, 31 August 1862, Kearny, *Letters from the Peninsula*, p. 167; Pope, "The Second Battle of Bull Run," *Battles and Leaders*, vol. 2, pp. 474–75; Halleck to McClellan, 6 September 1862, *OR*, vol. 19, pt. 2, p. 189; Howard, *Howard's Autobiography*, vol. 1, p. 281; Burnside's report, 14 February 1862, *OR*, vol. 9, p. 80.

76. Hooker to Marcy, 5 September 1862, *OR*, vol. 19, pt. 2, p. 184; Halleck to Nathaniel Banks, 9 September 1862, ibid., p. 227; McClellan to Banks, 9 September 1862, ibid., p. 228; Halleck to McClellan, 11 September 1862, ibid., p. 253; Lincoln to McClellan, 11 September 1862, ibid., p. 253.

77. Orlando Willcox, *Forgotten Valor: The Memoirs, Journals, and Civil War Letters of Orlando B. Willcox*, ed. Robert Garth Scott (Kent, OH: Kent State University Press, 1999), p. 355.

78. Jacob Cox, "The Battle of Antietam," *Battles and Leaders*, vol. 2, pp. 631–32; Special Orders No. [unknown], 15 September 1862, *OR*, vol. 19, pt. 2, p. 297; Hooker, *Army of the Potomac*, pp. 28–29.

79. McClellan to Mary Ellen McClellan, 15 July 1861, McClellan, *Selected Correspondence*, p. 58; McClellan to E. D. Townsend, 19 July 1861, ibid., p. 61; McClellan to Cox, 19 July 1861 and 22 July 1861, ibid., pp. 62, 67; Cox, "The Battle of Antietam," pp. 631–32; McClellan to Halleck, 5 October 1862, *OR*, vol. 19, pt. 2, p. 383; Cox to George Thomas, 4 November 1862, Cox Papers, reel 1.

80. McClellan to Mary Ellen McClellan, 12 September 1862, McClellan, *Selected Correspondence*, p. 450; Willcox, *Forgotten Valor*, pp. 356–57; Cox, "The Battle of Antietam," vol. 2, pp. 631–32; Richard Lewis to Seth Williams, 17 September 1862, *OR*, vol. 19, pt. 2, p. 314; Cox, *Military Reminiscences*, pp. 382–84, 387; [unknown] to Burnside, 16 September 1862, *OR*, vol. 19, pt. 2, p. 308; McClellan, *Own Story*, pp. 586–88.

81. Marcy to Meade, 17 September 1862, *OR*, vol. 19, pt. 2, p. 315; Gibbon, *Personal Recollections*, pp. 86–87; Meade to Margaret Meade, 13 September 1862, 18 September 1862, 20 September 1862, and 1 October 1862, Meade, *Life and Letters*, vol. 1, pp. 309–10, 311, 312, 315–16; McClellan, *Own Story*, p. 140; Porter's report, 7 July 1862, *OR*, vol. 11, pt. 2, p. 226; McDowell's report, 6 November 1862, ibid., vol. 16, p. 345.

82. Alpheus Williams, 20 March 1864, U.S. Army Generals' Reports, reel 2, vol. 3, p. 474.

83. Alpheus Williams to Irene Williams, 12 September 1862, Williams, *From the Cannon's Mouth*, p. 120; Willcox, *Forgotten Valor*, p. 250; Howard, *Howard's Autobiography*, vol. 1, p. 208; Nelson Miles, *Serving the Republic: Memoirs of the Civil and Military Life of Nelson A. Miles* (New York: Harper and Brothers, 1911), p. 46; Favill, 28 May 1862, *Diary of a Young Officer*, p. 103.

84. Wilson, *Under the Old Flag*, vol. 1, pp. 112–14.

85. Scrymser, *In Times of Peace and War*, p. 34; William Franklin, "Notes on Crampton's Gap and Antietam," *Battles and Leaders*, vol. 2, p. 597; Howard, *Howard's Autobiography*, vol. 1, p. 298; McClellan, *Own Story*, p. 601; Miles, *Serving the Republic*, p. 46; Franklin's testimony, 30 March 1863, U.S. Congress, *Reports of the Joint Committee*, pp. 626–27.

86. D. B. Sackett, 20 February 1876, McClellan, *Own Story*, pp. 609–10.

87. Ibid.; Wilson, *Under the Old Flag*, vol. 1, p. 110; McClellan, *Own Story*, pp. 602–4; Sackett, 9 March 1876, ibid., pp. 610–11.

88. Wilson, *Under the Old Flag*, vol. 1, p. 114; Swinton, *Campaigns*, p. 223; Burnside, *Army of the Potomac*, pp. 17–18; McClellan, *Own Story*, pp. 607–8; Edwin Sumner's testimony, 18 February 1863, U.S. Congress, *Reports of the Joint Committee*, p. 369.

89. McClellan to Mary Ellen McClellan, 18 September 1862, McClellan, *Selected Correspondence*, p. 469.

90. McClellan's report, 4 August 1863, OR, vol. 19, pt. 1, p. 69.

91. Marcy to John Reynolds, 30 September 1862, ibid., vol. 51, pt. 1, p. 872; James Biddle to Gertrude [unknown], 30 September 1862 and 17 October 1862, Biddle Letters.

92. Special Orders No. 266, 29 September 1862, OR, vol. 19, pt. 1, p. 367; Patrick, 24 September 1862, *Inside Lincoln's Army*, p. 153; McClellan to Halleck, 11 September 1862, OR, vol. 19, pt. 1, p. 252; Halleck to McClellan, 11 September 1862, ibid., p. 252; Hooker to Seth Williams, 12 September 1862, ibid., p. 273; Meade to Margaret Meade, 20 September 1862, 29 September 1862, and 1 October 1862, Meade, *Life and Letters*, vol. 1, pp. 312, 314–15, 315–16; Marcy to Reynolds, 30 September 1862, OR, vol. 51, pt. 1, p. 872; McClellan, *Own Story*, p. 140; McClellan to Cameron, 8 September 1861, McClellan, *Selected Correspondence*, p. 97.

93. Wainwright, 18 December 1862, *Diary of Battle*, p. 149; Porter, "Hanover House and Gaines' Mill," *Battles and Leaders*, vol. 2, p. 328; William Smith, "Franklin's 'Left Grand Division,'" ibid., vol. 3, pp. 132–33; Weld, *War Diary and Letters*, p. 200; Meade to Margaret Meade, 16 August 1862 and 30 December 1862, Meade, *Life and Letters*, vol. 1, pp. 301–2, 342–43; Howard, *Howard's Autobiography*, vol. 1, p. 402; Porter to Seth Williams, 16 July 1862, OR, vol. 51, pt. 1, p. 721; McClellan, *Own Story*, p. 140; Reynolds to his sisters, 1 July 1861, Reynolds Papers; Charles Veil, "An Old Boy's Personal Recollections and Reminiscences of the Civil War," Veil Folder, p. 51.

94. The quote is from McClellan to Halleck, 25 October 1862, OR, vol. 19, pt. 2, p. 483. See also Chase to Oran Follett, 25 September 1862, Chase, *Chase Papers*, vol. 3, pp. 284–85.

95. Darius Couch to Seth Williams, 21 July 1862, Couch Papers; Couch to Marcy, early June 1862, ibid.; Porter, "The Battle of Malvern Hill," *Battles and Leaders*, vol. 2, p. 424; Special Orders No. 274, 7 October 1862, OR, vol. 19, pt. 2, p. 400; McClellan, *Own Story*, p. 139; Favill, 12 May 1863, *Diary of a Young Officer*, p. 236; Heintzelman to McClellan, 1 June 1862, OR, vol. 51, pt. 1, p. 649; Couch to Andrew Johnson, 8 May 1865, ibid., vol. 48, pt. 3, p. 442; Wilson, *Under the Old Flag*, vol. 1, pp. 124–25.

96. Alpheus Williams to Irene and Mary Williams, 22 September 1862, Williams,

From the Cannon's Mouth, p. 131; Alpheus Williams to Mary Williams, 23 September 1862, ibid., p. 133; Alpheus Williams to Lew [unknown], 23 September 1862, ibid., pp. 134–35; Alpheus Williams to Mary Williams, 5 October 1862, ibid., Alpheus Williams to Marcy, 16 October 1862, *OR*, vol. 19, pt. 2, p. 434; Banks, June 1862, *OR*, vol. 15, p. 552.

97. Slocum to Franklin, 4 December 1862, Franklin Papers; Alpheus Williams to his daughter, 28 October 1862 and April 15, 1865, Williams, *From the Cannon's Mouth*, pp. 141, 294; Porter, "Hanover House and Gaines' Mill," *Battles and Leaders*, vol. 2, p. 335; Howard in Rossiter Johnson, *Campfire and Battlefield: The Classic Illustrated History of the Civil War* (New York: Fairfax Press, 1978), p. 518; Franklin, 17 May 1862, *OR*, vol. 11, pt. 1, p. 616; Franklin, 30 September 1862, ibid., vol. 19, pt. 1, p. 374; Slocum to Howland, 28 September 1862, 1 November 1862, 6 June 1863, Howland Papers; Charles Fessenden to [unknown], 7 May 1863, Charles Fessenden Morse, *Letters Written during the Civil War, 1861–1865* (Boston: privately printed, 1898), p. 138; Frank Haskell, 16 July 1863, *Haskell of Gettysburg: His Life and Civil War Papers*, ed. Frank L. Byrne and Andrew T. Weaver (Madison: State Historical Society of Wisconsin, 1970), p. 133.

98. Richard Irwin to Seth Williams, 13 October 1862, *OR*, vol. 19, pt. 2, p. 419; Marcy to Heintzelman, 1 November 1862, ibid. p. 526; Heintzelman to E. D. Townsend, 20 November 1864, Heintzelman Papers, reel 10, p. 8; [Indecipherable] to Heintzelman, 28 October 1862, ibid., p. 6; Heintzelman's notes on George McClellan's report, 28 February 1864, ibid., reel 9; Heintzelman's diary, 24 October 1862, 28 October 1862, 31 October 1862, 1 November 1862, and 13 November 1862, ibid., reel 7.

99. McClellan to Mary Ellen McClellan, 29 September 1862, McClellan, *Selected Correspondence*, p. 486.

100. Couch, "Sumner's 'Right Grand Division,'" *Battles and Leaders*, vol. 3, pp. 105–6; Special Orders No. 280, 13 October 1862, *OR*, vol. 19, pt. 2, p. 420; McClellan to Halleck, 23 October 1862, ibid., p. 469; Wilson, *Under the Old Flag*, vol. 1, pp. 124–25; McClellan, *Own Story*, p. 583.

101. Lincoln to McClellan (telegram), 25 October 1862, *OR*, vol. 19, pt. 2, p. 485.

102. The quote is from Couch, "Sumner's 'Right Grand Division,'" pp. 105–6. See also Lincoln to McClellan, 13 October 1862, *OR*, vol. 21, p. 97; Wilson, *Under the Old Flag*, vol. 1, pp. 121–23.

103. Smith, *Smith's Autobiography*, p. 57; Cox, *Military Reminiscences*, pp. 359–60; Wilson, *Under the Old Flag*, vol. 1, p. 126; Villard, *Villard Memoirs*, vol. 1, p. 337; John Cochrane, "Cochrane's Memoir," pp. 28–29.

104. Chase, 7 October 1862 and 11 October 1862, *Chase Papers*, vol. 1, pp. 415, 419; Wilson, *Under the Old Flag*, vol. 1, pp. 121–23; Cochrane, "Cochrane's Memoir," pp. 29–33.

105. Garfield to Rhodes, 26 September 1862, *Wild Life of the Army*, pp. 141–42; McClellan to Hooker, 20 September 1862, McClellan, *Selected Correspondence*, p. 474; McClellan to Lincoln, 20 September 1862, ibid., pp. 474–75; Chase, 23 September 1862 and 25 September 1862, *Chase Papers*, vol. 1, pp. 396, 400–01; Chase to Follett, 25 September 1862, ibid., vol. 3, pp. 284–85; Chase to Hiram Berry, 26 October 1862, ibid., p. 306; McClellan to Halleck, 19 September 1862, *OR*, vol. 19, pt. 1, p. 182.

106. Heintzelman's diary, 18 October 1862, Heintzelman Papers, reel 7.

107. Ibid., 24 October 1862.

108. Chase, 27 September 1862, *Chase Papers*, vol. 1, p. 404; Wainwright, 19 September 1862, *Diary of Battle*, pp. 103–4; Meade to Margaret Meade, 20 September 1862, Meade, *Life and Letters*, vol. 1, p. 312; Meade to George Sergeant Meade, 11 October

1862, ibid., p. 318; Meade to Margaret Meade, 12 October 1862, ibid., pp. 318–19; Charles Hamlin, Gould, *Berry*, pp. 228–29; Hooker to Henry Wilson, 8 December 1864, OR, vol. 45, pt. 2, p. 109.

109. The quote is from Foote, *Civil War*, vol. 1, p. 753. See also Welles, 4 November 1862, *Welles's Diary*, vol. 1, p. 179; Browning, 29 November 1862, *Browning's Diary*, vol. 1, p. 590; McClellan to Mary Ellen McClellan, 7 November 1862, McClellan, *Selected Correspondence*, p. 520.

110. McClellan to officers and soldiers of the Army of the Potomac, 7 November 1862, OR, vol. 19, pt. 2, p. 551.

111. The quote is from Meade to Margaret Meade, 2 January 1863, Meade, *Life and Letters*, vol. 1, p. 345. See also John Gibbon to his wife, 9 November 1862, Gibbon Letters; Patrick, 11 November 1862, *Inside Lincoln's Army*, pp. 174–75; Couch, "Sumner's 'Right Grand Division,'" pp. 106–7; Gibbon, *Personal Recollections*, pp. 96–97; Meade to Margaret Meade, 3 December 1862, Meade, *Life and Letters*, vol. 1, p. 335; Smith, *Smith's Autobiography*, p. 58; Wilson, *Under the Old Flag*, vol. 1, pp. 121–23, 126; John Haley, 16 November 1862, *The Rebel Yell and the Yankee Hurrah: The Civil War Journal of a Maine Volunteer*, ed. Ruth L. Silliker (Camden, ME: Down East Books, 1985), p. 50; Alexander Hays to John McFadden, 19 November 1862, Hays, *Hays's Life and Letters*, p. 279.

112. Wainwright, 25 January 1863, *Diary of Battle*, p. 161; Lincoln, 21 January 1863, "Order Approving Sentence of Fitz-John Porter," *Collected Works*, vol. 6, p. 67; Carl Schurz, *The Reminiscences of Carl Schurz*, vol. 2 (New York: McClure Company, 1907), pp. 381–82; Strong, 22 January 1863, *Diary of the Civil War*, p. 289; Lincoln, 5 November 1862, OR, vol. 19, pt. 2, p. 545; Browning, 29 November 1862, *Browning's Diary*, vol. 1, p. 589; Alexander McClure, *Colonel Alexander K. McClure's Recollections of Half a Century* (Salem, MA: Salem Press, 1902), pp. 435–36; Chandler to his wife, 25 January 1863, Chandler Papers, reel 1.

113. Seth Williams to William Burns, 29 October 1862, Burns Papers.

Chapter 2. Burnside's Unhappy and Insecure Tenure:
November 1862 to January 1863

1. Orlando Willcox, *Forgotten Valor: The Memoirs, Journals, and Civil War Letters of Orlando B. Willcox*, ed. Robert Garth Scott (Kent, OH: Kent State University Press, 1999), pp. 382–83.

2. The quote is from Herman Haupt, *Reminiscences of General Herman Haupt* (Milwaukee, WI: Wright and Joys, 1901), p. 160. See also Willcox, *Forgotten Valor*, pp. 382–83; Darius Couch, "Sumner's 'Right Grand Division,'" *Battles and Leaders of the Civil War*, vol. 3, ed. Robert Underwood Johnson and Clarence Clough Buel (New York: Thomas Yoseloff, 1956), p. 106; Ambrose Burnside, 19 December 1862, U.S. Congress, *Reports of the Joint Committee on the Conduct of the War*, 37th Cong., 3d sess. (Washington, DC: Government Printing Office, 1863), p. 650.

3. The quote is from Carl Schurz, *The Reminiscences of Carl Schurz*, vol. 2 (New York: McClure, 1907), pp. 397–98. See also John Gibbon, *Personal Recollections of the Civil War* (New York: G. P. Putnam's Sons, 1928), pp. 252–53; Alpheus Williams to Lew [unknown], 16 November 1862, Alpheus Williams, *From the Cannon's Mouth: The Civil War Letters of General Alpheus S. Williams*, ed. Milo M. Quaife (Detroit, MI: Wayne State University Press and the Detroit Historical Society, 1959), p. 151; Charles Wainwright,

10 November 1862, *A Diary of Battle: The Personal Journals of Colonel Charles S. Wainwright*, ed. Allan Nevins (New York: Harcourt, Brace and World, 1962), p. 125; Willcox, *Forgotten Valor*, p. 53; Willcox to Marie Willcox, 19 November 1862, ibid., p. 394; Couch, "Sumner's 'Right Grand Division,'" pp. 106–7; William Smith, "Franklin's 'Left Grand Division,'" *Battles and Leaders*, vol. 3, p. 133; George Meade to Margaret Meade, 8 November 1862, George Meade, *The Life and Letters of George Gordon Meade*, vol. 1, ed. George Meade (New York: Charles Scribner's Sons, 1913), p. 325; Howard, *Howard's Autobiography*, vol. 1, pp. 313–14; Smith, *Smith's Autobiography*, p. 59; Jacob Cox, *Military Reminiscences of the Civil War*, vol. 1 (New York: Charles Scribner's Sons, 1900), pp. 389–90; Alexander Hays to John McFadden, 19 November 1862, Hays, *Hays's Life and Letters*, p. 279; John Cochrane to Abraham Lincoln, 14 November 1862, Lincoln Papers; John Reynolds to his sisters, 30 November 1862, Reynolds Papers.

 4. Henry Halleck to Burnside, 10 November 1862, *OR*, vol. 19, pt. 2, p. 564; General Orders No. 184, 14 November 1862, ibid., p. 583.

 5. Meade to Margaret Meade, 24 November 1862, Meade, *Life and Letters*, vol. 1, pp. 331–32.

 6. The quote is from Willcox to Marie Willcox, n.d., *Forgotten Valor*, p. 413. See also ibid., p. 349; Willcox to Marie Willcox, 3 October 1862, 18 October 1862, 16 November 1862, 19 November 1862, 27 November 1862, and 3 December 1862, ibid., pp. 370, 374, 380, 394, 401, 402; Willcox to Zachariah Chandler, December 1862, Chandler Papers, reel 1; Burnside's report, 30 September 1862, *OR*, vol. 19, pt. 1, p. 421.

 7. Thomas Hyde, *Following the Greek Cross: Or, Memories of the Sixth Army Corps* (Boston: Houghton Mifflin, 1894), p. 117.

 8. William Franklin to William Wallace Burns, 20 October 1873, Burns Papers.

 9. The quote is from Smith, *Smith's Autobiography*, p. 50n. See also John Sedgwick to Ellen Sedgwick Welch, 27 April 1862, Sedgwick, *Sedgwick's Correspondence*, vol. 2, pp. 44–45; Smith, "Franklin's 'Left Grand Division,'" pp. 132–33; Theodore Lyman, 2 June 1864, *Meade's Headquarters, 1863–1865: Letters of Colonel Theodore Lyman from The Wilderness to Appomattox*, ed. George Agassiz (Boston: Atlantic Monthly Press, 1922), p. 139; Smith, *Smith's Autobiography*, pp. 38–39.

 10. Salmon Chase, 15 September 1862, *Chase Papers*, vol. 1, p. 389; William Averell, "With the Cavalry on the Peninsula," *Battles and Leaders*, vol. 2, p. 430; George McClellan's report, 4 August 1863, *OR*, vol. 11, pt. 1, p. 19; Samuel Heintzelman to Richard Irwin, 15 September 1862, ibid., vol. 19, pt. 2, p. 300; Charles Francis Adams Jr. to his Mom, 12 May 1863, Worthington Chauncey Ford, ed., *A Cycle of Adams Letters, 1861–1865*, vol. 2 (Boston: Houghton Mifflin, 1920), p. 8; James Harrison Wilson, *Under the Old Flag: Recollections of Military Operations in the War for the Union, the Spanish War and the Boxer Rebellion, etc.*, vol. 1 (Westport, CT: Greenwood Press, 1971), pp. 321, 362; Robert McAllister to Ellen McAllister, 7 January 1863, McAllister, *McAllister's Letters*, p. 253; Hiram Berry, 12 November 1862, Gould, *Berry*, p. 211; Special Orders No. 241, 22 August 1862, *OR*, vol. 51, pt. 1, p. 754; Regis de Trobriand, *Four Years with the Army of the Potomac*, trans. George K. Dauchy (Boston: Ticknor, 1889), p. 337; George Alfred Townsend, *Rustics in Rebellion: A Yankee Reporter on the Road to Richmond, 1861–65* (Chapel Hill: University of North Carolina Press, 1950), p. 77; Fitz John Porter, 5 July 1862, *OR*, vol. 11, pt. 2, p. 334; George Augustus Armes, *Ups and Downs of an Army Officer* (Washington, DC, 1900), pp. 141–42; Halleck to Nathaniel Banks, 15 September 1862, *OR*, vol. 19, pt. 2, p. 297.

 11. Williams to Irene and Mary Williams, 15 July 1864, Williams, *From the Cannon's*

Mouth, p. 331; Wainwright, 6 February 1863, *Diary of Battle*, pp. 162–63; John Hay, 9 September 1863, *Hay's Letters and Diaries*, p. 86; Special Orders No. 305, 30 October 1862, *OR*, vol. 19, pt. 2, p. 514; Stephen Weld to his Dad, 31 October 1862, Stephen Minot Weld, *War Diary and Letters of Stephen Minot Weld, 1861–1865* (Boston: Massachusetts Historical Society, 1979), p. 146; Philip Kearny to J. Watts de Peyster, 21 January 1862, Julia Lorrilard Butterfield, ed., *A Biographical Memorial of General Daniel Butterfield* (New York: Grafton Press, 1904), p. 31; Howard, *Howard's Autobiography*, vol. 1, p. 139; Porter to Seth Williams, 26 September 1862, *OR*, vol. 51, pt. 1, p. 863; Daniel Butterfield to Chandler, 8 February 1862, Chandler Papers, reel 1; Villard, *Villard Memoirs*, vol. 1, pp. 349–50; Theodore Ayrault Dodge, 12 March 1863, *On Campaign with the Army of the Potomac: The Civil War Journal of Theodore Ayrault Dodge*, ed. Stephen Sears (New York: First Cooper Square Press, 2001), p. 211.

12. James Garfield to Harry Garfield, 5 October 1862, James Garfield, *The Wild Life of the Army: Civil War Letters of James A. Garfield* (Lansing: Michigan State University Press, 1964), p. 153; Schurz, *Reminiscences*, vol. 2, pp. 348–50, 383–84; James Rusling to his friends, 25 November 1862, James Rusling, *Men and Things I Saw in Civil War Days* (New York: Eaton and Mains, 1899), p. 285; Schurz to Lincoln, 28 June 1862, *OR*, vol. 51, pt. 1, p. 708; Heintzelman's diary, 22 November 1862, Heintzelman Papers, reel 7; Adam De Gurowski, 25 September 1862, *Diary*, vol. 1 (Boston: Lee and Shepard, 1862), p. 281; Charles Sumner to Lincoln, September or October 1861, Lincoln Papers; Franz Sigel to Lincoln, 26 September 1862 and 9 October 1862, ibid.; Edwin Stanton to Lincoln, 17 October 1862, ibid.; Halleck to John Pope, 26 August 1862, *OR*, vol. 12, pt. 3, p. 666.

13. Meade to Margaret Meade, 20 November 1862 and 24 November 1862, *Life and Letters*, vol. 1, pp. 329, 331–33.

14. Halleck to Burnside, 15 November 1862, *OR*, vol. 19, pt. 2, p. 579.

15. Couch, "Sumner's 'Right Grand Division,'" pp. 109–10.

16. Ibid., pp. 107–8; Darius Couch's autobiographical sketch, 1873, Couch Papers, pp. 123–26; Willcox to Marie Willcox, 16 December 1862, Willcox, *Forgotten Valor*, p. 404; Willcox to Charles Willcox, 19 December 1862, ibid., p. 406; Rush Hawkins, "Why Burnside Did Not Renew the Attack on Fredericksburg," *Battles and Leaders*, vol. 3, p. 126; Smith, "Franklin's 'Left Grand Division,'" pp. 128–29; Howard, *Howard's Autobiography*, vol. 1, p. 321.

17. Smith, "Franklin's 'Left Grand Division,'" pp. 128–29; Joseph Hooker to Stanton, 19 November 1862 and 23 April 1863, *OR*, vol. 21, pp. 773, 855; Meade to Margaret Meade, 13 November 1862, 24 November 1862, and 2 December 1862, Meade, *Life and Letters*, vol. 1, pp. 327, 331–32, 335; Hooker to Henry Wilson, 8 December 1864, *OR*, vol. 45, pt. 2, p. 109; Smith, *Smith's Autobiography*, p. 59; Hooker, *Army of the Potomac. History of Its Campaigns, the Peninsula, Maryland, Fredericksburg. Testimony of Its Three Commanders, Maj.-Gen. G. B. McClellan, Maj.-Gen. A. E. Burnside, and Maj.-Gen. Joseph Hooker before the Congressional Committee on the Conduct of the War* (New York: Tribune Association, 1863), p. 29; Hooker to Stanton, 4 December 1862, Stanton Papers, vol. 9; Villard, *Villard Memoirs*, vol. 1, pp. 347–48.

18. The quote is from Harry Humphreys to his Mom, 18 December 1862, Humphreys Letters. See also Couch's autobiographical sketch, 1873, Couch Papers, pp. 123–26; Couch, "Sumner's 'Right Grand Division,'" pp. 113–14; Burnside, *Army of the Potomac*, p. 24; Hooker, ibid., p. 29; Burnside's Report, n.d., *OR*, vol. 21, p. 94; Villard, *Villard Memoirs*, vol. 1, p. 370; Elizabeth Blair Lee, 11 January 1863, *Wartime Washington: The*

Civil War Letters of Elizabeth Blair Lee, ed. Virginia Jeans Laas (Urbana: University of Illinois Press, 1991), p. 229.

19. Willcox to Charles Willcox, 19 December 1862, *Forgotten Valor*, p. 406; Couch, "Sumner's 'Right Grand Division,'" p. 117; Hawkins, "Why Burnside Did Not Renew the Attack on Fredericksburg," p. 127; Gibbon, *Personal Recollections*, p. 105; Burnside, *Army of the Potomac*, p. 20.

20. Burnside, *Army of the Potomac*, p. 20.

21. The quote is from Smith, "Franklin's 'Left Grand Division,'" p. 138. See also Willcox, *Forgotten Valor*, p. 391; Willcox to Charles Willcox, 19 December 1862, ibid., p. 406; Couch, "Sumner's 'Right Grand Division,'" pp. 117–18; Hawkins, "Why Burnside Did Not Renew the Attack on Fredericksburg," p. 127; Ambrose Burnside, *Army of the Potomac*, p. 20.

22. Smith, "Franklin's 'Left Grand Division,'" p. 138; Lincoln to Burnside (telegram), 30 December 1862, *OR*, vol. 21, p. 900; Smith, *Smith's Autobiography*, p. 62.

23. Franklin and Smith to Lincoln, 20 December 1862, *OR*, vol. 21, pp. 868–70; Lincoln to Franklin and Smith, 22 December 1862, Abraham Lincoln, *The Collected Works of Abraham Lincoln*, vol. 6, ed. Roy Basler (New Brunswick, NJ: Rutgers University Press, 1953), p. 15.

24. John Newton's testimony, 9 February 1863, U.S. Congress, *Reports of the Joint Committee*, pp. 730–31, 735–38; Franklin to Halleck, 1 June 1863, *OR*, vol. 21, p. 1009.

25. Newton's testimony, 9 February 1863, U.S. Congress, *Reports of the Joint Committee*, pp. 731–33; Cochrane's testimony, 9–10 February 1863, ibid., pp. 741–46; Cochrane, "Cochrane's Memoir," pp. 39–40, 48–52; Villard, *Villard Memoirs*, vol. 1, p. 390.

26. Lincoln to Halleck, 1 January 1862, Lincoln, *Collected Works*, vol. 6, p. 31; Lincoln to Burnside, 8 January 1863, ibid. p. 46; Burnside to Lincoln, 1 January 1863 and 5 January 1863, *OR*, vol. 21, pp. 941, 944–45; Halleck to Burnside, 9 May 1863, ibid., p. 1006; Halleck to Franklin, 29 May 1863, ibid., p. 1009; Smith to Franklin, 29 May 1863, ibid., p. 1010; Halleck to Franklin, 5 June 1863, ibid., p. 1011; Franklin to Halleck, 6 June 1863, ibid., p. 1011; Halleck to Franklin, 17 April 1866, ibid., p. 1012; Meade to Margaret Meade, 2 January 1863, Meade, *Life and Letters*, vol. 1, p. 344; Burnside, *Army of the Potomac*, p. 22; Henry Raymond, 22 January 1863, "Extracts from the Journal of Henry J. Raymond," *Scribner's Monthly*, November 1879 to April 1880, vol. 19, p. 422; John Parke's testimony, 28 January 1863, U.S. Congress, *Reports of the Joint Committee*, p. 728.

27. Wainwright, 25 December 1862, *Diary of Battle*, p. 149; Meade to Margaret Meade, 17 December 1862, 23 December 1862, and 26 December 1862, Meade, *Life and Letters*, vol. 1, pp. 339, 341, 341–42; Burnside's report, n.d., *OR*, vol. 21, p. 93.

28. Butterfield to Henry Wilson, 24 December 1862, Butterfield, *Biographical Memorial of Butterfield*, p. 112; Butterfield to Frederick Seward, 24 December 1862, Stanton Papers, vol. 10; Hooker to Stanton, 28 December 1862, ibid., vol. 10; Butterfield to Chandler, 25 December 1862, Chandler Papers, reel 1; Butterfield to Lincoln, 12 November 1863, Lincoln Papers.

29. Wainwright, 19 January 1863 and 21 January 1863, *Diary of Battle*, pp. 157–58, 159–60; Couch, "Sumner's 'Right Grand Division,'" pp. 118–19; Burnside, 5 January 1862, *OR*, vol. 21, p. 945; Meade to Margaret Meade, 23 January 1863, Meade, *Life and Letters*, vol. 1, pp. 348–49; Raymond, 22 January 1863, "Extracts," pp. 420–21, 421–22; *New York Times*, 6 February 1863, p. 5; Reynolds to his sisters, 23 January 1863, Reynolds Papers; Smith, *Smith's Autobiography*, p. 64.

30. The quote is from Smith, *Smith's Autobiography*, pp. 65–66. See also Meade to Margaret Meade, 23 January 1863, Meade, *Life and Letters*, vol. 1, pp. 348–49; George Templeton Strong, 11 February 1863, *Diary of the Civil War, 1860–1865*, ed. Allan Nevins (New York: Macmillan, 1962), p. 297; Smith, "Franklin's 'Left Grand Division,'" p. 138; Hooker to Stanton, 23 April 1863, OR, vol. 25, pt. 2, p. 855; Franklin, "Reply of Maj. Gen. William B. Franklin, to the report of the Joint Committee of Congress," 6 April 1863, ibid., vol. 51, pt. 1, p. 1026; Raymond, 22 January 1863, "Extracts," pp. 422–23; Marsena Patrick, 4 January 1863, *Inside Lincoln's Army: The Diary of Marsena Rudolph Patrick, Provost Marshal General, Army of the Potomac*, ed. David Sparks (New York: Thomas Yoseloff, 1964), p. 199; Couch, 1 August 1873, U.S. Army Generals' Reports, reel 5, vol. 9, pp. 77–79.

31. Willcox to Marie Willcox, 21 November 1862, *Forgotten Valor*, p. 396; J. L. Van Buren to Edward Ferrero, 26 April 1863, OR, vol. 21, p. 1123; General Orders No. 8, 23 January 1863, ibid., p. 998; Smith, *Smith's Autobiography*, pp. 30, 65–66; Brooks to his Dad, 17 February 1863, Brooks Papers, Civil War Letter Folder.

32. Burnside, *Army of the Potomac*, p. 23; Raymond, 23 January 1863 and 24 January 1863, "Extracts," pp. 423, 703–4.

33. Benjamin Charles, "Hooker's Appointment and Removal," *Battles and Leaders*, vol. 3, pp. 239–40; Alexander McClure, *Colonel Alexander K. McClure's Recollections of Half a Century* (Salem, MA: Salem Press, 1902), pp. 346–47; Raymond, 24 January 1863, "Extracts," pp. 704–6.

34. Charles, "Hooker's Appointment and Removal," pp. 239–40; General Orders No. 20, 25 January 1863, OR, vol. 21, p. 1004; Meade to Margaret Meade, 4 January 1863, Meade, *Life and Letters*, vol. 1, p. 346; Browning, 26 January 1863, *The Browning's Diary*, vol. 1, p. 619; Raymond, 24 January 1863, "Extracts," pp. 704–6; Horatio Nelson Taft, 4 January 1863, *The Diary of Horatio Nelson Taft*, vol. 2, http://memory.loc.gov/ ammem/tafthtml/tafthome.html.

35. The quote is from Zenas Bliss, Reminiscences of Zenas R. Bliss, vol. 4, USAMHI, pp. 48–49. See also Burnside, *Army of the Potomac*, pp. 23–24.

Chapter 3. Fighting Joe's Big Opportunity: January to June 1863

1. Abraham Lincoln to Joseph Hooker, 26 January 1863, Abraham Lincoln, *The Collected Works of Abraham Lincoln*, vol. 6, ed. Roy Basler (New Brunswick, NJ: Rutgers University Press, 1953), pp. 78–79. See also Browning, 23 January 1863, *Browning's Diary*, vol. 1, p. 619; Zachariah Chandler to his wife, 26 January 1863, Chandler Papers, reel 1; Noah Brooks, *Washington D.C. in Lincoln's Time*, ed. Herbert Mitgang (Athens: University of Georgia Press, 1989), pp. 56–57.

2. Stoneman's quote is found in Alexander McClure, *Colonel Alexander K. McClure's Recollections of Half a Century* (Salem, MA: Salem Press, 1902), p. 348. See also Gideon Welles, 24 January 1863, *Welles's Diary*, vol. 1, pp. 229–30; Hooker's testimony, 11 March 1865, U.S. Congress, *Reports of the Joint Committee on the Conduct of the War*, 38th Cong., 2d sess., pt. 1 (Washington, DC: Government Printing Office, 1865), pp. 111–12.

3. Charles Francis Adams, Jr., *Charles Francis Adams, 1835–1915: An Autobiography* (Boston: Houghton Mifflin, 1916), p. 161.

4. Charles Wainwright, 31 January 1863 and 19 April 1863, *A Diary of Battle: The Personal Journals of Colonel Charles S. Wainwright*, ed. Allan Nevins (New York: Harcourt,

Brace and World, 1962), pp. 161–62, 182–83; Charles Schurz, *The Reminiscences of Carl Schurz*, vol. 2 (New York: McClure Company, 1907), p. 403; Darius Couch, "Sumner's 'Right Grand Division,'" *Battles and Leaders of the Civil War*, vol. 3, ed. Robert Underwood Johnson and Clarence Clough Buel (New York: Thomas Yoseloff, 1956), p. 236; Darius Couch, "The Chancellorsville Campaign," ibid., p. 154; John Gibbon, *Personal Recollections of the Civil War* (New York: G. P. Putnam's Sons, 1928), pp. 107–9, 121–22; Abner Doubleday, *Chancellorsville and Gettysburg* (New York: Da Capo Press, 1994), pp. 1–3; Stephen Weld to his Dad, 7 March 1863, Stephen Minot Weld, *War Diary and Letters of Stephen Minot Weld, 1861–1865* (Boston: Massachusetts Historical Society, 1979), p. 158; George Meade to Margaret Meade, 26 January 1863, George Meade, *The Life and Letters of George Gordon Meade*, vol. 1, ed. George Meade (New York: Charles Scribner's Sons, 1913), p. 351; Regis de Trobriand, *Four Years with the Army of the Potomac*, trans. George K. Dauchy (Boston: Ticknor, 1889), pp. 413–14; Henry Slocum to Joseph Howland, 4 February 1863, Howland Papers; Daniel Sickles's testimony, 25 February 1864, U.S. Congress, *Reports of the Joint Committee*, pp. 14–15; David Birney's testimony, 7 March 1864, ibid., p. 37; Birney to George Gross, 26 February 1863, Birney Papers; William Brooks to his Dad, 17 February 1863, Brooks Papers, Civil War Letters Folder; Gouverneur Warren to Emily Chase, 17 April 1863, Warren Papers, Folder 2; Gould, *Berry*, pp. 234–35.

5. Marsena Patrick, 30 January 1863, 1 February 1863, 2 February 1863, 21 February 1863, and 11 March 1863, *Inside Lincoln's Army: The Diary of Marsena Rudolph Patrick, Provost Marshal General, Army of the Potomac*, ed. David Sparks (New York: Thomas Yoseloff, 1964), pp. 209, 210, 210, 215, 221; Couch, "The Chancellorsville Campaign," p. 154; Weld to his Dad, 28 April 1863, *War Diary and Letters*, p. 185; Meade to Margaret Meade, 26 January 1863 and 13 February 1863, Meade, *Life and Letters*, vol. 1, pp. 351, 354; Daniel Butterfield to Henry Scudder, 29 July 1863, Julia Lorrilard Butterfield, ed., *A Biographical Memorial of General Daniel Butterfield* (New York: Grafton Press, 1904), pp. 132–33; Birney to Gross, 31 January 1863, Birney Papers; Warren to Emily Chase, 20 May 1863, Warren Papers, Folder 3.

6. George McClellan to Mary Ellen McClellan, 18 August 1862 and 5 November 1862, George McClellan, *Selected Correspondence*, pp. 396, 518; Wainwright, 19 April 1863, *Diary of Battle*, p. 183; Patrick, 12 February 1863, *Inside Lincoln's Army*, p. 213; George Stoneman to Seth Williams, 23 February 1863, OR, vol. 25, pt. 2, p. 110; Trobriand, *Four Years with the Army of the Potomac*, pp. 426–27.

7. Wainwright, 19 February 1862, 30 March 1862, and 8 April 1863, *Diary of Battle*, pp. 17, 30, 178; George Templeton Strong, 17 May 1863, *Diary of the Civil War, 1860–1865*, ed. Allan Nevins (New York: Macmillan, 1962), p. 323; Meade to Margaret Meade, 26 January 1863, 28 January 1863, and 13 February 1863, Meade, *Life and Letters*, vol. 1, pp. 351, 352, 254; James Rusling to his friends, 28 September 1862, James F. Rusling, *Men and Things I Saw in Civil War Days* (New York: Eaton and Mains, 1899), p. 277; Rusling to his Dad, 20 October 1862, ibid., p. 281; Rusling to his friends, 28 December 1862, ibid., p. 292; Robert McAllister to Ellen McAllister, 27 September 1862, McAllister, *McAllister's Letters*, p. 211; Robert McAllister to Sarah McAllister, 28 September 1862, ibid., p. 212; Robert McAllister to Ellen McAllister, 3 October 1862, ibid., p. 214; Samuel Heintzelman's diary, 5 July 1862, Heintzelman Papers, reel 7; Trobriand, *Four Years with the Army of the Potomac*, pp. 398, 426–27; Hooker's report, 8 June 1862, OR, vol. 11, pt. 1, p. 819; Hooker's report, 14 July 1862, ibid., pt. 2, p. 110; W. A. Swanberg, *Sickles the Incredible* (New York: Charles Scribner's Sons, 1956), pp. 127–28, 156–58; Birney to Gross, 16 March 1863, Birney Papers; Thurlow Weed to Lincoln, 23

May 1861, Lincoln Papers; Ira Harris to Lincoln, 2 October 1862, ibid.; Warren to Emily Chase, 17 April 1863, Warren Papers, Folder 2.

8. Hooker to J. C. Kelton, 6 February 1863, *OR*, vol. 25, pt. 2, p. 52.

9. Orlando Willcox to Charles Willcox, 30 January 1863, Orlando Willcox, *Forgotten Valor: The Memoirs, Journals, and Civil War Letters of Orlando B. Willcox*, ed. Robert Garth Scott (Kent, OH: Kent State University Press, 1999), p. 415; Willcox to Marie Willcox, 5 February 1863, ibid., p. 416; Hooker to Henry Halleck, 3 February 1863, *OR*, vol. 25, pt. 2, p. 44; Halleck to Hooker, 4 February 1863, ibid.; Hooker to Edwin Stanton, 25 February 1864, ibid., vol. 32, pt. 2, pp. 467–68; Smith, *Smith's Autobiography*, pp. 66–67.

10. John Sedgwick to Ellen Sedgwick Welch, 4 June 1862 and 1 September 1863, Sedgwick, *Sedgwick's Correspondence*, vol. 2, pp. 49, 155; Special Orders No. 254, 13 September 1862, *OR*, vol. 19, pt. 2, p. 283; Gibbon, *Personal Recollections*, pp. 71–73; McClellan, *Own Story*, p. 140.

11. Franz Sigel to Stanton, 11 March 1863, Lincoln, *Collected Works*, vol. 6, p. 93n; Lincoln to Ambrose Burnside, 4 May 1863, ibid., p. 196; Schurz, *Reminiscences*, vol. 2, pp. 403–4; Sigel to Hooker, 12 February 1863, *OR*, vol. 25, pt. 2, p. 70; Sigel to Joseph Dickinson, 12 February 1863, ibid.; Hooker to Dickinson, 12 February 1863, ibid., p. 71.

12. Lincoln to Sigel, 26 January 1863, Lincoln, *Collected Works*, vol. 6, pp. 79–80; Sigel to Lincoln, 29 January 1863, ibid., p. 80n; Schurz to Lincoln, 24 February 1863, Lincoln Papers; Adolph von Steinwehr to Sigel, 20 January 1863, ibid.; Lincoln to Schurz, 11 April 1863, Lincoln, *Collected Works*, vol. 6, p. 168; Schurz to Lincoln, 6 April 1863, ibid., p. 168n; Adolph von Steinwehr to Lincoln, 30 January 1863, Lincoln Papers; Schurz to Lincoln, 14 February 1863, ibid.; Alpheus Williams to his daughter, 22 February 1863, Alpheus Williams, *From the Cannon's Mouth: The Civil War Letters of General Alpheus S. Williams*, ed. Milo M. Quaife (Detroit, MI: Wayne State University Press and the Detroit Historical Society, 1959), p. 166; Adolph von Steinwehr to Oliver Otis Howard, 5 April 1863, Lincoln, *Collected Works*, vol. 6, p. 168n; Lincoln to Sigel, 5 February 1863, ibid., p. 93; Lincoln to Hooker, 13 March 1863, ibid., p. 135.

13. Quoted in Stephen Sears, *Chancellorsville* (Boston: Houghton Mifflin, 1996), p. 64.

14. Howard, *Howard's Autobiography*, vol. 1, p. 251.

15. George McClellan's report, 4 August 1863, *OR*, vol. 11, pt. 1, p. 42; Wainwright, 19 April 1863 and 24 May 1863, *Diary of Battle*, pp. 183, 210; Howard, *Howard's Autobiography*, vol. 1, pp. 255, 348–49; Josiah Marshall Favill, 3 June 1862, *The Diary of a Young Officer* (Baltimore: Butternut and Blue, 2000), p. 112; Schurz, *Reminiscences*, vol. 2, pp. 405, 441–42; Special Orders No. 87, 31 March 1863, *OR*, vol. 25, pt. 2, p. 176; Doubleday, *Chancellorsville and Gettysburg*, p. 3; Robert Hubbard to Nellie Hubbard, 7 April 1863, Hubbard Letters, p. 27; Theodore Ayrault Dodge, 3 April 1863, *On Campaign with the Army of the Potomac: The Civil War Journal of Theodore Ayrault Dodge*, ed. Stephen Sears (New York: First Cooper Square Press, 2001), p. 227.

16. Brooks, *Washington, D.C. in Lincoln's Time*, p. 56.

17. Couch, "Sumner's 'Right Grand Division,'" pp. 119–20. Couch gave a slightly different version of this quote in Couch, "The Chancellorsville Campaign," p. 155.

18. Alpheus Williams to his daughter, 18 May 1863, Williams, *From the Cannon's Mouth*, p. 186; Wainwright, 19 April 1863, *Diary of Battle*, pp. 182–83; Welles, 26 June 1863, *Welles's Diary*, vol. 1, p. 344; Weld to his Dad, 7 March 1863, *War Diary and Letters*, p. 158; Meade to Margaret Meade, 26 April 1863, Meade, *Life and Letters*, vol. 1, p.

369; James Roberts Gilmore, *Personal Recollections of Abraham Lincoln and the Civil War* (Boston: L. C. Page, 1898), pp. 95–96.

19. Charles Fessenden Morse to [unknown], 7 May 1863, Charles Fessenden Morse, *Letters Written during the Civil War, 1861–1865* (Boston: privately printed, 1898), p. 129; James Biddle to Alexander Webb, 21 November 1886, *The Meade Archive*, http://patriot.net/~jcampi/webb.htm; Biddle to Gertrude Biddle, 7 May 1863, Biddle Letters.

20. Biddle to Webb, 21 November 1886, *The Meade Archive*.

21. Couch recorded his impressions in Couch, "The Chancellorsville Campaign," pp. 159–61.

22. J. H. Van Allen to Howard and Slocum, *OR*, vol. 25, pt. 2, p. 360; Schurz, *Reminiscences*, vol. 2, pp. 416, 431; Hooker, 11 March 1865, U.S. Congress, *Reports of the Joint Committee*, p. 127; Howard to Hooker, 2 May 1863, Samuel Bates Papers; Schurz to Hooker, 22 April 1876, ibid.

23. Couch's account is from Couch, "The Chancellorsville Campaign," pp. 164–70. See also Jonathan Letterman, *Medical Recollections of the Army of the Potomac* (Knoxville, TN: Bohemian Brigade Publishers, 1994), p. 137; Biddle to Webb, 21 November 1886, *The Meade Archive*; Schurz, *Reminiscences*, vol. 2, p. 416; Samuel Bates, "Hooker's Comments on Chancellorsville," *Battles and Leaders*, vol. 3, pp. 220–21; Meade to Margaret Meade, 23 May 1863, Meade, *Life and Letters*, vol. 1, p. 380; Rusling to his friends, 10 May 1863, *Men and Things I Saw*, pp. 302–3; Alfred Pleasonton's testimony, 7 March 1864, U.S. Congress, *Reports of the Joint Committee*, p. 31; Butterfield's testimony, 29 March 1864, ibid., pp. 85–86; Morse to [unknown], 7 May 1863, Morse, *Letters Written during the Civil War*, pp. 132–33; Andrew Humphreys to Meade, 16 June 1867, *The Meade Archive*.

24. The quote is from Couch, "The Chancellorsville Campaign," p. 171. For other accounts of this meeting, see Warren, n.d., *OR*, vol. 25, pt. 1, p. 511; Sickles to Meade, n.d., in Swanberg, *Sickles*, p. 195; Butterfield's testimony, 28 March 1864, U.S. Congress, *Reports of the Joint Committee*, p. 78; Hooker's testimony, 11 March 1865, ibid., pp. 134–36; Reynolds to George Meade, 24 May 1863, Reynolds Papers; Gibbon, 25 May 1863, *Personal Recollections*, p. 120.

25. Schurz, *Reminiscences*, vol. 2, pp. 430–31; Salmon Chase to William Aspinwall and John Murray Forbes, 14 May 1863, Chase, *Chase Papers*, vol. 4: *Correspondence, April 1863–1864*, p. 32; Couch, "The Chancellorsville Campaign," p. 170; Rusling, 10 May 1863, *Men and Things I Saw*, pp. 302–3; Slocum to Howland, 29 May 1863, Howland Papers; Pleasonton's testimony, 7 March 1864, U.S. Congress, *Reports of the Joint Committee*, p. 31; Butterfield's testimony, 29 March 1864, ibid., pp. 84–86; Welles, 18 May 1863 and 20 June 1863, *Welles's Diary*, vol. 1, pp. 305–6, 336.

26. Welles, 14 June 1863, 20 June 1863, 26 June 1863, 15 June 1863, *Welles' Diary*, vol. 1, pp. 329, 336, 344, 329; Chase to Benjamin Ludlow, 12 May 1863, Chase, *Chase Papers*, vol. 4, p. 28; Chase to Hooker, 23 May 1863, ibid., pp. 36–37; Chase to James Garfield, 31 May 1863, ibid., p. 47; Francis Blair Sr. to Lincoln, 17 May 1863, Lincoln Papers.

27. Brooks, *Washington, D.C. in Lincoln's Time*, pp. 60–61.

28. Darius Couch's autobiographical sketch, 1873, Couch Papers, pp. 131–32; Welles, 14 June 1863, 20 June 1863, and 26 June 1863, *Welles's Diary*, vol. 1, pp. 329, 336, 344; Charles Benjamin, "Hooker's Appointment and Removal," *Battles and Leaders*, vol. 3, pp. 240–41; Meade to Margaret Meade, 8 May 1863, 26 May 1863, and 13 June 1863, Meade, *Life and Letters*, vol. 1, pp. 372–73, 382, 385; Hooker's testimony, 13 March

1865, U.S. Congress, *Reports of the Joint Committee*, p. 151; Lincoln to Hooker, 14 May 1863, *Collected Works*, vol. 6, p. 217.

29. Hooker to Lincoln, 6 May 1863, *OR*, vol. 25, pt. 2, p. 435.

30. Meade to Margaret Meade, 8 May 1863, Meade, *Life and Letters*, vol. 1, pp. 372–73; Hooker to Lincoln, 7 May 1863, *OR*, vol. 25, pt. 2, p. 438; Biddle to Gertrude Biddle, 9 May 1863, Biddle Letters.

31. Sears, *Chancellorsville*, p. 146; Hooker to Lincoln, 7 May 1863, *OR*, vol. 25, pt. 2, p. 438; Nelson Miles to [unknown], n.d., Miles Papers, Civil War Correspondence File; Chase to Aspinwall and Forbes, 14 May 1863, Chase, *Chase Papers*, vol. 4, p. 32; Butterfield's testimony, 29 March 1864, U.S. Congress, *Reports of the Joint Committee*, p. 85; Hooker's testimony, 11 March 1865, ibid., p. 127; Wainwright, 24 May 1863, *Diary of Battle*, p. 210; Schurz, *Reminiscences*, vol. 2, pp. 432–33, 439–42; Couch, "The Chancellorsville Campaign," p. 163; Howard, *Howard's Autobiography*, vol. 1, p. 353; McAllister to Ellen McAllister, n.d., McAllister, *McAllister's Letters*, p. 305; Dodge, 10 May 1863, *On Campaign*, p. 262; Weld to his Dad, 7 May 1863, *War Diary and Letters*, p. 194; Rusling to his friends, 10 May 1863, *Men and Things I Saw*, p. 303; Frank Haskell, *Haskell of Gettysburg: His Life and Civil War Papers*, ed. Frank L. Byrne and Andrew T. Weaver (Madison: State Historical Society of Wisconsin, 1970), p. 80; Biddle to Gertrude Biddle, 7 May 1863, Biddle Letters.

32. Hooker to Stanton, 10 May 1863, *OR*, vol. 25, pt. 2, p. 463.

33. Biddle to Gertrude Biddle, 17 May 1863, Biddle Letters; Wainwright, 7 April 1864, *Diary of Battle*, p. 341; Seth Williams to Stoneman, 15 April 1863, *OR*, vol. 25, pt. 2, p. 213; Hooker to Lincoln, 17 April 1863, ibid., p. 220; Seth Williams to Stoneman, 22 April 1863, ibid., p. 242; Butterfield to Stoneman, 8 May 1863, ibid., p. 450; General Orders No. 11, 22 May 1863, ibid., p. 513; Hooker to Stanton, 28 May 1863, ibid., p. 543; Gibbon, *Personal Recollections*, pp. 121–22; Meade to Margaret Meade, 26 May 1863, Meade, *Life and Letters*, vol. 1, pp. 381–82; Hooker's testimony, 11 March 1865, U.S. Congress, *Reports of the Joint Committee*, p. 140; James Harrison Wilson, *Under the Old Flag: Recollections of Military Operations in the War for the Union, the Spanish War and the Boxer Rebellion, etc.*, vol. 1 (Westport, CT: Greenwood Press, 1971), p. 327.

34. John Gibbon to his wife, 2 June 1863, Gibbon Letters; McClellan to Mary Ellen McClellan, 18 August 1862 and 5 November 1862, McClellan, *Selected Correspondence*, pp. 396, 518; John Hay, 10 September 1863, *Hay's Letters and Diaries*, p. 88; Patrick, 12 February 1863, *Inside Lincoln's Army*, p. 213; General Orders No. 11, 22 May 1863, *OR*, vol. 25, pt. 2, p. 513; Hooker to Halleck, 18 June 1863, ibid., vol. 27, pt. 1, p. 51; Charles Francis Adams Jr. to his Mom, 12 May 1863, Worthington Chauncey Ford, ed., *A Cycle of Adams Letters, 1861–1865*, vol. 2 (Boston: Houghton Mifflin, 1920), p. 8; Sickles to Seth Williams, 5 May 1863, *OR*, vol. 51, pt. 1, p. 1036; Sickles to Seth Williams, 14 May 1863, ibid., vol. 25, pt. 2, p. 1039; Hooker to Halleck, 18 June 1863, ibid., vol. 27, pt. 1, p. 51; Slocum, 17 May 1863, ibid., vol. 25, pt. 1, p. 672; Haskell, *Haskell of Gettysburg*, pp. 133–34; Blair to Lincoln, 6 June 1863, Lincoln Papers.

35. Butterfield to Lincoln, 5 May 1863, *OR*, vol. 25, pt. 2, p. 421.

36. Sedgwick to Ellen Sedgwick Welch, 6 May 1863 and 9 May 1863, Sedgwick, *Sedgwick's Correspondence*, vol. 2, pp. 92, 109; R. F. Halsted to Ellen Sedgwick Welch, 13 May 1863, ibid., pp. 125–27; Sedgwick to Welch, 15 May 1863, ibid., p. 128; Gibbon, *Personal Recollections*, pp. 121–22; Winfield Scott Hancock to Alma Hancock, n.d., Hancock, *Hancock Reminiscences*, p. 94; Butterfield's testimony, 28 March 1864, U.S. Congress, *Reports of the Joint Committee*, p. 76; Hooker's testimony, 11 March 1865, ibid., pp. 129–33, 146.

37. Gibbon to his wife, 13 May 1863, Gibbon Letters; Butterfield's testimony, 28 March 1864, U.S. Congress, *Report of the Joint Committee*, p. 83.

38. Slocum to Howland, 29 May 1863, Howland Papers.

39. Ibid.; Alpheus Williams to his daughter, 18 May 1863, Williams, *From the Cannon's Mouth*, p. 180; Meade to Margaret Meade, 10 May 1863 and 20 May 1863, Meade, *Life and Letters*, vol. 1, pp. 373–74, 379; Slocum to Howland, 4 February 1863 and 22 October 1863, Howland Papers; William Seward to Lincoln, 18 May 1863, Lincoln Papers; Slocum to Seward, 14 November 1863, ibid.

40. Gibbon, *Personal Recollections*, p. 119.

41. Bates, "Hooker's Comments on Chancellorsville," p. 222; Weld, *War Diary and Letters*, p. 227n; Meade to Margaret Meade, 13 June 1863, Meade, *Life and Letters*, vol. 1, p. 385; Wainwright, 29 June 1863, *Diary of Battle*, p. 229.

42. The quote is from Meade to Margaret Meade, 10 May 1863, Meade, *Life and Letters*, vol. 1, pp. 373–74. See also Gibbon to his wife, 10 May 1863, Gibbon Letters; Couch's autobiographical sketch, 1873, Couch Papers, pp. 131–32; Biddle to Gertrude Biddle, 14 May 1863 and 16 May 1863, Biddle Letters; Wainwright, 6 May 1863, *Diary of Battle*, p. 202; Gibbon, 10 May 1863, *Personal Recollections*, p. 119; Meade to Margaret Meade, 20 May 1863 and 25 June 1863, Meade, *Life and Letters*, vol. 1, pp. 379, 385; Adams to John Quincy Adams, 25 June 1863, Ford, *Cycle of Adams Letters*, vol. 2, p. 38.

43. Biddle to Gertrude Biddle, 20 May 1863, Biddle Letters; Meade to Margaret Meade, 15 May 1863 and 19 May 1863, Meade, *Life and Letters*, vol. 1, pp. 376, 377–78; Butterfield's testimony, 29 March 1864, U.S. Congress, *Reports of the Joint Committee*, pp. 84–85; Hooker's testimony, 13 March 1865, ibid., pp. 151, 176; Meade to Andrew Curtin, 15 May 1863, Lincoln Papers; Warren to Emily Chase, 15 May 1863, Warren Papers, Folder 3.

44. Gibbon to his wife, 30 May 1863, Gibbon Letters; Biddle to Gertrude Biddle, 14 May 1863, Biddle Letters; Schurz, *Reminiscences*, vol. 2, pp. 432–33; Chase to Hooker, 23 May 1863, Chase, *Chase Papers*, vol. 4, p. 36; Meade to Margaret Meade, 10 May 1863 and 20 May 1863, Meade, *Life and Letters*, vol. 1, pp. 373–74, 379; Favill, 12 May 1863, *Diary of a Young Officer*, p. 236; Francis Walker, *History of the Second Army Corps in the Army of the Potomac* (New York: Charles Scribner's Sons, 1886), pp. 253–54.

45. E. D. Townsend to Hooker, 25 June 1863, OR, vol. 37, pt. 1, p. 57; Special Orders No. 186, 24 June 1863, OR, vol. 37, pt. 3, p. 299.

46. Gibbon to his wife, 10 May 1863 and 21 May 1863, Gibbon Letters; McClellan to Mary Ellen McClellan, 6 May 1862, McClellan, *Selected Correspondence*, pp. 256–57; Wainwright, 28 August 1864, *Diary of Battle*, p. 460; Hancock to Hancock, n.d., Hancock, *Hancock Reminiscences*, p. 94; Hancock, *Hancock Reminiscences*, pp. 182–83; Favill, 25 February 1863, *Diary of a Young Officer*, p. 223; Trobriand, *Four Years with the Army of the Potomac*, pp. 596–98; Haskell, 16 July 1863, *Haskell of Gettysburg*, p. 133.

47. Hooker to Halleck, 18 June 1863, OR, vol. 27, pt. 1, p. 51.

48. Welles, 28 June 1863, *Welles's Diary*, vol. 1, pp. 348–49; Lincoln to Hooker, 16 June 1863, Lincoln, *Collected Works*, vol. 6, p. 281, 282; Benjamin, "Hooker's Appointment and Removal," pp. 240–41; Hooker to Lincoln, 16 June 1863, OR, vol. 27, pt. 1, p. 45; Caleb Cushing to Benjamin Butler, 15 May 1863, Butler, *Butler's Correspondence*, vol. 3, p. 73.

49. Welles, 28 June 1863, *Welles's Diary*, vol. 1, pp. 348–49; Chase to Kate Chase, 29 June 1863, Chase, *Chase Papers*, vol. 4, pp. 72–73; Benjamin, "Hooker's Appointment and Removal," pp. 240–41; Sickles's testimony, 25 February 1864, U.S. Congress, *Reports*

of the Joint Committee, pp. 14–15; Butterfield's testimony, 28 March 1864, ibid., pp. 81–82; Hay, 9 September 1863, *Hay's Letters and Diaries,* p. 84; Hooker to Halleck, 27 June 1863, *OR,* vol. 27, pt. 1, p. 60.

50. Thomas Hyde, *Following the Greek Cross: Or, Memories of the Sixth Army Corps* (Boston: Houghton, Mifflin, 1894), p. 140; Welles, 28 June 1863 and 29 June 1863, *Welles's Diary,* vol. 1, pp. 348–49, 351; Chase to David Dudley Field, 30 June 1863, Chase, *Chase Papers,* vol. 4, p. 74; Chase to Kate Chase, 29 June 1863, ibid., pp. 72–73.

Chapter 4. Meade Marks Time: June 1863 to March 1864

1. Hardie, "Hardie Memoir," pp. 38–39; Charles Benjamin, "Hooker's Appointment and Removal," *Battles and Leaders of the Civil War,* vol. 3, ed. Robert Underwood Johnson and Clarence Clough Buel (New York: Thomas Yoseloff, 1956), pp. 240–43.

2. Hardie, "Hardie Memoir," pp. 38–40; Benjamin, "Hooker's Appointment and Removal," pp. 242–43; George Meade to Margaret Meade, 29 June 1863, George Meade, *The Life and Letters of George Gordon Meade,* vol. 2, ed. George Meade (New York: Charles Scribner's Sons, 1913), pp. 11–12; Joseph Hooker to Abraham Lincoln, 7 July 1863, *OR,* vol. 51, pt. 1, p. 1071; Noah Brooks, *Washington D.C. in Lincoln's Time,* ed. Herbert Mitgang (Athens: University of Georgia Press, 1989), pp. 62–63; Hooker's testimony, 13 March 1865, U.S. Congress, *Reports of the Joint Committee on the Conduct of the War,* 38th Cong., 2d sess., pt. 1 (Washington, DC: Government Printing Office, 1865), p. 175; Hay, 27 September 1863, *Hay's Letters and Diaries,* p. 94.

3. Horace Porter, *Campaigning with Grant* (Bloomington: Indiana University Press, 1961), pp. 246–48; Herman Haupt, *Reminiscences of General Herman Haupt* (Milwaukee, WI: Wright and Joys, 1901), pp. 310–11; Theodore Lyman, 29 September 1863, *Meade's Headquarters, 1863–1865: Letters of Colonel Theodore Lyman from the Wilderness to Appomattox,* ed. George Agassiz (Boston: Atlantic Monthly Press, 1922), p. 25; James Rusling, *Men and Things I Saw in Civil War Days* (New York: Eaton and Mains, 1899), p. 67; Regis de Trobriand, *Four Years with the Army of the Potomac,* trans. George K. Dauchy (Boston: Ticknor, 1889), pp. 518–19; Brooks, *Washington D.C. in Lincoln's Time,* p. 85; Frank Haskell, 16 July 1863, *Haskell of Gettysburg: His Life and Civil War Papers,* ed. Frank L. Byrne and Andrew T. Weaver (Madison: State Historical Society of Wisconsin, 1970), p. 132; Ulysses Grant, *Personal Memoirs of U. S. Grant,* vol. 2 (New York: Century, 1917), pp. 382–83.

4. John Gibbon to his wife, 30 June 1863, Gibbon Letters; Alpheus Williams, 6 July 1863, *From the Cannon's Mouth: The Civil War Letters of General Alpheus S. Williams,* ed. Milo M. Quaife (Detroit, MI: Wayne State University Press and the Detroit Historical Society, 1959), p. 223; Charles Wainwright, 28 June 1863, *A Diary of Battle: The Personal Journals of Colonel Charles S. Wainwright,* ed. Allan Nevins (New York: Harcourt, Brace and World, 1962), p. 227; Henry Hunt, "The First Day at Gettysburg," *Battles and Leaders,* vol. 3, p. 270; John Gibbon, *Personal Recollections of the Civil War* (New York: G. P. Putnam's Sons, 1928), p. 128; Howard, *Howard's Autobiography,* vol. 1, pp. 395–96; Rufus Ingalls to Montgomery Meigs, 28 June 1863, *OR,* vol. 27, pt. 3, p. 378; Albion Howe's testimony, 4 March 1864, U.S. Congress, *Report of the Joint Committee,* p. 327; Levi Bird Duff to Harriet Duff, 29 June 1963, Blake Collection, David Birney Folder; Thomas Hyde, *Following the Greek Cross: Or, Memories of the Sixth Army Corps* (Boston: Houghton, Mifflin, 1894), p. 140.

5. Meade, "A Letter from General Meade," *Battles and Leaders*, vol. 3, p. 413; Gouverneur Warren, n.d., Taylor, *Life and Letters of an American Soldier*, pp. 119–20; Andrew Humphreys' testimony, 21 March 1864, U.S. Congress, *Report of the Joint Committee*, p. 388; Daniel Butterfield's testimony, 25 March 1864, ibid., pp. 418–19; Warren to Emily Warren, 28 June 1863 and 9 July 1863, Warren Papers, Folder 3.

6. Andrew Humphreys to his wife, 27 March 1864, Humphreys Letters; William Averell, *Ten Years in the Saddle: The Memoir of William Woods Averell*, ed. Edward Eckert and Nicholas Amato (San Rafael, CA: Presidio Press, 1978), p. 120; Gibbon, *Personal Recollections*, p. 131; Lyman, 6 September 1863 and 27 November 1863, *Meade's Headquarters*, pp. 9, 52; Meade to Margaret Meade, 29 March 1864, Meade, *Life and Letters*, vol. 2, p. 185; Stephen Weld to his Dad, 4 September 1862, Stephen Minot Weld, *War Diary and Letters of Stephen Minot Weld, 1861–1865* (Boston: Massachusetts Historical Society, 1979), p. 136; Howard, *Howard's Autobiography*, vol. 1, p. 298; Fitz John Porter to McClellan, 30 August 1862, *OR*, vol. 12, pt. 3, p. 768; Porter to Seth Williams, 26 September 1862, ibid., vol. 51, pt. 1, p. 865; Meade, 12 May 1863, ibid., vol. 25, pt. 1, p. 508; Haskell, 16 July 1863, *Haskell of Gettysburg*, p. 133; George Sykes's testimony, 30 December 1862, *OR*, vol. 12, pt. 2, supplement, p. 999; David Birney to George Gross, 28 October 1863, Birney Papers; Henry Halleck to Meade, 27 June 1863, *OR*, vol. 27, pt. 1, p. 61.

7. Weld, *War Diary and Letters*, pp. 231–32.

8. The quote is from Haskell, 16 July 1863, *Haskell of Gettysburg*, p. 100. See also Wainwright, 1 July 1863, *Diary of Battle*, p. 232; Abner Doubleday, *Chancellorsville and Gettysburg* (New York: Da Capo Press, 1994), p. 122; Weld, 1 July 1863, *War Diary and Letters*, pp. 229–30; Weld, ibid., pp. 231–32; Weld, 4 July 1863, ibid., p. 237; Howard, *Howard's Autobiography*, vol. 1, pp. 403–4; Veil, "An Old Boy's Personal Recollections and Reminiscences of the Civil War," Veil Folder, pp. 41–42, 51; James Biddle to Alexander Webb, 21 November 1886, *The Meade Archive*, http://patriot.net/~jcampi/webb.htm.

9. Weld, *War Diary and Letters*, pp. 231–32.

10. Gibbon to his wife, 14 June 1862, Gibbon Letters; Meade to Margaret Meade, 23 January 1863, Meade, *Life and Letters*, vol. 1, p. 349; Wainwright, 8 March 1863 and 1 July 1863, *Diary of Battle*, pp. 172, 232–33; Marsena Patrick, 23 May 1862 and 14 June 1862, *Inside Lincoln's Army: The Diary of Marsena Rudolph Patrick, Provost Marshal General, Army of the Potomac*, ed. David Sparks (New York: Thomas Yoseloff, 1964), pp. 82, 95; William Doubleday to Zachariah Chandler, 5 July 1861, Chandler Papers, reel 1; Abner Doubleday's testimony, 1 March 1864, U.S. Congress, *Reports of the Joint Committee*, p. 311.

11. Gibbon to his wife, 22 June 1863, Gibbon Letters; Winfield Scott Hancock's testimony, 22 March 1864, U.S. Congress, *Reports of the Joint Committee*, p. 404; Butterfield to Hancock, 1 July 1863, *OR*, vol. 27, pt. 3, p. 461.

12. Hancock, *Hancock's Reminiscences*, p. 190.

13. The quote about Hancock is from Hunt, "The First Day at Gettysburg," p. 283. The conversation between Howard and Hancock, as well as the accompanying quotes, comes from E. P. Halstead, "Incidents of the First Day at Gettysburg," *Battles and Leaders*, vol. 3, p. 285. See also Wainwright, 1 July 1863, *Diary of Battle*, p. 237; Howard, *Howard's Autobiography*, vol. 1, p. 418; Hancock, *Hancock Reminiscences*, pp. 189–90; Haskell, 16 July 1863, *Haskell of Gettysburg*, p. 101.

14. The quote is from Howard, *Howard's Autobiography*, vol. 1, p. 423. See also Hyde to his Mom, 6 September 1863, Thomas W. Hyde, *Civil War Letters* (N.p.: privately published, 1933), pp. 96–97.

15. Gibbon to his wife, 31 March 1863, Gibbon Letters; Hyde to his Mom, 6 September 1863, Hyde, *Civil War Letters*, p. 97; Abner Doubleday, n.d., U.S. Army Generals' Reports, reel 8, vol. 13, p. 357; Wainwright, 6 July 1863, 22 July 1863, 26 July 1863, 3 September 1863, and 14 October 1863, *Diary of Battle*, pp. 256, 268, 268–69, 279–80, 292; John Sedgwick to Seth Williams, 7 May 1863, Sedgwick, *Sedgwick's Correspondence*, vol. 2, p. 105; Patrick, 28 April 1863 and 28 November 1863, *Inside Lincoln's Army*, pp. 237–38, 317; Huntington Jackson, "Sedgwick at Fredericksburg and Salem Heights," *Battles and Leaders*, vol. 3, pp. 228–32; John Gibbon, "The Council of War on the Second Day," ibid., p. 313; Lyman, 6 September 1863, *Meade's Headquarters*, p. 9; Weld to his Dad, 30 July 1863, *War Diary and Letters*, p. 252; Special Orders No. 178, 1 July 1863, OR, vol. 27, pt. 3, p. 1066; William Franklin, 17 May 1862, ibid., vol. 11, pt. 1, p. 616; Franklin, 30 September 1862, ibid., vol. 19, pt. 1, p. 376; William Doubleday to Chandler, 6 December 1861, Chandler Papers, reel 1; Haskell, 16 July 1863, *Haskell of Gettysburg*, p. 133; Henry Slocum to Joseph Howland, 4 February 1863, Howland Papers; Birney to Gross, 28 October 1863, Birney Papers; Abner Doubleday to Samuel Bates, 4 April 1874, Blake Collection, Abner Doubleday Folder; John Cochrane to Lincoln, 23 February 1863, Lincoln Papers; Special Orders No. 181, 5 July 1863, OR, vol. 27, pt. 3, p. 542.

16. Quoted in Shelby Foote, *The Civil War: A Narrative*, vol. 2 (New York: Vintage Books, 1986), p. 496.

17. Rusling, *Men and Things I Saw*, pp. 12–14; Rusling to his friends, 5 July 1863, ibid., pp. 306–7; Henry Edwin Tremain, *Two Days of War: A Gettysburg Narrative and Other Excursions* (New York: Bonnell, Silver and Bowers, 1905), p. 89.

18. Trobriand, *Four Years with the Army of the Potomac*, p. 505.

19. Gibbon, "The Council of War on the Second Day," vol. 3, p. 314.

20. Ibid.; Minutes of War, 2 July 1863, OR, vol. 27, pt. 1, p. 72; Gibbon, *Personal Recollections*, p. 144; Gibbon's testimony, 1 April 1864, U.S. Congress, *Reports of the Joint Committee*, p. 442.

21. R. F. Halsted to Ellen Sedgwick Welch, 17 July 1863, Sedgwick, *Sedgwick's Correspondence*, vol. 2, pp. 134–35; Meade to Margaret Meade, 8 July 1863, Meade, *Life and Letters*, vol. 2, p. 132; Weld, 7 July 1863, *War Diary and Letters*, p. 238.

22. Hay, 14 July 1863, *Hay's Letters and Diaries*, pp. 66–67.

23. The quote is from Meade to Margaret Meade, 22 July 1863, Meade, *Life and Letters*, vol. 2, p. 136. See also Gideon Welles, 7 July 1863, 14 July 1863, and 17 July 1863, *Welles's Diary*, vol. 1, pp. 363, 370, 374; Lincoln to Meade, 14 July 1863, *The Collected Works of Abraham Lincoln*, vol. 6, ed. Roy Basler (New Brunswick, NJ: Rutgers University Press, 1953), pp. 327–28; Salmon Chase to William Sprague, 15 July 1863, Chase, *Chase Papers, vol. 4: Correspondence, April 1863–1864*, p. 82; Meade to Halleck, 14 July 1863, OR, vol. 27, pt. 1, p. 93; Halleck to Meade, 14 July 1863, ibid.; Halleck to Meade, 28 July 1863, ibid., p. 104; Meade to Margaret Meade, 14 July 1863, Meade, *Life and Letters*, vol. 2, p. 134.

24. Meade to Halleck, 14 September 1863, OR, vol. 29, pt. 2, p. 179; Halleck to Meade, 15 September 1863, ibid., p. 185; Lincoln to Halleck, 19 September 1863, ibid., p. 207.

25. Meade to Butterfield, n.d., Julia Lorrilard Butterfield, *A Biographical Memorial of General Daniel Butterfield* (New York: Grafton Press, 1904), pp. 126–27.

26. Ibid., 14 July 1863 and n.d., pp. 125–26, 126–27; Patrick, 9 July 1863, *Inside Lincoln's Army*, p. 270.

27. Ambrose Burnside to Lincoln, 14 February 1863, OR, vol. 21, p. 1006; Lyman, 24

February 1864, *Meade's Headquarters*, p. 73; Meade to Margaret Meade, 28 January 1863 and 19 May 1863, Meade, *Life and Letters*, vol. 1, pp. 352, 378; Robert McAllister to Ellen McAllister, 25 May 1863, McAllister, *McAllister's Letters*, p. 317; Halleck, 13 September 1862 and 3 April 1863, OR, vol. 51, pt. 1, pp. 818, 1000; Humphreys to McClellan, 13 April 1863, ibid., p. 1004; Burnside's report, n.d., ibid., vol. 21, p. 94; Trobriand, *Four Years with the Army of the Potomac*, pp. 687–88; Meade, 12 May 1863, OR, vol. 25, pt. 1, p. 508; Birney to Gross, 16 March 1864, Birney Papers; Humphreys, *Humphreys's Biography*, p. 257.

28. Quoted in Humphreys, *Humphreys's Biography*, p. 207.

29. Humphreys to his wife, 24 August 1663, Humphreys Letters; Patrick, 28 March 1864, *Inside Lincoln's Army*, p. 353; Lyman, 5 September 1863, 24 February 1864, and 5 March 1864, *Meade's Headquarters*, pp. 6–7, 73, 78; Charles Dana, *Recollections of the Civil War: With the Leaders at Washington and in the Field in the Sixties* (Lincoln: University of Nebraska Press, 1996), p. 192; McAllister to McAllister, 25 May 1863, McAllister, *McAllister's Letters*, p. 317; Charles Francis Adams Jr., *Charles Francis Adams, 1835–1915: An Autobiography* (Boston: Houghton Mifflin, 1916), pp. 157–58; Trobriand, *Four Years with the Army of the Potomac*, pp. 687–88; Warren to Emily Warren, 1 August 1863, Warren Papers, Folder 4.

30. Josiah Marshall Favill, 3 June 1862, *The Diary of a Young Officer* (Baltimore: Butternut and Blue, 2000), p. 112.

31. John Haley, 17 July 1863, *The Rebel Yell and the Yankee Hurrah: The Civil War Journal of a Maine Volunteer*, ed. Ruth L. Silliker (Camden, ME: Down East Books, 1985), p. 112.

32. Hay, 20 October 1863, *Hay's Letters and Diaries*, p. 103; Patrick, 28 November 1863, *Inside Lincoln's Army*, p. 317; Howard, *Howard's Autobiography*, vol. 1, pp. 186–87; James Harrison Wilson, *Under the Old Flag: Recollections of Military Operations in the War for the Union, the Spanish War and the Boxer Rebellion, etc.*, vol. 1 (Westport, CT: Greenwood Press, 1971), pp. 112–14; McAllister to Ellen McAllister and his family, 18 October 1863, McAllister, *McAllister's Letters*, pp. 345–46; Trobriand, *Four Years with the Army of the Potomac*, pp. 517–18, 530–31, 547–48; Darius Couch, 20 May 1863, OR, vol. 25, pt. 1, p. 307; Favill, 3 June 1862, *Diary of a Young Officer*, p. 120; Henry Blake, *Three Years in the Army of the Potomac* (Boston: Lee and Shepard, 1865), p. 257; Birney's testimony, 7 March 1864, U.S. Congress, *Report of the Joint Committee*, p. 369; Birney to Gross, 28 October 1863, Birney Papers.

33. The quote is from Birney to Gross, 28 October 1863, Birney Papers. See also Hay, 20 October 1863, *Hay's Letters and Diaries*, p. 103; McAllister to Ellen McAllister and his family, 18 October 1863, McAllister, *McAllister's Letters*, pp. 345–46; Rusling to his brother, 13 November 1863, *Men and Things I Saw*, pp. 309–10; Trobriand, *Four Years with the Army of the Potomac*, pp. 545–46; Haley, 2 July 1863 and 17 October 1863, *Rebel Yell*, pp. 102, 125; Daniel Sickles to Edwin Stanton, 7 August 1863, Stanton Papers, vol. 14; Sickles's letter, 1 August 1863, W. A. Swanberg, *Sickles the Incredible* (New York: Charles Scribner's Sons, 1956), p. 227.

34. Alexander Hays to John McFadden, 2 November 1863, Hays, *Hays's Life and Letters*, p. 512; Biddle to Gertrude Biddle, 13 August 1863, Biddle Letters; Humphreys to Alexander Webb, 6 April 1865, OR, vol. 46, pt. 3, p. 597.

35. George to Halleck, 19 July 1863, OR, vol. 27, pt. 1, p. 96; Halleck to Meade, 26 July 1863, ibid.; Butterfield, December 1862, ibid., vol. 11, p. 402; Couch, 20 May 1863, ibid., vol. 25, pt. 1, p. 306; Sykes, 8 May 1863, ibid., p. 526; Warren to Emily Warren, 24 August 1863, Warren Papers, Folder 4.

36. Grant, *Personal Memoirs*, vol. 2, pp. 306–7.

37. The quote is from Warren to Emily Warren, 16 August 1863, Warren Papers, Folder 4. See also Sylvanus Cadwallader, *Three Years with Grant: As Recalled by War Correspondent Sylvanus Cadwallader*, ed. Benjamin Thomas (New York: Alfred A. Knopf, 1956), pp. 203, 303; Wainwright, 31 March 1864, *Diary of Battle*, pp. 338–39; Wainwright, 1 June 1864 and 4 June 1864, *Diary of Battle*, pp. 396, 405; Grant, *Personal Memoirs*, vol. 2, pp. 124–25; Lyman, 1 October 1863 and 3 June 1864, *Meade's Headquarters*, pp. 26, 147; Wilson, *Under the Old Flag*, vol. 1, p. 397; Adam Badeau, *Military History of Ulysses S. Grant, from April, 1861, to April, 1865*, vol. 3 (New York: D. Appleton, 1881), pp. 479–99; Haskell, 31 October 1863, *Haskell of Gettysburg*, p. 225; Favill, 8 January 1864, *Diary of a Young Officer*, p. 274; Schaff, *Wilderness*, p. 30; Hays to Annie Hays, 16 October 1863 and 28 October 1863, *Hays's Life and Letters*, pp. 497, 508; Warren to Emily Chase, 27 July 1862, Warren Papers, Folder 1; Warren to Emily Chase, 16 May 1863, ibid., Folder 3; Warren to Emily Chase, 22 September 1863, ibid., Folder 4.

38. Meade to Margaret Meade, 18 July 1863, Meade, *Life and Letters*, vol. 2, p. 136.

39. Alfred Pleasonton to Stanton, 15 August 1863, Stanton Papers, vol. 14; Hay, 31 July 1863, *Hay's Letters and Diaries*, p. 73; Humphreys to Sedgwick, 7 November 1863, OR, vol. 29, pt. 2, p. 433; Rusling, *Men and Things I Saw*, pp. 72–73; Meade to Halleck, 10 July 1863, OR, vol. 27, pt. 1, p. 89; Halleck to Meade, 11 July 1863, ibid., p. 89; Meade to Margaret Meade, 24 March 1864, Meade, *Life and Letters*, vol. 2, pp. 182–83.

40. Howard to Lincoln, 18 July 1863, *Collected Works*, vol. 6, p. 341n; Meade to Halleck, 29 July 1863, OR, vol. 27, pt. 1, p. 105; Adolphus Buschbeck to Adolph von Steinwehr, 30 July 1863, ibid., p. 785; von Steinwehr to Howard, 29 July 1863, ibid., pp. 779–80; Orland Smith to von Steinwehr, 30 July 1863, ibid., p. 786; Seth Williams to John Newton, 14 September 1863, ibid., vol. 29, pt. 2, p. 181; Warren to William Warren, n.d., Taylor, *Life and Letters of an American Soldier*, p. 148; Warren's testimony, 9 March 1864, U.S. Congress, *Reports of the Joint Committee*, p. 381; Warren to Sykes, 31 October 1863, John Bates Papers, Correspondence of Maj. Gen. George Sykes; Carl Schurz to Lincoln, 8 August 1863, Lincoln Papers; Warren to Emily Warren, 15 October 1863, Warren Papers, Folder 4.

41. Lincoln to Meade, 27 July 1863, *Collected Works*, vol. 6, p. 350; Meade to Lincoln, 30 July 1863, ibid., p. 350n; Lincoln to Meade, 11 August 1863, ibid., p. 381; Meade to Lincoln, 12 August 1863, ibid., p. 381n; Hay, 14 August 1863, *Hay's Letters and Diaries*, pp. 80–81; Meade to Margaret Meade, 6 August 1863, Meade, *Life and Letters*, vol. 2, p. 142.

42. Biddle to Gerturde Biddle, 29 September 1863, Biddle Letters; Lincoln to William Rosecrans, 28 September 1863, *Collected Works*, vol. 6, p. 486; Slocum to Lincoln, 25 September 1863, ibid., p. 486n; Hooker to Lincoln, 12 October 1863, OR, vol. 30, pt. 4, p. 322; Dana to Stanton, 29 October 1863, ibid., vol. 31, pt. 1, p. 73; Slocum to Howland, 22 October 1863, Howland Papers; Slocum to William Seward, 14 November 1863, Lincoln Papers.

43. Patrick, 26 November 1863, 27 November 1863, and 28 November 1863, *Inside Lincoln's Army*, pp. 313, 314, 317; Humphreys to William French, 26 November 1863, 27 November 1863, and 29 November 1863, OR, vol. 29, pt. 2, pp. 490, 500, 515; Adam De Gurowski, 29 November 1863, *Diary*, vol. 3 (Boston: Lee and Shepard, 1866), pp. 55–56.

44. Lyman, 30 November 1863, *Meade's Headquarters*, pp. 57–58; Patrick, 28 November 1863, *Inside Lincoln's Army*, p. 317.

45. Hyde to his Mom, 4 December 1863, *Civil War Letters*, p. 120; Warren to Emily Warren, 4 December 1863, 7 December 1863, and 8 December 1863, Warren Papers, Folder 4; Lyman, 30 November 1863, *Meade's Headquarters*, p. 57; Meade to Margaret

Meade, 2 December 1863, Meade, *Life and Letters*, vol. 2, p. 157; Humphreys to French, 26 November 1863, *OR*, vol. 29, pt. 2, p. 490; Humphreys to French, 3 December 1863, ibid., pt. 1, p. 746; French to Humphreys, 8 December 1863, ibid.; French to Seth Williams, 8 January 1864, ibid., p. 747; Seth Williams to French, 8 January 1864, ibid.; Sedgwick to French, 17 January 1864, *New York Times*, p. 5; Gurowski, 29 November 1863, *Diary*, vol. 3, pp. 55–56; French to Humphreys, 4 December 1863, *OR*, vol. 29, pt. 1, p. 739; George Meade's testimony, 5 March 1864, U.S. Congress, *Reports of the Joint Committee*, p. 344; Warren to Emily Warren, 20 December 1863, Warren Papers, Folder 4.

46. Wainwright, 10 December 1863, *Diary of Battle*, p. 308; Welles, 17 July 1863, 24 July 1863, 14 August 1863, and 21 September 1863, *Welles's Diary*, vol. 1, pp. 374–75, 382, 404, 439–40; Patrick, 27 December 1863, *Inside Lincoln's Army*, p. 325; Lyman, 26 October 1863, 10 December 1863, and 12 December 1863, *Meade's Headquarters*, pp. 38–39, 60, 61; George Meade to Margaret Meade, 26 July 1863, 24 September 1863, 11 December 1863, and 28 December 1863, Meade, *Life and Letters*, vol. 2, pp. 137, 150, 160–61, 163–64; Horatio Nelson Taft, 23 October 1863, *The Diary of Horatio Nelson Taft*, vol. 2, http://memory.loc.gov/ammem/tafthtml/tafthome.html.

47. The quote is from Birney to Gross, 16 March 1864, Birney Papers. See also Chase to Hooker, 21 December 1863, Chase, *Chase Papers*, vol. 4, p. 223; Meade to Margaret Meade, 14 March 1864, Meade, *Life and Letters*, vol. 2, pp. 177–78; Meade to Henry Cram, 15 March 1864, ibid., p. 179; Hooker to Henry Wilson, 17 December 1864, *OR*, vol. 45, pt. 2, pp. 246, 248; Sickles to Chandler, December 1863, Chandler Papers, reel 1; Howe's testimony, 4 March 1864, U.S. Congress, *Reports of the Joint Committee*, p. 327; Birney to Gross, 16 March 1864, Birney Papers.

48. Humphreys to his wife, January 1864, Humphreys Letters; Meade to Margaret Meade, 6 March 1864, 8 March 1864, and 20 March 1864, Meade, *Life and Letters*, vol. 2, pp. 169–70, 176, 181–82; Sickles to Chandler, December 1863, Chandler Papers, reel 1.

49. Meade to Margaret Meade, 9 March 1864 and 20 March 1864, Meade, *Life and Letters*, vol. 2, pp. 176, 181–82; Sickles to Chandler, December 1863, Chandler Papers, reel 1; Howe's testimony, 4 March 1864, U.S. Congress, *Reports of the Joint Committee*, p. 327; Pleasonton's testimony, 7 March 1864, ibid., p. 365; Birney's testimony, 7 March 1864, ibid., pp. 373–74; Butterfield's testimony, 25 March 1864, ibid., p. 424.

50. Patrick, 9 March 1864, *Inside Lincoln's Army*, p. 344; Halleck to Meade, 20 March 1864, *OR*, vol. 27, pt. 1, p. 137; Meade to Halleck, 22 March 1864, ibid., pp. 137–38; Lincoln to Meade, 29 March 1864, ibid., 139; Meade to Margaret Meade, 6 March 1864, 9 March 1864, 14 March 1864, 16 March 1864, 26 March 1864, and 6 April 1864, Meade, *Life and Letters*, vol. 2, pp. 169–70, 176, 177–78, 180, 183–84, 188; Meade to E. D. Townsend, 4 March 1864, *OR*, vol. 27, pt. 1, p. 128;

51. Meade to Margaret Meade, 6 March 1864, 14 March 1864, and 4 April 1864, Meade, *Life and Letters*, vol. 2, pp. 169–70, 177–78, 187; Warren to Emily Warren, 6 April 1864, Warren Papers, Folder 5; Grant, *Personal Memoirs*, vol. 2, p. 383.

52. Birney to Meade, 10 March 1864, *OR*, vol. 27, pt. 1, p. 122; Meade to Margaret Meade, 9 March 1864, 11 April 1864, and 18 April 1864, Meade, *Life and Letters*, vol. 2, pp. 176, 289, 190; Birney to Gross, 16 March 1864 and 18 April 1864, Birney Papers.

Chapter 5. Grant as General in Chief: March 1864 to April 1865

1. Sylvanus Cadwallader, *Three Years with Grant: As Recalled by War Correspondent Sylvanus Cadwallader*, ed. Benjamin Thomas (New York: Alfred A. Knopf, 1956), pp.

347–53; Charles Wainwright, 24 March 1864, A *Diary of Battle: The Personal Journals of Colonel Charles S. Wainwright*, ed. Allan Nevins (New York: Harcourt, Brace and World, 1962), p. 338; John Sedgwick to Ellen Sedgwick Welch, 14 March 1864, Sedgwick, *Sedgwick's Correspondence*, vol. 2, p. 177; Horace Porter, *Campaigning with Grant* (Bloomington: Indiana University Press, 1961), p. 272; Orlando Willcox, *Forgotten Valor: The Memoirs, Journals, and Civil War Letters of Orlando B. Willcox*, ed. Robert Garth Scott (Kent, OH: Kent State University Press, 1999), pp. 498–501; Welles, 11 March 1864, *Welles's Diary*, vol. 1, pp. 539–40; Hay, 27 March 1864, *Hay's Letters and Diaries*, p. 168; George Meade to Margaret Meade, 24 April 1864, George Meade, *The Life and Letters of George Gordon Meade*, vol. 2, ed. George Meade (New York: Charles Scribner's Sons, 1913), p. 191; Meade to Henry Cram, 24 November 1864, ibid., p. 246; Charles Francis Adams Jr. to his Dad, 29 May 1864, Worthington Chauncey Ford, ed., *A Cycle of Adams Letters, 1861–1865*, vol. 2 (Boston: Houghton Mifflin, 1920), pp. 133–34; James Harrison Wilson, *Under the Old Flag: Recollections of Military Operations in the War for the Union, the Spanish War and the Boxer Rebellion, etc.*, vol. 1 (Westport, CT: Greenwood Press, 1971), pp. 322–23; James Rusling, *Men and Things I Saw in Civil War Days* (New York: Eaton and Mains, 1899), p. 136; Robert McAllister to Henrietta McAllister, 24 April 1864, McAllister, *McAllister's Letters*, p. 408; Adam Badeau, *Military History of Ulysses S. Grant, from April, 1861, to April, 1865*, vol. 3 (New York: D. Appleton, 1881), pp. 589–90; Noah Brooks, *Washington D.C. in Lincoln's Time*, ed. Herbert Mitgang (Athens: University of Georgia Press, 1989), p. 134; Morris Schaff, *The Battle of the Wilderness* (Boston: Houghton Mifflin, 1910), p. 47; James Barnet Fry, *Military Miscellanies* (New York: Brentano's, 1889), p. 295.

2. Ulysses Grant, *Personal Memoirs of U. S. Grant*, vol. 2 (New York: Century, 1917), pp. 45–46, 50–51; General Orders No. 98, 12 March 1864, *OR*, vol. 33, p. 669; James Nesmith, 11 February 1864, John C. Rives, ed., "The Debates and Proceedings of Congress for the 37th and 38th Sessions," *The Congressional Globe*, vol. 33, 38th Cong., sess. 1, Reel 22, p. 587; Henry Wilson, 11 February 1864, ibid., p. 589.

3. The quote is from Grenville Dodge, *Personal Recollections of President Abraham Lincoln, General Ulysses S. Grant and General William T. Sherman* (Denver: Sage Books, 1965), pp. 69–70. See also James Biddle to Gertrude Biddle, 20 March 1864, Biddle Letters; Porter, *Campaigning with Grant*, pp. 28–29; Grant, *Personal Memoirs*, vol. 2, pp. 46–47; Meade to Margaret Meade, 8 March 1864, 14 March 1864, and 4 April 1864, Meade, *Life and Letters*, vol. 2, pp. 176, 177–78, 187; Comstock, 10 March 1864 and 17 March 1864, *Comstock's Diary*, p. 260, 261; Badeau, *Military History of Grant*, vol. 3, p. 16; Smith, *Smith's Autobiography*, pp. 82–84.

4. Porter, *Campaigning with Grant*, pp. 114–15; Grant, *Personal Memoirs*, vol. 2, pp. 46–47; Wilson, *Life of Rawlings*, pp. 195–96; Badeau, *Military History of Grant*, vol. 3, pp. 186–90.

5. Meade to Margaret Meade, 22 March 1864, 26 March 1864, and 24 April 1864, Meade, *Life and Letters*, vol. 2, pp. 181–82, 183, 191; Badeau, *Military History of Grant*, vol. 3, pp. 186–90; Andrew Humphreys to [unknown], n.d., *Humphreys's Biography*, p. 219.

6. Wainwright, 10 January 1864, 10 March 1864, and 24 March 1864, *Diary of Battle*, pp. 314–15, 329, 335; Sedgwick to Charles Townsend, 16 December 1863, Sedgwick, *Sedgwick's Correspondence*, vol. 2, p. 168; Meade to Margaret Meade, 16 April 1864, Meade, *Life and Letters*, vol. 2, p. 190; Meade to Henry Halleck, 4 March 1864, *OR*, vol. 33, p. 638; General Orders No. 115, 23 March 1864, ibid., p. 717; General Orders No. 10, 24 March 1864, ibid., p. 722; Special Orders No. 75, 24 March 1864, ibid., vol. 51,

pt. 1, p. 1152; John Haley, 3 March to 30 April 1864, *The Rebel Yell and the Yankee Hurrah: The Civil War Journal of a Maine Volunteer*, ed. Ruth L. Silliker (Camden, ME: Down East Books, 1985), p. 139; Adam De Gurowski, 24 March 1864, *Diary*, vol. 3 (Boston: Lee and Shepard, 1866), p. 148; David Birney to George Gross, 5 April 1864, Birney Papers; Alexander Hays to Annie Hays, 25 March 1864, Hays, *Hays's Life and Letters*, p. 562.

7. John Gibbon to his wife, 4 April 1864, Gibbon Letters; Meade to Margaret Meade, 29 March 1864, Meade, *Life and Letters*, vol. 2, p. 185; Comstock, 16 March 1864 and 24 March 1864, *Comstock's Diary*, p. 261; Ulysses Grant to Halleck, 25 March 1864, *OR*, vol. 33, p. 730.

8. The quote is from Gouverneur Warren to Emily Warren, 27 March 1864, Warren Papers, Folder 5. See also Biddle to Gertrude Biddle, 24 March 1864, Biddle Letters; Wainwright, 24 March 1864, *Diary of Battle*, p. 335; Grant, *Personal Memoirs*, vol. 2, p. 125; Theodore Lyman, 30 March 1864, *Meade's Headquarters, 1863–1865: Letters of Colonel Theodore Lyman from The Wilderness to Appomattox*, ed. George Agassiz (Boston: Atlantic Monthly Press, 1922), pp. 80–81; Meade to Margaret Meade, 29 March 1864, Meade, *Life and Letters*, vol. 2, p. 185; Meade to Halleck, 4 March 1864, *OR*, vol. 33, p. 638; General Orders No. 115, 23 March 1864, ibid., p. 717; Special Orders No. 126, 24 March 1864, ibid., p. 722; Grant to Halleck, 25 March 1864, ibid., p. 730; Gurowski, 24 March 1864, *Diary*, vol. 3, p. 148; Warren to Emily Warren, 30 March 1864, Warren Papers, Folder 5.

9. Grant, *Personal Memoirs*, vol. 2, pp. 60–61; Meade to Margaret Meade, 24 March 1864 and 29 March 1864, Meade, *Life and Letters*, vol. 2, pp. 182–83, 185; Grant to Edwin Stanton, 24 March 1864, *OR*, vol. 33, p. 720.

10. The quote is from Porter, *Campaigning with Grant*, pp. 23–24. See also Cadwallader, *Three Years with Grant*, pp. 305–6; John Pope, *The Military Memoirs of General John Pope*, ed. Peter Cozzens and Robert Girardi (Chapel Hill: University of North Carolina Press, 1998), p. 93; Wainwright, 3 April 1865, *Diary of Battle*, p. 517; Porter, *Campaigning with Grant*, p. 228; Sheridan, *Sheridan's Memoirs*, pp. 140, 213–14; Grant, *Personal Memoirs*, vol. 2, p. 60; Theodore Rodenbough, "Sheridan's Richmond Raid," *Battles and Leaders of the Civil War*, vol. 4, ed. Robert Underwood Johnson and Clarence Clough Buel (New York: Thomas Yoseloff, 1956), p. 188; Marsena Patrick, 6 April 1864, *Inside Lincoln's Army: The Diary of Marsena Rudolph Patrick, Provost Marshal General, Army of the Potomac*, ed. David Sparks (New York: Thomas Yoseloff, 1964), p. 355; Lyman, 13 April 1864, *Meade's Headquarters*, p. 82; Comstock, 18 February 1864, *Comstock's Diary*, p. 257; Badeau, *Military History of Grant*, vol. 2, pp. 500–01.

11. Gibbon to his wife, 22 April 1864, Gibbon Letters; Meade to Halleck, 18 March 1864, *OR*, vol. 33, p. 688; Winfield Scott Hancock to Seth Williams, 1 May 1864, ibid., vol. 36, pt. 2, p. 320; E. D. Townsend to Hancock, 7 May 1864, ibid., p. 485; Hancock, *Hancock Reminiscences*, pp. 97–101.

12. Charles Benjamin, "Hooker's Appointment and Removal," *Battles and Leaders*, vol. 3, p. 239n.

13. Sedgwick to Ellen Sedgwick Welch, 17 February 1864, Sedgwick, *Sedgwick's Correspondence*, vol. 2, p. 175.

14. Meade to Margaret Meade, 29 March 1864, Meade, *Life and Letters*, vol. 2, p. 185; John Gibbon, *Personal Recollections of the Civil War* (New York: G. P. Putnam's Sons, 1928), pp. 209–10; Sedgwick to Charles Townsend, 16 December 1863, Sedgwick, *Sedgwick's Correspondence*, vol. 2, p. 168.

15. The quote is from Wainwright, 19 January 1864, *Diary of Battle*, pp. 316–17. See also Charles Mills to his Mom, 27 April 1864, Charles Mills, *Through Blood and Fire: The Civil War Letters of Major Charles A. Mills, 1862–1865*, ed. Gregory Coco (Gettysburg, PA: Gregory Coco, 1982), pp. 68–69.

16. Lyman, 5 May 1864, *Meade's Headquarters*, p. 91n.

17. Schaff, *Wilderness*, pp. 225–26.

18. Porter, *Campaigning with Grant*, pp. 57–58.

19. Quoted in Shelby Foote, *The Civil War: A Narrative*, vol. 3 (New York: Vintage Books, 1986), p. 168.

20. Lyman, 16 May 1864, *Meade's Headquarters*, p. 94.

21. Horatio Wright interview, Garland Collection.

22. Quoted in Bruce Catton, *Bruce Catton's Civil War: Three Volumes in One (A Stillness at Appomattox)* (New York: Fairfax Press, 1984), p. 513.

23. Wilson, *Under the Old Flag*, vol. 1, p. 390.

24. Warren to Meade, 8 May 1864, *OR*, vol. 33, pt. 2, p. 542.

25. Rodenbough, "Sheridan's Richmond Raid," p. 189.

26. Sheridan, *Sheridan's Memoirs*, pp. 154–55.

27. Ibid., pp. 145–48, 154–55; Porter, *Campaigning with Grant*, pp. 83–84; Lyman, *Meade's Headquarters*, pp. 105–6n.

28. The quote is from Wainwright, 9 May 1864, *Diary of Battle*, p. 360. Most of the information on Sedgwick's death is from his chief of staff, Martin McMahon, "The Death of General John Sedgwick," *Battles and Leaders*, vol. 4, p. 175. See also Porter, *Campaigning with Grant*, pp. 89–90; Gibbon, *Personal Recollections*, p. 217; Badeau, *Military History of Grant*, vol. 2, p. 150.

29. Biddle to Gertrude Biddle, 22 May 1864, Biddle Letters; McMahon, "The Death of General John Sedgwick," p. 175; General Orders No. 199, 16 May 1864, *OR*, vol. 36, pt. 2, p. 822.

30. Wright interview, Garland Collection; Elizabeth Blair Lee, 17 March 1863, *Wartime Washington: The Civil War Letters of Elizabeth Blair Lee*, ed. Virginia Jeans Laas (Urbana: University of Illinois Press, 1991), p. 252; Wainwright, 9 May 1864, *Diary of Battle*, p. 360; Sheridan, *Sheridan's Memoirs*, p. 220; Martin McMahon, "Cold Harbor," *Battles and Leaders*, vol. 4, p. 213; John Sherman to Chase, 10 September 1862 and 28 September 1862, Chase, *Chase Papers*, vol. 3, pp. 262–63, 286–87; Lyman, 17 May 1864, *Meade's Headquarters*, p. 98; Meade to Margaret Meade, 17 March 1863, Meade, *Life and Letters*, vol. 1, p. 360; Charles Dana, *Recollections of the Civil War: With the Leaders at Washington and in the Field in the Sixties* (Lincoln: University of Nebraska Press, 1996), p. 191; Meade, 8 May 1864, *OR*, vol. 36, pt. 2, p. 540; Pope to Halleck, 16 August 1862, ibid., vol. 12, pt. 3, p. 576; John Rawlins to his wife, 9 May 1864, Wilson, *Life of Rawlins*, p. 218; Charles Page, *Letters of a War Correspondent* (Boston: L. C. Page, 1899), p. 66; Jesse Reno to Pope, 16 August 1862, *OR*, vol. 51, pt. 1, p. 740; Halleck to Ambrose Burnside, 30 March 1863, ibid., vol. 23, pt. 2, p. 193.

31. Quoted from Catton, *Catton's Civil War*, p. 535. See also Lyman, 23 May 1864, *Meade's Headquarters*, p. 112; Hancock, 12 May 1864, *OR*, vol. 36, pt. 2, p. 657.

32. Badeau, *Military History of Grant*, vol. 2, pp. 177–78.

33. Grant, *Personal Memoirs*, vol. 2, p. 137.

34. Ibid., pp. 137–38; Wainwright, 10 May 1864, *Diary of Battle*, p. 364; Grant to Meade, 12 May 1864, Grant, *Grant Papers*, vol. 10, p. 433; Porter, *Campaigning with Grant*, p. 118; Grant to Halleck, 11 May 1864, *OR*, vol. 36, pt. 2, p. 627; Meade to

Grant, 12 May 1864, ibid., p. 654; Warren to Meade, 12 May 1864, ibid., p. 657; Humphreys to Warren, 12 May 1864, ibid., p. 663; Warren to Charles Griffin, 12 May 1864, ibid., p. 667; Warren to Samuel Crawford, 12 May 1864, ibid., p. 669; Warren to Cutler, 12 May 1864, ibid., p. 671; Dana to Stanton, 12 May 1864, ibid., pt. 1, p. 67; Badeau, *Military History of Grant*, vol. 2, pp. 183–84; Washington Roebling to Emily Warren, 15 May 1864, Washington Roebling, *Wash Roebling's War: Being a Selection from the Unpublished Letters of Washington Augustus Roebling*, ed. Earl Schenck Miers (Newark, DE: Curtis Paper, 1961), p. 24.

35. Grant to Stanton, 13 May 1864, Grant, *Grant Papers*, vol. 10, p. 434.

36. Ibid.; Stanton to Grant, 14 May 1864, *OR*, vol. 36, pt. 2, p. 746; Halleck to Grant, 23 May 1864, ibid., pt. 3, p. 115; George Augustus Armes, *Ups and Downs of an Army Officer* (Washington, DC, 1900), p. 88.

37. Gibbon, *Personal Recollections*, pp. 227–28.

38. Lyman, 3 June 1864, *Meade's Headquarters*, p. 147.

39. Wainwright, 3 June 1864, *Diary of Battle*, p. 405.

40. Ibid., 1 June 1864 and 7 June 1864, pp. 396, 409; Wilson, *Under the Old Flag*, vol. 1, pp. 397–401; Warren to Emily Warren, 26 May 1864, Warren Papers, Folder 5.

41. Badeau, *Military History of Grant*, vol. 2, pp. 260–61.

42. Wainwright, 25 May 1864, *Diary of Battle*, p. 387; Porter, *Campaigning with Grant*, pp. 144–45; Patrick, 23 May 1864, *Inside Lincoln's Army*, p. 376; Lyman, 4 June 1864, *Meade's Headquarters*, pp. 148–49; Special Orders No. 25, 24 May 1864, *OR*, vol. 36, pt. 3, p. 169; Burnside to Seth Williams, 27 May 1864, ibid., p. 256; Seth Williams to Burnside, 27 May 1864, ibid., p. 258.

43. Thomas Hyde to his Mom, 24 May 1864, Thomas W. Hyde, *Civil War Letters* (N.p.: privately printed, 1933), p. 134; Porter, *Campaigning with Grant*, p. 190; Lyman, 24 May 1864 and 1 June 1864, *Meade's Headquarters*, pp. 125–26, 138; Hancock to Seth Williams, 30 May 1864, *OR*, vol. 36, pt. 3, p. 328; Dana to Stanton, 1 June 1864, ibid., pt. 1, p. 85; Dana to Stanton, 7 July 1864, ibid., vol. 40, pt. 1, p. 35; Wilson, *Under the Old Flag*, vol. 1, p. 443; Gouverneur to Warren, 26 May 1864, Warren Papers, Folder 5; William Smith, "The Eighteenth Corps at Cold Harbor," *Battles and Leaders*, vol. 4, p. 228; Gibbon, *Personal Recollections*, pp. 239–40.

44. Lyman, 24 May 1864, *Meade's Headquarters*, p. 126; Wilson, *Under the Old Flag*, vol. 1, pp. 397–404; Rawlins to his wife, 9 May 1864, Wilson, *Life of Rawlins*, p. 229.

45. Meade to John Martindale, 18 June 1864, *OR*, vol. 40, pt. 2, p. 205.

46. Gibbon, *Personal Recollections*, pp. 243–45; William Farrar Smith, *From Chattanooga to Petersburg under Generals Grant and Butler* (Boston: Houghton, Mifflin, 1893), p. 33; Meade to Grant, 17 June 1864, *OR*, vol. 40, pt. 2, p. 118; Meade to Burnside, 17 June 1864, ibid., p. 135; Seth Williams, 18 June 1864, ibid., p. 161; Meade to Birney, 18 June 1864, ibid., p. 167.

47. Wainwright, 12 July 1864, *Diary of Battle*, p. 436; Henry Lockwood to Seth Williams, 10 June 1864, *OR*, vol. 36, pt. 3, pp. 726–28; Meade to Warren and Burnside, 18 June 1864, ibid., vol. 40, pt. 2, p. 179; Wilson, *Under the Old Flag*, vol. 1, p. 455; Warren to Humphreys [?], 20 July 1864, *OR*, vol. 40, pt. 2, p. 350; Dana to Stanton, 1 July 1864, ibid., pt. 1, p. 28; Warren to Emily Warren, 20 June 1864, 25 June 1864, 20 July 1864, and 26 August 1864, Warren Papers, Folder 6.

48. Armes to [unknown], 21 June 1864, Armes, *Ups and Downs*, p. 104.

49. Meade to Margaret Meade, 25 June 1864, Meade, *Life and Letters*, vol. 2, pp. 208–9; Nelson Miles to his uncle, 28 June 1864, Miles Papers, Civil War Correspon-

dence File; Armes to [unknown], 18 June 1864, Armes, *Ups and Downs*, p. 103; Armes to [unknown], 20 June 1864, ibid., p. 104; Armes to [unknown], 22 June 1864, ibid., p. 106.

50. Lyman, 20 July 1864, *Meade's Headquarters*, p. 192.

51. Porter, *Campaigning with Grant*, p. 246; Welles, 29 December 1862 and 16 July 1863, *Welles's Diary*, vol. 1, pp. 209–10, 373; Abraham Lincoln, 26 February 1864, "Memorandum concerning Benjamin F. Butler," *The Collected Works of Abraham Lincoln*, vol. 7, ed. Roy Basler (New Brunswick, NJ: Rutgers University Press, 1953), p. 207; Smith, *Smith's Autobiography*, p. 119; Browning, 2 January 1863 and 12 July 1864, *Browning's Diary*, vol. 1, pp. 609, 676; Comstock, 27 October 1864, *Comstock's Diary*, p. 293; Badeau, *Military History of Grant*, vol. 2, pp. 44, 259; Miles to his brother, 26 July 1864, Miles Papers, Civil War Correspondence File; Hay, 21 May 1864, *Hay's Letters and Diaries*, p. 183; Benjamin Butler, *Butler's Book: Autobiography and Personal Reminiscences of Major-General Benjamin Butler* (Boston: A M Thayer, 1892), pp. 631–34.

52. Smith to Franklin, 28 April 1864, Franklin Papers; Porter, *Campaigning with Grant*, p. 246; Badeau, *Military History of Grant*, vol. 2, p. 44; Grant to Halleck, 28 March 1864, Grant, *Grant Papers*, vol. 10, p. 231; Grant, *Personal Memoirs*, vol. 2, p. 60; Grant to Stanton, 12 November 1863, *OR*, vol. 31, pt. 3, p. 121; Grant to Lincoln, 30 November 1863, ibid., p. 277; Smith, *From Chattanooga to Petersburg*, p. 16; Smith, *Smith's Autobiography*, p. 84.

53. Welles, 24 October 1863, *Welles's Diary*, vol. 1, pp. 474–75; Grant, *Personal Memoirs*, vol. 2, p. 56; Hay, 27 March 1864 and 25 June 1864, *Hay's Letters and Diaries*, pp. 168, 198; Grant to Butler, 2 April 1864, *OR*, vol. 33, p. 795; Quincy Gillmore to Halleck, 19 March 1864, ibid., vol. 35, pt. 2, p. 24; Butler to Henry Wilson, 23 April 1864, ibid., vol. 33, p. 959; John Turner to Butler, 20 April 1864, Butler, *Butler's Correspondence*, vol. 4, p. 108.

54. William Smith, "Butler's Attack on Drewry's Bluff," *Battles and Leaders*, vol. 4, p. 208.

55. Butler to Henry Wilson, 28 May 1864, *OR*, vol. 36, pt. 3, p. 279.

56. Smith, "Butler's Attack on Drewry's Bluff," p. 208; Smith, *From Chattanooga to Petersburg*, p. 137; Butler to Henry Wilson, 7 May 1864, *OR*, vol. 36, pt. 2, p. 518; Charles Sumner to Butler, 23 May 1864, ibid., pt. 3, p. 139; Smith, *Smith's Autobiography*, pp. 86–87, 90; Butler, *Butler's Book*, p. 639; Gillmore to Butler, 17 May 1864, *OR*, vol. 51, pt. 1, p. 1163; Butler to Gillmore, 4 May 1864, Butler, *Butler's Correspondence*, vol. 4, p. 162; J. K. Herbert to Butler, 26 May 1864, ibid., pp. 269–70; Herbert to Butler, 31 May 1864, ibid, p. 292.

57. Grant to Halleck, 21 May 1864, Grant, *Grant Papers*, vol. 10, p. 475; Montgomery Meigs and John Barnard to Halleck, 23 May 1864 and 24 May 1864, *OR*, vol. 36, pt. 3, pp. 141, 177; Halleck to Butler, 26 May 1864, ibid., p. 234; Butler to Sarah Butler, 25 May 1864, Butler, *Butler's Correspondence*, vol. 4, p. 263.

58. Hay, 21 June 1864, *Hay's Letters and Diaries*, p. 195; Butler to Gillmore, 26 May 1864, *OR*, vol. 36, pt. 3, p. 238; Butler to Henry Wilson, 28 May 1864, ibid., p. 279; Butler to Gillmore, 29 May 1864, ibid., p. 317; Gillmore to Halleck, 30 May 1864, ibid., p. 368; Butler to Stanton, 9 June 1864, ibid., p. 717; R. S. Davis, 14 June 1864, ibid., vol. 40, pt. 2, p. 39; Grant to Butler, 17 June 1864, ibid., p. 142; Butler to Grant, 17 June 1864, ibid.; Davis, 17 June 1864, ibid., p. 148; Butler to Grant, 21 June 1864, p. 302; Dana to Stanton, 17 June 1864, ibid., pt. 1, p. 23; Butler to Gillmore, 11 June 1864, Butler, *Butler's Correspondence*, vol. 4, pp. 343–54; Butler to Butler, 13 June 1864 and 14 June 1864, ibid., pp. 362, 365; John Shaffer to Gillmore, 14 June 1864, ibid., pp. 368–71.

59. Gibbon to his wife, 31 March 1863, Gibbon Letters; Sedgwick, 15 May 1863, OR, vol. 35, pt. 1, p. 561; McClellan, 4 August 1863, ibid., vol. 11, pt. 1, p. 63.

60. Sedgwick to Lincoln, 8 May 1863, Sedgwick, *Sedgwick's Correspondence*, vol. 2, pp. 108–9; Patrick, 4 January 1863, *Inside Lincoln's Army*, p. 199; General Orders No. 8, 23 January 1863, OR, vol. 21, p. 98; William Doubleday to Zachariah Chandler, 6 December 1861, Chandler Papers, reel 1; Chandler to his wife, 26 January 1863, ibid.; Henry Slocum to Joseph Howland, 4 February 1863, Howland Papers; William Brooks to his Dad, 22 June 1862, 2 October 1862, 17 February 1863, 18 March 1863, 6 April 1863, 25 April 1863, and 11 May 1863, Brooks Papers, Civil War Letters Folder.

61. Meigs and Barnard to Halleck, 24 May 1864, OR, vol. 36, pt. 3, p. 177; Grant to Butler, 17 June 1864, ibid., vol. 40, pt. 2, p. 141; Butler to Grant, 17 June 1864, p. 142; Smith, *Smith's Autobiography*, p. 30; Grant to Butler, 5 April 1864, Butler, *Butler's Correspondence*, vol. 4, p. 24; Butler to Grant, 8 April 1864, ibid., p. 42; Grant to Brooks, 6 July 1864, Grant, *Grant Papers*, vol. 11, p. 181; Butler to Brooks, 10 July 1864, OR, vol. 40, pt. 3, p. 139; Grant to Halleck, 11 July 1864, ibid., p. 144; Butler to Brooks, 18 July 1864, ibid., p. 329.

62. Smith to Franklin, 28 April 1864, Franklin Papers; Patrick, 22 July 1864, *Inside Lincoln's Army*, pp. 401–2; Smith, *From Chattanooga to Petersburg*, p. 33, 175–77; Meade to Margaret Meade, 7 July 1864 and 23 July 1864, Meade, *Life and Letters*, vol. 2, pp. 210, 215; Dana, *Recollections*, pp. 220–21; Smith to Grant, 2 July 1864, OR, vol. 40, pt. 2, pp. 594–95; Smith, *Smith's Autobiography*, p. 111; Wilson, *Life of Rawlins*, p. 228; Comstock, 17 July 1864, *Comstock's Diary*, p. 282; Sarah Butler to Fisher Hildreth, 14 June 1864, Butler, *Butler's Correspondence*, vol. 4, pp. 364–65.

63. Smith to Grant, 2 July 1864, OR, vol. 40, pt. 2, p. 595.

64. Ibid.; Porter, *Campaigning with Grant*, pp. 245–46; Smith to Butler, 10 May 1864, OR, vol. 36, pt. 2, p. 624; Butler to Smith, 21 June 1864, ibid., vol. 40, pt. 2, p. 299; Smith to Butler, 21 June 1864, ibid., p. 300; Butler to Smith, 21 June 1864, ibid.; Smith to Rawlins, 21 June 1864 and 30 June 1864, ibid., pp. 301, 538.

65. Grant to Halleck, 1 July 1864, Grant, *Grant Papers*, vol. 11, pp. 155–56; Butler to Horatio Wright, 17 June 1864, OR, vol. 40, pt. 2, p. 132; Wright to Butler, 17 June 1864, ibid.; Halleck to Grant, 3 July 1864, ibid., p. 598; Grant to Halleck, 6 July 1864, ibid., pt. 3, p. 31; Stanton to Halleck, 7 July 1864, ibid., p. 59; General Orders No. 225, 7 July 1864, ibid., p. 69; Dana to Stanton, 1 July 1864, ibid., pt. 1, p. 28; Comstock, 26 June 1864, *Comstock's Diary*, p. 276.

66. Butler to Butler, 3 July 1864, Butler, *Butler's Correspondence*, vol. 4, p. 461.

67. Ibid., 10 July 1864, pp. 481–82.

68. Ibid.

69. The quote is from Butler to Butler, 15 July 1864, *Butler's Correspondence*, vol. 4, p. 503. See also Grant to Butler, 18 July 1864, Grant, *Grant Papers*, vol. 11, pp. 275–76; Patrick, 27 July 1864, *Inside Lincoln's Army*, pp. 403–4; Butler to Grant, 14 July 1864, OR, vol. 40, pt. 3, p. 247; Butler, *Butler's Book*, p. 878; Butler to Butler, 10 July 1864, *Butler's Correspondence*, vol. 4, pp. 481–82; Shaffer to Butler, 27 July 1864, ibid., pp. 547–48.

70. Smith, *Smith's Autobiography*, p. 116.

71. Rawlins to his wife, 19 July 1864, Wilson, *Life of Rawlins*, p. 247.

72. Biddle to Gertrude Biddle, 22 July 1864, Biddle Letters; Grant to Smith, 2 July 1864, Grant, *Grant Papers*, vol. 11, p. 162; Porter, *Campaigning with Grant*, pp. 245–46; George Templeton Strong, 8 August 1864, *Diary of the Civil War, 1860–1865*, ed. Allan Nevins (New York: Macmillan, 1962), p. 471; Patrick, 22 July 1864, *Inside Lincoln's*

Army, pp. 401–2; Smith, *From Chattanooga to Petersburg*, pp. 46–47, 52–58, 174–75; Rawlins to Smith, 30 June 1864, Smith, *Smith's Autobiography*, p. 110n; Smith, *Smith's Autobiography*, pp. 111–12; Special Orders No. 62, 19 July 1862, *OR*, vol. 40, pt. 3, p. 334; Comstock, 17 July 1864, *Comstock's Diary*, p. 282; Butler, *Butler's Book*, pp. 694–96.

73. Humphreys to Grant, 15 July 1864, Grant, *Grant Papers*, vol. 11, pp. 259n–60n.

74. Ibid.; Patrick, 27 July 1864, *Inside Lincoln's Army*, pp. 403–4; Humphreys to his wife, 31 July 1864, Humphreys Letters; Grant to Meade, 15 July 1864, Grant, *Grant Papers*, vol. 11, p. 259; Meade to Grant, 15 July 1864, *OR*, vol. 40, pt. 3, p. 255; Grant to Meade, 16 July 1864, ibid., p. 276; Humphreys to [unknown], 6 June 1864, Humphreys, *Humphreys's Biography*, p. 229; Humphreys to [unknown], 19 June 1864, ibid., p. 237; Humphreys to his wife, 20 July 1864, Humphreys Letters.

75. Grant to Halleck, 8 July 1864 and 10 July 1864, Grant, *Grant Papers*, vol. 11, pp. 192, 204; Halleck to Grant, 12 July 1864, *OR*, vol. 40, pt. 3, p. 175; Halleck to Grant, 7 July 1864, ibid., vol. 37, pt. 2, p. 98; General Orders No. 236, 28 July 1864, ibid., vol. 40, pt. 3, p. 577; Porter, *Campaigning with Grant*, p. 453; Patrick, 20 May 1865, *Inside Lincoln's Army*, p. 509; Meade to Margaret Meade, 27 December 1861, Meade, *Life and Letters*, vol. 1, p. 239; Charles Veil, "An Old Boy's Personal Recollections and Reminiscences of the Civil War," Veil Folder, Civil War Miscellaneous, p. 17; Edward Ord to William Seward, 23 May 1864, Lincoln Papers.

76. Grant to Butler, 20 July 1864, Grant, *Grant Papers*, vol. 11, pp. 287–88; Special Orders No. 64, 21 July 1864, *OR*, vol. 40, pt. 3, p. 361; Butler to Grant, 21 July 1864, ibid., p. 376; Birney to Gross, 23 July 1864, Birney Papers.

77. Lyman, 12 November 1864, *Meade's Headquarters*, p. 266.

78. Biddle to Gertrude Biddle, 25 June 1864, Biddle Letters; Chase, 10 September 1862 and 13 September 1862, Chase, *Chase Papers*, vol. 1, pp. 378, 386; Philip Kearny to Cortlandt Parker, 10 July 1862, Philip Kearney, *Letters from the Peninsula: The Civil War Letters of General Philip Kearny*, ed. William Styple (Kearny, NJ: Belle Grove Publishing, 1988), p. 130; Kearny's report, 6 July 1864, ibid., p. 124; Lyman, 10 July 1864, *Meade's Headquarters*, p. 188; Meade to Margaret Meade, 25 June 1864, Meade, *Life and Letters*, vol. 2, pp. 208–9; Robert McAllister to Ellen McAllister, 9 April 1864, McAllister, *McAllister's Letters*, p. 404; Daniel Sickles to Seth Williams, 14 May 1863, *OR*, vol. 41, pt. 1, p. 1040; Regis de Trobriand, *Four Years with the Army of the Potomac*, trans. George K. Dauchy (Boston: Ticknor, 1889), pp. 316–17; Burnside, n.d., *OR*, vol. 21, p. 93; George Stoneman, 20 December 1862, ibid., p. 361; William French, 3 December 1863, ibid., vol. 29, p. 743; Birney to Gross, 7 August 1862, 28 December 1862, 16 March 1863, 27 February 1864, and 26 May 1864, Birney Papers; Armes to [unknown], 22 June 1864, Armes, *Ups and Downs*, p. 106.

79. Humphreys to his wife, 20 October 1864, Humphreys Letters; Meade to Margaret Meade, 19 October 1864, Meade, *Life and Letters*, vol. 2, p. 235; Butler to Grant, 9 October 1864, *OR*, vol. 42, pt. 3, p. 149; Birney to Gross, 21 July 1864 and 6 September 1864, Birney Papers.

80. Meade to Margaret Meade, 25 November 1864, Meade, *Life and Letters*, vol. 2, p. 248; Butler to Rawlins, 30 November 1864, *OR*, vol. 42, pt. 3, p. 761; General Orders No. 297, 3 December 1864, ibid., p. 791; Page, 2 December 1864, *Letters of a War Correspondent*, p. 285.

81. Grant to Stanton, 15 November 1864, Grant, *Grant Papers*, vol. 12, p. 418; George Denison to Chase, 15 July 1863, Chase, *Chase Papers*, vol. 4, pp. 86–87; Meigs and Barnard to Halleck, 23 May 1864 and 24 May 1864, *OR*, vol. 36, pt. 3, pp. 141, 177;

General Orders No. 116, 30 September 1864, ibid., vol. 42, pt. 2, p. 1146; Comstock, 23 July 1864, *Comstock's Diary*, p. 283; Page, 22 June 1864 and 11 September 1864, *Letters of a War Correspondent*, pp. 132–33, 250; Butler to David Farragut, 9 September 1862, *OR*, vol. 15, p. 564; Godfrey Weitzel to Smith, 5 July 1864, ibid., vol. 40, pt. 3, p. 28; Peter Michie, 10 September 1864, ibid., vol. 42, pt. 1, p. 657.

82. Grant to Halleck, 26 April 1864, Grant, *Grant Papers*, vol. 10, p. 356; Grant to Halleck, 1 July 1864, 10 July 1864, and 18 July 1864, ibid., vol. 11, pp. 155, 206, 275; Grant to Butler, 18 July 1864, Grant, *Grant Papers*, vol. 11, pp. 275–76; Grant to Lincoln, 25 July 1864, ibid., pp. 309–11; Grant to Halleck, 1 August 1864, ibid., pp. 358–59; Grant to Julia Grant, 8 August 1864, ibid., p. 383; Ulysses Grant, *Personal Memoirs*, vol. 2, pp. 205–6; Strong, 8 August 1864, *Diary of the Civil War*, p. 471; Patrick, 5 August 1864, *Inside Lincoln's Army*, pp. 409–10; Meade to Margaret Meade, 29 July 1864 and 3 August 1864, Meade, *Life and Letters*, vol. 2, pp. 216–17, 218–19; Halleck to Grant, 21 July 1864, *OR*, vol. 40, pt. 3, p. 360.

83. Dana to Stanton, 7 July 1864, *OR*, vol. 40, pt. 1, p. 35.

84. Ibid.; Biddle to Gertrude Biddle, 25 November 1864, Biddle Letters; Smith, "The Eighteenth Corps at Cold Harbor," p. 228; Patrick, 19 June 1864, 6 July 1864, 27 July 1864, and 23 August 1864, *Inside Lincoln's Army*, pp. 386, 393–94, 403–4, 416; Lyman, 1 June 1864, *Meade's Headquarters*, p. 138; George Meade to Margaret Meade, 19 May 1864, 23 May 1864, 9 June 1864, 12 July 1864, 15 July 1864, 10 August 1864, 13 August 1864, 24 August 1864, 22 September 1864, 25 October 1864, 20 November 1864, 25 November 1864, and 6 December 1864, Meade, *Life and Letters*, vol. 2, pp. 197, 198, 202–3, 212, 212–13, 220–21, 221–22, 223–24, 229, 236–37, 244, 247–48, 249; Seth Williams, 7 June 1864, *OR*, vol. 36, pt. 3, p. 670; Wilson, *Under the Old Flag*, vol. 1, p. 443; Dana to Stanton, 9 June 1864, *OR*, vol. 36, pt. 1, p. 94; Comstock, 7 July 1864, *Comstock's Diary*, p. 279; Warren to Emily Warren, 24 July 1864, Warren Papers, Folder 6.

85. The quote is from Grant to Meade, 24 October 1864, Grant, *Grant Papers*, vol. 12, p. 342. See also Biddle to Gertrude Biddle, 26 August 1864, Biddle Letters; Gibbon, *Personal Recollections*, pp. 239–40; Lyman, 12 July 1864, *Meade's Headquarters*, p. 189; Dana, *Recollections*, pp. 226–28; Dana to Stanton, 9 June 1864, *OR*, vol. 36, pt. 1, p. 94; Badeau, *Military History of Grant*, vol. 2, p. 190; Meade to Margaret Meade, 23 July 1864, Meade, *Life and Letters*, vol. 2, p. 215.

86. The quote is from Warren to Emily Warren, 24 July 1864, Warren Papers, Folder 6. See also Grant to Meade, 19 August 1864, Grant, *Grant Papers*, vol. 12, p. 47; Porter, *Campaigning with Grant*, pp. 251–52; Warren to Meade, 22 July 1864, *OR*, vol. 40, pt. 3, p. 393; Meade to Warren, 22 July 1864, ibid.; Warren to Emily Warren, 25 June 1864, 31 July 1864, 14 August 1864, 22 August 1864, 26 August 1864, and 27 August 1864, Warren Papers, Folder 6.

87. Biddle to Gertrude Biddle, 26 August 1864, Biddle Letters; Patrick, 27 July 1864, *Inside Lincoln's Army*, p. 404; Burnside, 4 July 1864, *OR*, vol. 40, pt. 2, pp. 629–30; Meade to Burnside, 4 July 1864, ibid., p. 630; Comstock, 7 July 1864, *Comstock's Diary*, p. 279; Gouverneur Warren to [unknown], n.d., Taylor, *Life and Letters of an American Soldier*, pp. 186–87; Warren to Emily Warren, 24 July 1864, Warren Papers, Folder 6.

88. Burnside to Grant, 5 June 1864, *OR*, vol. 36, pt. 3, p. 619; Stephen Minot Weld, *War Diary and Letters of Stephen Minot Weld, 1861–1865* (Boston: Massachusetts Historical Society, 1979), pp. 311–12; Gibbon, *Personal Recollections*, pp. 252–53; Grant's testimony, 20 December 1864, Grant, *Grant Papers*, vol. 12, pp. 139–40; Meade to Margaret Meade, 29 July 1864, Meade, *Life and Letters*, vol. 2, p. 217.

89. Meade to Burnside, 30 July 1864, *OR*, vol. 40, pt. 3, p. 660.

90. Burnside to Meade, ibid., p. 660.

91. Porter, *Campaigning with Grant*, pp. 267–68.

92. Biddle to Gertrude Biddle, 25 August 1864, Biddle Letters; Wainwright, 2 August 1864, *Diary of Battle*, pp. 448–49; Grant to Julia Grant, 13 August 1864, Grant, *Grant Papers*, vol. 11, pp. 413–14; Willcox to Marie Willcox, 8 August 1864 and 14 August 1864, Willcox, *Forgotten Valor*, pp. 562–63, 564; Grant, *Personal Memoirs*, vol. 2, p. 203; Patrick, 13 August 1864, *Inside Lincoln's Army*, p. 413; Lyman, 31 July 1864, *Meade's Headquarters*, p. 200; Meade to Margaret Meade, 31 July 1864, 3 August 1864, and 13 August 1864, Meade, *Life and Letters*, vol. 2, pp. 217–18, 218, 223; Burnside to Grant, 31 August 1864, *OR*, vol. 42, pt. 2, p. 603; Theodore Bowers to Burnside, 1 September 1864, ibid., p. 641; Special Orders No. 132, 4 August 1864, ibid., p. 44; Meade to Grant, 8 December 1864, ibid., pt. 3, p. 867; Seth Williams to James Ledlie, 9 December 1864, ibid., p. 919.

93. Burnside to Stanton, 23 March 1865, *OR*, vol. 46, pt. 3, p. 96.

94. Grant to Burnside, 17 October 1864, Grant, *Grant Papers*, vol. 12, p. 317; Grant to Meade, 9 February 1865, Grant, *Grant Papers*, vol. 13, p. 399; Willcox to Marie Willcox, 3 November 1864, Willcox, *Forgotten Valor*, p. 585; Burnside to Willcox, 4 December 1864, ibid., p. 593; Strong, 22 November 1864 and 22 January 1865, *Diary of the Civil War*, pp. 518, 546; Bowers to Burnside, 1 September 1864, *OR*, vol. 42, pt. 2, p. 641; Record of the Court of Inquiry on the Mine Explosion, 9 September 1864, ibid., vol. 40, pt. 1, p. 128; Burnside to Lincoln, 14 April 1865, Lincoln Papers.

95. Mills to his Mom, 20 September 1864, Mills, *Through Blood and Fire*, p. 172; Humphreys to his wife, 7 September 1864, Humphreys Letters; McClellan to Burnside, 19 April 1862, McClellan, *Selected Correspondence*, p. 242; Patrick, 16 August 1864, *Inside Lincoln's Army*, p. 414; Lyman, 14 August 1864 and 10 November 1864, *Meade's Headquarters*, pp. 213, 261; Burnside to Seth Williams, 3 July 1864, *OR*, vol. 40, pt. 2, p. 609; Jacob Cox, *Military Reminiscences of the Civil War*, vol. 1 (New York: Charles Scribner's Sons, 1900), pp. 264–65; Grant to Meade, 13 August 1864, *OR*, vol. 42, pt. 2, p. 142; Henry Raymond, 22 January 1863, "Extracts from the Journal of Henry J. Raymond," *Scribner's Monthly*, November 1879 to April 1880, vol. 19, p. 422; John Parke's testimony, 24 December 1862, *OR*, vol. 12, pt. 2, supplement, p. 937; William Sherman to Parke, 10 July 1863, ibid., vol. 24, pt. 3, p. 563; Burnside, 14 February 1862, ibid., vol. 9, p. 80; Burnside, 30 September 1862, ibid., vol. 19, pt. 1, p. 421; General Orders No. 37, 14 August 1864, ibid., vol. 42, pt. 2, p. 177.

96. Gibbon to his wife, 21 August 1864, Gibbon Letters; Humphreys to his wife, 16 July 1864, Humphreys Letters; Grant to Meade, 28 June 1864, Grant, *Grant Papers*, vol. 11, pp. 145–46; Orlando Willcox, "Actions on the Weldon Railroad," *Battles and Leaders*, vol. 4, p. 573; Patrick, 28 August 1864, *Inside Lincoln's Army*, p. 417; Gibbon, *Personal Recollections*, pp. 243–45, 248–51, 259–63, 265–68; Meade to Margaret Meade, 3 August 1864, Meade, *Life and Letters*, vol. 2, p. 219; Dana, *Recollections*, pp. 220–21; General Orders No. 22, 27 June 1864, *OR*, vol. 40, pt. 2, p. 467; Meade to Hancock, 25 August 1864, ibid., p. 486; Hancock to Seth Williams, 17 September 1864, ibid., p. 886; Comstock, 2 July 1864, *Comstock's Diary*, p. 278; Miles to his uncle, 28 June 1864, Miles Papers, Civil War Correspondence File.

97. Stanton to Grant, 25 October 1864, *OR*, vol. 42, pt. 3, p. 337; Grant to Stanton, 15 November 1864, ibid., p. 619; Hancock, *Hancock Reminiscences*, p. 106; McAllister to McAllister, 7 November 1864, McAllister, *McAllister's Letters*, p. 537; Hancock to

Meade, 16 November 1864, OR, vol. 42, pt. 3, p. 628; Humpheys to [unknown], n.d., *Humphreys's Biography*, pp. 256–57, 260–61; Dodge, *Personal Recollections*, p. 79.

98. Humphreys to his wife, 20 July 1864, 10 November 1864, 16 March 1865, and 27 March 1865, Humphreys Letters; Grant to Meade, 30 November 1864, Grant, *Grant Papers*, vol. 13, pp. 43–44; Grant to Stanton, 22 February 1865, ibid., vol. 14, p. 13; Patrick, 11 August 1864, *Inside Lincoln's Army*, p. 413; Lyman, 27 November 1864, *Meade's Headquarters*, p. 279; McAllister to McAllister, 26 November 1864, McAllister, *McAllister's Letters*, p. 547; General Orders No. 45, 26 November 1864, OR, vol. 42, pt. 3, p. 714; Humphreys to [unknown], n.d., *Humphreys's Biography*, p. 219; Humphreys to [unknown], 6 June 1864, ibid., p. 229; Humphreys to [unknown], 19 June 1864, ibid., p. 237; Humphreys to [unknown], 30 August 1864, ibid., p. 249; Humphreys to [unknown], 6 September 1864, ibid., pp. 249–50; Humphreys to [unknown], n.d., ibid., p. 257; Humphreys to [unknown], 25 November 1864, ibid., pp. 258–59; Humphreys to [unknown], n.d., ibid., pp. 261–62; Birney to Gross, 23 March 1864, Birney Papers.

99. Grant to Meade, Grant, *Grant Papers*, vol. 13, pp. 43–44.

100. Ibid.; Gibbon to his wife, 27 August 1864, 7 September 1864, 26 November 1864, 3 December 1864, and 6 December 1864, Gibbon Letters; Gibbon, *Personal Recollections*, pp. 273–74; Gibbon to Seth Williams, 26 November 1864, OR, vol. 42, pt. 3, p. 714; Meade, 27 November 1864, ibid., vol. 51, pt. 1, p. 1191; Seth Williams to Humphreys, 28 November 1864, ibid., vol. 42, pt. 3, p. 730; Humphreys to Seth Williams, 28 November 1864, ibid.; Gibbon to Humphreys, 28 November 1864, ibid., p. 731; Gibbon to Seth Williams, 3 December 1864, ibid., p. 788; Shaffer to Butler, 25 September 1864, Butler, *Butler's Correspondence*, vol. 5, p. 159.

101. Porter, *Campaigning with Grant*, p. 338.

102. Grant's testimony, 11 February 1865, Grant, *Grant Papers*, vol. 13, pp. 400–2; Welles, 26 December 1864, 27 December 1864, and 29 December 1864, *Welles's Diary*, vol. 2, pp. 209, 210, 213; Grant, *Personal Memoirs*, vol. 2, pp. 262–66; Meade to Margaret Meade, 18 December 1864, Meade, *Life and Letters*, vol. 2, p. 253; Butler to David Porter, 25 December 1864, OR, vol. 42, pt. 3, p. 1075; Grant to Stanton, 2 January 1865, ibid., vol. 46, pt. 2, p. 9; Butler to Weitzel, 23 January 1865, ibid., p. 211; Weitzel to Rawlins, 16 January 1865, ibid., p. 184.

103. Grant to Stanton, 4 January 1865, OR, vol. 46, pt. 2, p. 28.

104. Porter, *Campaigning with Grant*, pp. 373–74; Grant to Stanton, 7 January 1865, Grant, *Grant Papers*, vol. 13, ed, p. 241; Welles, 30 December 1864 and 14 January 1865, *Welles's Diary*, vol. 2, pp. 215, 223–24; Patrick, 9 January 1865, *Inside Lincoln's Army*, p. 457; Browning, 12 July 1864, *Browning's Diary*, vol. 1, p. 676; Lincoln to Grant, 28 December 1864, OR, vol. 42, pt. 3, p. 1087; Grant to Stanton, 2 January 1865, ibid., vol. 46, pt. 2, p. 9; Grant to Lincoln, 6 January 1865, ibid., p. 52; Halleck to Grant, 7 January 1865, ibid., p. 60; General Orders No. 1, 7 January 1865, ibid.; Francis Pierpoint to Lincoln, 2 December 1864, Lincoln Papers.

105. Butler to the Soldiers of the Army of the James, 8 January 1865, OR, vol. 46, pt. 2, p. 60.

106. Butler to Rawlins, 13 January 1865, ibid., pp. 120–21; Butler to Weitzel, 23 January 1865, ibid., p. 211; Weitzel to Butler, 25 January 1865, Butler, *Butler's Correspondence*, vol. 5, p. 513; Butler to Weitzel, 30 January 1865, ibid., p. 515; Weitzel to Butler, 12 February 1865, ibid., p. 548; William Birney to Butler, 23 April 1865, ibid., p. 600; George Henry Gordon, *A War Diary of Events in the War of the Great Rebellion* (Boston: James R. Osgood, 1882), pp. 370–71; Grant to Stanton, 23 February 1865, Grant, *Grant Papers*, vol. 14, pp. 23–24.

107. Grant to Halleck, 4 February 1865, *Grant Papers*, vol. 13, p. 363; Butler, 25 August 1864, *OR*, vol. 42, pt. 2, p. 498; Grant to Stanton, 6 January 1865, ibid., vol. 37, pt. 2, p. 18; Butler to the Soldiers of the Army of the James, 11 October 1864, ibid., vol. 42, pt. 3, p. 163; Special Orders No. 5, 7 January 1865, ibid., vol. 36, pt. 2, p. 61; Halleck to Grant, 6 February 1865, ibid., p. 415; General Orders No. 14, 6 February 1865, ibid., p. 421; Shaffer to Butler, 2 September 1864, Butler, *Butler's Correspondence*, vol. 5, p. 119; Weitzel to Butler, 26 April 1865, ibid., p. 585; William Birney to Butler, 23 April 1865, ibid., pp. 600–01; Gibbon, *Personal Recollections*, pp. 277–78, 284.

108. Gibbon to his wife, 26 February 1862, Gibbon Letters.

109. Ibid., 24 April 1862; Kearny to Kearny, 31 August 1862, *Letters from the Peninsula*, p. 166; Willcox, 5 November 1862, *Forgotten Valor*, p. 377; Gibbon, *Personal Recollections*, pp. 26, 109; Frank Haskell, 16 July 1863, *Haskell of Gettysburg: His Life and Civil War Papers*, ed. Frank L. Byrne and Andrew T. Weaver (Madison: State Historical Society of Wisconsin, 1970), p. 93; Hancock's testimony, 22 March 1864, U.S. Congress, *Reports of the Joint Committee on the Conduct of the War*, 38th Cong., 2d sess., pt. 1 (Washington, DC: Government Printing Office, 1865), p. 404.

110. Gibbon to his wife, 5 March 1865, Gibbon Letters; Grant to Stanton, 13 May 1864, Grant, *Grant Papers*, vol. 10, p. 434; Grant to Butler, 20 July 1864, ibid., vol. 11, pp. 287–88; Grant to Lincoln, 25 July 1864, ibid., pp. 309–11; Gibbon, *Personal Recollections*, pp. 198, 209–10, 273–74, 277–78, 284, 289; Lyman, 18 May 1864, *Meade's Headquarters*, p. 103; Meade to Margaret Meade, 12 October 1863 and 14 January 1865, Meade, *Life and Letters*, vol. 2, pp. 153, 256; Warren to Humphreys, 24 June 1864, *OR*, vol. 40, pt. 2, p. 384; Meade to Grant, 13 January 1865, ibid., vol. 36, pt. 2, p. 113; Shaffer to Butler, 25 September 1864, Butler, *Butler's Correspondence*, vol. 5, p. 159; David Birney to Gross, 4 July 1864, Birney Papers.

111. Meade to Grant, 26 March 1865, *OR*, vol. 46, pt. 3, p. 170.

112. Grant to Sheridan, 31 March 1865, Grant, *Grant Papers*, vol. 14, p. 289; Sheridan, *Sheridan's Memoirs*, p. 315; Porter, *Campaigning with Grant*, p. 435.

113. Sheridan, *Sheridan's Memoirs*, pp. 326.

114. The quote is from Joshua Chamberlain, *The Passing of the Armies: An Account of the Final Campaign of the Army of the Potomac, Based upon Personal Reminiscences of the Fifth Corps* (Lincoln: University of Nebraska Press, 1998), p. 104. See also Wainwright, 29 March 1865, *Diary of Battle*, pp. 508–9; Grant to Stanton, 21 February 1865, Grant, *Grant Papers*, vol. 14, p. 5; Grant to Sheridan, 31 March 1865, ibid., pp. 287–88; Sheridan, *Sheridan's Memoirs*, p. 315, 323–26; Grant, *Personal Memoirs*, vol. 2, pp. 306–7; Meade to Margaret Meade, 2 March 1865, Meade, *Life and Letters*, vol. 2, p. 265; Stanton to Grant, 21 February 1865, *OR*, vol. 46, pt. 2, p. 608; Warren to [unknown], 5 March 1865, Taylor, *Life and Letters of an American Soldier*, p. 204; Roebling to Rusling, 18 February 1916, Roebling, *Wash Roebling's War*, p. 32.

115. Cadwallader, *Three Years with Grant*, pp. 299–302.

116. For an account of Sheridan's meeting with Warren, see Chamberlain, *The Passing of the Armies*, pp. 142, 151.

117. Cadwallader, *Three Years with Grant*, p. 303; Porter, *Campaigning with Grant*, pp. 440–41; Sheridan, *Sheridan's Memoirs*, pp. 328–30; Lyman, 1 April 1865, *Meade's Headquarters*, pp. 333–34; Warren to Emily Warren, 2 April 1865, Taylor, *Life and Letters of an American Soldier*, pp. 228–29; Channing Clapp to Warren, 2 April 1865, *OR*, vol. 46, pt. 3, p. 505; Warren to Rawlins, 9 April 1865, ibid., p. 574.

118. Chamberlain, *The Passing of the Armies*, p. 122; Alpheus Williams to his daughter, 3 September 1863, Alpheus Williams, *From the Cannon's Mouth: The Civil War Letters*

of General Alpheus S. Williams, ed. Milo M. Quaife (Detroit: Wayne State University Press and the Detroit Historical Society, 1959), p. 255; Wainwright, 10 May 1864, 5 June 1864, 3 July 1864, 16 October 1864, 20 October 1864, 31 March 1865, and 3 April 1865, *Diary of Battle,* pp. 364, 407, 431, 472–73, 473, 514, 518; Porter, *Campaigning with Grant,* pp. 247–48; Warren to Meade, 13 May 1864, *OR,* vol. 36, pt. 2, p. 714.

119. Lee, 8 August 1862, *Wartime Washington,* p. 175; Cadwallader, *Three Years with Grant,* pp. 331–33; Wainwright, 19 February 1863, 4 October 1863, and 3 May 1864, *Diary of Battle,* pp. 167, 285, 348; Lyman, *Meade's Headquarters,* p. 168n; Warren to Seth Williams, 18 July 1864, *OR,* vol. 40, pt. 3, p. 319; Daniel Butterfield, December 1862, ibid., vol. 21, p. 401; Meade, 12 May 1863, ibid., vol. 25, pt. 1, p. 508; Pope, 3 September 1862, ibid., vol.12, pt. 2, p. 15; Speed Butler, 3 September 1862, ibid., p. 18; Sallie Griffin to Lincoln, 18 July 1862 and 1 July 1863, Lincoln Papers; Warren to Emily Warren, 20 July 1863, Warren Papers, Folder 6.

120. Grant to Meade, 1 April 1865, *OR,* vol. 46, pt. 3, p. 399.

121. Badeau, *Military History of Grant,* vol. 3, p. 504; Wright to Alexander Webb, 30 March 1865 and 1 April 1865, *OR,* vol. 46, pt. 3, pp. 314, 423; Sheridan to Grant, 19 September 1864, ibid., vol. 43, pt. 1, p. 24.

BIBLIOGRAPHY

Archival Sources

Cushing Memorial Library, Texas A & M University, College Station, Texas. William Wallace Burns Papers.

Doheny Memorial Library, University of Southern California, Los Angeles, California. Hamlin Garland Collection.

Historical Society of Pennsylvania, Philadelphia, Pennsylvania. Letters of James Biddle, John Gibbon, and Andrew Humphreys.

Lawrence Lee Pelletier Library, Allegheny College, Meadville, Pennsylvania. Samuel Bates Papers.

Library of Congress, Washington, D.C. Papers of the Blair Family, Zachariah Chandler, William Franklin, Samuel Heintzelman, Abraham Lincoln, George McClellan, John Sherman, Edwin Stanton, and Benjamin Wade.

National Archives and Records Administration, College Park, Maryland. U.S. Army Generals' Reports of Civil War Service, 1864–1887.

New-York Historical Society, New York, New York. Joseph Howland Papers.

New York State Library, Albany, New York. Gouverneur Warren Papers.

Oberlin College Library, Oberlin College, Oberlin, Ohio. Jacob Cox Papers.

Old Colony Historical Society, Taunton, Massachusetts. Darius Couch Papers.

Shadeck-Fackenthal Library, Franklin and Marshall College, Lancaster, Pennsylvania. Reynolds Family Papers.

United States Army Military History Institute, Carlisle, Pennsylvania. Papers of John C. Bates, David Birney, Robert Blake, Zemas Bliss, William Brooks, Solon Carter, Quincy Gillmore, Winfield Scott Hancock, Robert Hubbard, Nelson Miles, Fitz John Porter, and Charles Veil.

Primary Sources

Adams, Charles Francis, Jr. *Charles Francis Adams, 1835–1915: An Autobiography.* Boston: Houghton Mifflin, 1916.

Ames, Adelbert. *Chronicles from the Nineteenth Century: Family Letters of Blanche Butler and Adelbert Ames, Married July 21st, 1870*, vol. 1. Compiled by Blanche Butler Ames. N.p.: privately published, 1957.

Armes, George Augustus. *Ups and Downs of an Army Officer*. Washington, DC, 1900.

Army of the Potomac. History of Its Campaigns, the Peninsula, Maryland, Fredericksburg. Testimony of Its Three Commanders, Maj.-Gen. G. B. McClellan, Maj.-Gen. A. E. Burnside, and Maj.-Gen. Joseph Hooker before the Congressional Committee on the Conduct of the War. New York: Tribune Association, 1863.

Averell, William. *Ten Years in the Saddle: The Memoir of William Woods Averell*. Ed. Edward Eckert and Nicholas Amato. San Rafael, CA: Presidio Press, 1978.

Bates, Edward. *The Diary of Edward Bates, 1859–1866*. Ed. Howard Beale. New York: Da Capo Press, 1971.

Battles and Leaders of the Civil War, vols. 1–4. Ed. Robert Underwood Johnson and Clarence Clough Buel. New York: Thomas Yoseloff, 1956.

Beaudry, Louis. *War Journal of Louis N. Beaudry, Fifth New York Cavalry: The Diary of a Union Chaplain, Commencing February 16, 1863*. Ed. Richard Beaudry. Jefferson, NC: McFarland and Company, 1996.

Blaine, James G. *Twenty Years of Congress from Lincoln to Garfield*, vol. 1. Norwich, CT: Henry Bill Publishing, 1884.

Blake, Henry N. *Three Years in the Army of the Potomac*. Boston: Lee and Shepard, 1865.

Brooks, Noah. *Washington, D.C. in Lincoln's Time*. Ed. Herbert Mitgang. Athens: University of Georgia Press, 1989.

Browning, Orville Hickman. *The Diary of Orville Hickman Browning*, vols. 1–2. Ed. Theodore Calvin Peade and James Randall. Springfield: Illinois State Historical Library, 1927 and 1933.

Butler, Benjamin. *Butler's Book: Autobiography and Personal Reminiscences of Major-General Benjamin F. Butler*. Boston: A. M. Thayer, 1892.

———. *Private and Official Correspondence of Gen. Benjamin F. Butler during the Period of the Civil War*, vols. 3–5. Norwood, MA: Plimpton Press, 1917.

Cadwallader, Sylvanus. *Three Years with Grant: As Recalled by War Correspondent Sylvanus Cadwallader*. Ed. Benjamin Thomas. New York: Alfred A. Knopf, 1956.

Chamberlain, Joshua. *The Passing of the Armies: An Account of the Final Campaign of the Army of the Potomac, Based upon Personal Reminiscences of the Fifth Corps*. Lincoln: University of Nebraska Press, 1998.

Chase, Salmon. *The Salmon P. Chase Papers*, vols. 1, 3–4. Ed. John Niven. Kent, OH: Kent State University Press, 1993–1997.

Cochrane, John. "The War for the Union: Memoir of Gen. John Cochrane." In *American Civil War: Memories of the Rebellion*. New York: Rogers and Sherwood, 1879.

Coffin, Charles Carleton. *Four Years of Fighting: A Volume of Personal Observation with the Army and Navy, from the First Battle of Bull Run to the Fall of Richmond*. Boston: Ticknor and Fields, 1866.

Comstock, Cyrus B. *The Diary of Cyrus B. Comstock*. Ed. Merlin E. Sumner. Dayton, OH: Morningside House, 1987.

Cox, Jacob. *Military Reminiscences of the Civil War*, vol. 1. New York: Charles Scribner's Sons, 1900.

Crook, George. *General George Crook: His Autobiography*. Ed. Martin Schmitt. Norman: University of Oklahoma Press, 1946.

Dana, Charles. *Recollections of the Civil War: With the Leaders at Washington and in the Field in the Sixties*. Lincoln: University of Nebraska Press, 1996.

Dodge, Grenville. *Personal Recollections of President Abraham Lincoln, General Ulysses S. Grant and General William T. Sherman*. Denver: Sage Books, 1965.

Dodge, Theodore Ayrault. *On Campaign with the Army of the Potomac: The Civil War Journal of Theodore Ayrault Dodge*. Ed. Stephen Sears. New York: First Cooper Square Press, 2001.

Doubleday, Abner. *Chancellorsville and Gettysburg*. New York: Da Capo Press, 1994.

Favill, Josiah Marshall. *The Diary of a Young Officer*. Baltimore: Butternut and Blue, 2000.

Ford, Worthington Chauncey, ed. *A Cycle of Adams Letters, 1861–1865*, vol. 2. Boston: Houghton Mifflin, 1920.

Fry, James Barnet. *Military Miscellanies*. New York: Brentano's, 1889.

Garfield, James. *The Wild Life of the Army: Civil War Letters of James A. Garfield*. Lansing: Michigan State University Press, 1964.

Geary, John. *A Politician Goes to War: The Civil War Letters of John White Geary*. Ed. William Alan Blair. University Park: Pennsylvania State University Press, 1995.

Gibbon, John. *Personal Recollections of the Civil War*. New York: G. P. Putnam's Sons, 1928.

Gilmore, James Roberts. *Personal Recollections of Abraham Lincoln and the Civil War*. Boston: L. C. Page, 1898.

Gordon, George Henry. *A War Diary of Events in the War of the Great Rebellion*. Boston: James R. Osgood, 1882.

Grant, Ulysses. *The Papers of Ulysses S. Grant*, vols. 10–13. Ed. John Simon. Carbondale: Southern Illinois University Press, 1982–85.

———. *Personal Memoirs of U. S. Grant*, vol. 2. New York: Century, 1917.

De Gurowski, Adam. *Diary*, vols. 1–3. Boston: Lee and Shepard, 1862–1866.

Haley, John. *The Rebel Yell and the Yankee Hurrah: The Civil War Journal of a Maine Volunteer*. Ed. Ruth L. Silliker. Camden, ME: Down East Books, 1985.

Hardie, James. "Memoir of James A. Hardie." *Western Americana: Frontier History of the Trans-Mississippi West, 1550–1900*. New Haven, CT: Research Publications, 1975.

Haskell, Frank. *Haskell of Gettysburg: His Life and Civil War Papers*. Ed. Frank L. Byrne and Andrew T. Weaver. Madison: State Historical Society of Wisconsin, 1970.

Haupt, Herman. *Reminiscences of General Herman Haupt*. Milwaukee, WI: Wright and Joys, 1901.

Hay, John. *Lincoln's Journalist: John Hay's Anonymous Writings for the Press, 1860–1864*. Ed. Michael Burlingame. Carbondale: Southern Illinois University Press, 1998.

———. *Lincoln and the Civil War in the Letters and Diaries of John Hay*. Ed. Tyler Dennett. Westport, CT: Negro Universities Press, 1972.

Hays, Alexander. *Life and Letters of Alexander Hays*. Ed. George Thornton Fleming. Pittsburgh, PA, 1919.

Hitchcock, Ethan Allen. *Fifty Years in Camp and Field: Diary of Major-General Ethan Allen Hitchcock, U.S.A.* Ed. W. A. Croffut. New York: G. P. Putnam's Sons, 1909.

Howard, Oliver Otis. *Autobiography of Oliver Otis Howard*, vol. 1. New York: Baker and Taylor, 1908.

Humphreys, Andrew. *From Gettysburg to the Rapidan: The Army of the Potomac, July, 1863, to April, 1864*. New York: Scribner's Sons, 1883.

———. *The Virginia Campaign of '64 and '65*. New York: Thomas Yoseloff, 1963.

Hyde, Thomas W. *Civil War Letters*. N.p.: privately published, 1933.

———. *Following the Greek Cross: Or, Memories of the Sixth Army Corps*. Boston: Houghton Mifflin, 1894.

Julian, George W. *Political Recollections, 1840 to 1872*. Chicago: Jansen, McClurg, 1884.

Kearny, Philip. *Letters from the Peninsula: The Civil War Letters of General Philip Kearny*. Ed. William Styple. Kearny, NJ: Belle Grove Publishing, 1988.

Keyes, Erasmus. *Fifty Years' Observations of Men and Events, Civil and Military*. New York: Charles Scribner's Sons, 1884.

Lee, Elizabeth Blair. *Wartime Washington: The Civil War Letters of Elizabeth Blair Lee*. Ed. Virginia Jeans Laas. Urbana: University of Illinois Press, 1991.

Letterman, Jonathan. *Medical Recollections of the Army of the Potomac*. Knoxville, TN: Bohemian Brigade Publishers, 1994.

Lincoln, Abraham. *The Collected Works of Abraham Lincoln*, vols. 5–8, supplements 1–2. Ed. Roy Basler. New Brunswick, NJ: Rutgers University Press, 1953 and 1990.

Lyman, Theodore. *Meade's Headquarters, 1863–1865: Letters of Colonel Theodore Lyman from the Wilderness to Appomattox*. Ed. George Agassiz. Boston: Atlantic Monthly Press, 1922.

McAllister, Robert. *Civil War Letters of General Robert McAllister*. Ed. James Robetson Jr. Baton Rouge: Louisiana State University Press, 1998.

McClellan, George. *The Civil War Papers of George B. McClellan: Selected Correspondence, 1860–1865*. Ed. Stephen W. Sears. New York: Ticknor and Fields, 1989.

_____. *McClellan's Own Story*. Harrisburg, PA: Archive Society, 1997.

McClure, Alexander. *Colonel Alexander K. McClure's Recollections of Half a Century*. Salem, MA: Salem Press, 1902.

Meade, George. *The Life and Letters of George Gordon Meade*, vols. 1–2. Ed. George Meade. New York: Charles Scribner's Sons, 1913.

The Meade Archive, http://patriot.net/~jcampi/webb.htm.

Meigs, Montgomery. "General M. C. Meigs on the Conduct of the Civil War." *The American Historical Review*, January 1921, vol. 26, no. 2, pp. 285–303.

Miles, Nelson. *Serving the Republic: Memoirs of the Civil and Military Life of Nelson A. Miles*. New York: Harper and Brothers, 1911.

Mills, Charles. *Through Blood and Fire: The Civil War Letters of Major Charles J. Mills, 1862–1865*. Ed. Gregory Coco. Gettysburg, PA: Gregory Coco, 1982.

Morse, Charles Fessenden. *Letters Written during the Civil War, 1861–1865*. Boston: privately printed, 1898.

Newton, John. *Memories of Incidents*. New York: Rogers and Sherwood, 1879.

Page, Charles A. *Letters of a War Correspondent*. Boston: L. C. Page, 1899.

Patrick, Marsena. *Inside Lincoln's Army: The Diary of Marsena Rudolph Patrick, Provost Marshal General, Army of the Potomac*. Ed. David Sparks. New York: Thomas Yoseloff, 1964.

Pope, John. *The Military Memoirs of General John Pope*. Ed. Peter Cozzens and Robert Girardi. Chapel Hill: University of North Carolina Press, 1998.

Porter, Horace. *Campaigning with Grant*. Bloomington: Indiana University Press, 1961.

Raymond, Henry. "Extracts from the Journal of Henry J. Raymond." *Scribner's Monthly*, November 1879 to April 1880, vol. 19, pp. 419–23, 703–10.

Reid, Whitelaw. *A Radical View: The "Agate" Dispatches of Whitelaw Reid, 1861–1865*, vols. 1–2. Ed. James G. Smart. Memphis, TN: Memphis State University Press, 1976.

Revere, Joseph. *Keel and Saddle: A Retrospect of Forty Years of Military and Naval Service*. Boston: James R. Osgood, 1873.

Riddle, Albert Gallatin. *Recollections of War Times: Reminiscences of Men and Events in Washington, 1860–1865*. New York: G. P. Putnam's Sons, 1895.

Rives, John C., ed. "The Debates and Proceedings of Congress for the 37th and 38th Sessions." *Congressional Globe*, vols. 32–35. Washington, DC, 1862–1865, reels 21–23.

Roebling, Washington. *Wash Roebling's War: Being a Selection from the Unpublished Letters of Washington Augustus Roebling*. Ed. Earl Schenck Miers. Newark, DE: Curtis Paper, 1961.

Rusling, James F. *Men and Things I Saw in Civil War Days*. New York: Eaton and Mains, 1899.

Schurz, Carl. *Intimate Letters of Carl Schurz, 1841–1869*. Madison: State Historical Society of Wisconsin, 1928.

_____. *The Reminiscences of Carl Schurz*, vol. 2. New York: McClure Company, 1907.

Scrymser, James. *Personal Reminiscences of James A. Scrymser in Times of Peace and War*. Easton, PA: James A Scrymser, 1915.

Sedgwick, John. *Correspondence of John Sedgwick*, vol. 2. New York: Devinne Press, 1903.

Sheridan, Philip. *Civil War Memoirs: Philip Sheridan*. Ed. Paul Andrew Hutton. New York: Bantam Books, 1991.

Smith, William Farrar. *Autobiography of Major General William F. Smith, 1861–1864*. Ed. Herbert Schiller. Dayton, OH: Morningside, 1990.

_____. *From Chattanooga to Petersburg under Generals Grant and Butler*. Boston: Houghton Mifflin, 1893.

Spiegel, Marcus. *Your True Marcus: The Civil War Letters of a Jewish Colonel*. Ed. Frank Byrne and Jean Powers Soman. Kent, OH: Kent State University Press, 1985.

Stoddard, William. *Dispatches from Lincoln's White House: The Anonymous Civil War Journalism of Presidential Secretary William O. Stoddard*. Ed. Michael Burningame. Lincoln: University of Nebraska Press, 2002.

Strong, George Templeton. *Diary of the Civil War, 1860–1865*. Ed. Allan Nevins. New York: Macmillan, 1962.

Taft, Horatio Nelson. *The Diary of Horatio Nelson Taft, 1861–1865*, vols. 1–3. Manuscript Collection, Library of Congress, Washington, DC (http://memory.loc.gov/ammem/tafthtml/tafthome.html).

Townsend, George Alfred. *Rustics in Rebellion: A Yankee Reporter on the Road to Richmond, 1861–65*. Chapel Hill: University of North Carolina Press, 1950.

Tremain, Henry Edwin. *Two Days of War: A Gettysburg Narrative and Other Excursions*. New York: Bonnell, Silver and Bowers, 1905.

Trobriand, Regis de. *Four Years with the Army of the Potomac*. Trans. by George K. Dauchy. Boston: Ticknor, 1889.

U.S. Congress. *Reports of the Joint Committee on the Conduct of the War*. Washington, DC: Government Printing Office, 1863–1865.

Villard, Henry. *Memoirs of Henry Villard*, vol. 1. Boston: Houghton Mifflin, 1904.

Wainwright, Charles. *A Diary of Battle: The Personal Journals of Colonel Charles S. Wainwright*. Ed. Allan Nevins. New York: Harcourt, Brace and World, 1962.

Walker, Francis. *History of the Second Army Corps in the Army of the Potomac*. New York: Charles Scribner's Sons, 1886.

The War of the Rebellion: A Compilation of the Official Records of the Union and Confederate Armies, vols. 1–128. Washington, DC: Government Printing Office, 1880–1901. All notations from Series 1.

Weld, Stephen Minot. *War Diary and Letters of Stephen Minot Weld, 1861–1865*. Boston: Massachusetts Historical Society, 1979.

Welles, Gideon. *Diary of Gideon Welles: Secretary of the Navy under Lincoln and Johnson*, vols. 1–2. Boston: Houghton Mifflin, 1911.

Willcox, Orlando. *Forgotten Valor: The Memoirs, Journals, and Civil War Letters of Orlando B. Willcox.* Ed. Robert Garth Scott. Kent, OH: Kent State University Press, 1999.

Williams, Alpheus. *From the Cannon's Mouth: The Civil War Letters of General Alpheus S. Williams.* Ed. Milo M. Quaife. Detroit, MI: Wayne State University Press and Detroit Historical Society, 1959.

Wilson, Henry. *Military Measures of the United States Congress, 1861–1865.* New York: D. Van Nostrand, 1866.

Wilson, James Harrison. *Under the Old Flag: Recollections of Military Operations in the War for the Union, the Spanish War and the Boxer Rebellion, etc.,* vol. 1. Westport, CT: Greenwood Press, 1971.

Secondary Sources

Adams, Michael C.C. *Our Masters the Rebels: A Speculation on Union Military Failure in the East, 1861–1865.* Cambridge, MA: Harvard University Press, 1978.

Ambrose, Stephen E. *Halleck: Lincoln's Chief of Staff.* Baton Rouge: Louisiana State University Press, 1962.

Badeau, Adam. *Military History of Ulysses S. Grant, from April, 1861, to April, 1865,* vols. 1–3. New York: D. Appleton, 1881.

Bayard, Samuel. *The Life of George Dashiell Bayard.* New York: G. P. Putnam's Sons, 1874.

Bogue, Allan G. *The Earnest Men: Republicans of the Civil War Senate.* Ithaca, NY: Cornell University Press, 1981.

Butterfield, Julia Lorrilard, ed. *A Biographical Memorial of General Daniel Butterfield.* New York: Grafton Press, 1904.

Carpenter, John A. *Sword and Olive Branch: Oliver Otis Howard.* Pittsburgh, PA: University of Pittsburgh Press, 1964.

Catton, Bruce. *Bruce Catton's Civil War: Three Volumes in One (Mr. Lincoln's Army, Glory Road, A Stillness at Appomattox).* New York: Fairfax Press, 1984.

———. *Grant Takes Command.* Boston: Little, Brown, 1968.

Cleaves, Freeman. *Meade of Gettysburg.* Norman: University of Oklahoma Press, 1960.

Cresap, Bernarr. *Appomattox Commander: The Story of General E.O.C. Ord.* New York: A. S. Barnes and Company, 1981.

Cullen, Joseph P. *The Peninsula Campaign 1862: McClellan and Lee Struggle for Richmond.* Harrisburg, PA: Stackpole Books, 1973.

Engle, Stephen Douglas. *Yankee Dutchman: The Life of Franz Sigel.* Baton Rouge: Louisiana State University Press, 1999.

Foote, Shelby. *The Civil War: A Narrative,* vols. 1–3. New York: Vintage Books, 1986.

Furgurson, Ernest B. *Chancellorsville 1863: The Souls of the Brave.* New York: Alfred A. Knopf, 1992.

Gallagher, Gary W., ed. *The Antietam Campaign.* Chapel Hill: University of North Carolina Press, 1999.

———. *Chancellorsville: The Battle and Its Aftermath.* Chapel Hill: University of North Carolina Press, 1996.

———. *The Fredericksburg Campaign: Decision on the Rappahannock.* Chapel Hill: University of North Carolina Press, 1995.

———. *The Spotsylvania Campaign.* Chapel Hill: University of North Carolina Press, 1998.

_____. *Three Days at Gettysburg: Essays on Confederate and Union Leadership*. Kent, OH: Kent State University Press, 1999.

_____. *The Wilderness Campaign*. Chapel Hill: University of North Carolina Press, 1997.

Gambone, A. M. *Major-General Darius Nash Couch: Enigmatic Valor*. Baltimore: Butternut and Blue, 2000.

George, Mary Karl. *Zachariah Chandler: A Political Biography*. East Lansing: Michigan State University, 1969.

Glatthaar, Joseph T. *Partners in Command: The Relationships between Leaders in the Civil War*. New York: Free Press, 1994.

Goss, Thomas. *The War within the Union High Command: Politics and Generalship during the Civil War*. Lawrence: University Press of Kansas, 2003.

Gould, Edward K. *Major-General Hiram G. Berry*. Rockland, ME: Press of the Courier-Gazette, 1899.

Hancock, Alma. *Reminiscences of Winfield Scott Hancock*. New York: Charles L. Webster, 1887.

Hassler, Warren W., Jr. *Commanders of the Army of the Potomac*. Baton Rouge: Louisiana State University Press, 1962.

Hebert, Walter H. *Fighting Joe Hooker*. Lincoln: University of Nebraska Press, 1999.

Hendrick, Burton J. *Lincoln's War Cabinet*. Gloucester, MA: Peter Smith, 1965.

Humphreys, Henry H. *Andrew Atkinson Humphreys: A Biography*. Philadelphia: John C. Winston, 1924.

Johnson, Rossiter. *Campfire and Battlefield: The Classic Illustrated History of the Civil War*. New York: Fairfax Press, 1978.

Johnson, Timothy D. *Winfield Scott: The Quest for Military Glory*. Lawrence: University Press of Kansas, 1998.

Jones, Archer. *Civil War Command and Strategy: The Process of Victory and Defeat*. New York: Free Press, 1992.

Jordan, David M. *"Happiness Is Not My Companion": The Life of General G. K. Warren*. Bloomington: Indiana University Press, 2001.

_____. *Winfield Scott Hancock: A Soldier's Life*. Bloomington: Indiana University Press, 1988.

Keneally, Thomas. *American Scoundrel: The Life of the Notorious Civil War General Dan Sickles*. New York: Doubleday, 2002.

Lavery, Dennis S., and Mark H. Jordan. *Iron Brigade General: John Gibbon, A Rebel in Blue*. Westport, CT: Greenwood Press, 1993.

Macartney, Clarence Edward. *Grant and His Generals*. New York: McBride, 1953.

Martin, Samuel J. *"Kill-Cavalry," Sherman's Merchant of Terror: The Life of Union General Hugh Judson Kilpatrick*. Madison, NJ: Fairleigh Dickinson University Press, 1996.

Marvel, William. *Burnside*. Chapel Hill: University of North Carolina Press, 1991.

McConnell, William F. *Remember Reno: A Biography of Major General Jesse Lee Reno*. Shippensburg, PA: White Mane Publishing, 1996.

McPherson, James M. *Ordeal by Fire: The Civil War*. New York: Alfred A. Knopf, 1982.

Michie, Peter. *The Life and Letters of Emory Upton*. New York: D. Appleton, 1885.

Morris, Roy, Jr. *Sheridan: The Life and Wars of General Phil Sheridan*. New York: Crown Publishers, 1992.

Nash, Howard, Jr. *Stormy Petrel: The Life and Times of General Benjamin F. Butler, 1818–1893*. Rutherford, NJ: Fairleigh Dickinson University Press, 1969.

Nichols, Edward J. *Toward Gettysburg: A Biography of General John F. Reynolds*. University Park: Pennsylvania State University Press, 1958.

Palfrey, Francis Winthrop. *The Antietam and Fredericksburg*. New York: Thomas Yoseloff, 1963.

Paludan, Phillip Shaw. *The Presidency of Abraham Lincoln*. Lawrence: University Press of Kansas, 1994.

Pierce, Edward L. *Memoir and Letters of Charles Sumner*, vol. 4. New York: Arno Press and New York Times, 1969.

Pratt, Fletcher. *Stanton: Lincoln's Secretary of War*. Westport, CT: Greenwood Press, 1953.

Rhea, Gordon C. *The Battles for Spotsylvania Court House and the Road to Yellow Tavern, May 7–12, 1864*. Baton Rouge: Louisiana State University Press, 1997.

Robertson, William Glenn. *Back Door to Richmond: The Bermuda Hundred Campaign, April–June 1864*. Newark: University of Delaware Press, 1987.

Schaff, Morris. *The Battle of the Wilderness*. Boston: Houghton Mifflin, 1910.

Schutz, Wallace J., and Walter N. Trenerry. *Abandoned by Lincoln: A Military Biography of General John Pope*. Chicago: University of Illinois Press, 1990.

Sears, Stephen W. *Chancellorsville*. Boston: Houghton Mifflin, 1996.

———. *Controversies and Commanders: Dispatches from the Army of the Potomac*. Boston: Houghton Mifflin, 1999.

———. *George B. McClellan: The Young Napoleon*. New York: Ticknor and Fields, 1988.

———. *To the Gates of Richmond: The Peninsula Campaign*. New York: Ticknor and Fields, 1992.

Simpson, Brooks. *Ulysses S. Grant: Triumph over Adversity, 1822–1865*. Boston: Houghton Mifflin, 2000.

Snell, Mark A. *From First to Last: The Life of Major General William B. Franklin*. New York: Fordham University Press, 2002.

Sommers, Richard J. *Richmond Redeemed: The Siege of Petersburg*. Garden City, NY: Doubleday, 1981.

Swanberg, W. A. *Sickles the Incredible*. New York: Charles Scribner's Sons, 1956.

Swinton, William. *Campaigns of the Army of the Potomac*. New York: Charles B. Richardson, 1866.

Tap, Bruce. *Over Lincoln's Shoulder: The Committee on the Conduct of the War*. Lawrence: University Press of Kansas, 1998.

Taylor, Emerson Gifford. *Gouverneur Kemble Warren: The Life and Letters of an American Soldier, 1830–1882*. Boston: Houghton Mifflin, 1932.

Trefousse, Hans L. *Ben Butler: The South Called Him Beast!* New York: Twayne Publishers, 1957.

Trudeau, Noah Andre. *Bloody Roads South: The Wilderness to Cold Harbor, May–June 1864*. Boston: Little, Brown, 1989.

———. *The Last Citadel: Petersburg, Virginia, June 1864–April 1865*. Boston: Little, Brown, 1991.

Utley, Robert M. *Frontiersmen in Blue: The United States Army and the Indian, 1848–1865*. New York: Macmillan, 1973.

Warner, Ezra. *Generals in Blue: Lives of the Union Commanders*. Baton Rouge: Louisiana State University Press, 1964.

Webb, Alexander. *The Peninsula: McClellan's Campaign of 1862*. New York: Thomas Yoseloff, 1963.

Weigley, Russell F. *Quartermaster General of the Union Army: A Biography of* M. C. Meigs. New York: Columbia University Press, 1959.

Wert, Jeffry. *The Sword of Lincoln: The Army of the Potomac.* New York: Simon and Schuster, 2005.

Williams, T. Harry. *Lincoln and His Generals.* New York: Alfred A. Knopf, 1952.

Wilson, James Harrison. *The Life of John A. Rawlins: Lawyer, Assistant Adjutant-General, Chief of Staff, Major General of Volunteers, and Secretary of War.* New York: Neale, 1916.

Winslow, Richard Elliott, III. *General John Sedgwick: The Story of a Union Corps Commander.* Novato, CA: Presidio Press, 1982.

INDEX

Alexandria, Virginia, 14, 31, 32
Andrews, John, 55
Annapolis, Maryland, 151
Antietam, Battle of, 42–47
Antietam Creek, 41, 46
Appomattox campaign, 205–6
Appomattox Courthouse, Virginia, 205–6
Appomattox River, 165, 172, 184, 200
Aquia, Virginia, 32, 40
Army of Georgia, 132
Army of the Cumberland, 73, 122, 130, 147, 149, 152
Army of the James, 168–83, 184, 185, 196, 197, 206, 207, 213, 214, 215, 218
Army of the Ohio, 152
Army of the Shenandoah, 186, 214
Army of the Tennessee, 131, 152
Army of Virginia, 31, 33
Atlanta, Georgia, 152, 184, 195
Atlanta campaign, 100, 136
Ayres, Romeyn, 203

Ball's Bluff, Battle of, 84
Banks, Nathaniel, 31, 45, 52, 80, 152, 183
   background and character, 39
   removed as Twelfth Corps commander, 39
   and Williams, 51
Banks Ford, Virginia, 95, 100–101
Barlow, Francis, 155
Barnard, John, 173
Bates, Edward, 35

Bermuda Hundred, Virginia, 165, 171, 184, 203
Bermuda Hundred campaign, 168–72
Berry, Hiram, 20, 28, 55, 84, 87, 93, 124, 209, 212, 217
Big Bethel, Battle of, 169
Birney, David, 20, 28, 55, 84, 110, 124, 125, 126, 127, 129, 147, 179, 209, 211, 212, 214, 216, 217
   appointed Tenth Corps commander, 181
   background and character, 181–82
   and Burnside, 181
   court martial of, 22–23
   death of, 182
   and French, 125, 181
   and Gettysburg, 118–19
   and Hancock, 181, 182
   and Humphreys, 182
   and Kearny, 181
   and Meade, 119, 137, 182
   serves as temporary Second Corps commander, 166, 167–68, 192
   and Stoneman, 181
   works against Meade, 134–37
Birney, William, 182, 197, 198
Blair, Francis, 56
Blair, Montgomery, 35, 37, 98
Bloody Angle, 160
Bloody Lane, 45
Blue Ridge Mountains, 67, 105
Brandy Station, Battle of, 105
Bristoe, Battle of, 123, 128

271

Brock Road, 154, 155
Brooks, William, 95, 101, 159, 214
    appointed Tenth Corps commander,
        174–75
    and Butler, 175–76
    arrested by Burnside, 77
    background and character, 174–75
    and General Orders Number Eight, 78
    and McClellan, 174
    resignation from the army, 175–76
    and Sedgwick, 174
    and Smith, William, 175
    and Stanton, 175
    subsequent career, 176
Buckingham, Catharinus, 56, 60
Buell, Don Carlos, 15–16, 31
Buford, John, 100, 112
Bull Run, First Battle of, 2
Bull Run, Second Battle of, 33–34
Burnside, Ambrose, 15, 29, 32, 35, 40, 82,
        90, 102, 107, 116, 117, 121, 129, 130,
        134, 137, 207, 209, 214, 215, 217, 218
    and Antietam, 41–42, 46, 47
    appointed Army of the Potomac
        commander, 56, 60–61
    background and character, 27, 61–62
    becomes Ninth Corps commander, 27
    and Birney, 181
    and the Crater, 188–90
    evaluation of, 80–81
    forwards Porter's messages to Lincoln
        administration, 33
    and Franklin, 77
    and Fredericksburg, 67–72
    and Grant, 162, 191
    and Hancock, 63, 191
    and Harrison's Landing, 27
    and Hooker, 61, 63, 70, 72, 76, 77–78
    and Humphreys, 124
    issues General Orders Number Eight,
        77–78
    and Lincoln, 27–28, 62, 67, 73–75
    and McClellan, 27–28, 42, 53
    and Meade, 66–67, 75, 164, 188, 190–91
    and Mud March, 76–77
    Ninth Corps incorporated into Meade's
        Army of the Potomac command, 164
    offered command of McClellan's Army of
        the Potomac, 27–28, 35
    and officer corps, 61–62

and Parke, 191
and Petersburg, 166
rejoins the Army of the Potomac, 151
relieved as Army of the Potomac
    commander, 78–79, 80
relieved as Ninth Corps commander,
    190–91
and Reno, 40
reorganizes Army of the Potomac, 62–67
and Smith, 73–74, 76–77
and Spotsylvania, 161
subsequent career, 190–91
and Turner's Gap, 41
undermined by officer corps after
    Fredericksburg, 73–75, 76–77
and Wilderness, 154, 155, 156
Burnside's Bridge, 46
Butler, Benjamin, 52, 86, 152, 181, 185, 195,
        206, 212, 217
    appointed Army of the James commander,
        168–69
    background and character, 169–70
    and Birney, 181, 182
    and Brooks, 175–76
    and confinement in Bermuda Hundred,
        171–73
    and Fort Fisher, 196
    and General Orders Number 225, 177–78
    and Gillmore, 171, 172–73, 173–74, 177
    and Grant, 170, 173, 177–78, 196–97
    and Halleck, 177
    removed from Army of the James
        command, 196–97
    and Smith, 170, 172, 176, 177
    subsequent career, 197–98
    and Weitzel, 183, 196
    and Wright, 177
Butterfield, Daniel, 3, 72, 96, 101, 104, 110,
        111, 112, 119, 146, 204, 212, 214, 217
    appointed Fifth Corps commander, 65
    appointed Hooker's chief of staff, 84
    background and character, 1, 65–66
    creates corps badges, 1–2
    and Hooker, 75–76, 101, 123
    as Hooker's chief of staff, 84–85, 90
    and Meade, 75, 110–11, 112, 123, 134–37
    passed over as First Corps commander, 116
    and Porter, 65
    removed as Meade's chief of staff, 110–11,
        123

subsequent career, 136
supplanted by Meade as Fifth Corps
    commander, 75–76

Caldwell, John, 126
Cameron, Simon, 9, 48
Casey, Silas, 21, 22
Cedar Creek, Battle of, 186
Cedar Mountain, Battle of, 39, 43
Cemetery Hill, 114, 115, 117
Cemetery Ridge, 117, 118, 119, 120
Centreville, Virginia, 14
Chaffin's Farm, Battle of, 183
Chancellorsville, Battle of, 90–97
Chancellorsville, Virginia, 91, 92, 95, 97
Chandler, Zachariah, 8, 58, 64, 65, 76, 82,
    98, 134, 135
Chantilly, Battle of, 34
Charleston, South Carolina, 123, 171, 197,
    199
Chase, Salmon, 10, 12, 22, 37, 39, 49, 65,
    121
    and Hooker, 55, 79, 82, 98, 106, 134
    and McClellan, 6, 9, 34–35, 54
Chattanooga, Battle of, 131
Chattanooga, Tennessee, 122, 123, 130,
    144
Chickahominy River, 21, 22, 23, 24, 162,
    165
Chickamauga, Battle of, 130
Chickasaw Bluffs, Battle of, 73
City Point, Virginia, 177, 184, 196, 203
Cleveland, Grover, 58
Cochrane, John, 54, 74, 78
Cold Harbor, Battle of, 162
Combat commanders, 5, 218
Committee on the Conduct of the War, 9,
    74, 76, 135, 136, 149, 197, 212
Corinth, Battle of, 47
Corinth, Mississippi, 16, 25, 30, 31, 144
Cornfield, 43
Corps commanders
    criteria for, 4, 208–13
    importance of, 2–4
    reasons for removal from, 213–15
    types of, 4–5, 215–18
Couch, Darius, 21, 28, 32, 40, 46, 49, 53, 58,
    77, 79, 81, 87, 90, 102, 107, 125, 214
    appointed Second Corps commander, 50,
    63

background and character, 50–51
and Chancellorsville, 91–92, 94, 96, 97
and Fredericksburg, 68, 71, 72
and Hooker, 94, 101, 103–4
and McClellan, 50–51
relieved as Second Corps commander,
    103–4
subsequent career, 104
Cox, Jacob, 49, 212, 216
    background and character, 41–42
    becomes Ninth Corps commander,
    41–42
    and McClellan, 42, 54
Crampton's Gap, Battle of, 41
Crater, Battle of the, 188–91
Crawford, Samuel, 202
    background and character, 203
    passed over as Fifth Corps commander,
    203
Crook, George, 185
Culpeper, Virginia, 145
Culp's Hill, 117, 119
Curtin, Andrew, 48, 103
Curtis, Samuel, 15

Deep Bottom, Virginia, 182
Departments
    the Gulf, 52
    Kansas, 148
    the Mississippi, 25
    Missouri, 25, 80, 149
    the Monongahela, 174
    the North, 52, 131
    the Northwest, 35
    the Ohio, 6, 159, 192
    the South, 174, 198
    the Susquehanna, 88, 104
    Vicksburg, 132
    Virginia, 32
    Virginia and North Carolina, 169, 173,
        177, 196, 198
    West Virginia, 193, 201
Dinwiddie Courthouse, Virginia, 200, 201
District of West Florida, 148
Dix, John, 32
Doubleday, Abner, 70, 86, 114–15, 116, 117,
    122, 135
Dranesville, Battle of, 180
Drewry's Bluff, Battle of, 172
Dunker Church, 43

Ely's Ford, Virginia, 132, 152
Emory, William, 185

Fair Oaks, Battle of, 21–22
Falmouth, Virginia, 32, 75, 98
Farragut, David, 16
Ferrero, Edward, 78, 189, 190
Fisher's Hill, Battle of, 186
Five Forks, Battle of, 200–203, 204
Forts, fortresses, and batteries
   Donelson, 15, 25, 144
   Fisher, 196, 197
   Gilmer, 182
   Gregg, 205
   Harrison, 183
   Henry, 25
   Monroe, 14, 87, 165, 170, 196
   Pulaski, 171
   Stedman, 200, 204
   Wagner, 171
   Whitworth, 205
Foster, John, 80
Franklin, William, 10, 15, 17, 19, 21, 25, 26,
      28, 32, 40, 50, 52, 58, 60, 66, 75, 79,
      81, 90, 138, 176, 206, 211, 214, 215
   and Antietam, 45, 46
   appointed Left Grand Division
      commander, 62–63
   appointed Sixth Corps commander, 17
   background and character, 18
   and Burnside, 73–74, 76–77
   considered for command by Grant, 185
   and Crampton's Gap, 41
   and Fredericksburg, 68, 69
   and General Orders Number Eight, 78
   and Grant, 184
   and Lincoln, 73, 80
   and McClellan, 18, 30
   and Newton, 117
   reinstated as Sixth Corps commander, 38
   relieved as Sixth Corps commander after
      Fredericksburg, 80
   removed as Sixth Corps commander after
      Second Bull Run, 36, 37
   and Reynolds, 49
   and Slocum, 51
   and Smith, William, 64, 66
   subsequent career, 80
Frederick, Maryland, 41, 108, 120
Fredericksburg, Battle of, 67–72

Fredericksburg, Virginia, 31, 67–68, 71, 72,
      73, 76, 91
Frémont, John, 25
French, William, 45, 59, 68, 71, 86, 104,
      126, 129, 137, 150, 210, 214, 215
   appointed Third Corps commander, 125
   background and character, 125
   and Birney, 125, 181
   and Meade, 132, 133
   and Mine Run, 132–33
   relieved as Third Corps commander,
      147–48
   subsequent career, 147–48

Gaines's Mill, Battle of, 23, 24
Garfield, James, 193
General Orders Number Eight, 77–78
General Orders Number 225, 177–78, 185
Germanna Ford, Virginia, 132, 152
Getty, George, 71, 154
Gettysburg, Battle of, 112–20
Gettysburg, Pennsylvania, 112
Gettysburg campaign, 105, 108–22
Gibbon, John, 31, 34, 70, 93, 95, 102, 129,
      136, 151, 163, 181, 187, 189, 200, 204,
      206, 210, 215
   appointed Twenty-Fourth Corps
      commander, 198–99
   background and character, 198–99
   demoralized by failure to attain corps
      command, 194–95, 199
   and Gettysburg, 115, 119, 120
   and Grant, 162, 194–95, 199
   and Hancock, 193, 199
   and Hooker, 199
   and Humphreys, 194–95
   and Kearny, 199
   and McClellan, 199
   and Meade, 110, 115, 187, 199
   subsequent career, 219
   and Willcox, 199
Gillmore, Quincy, 198, 206, 214
   appointed Tenth Corps commander,
      170–71
   background and character, 170–71
   and Bermuda Hundred campaign, 171
   and Butler, 171, 172–73, 173–74, 177
   relieved as Tenth Corps commander,
      172–73, 173–74
   subsequent career, 174

Glendale, Battle of, 23
Grant, Ulysses, 15, 16, 31, 47, 110, 122, 131,
    136, 137, 151, 168, 174, 176, 193, 200,
    209, 211, 213
  appointed general in chief, 144–45
  and Appomattox campaign, 205–6
  background and character, 143–44
  and Burnside, 162, 164, 190–91
  and Butler, 170, 173, 177–78, 179,
    196–97
  and Cold Harbor, 162
  concerned with Army of the Potomac,
    164–65
  and the Crater, 189, 190
  establishes national command structure,
    144–45
  evaluation of, 206–7
  and Fort Fisher, 195, 196
  and Franklin, 184
  and Gibbon, 162, 194–95, 199
  and Hancock, 162, 192
  and Humphreys, 162, 194
  and Lincoln, 144–45, 185
  and Meade, 145–47, 162, 164, 185,
    186–87
  and Ord, 180
  and Parke, 191
  and Petersburg assault, 165, 167
  and Petersburg breakthrough, 199–201,
    204–5
  and Sedgwick, 158
  and Shenandoah Valley, 185
  and Sheridan, 149–50, 157, 185–86
  and Smith, William, 145, 176, 178–79
  and Spotsylvania, 156–62
  strategic plan, 152, 168
  subsequent career, 219
  and Warren, 128, 148, 161, 162, 163, 164,
    167, 188, 201, 203
  and Wilderness, 152–56
  and Wright, 162, 164, 205
Gravelly Run, Virginia, 200
Griffin, Charles, 92, 203
  appointed Fifth Corps commander, 204
  and Appomattox campaign, 205, 206
  background and character, 204
  and Petersburg breakthrough, 205
  reinstated to command, 38
  relieved of command after Second Bull
    Run, 36, 37

subsequent career, 219
  and Warren, 204
  and Wilderness, 153–54
Groveton, Battle of, 31

Halleck, Henry, 26, 30, 35, 36, 52, 54, 55,
    67, 73, 74, 75, 78–79, 98, 111, 115,
    124, 130, 131, 147, 148, 149, 162, 169,
    173, 174, 185, 206, 209, 211, 213
  appointment as general in chief, 25–26
  background and character, 25–26
  and Butler, 177
  and Hooker, 79, 82, 105–6, 109
  and Keyes, 32
  and Lincoln, 26, 34
  made Grant's chief of staff, 144–45
  and McClellan, 26–27, 29, 32–33
  and Meade, 120, 121, 136
  and Sigel, 66
  and Stoneman, 66, 100
  subsequent career, 219
Hamilton, Charles, 17, 19
Hamlin, Hannibal, 55
Hampton Roads, Virginia, 171, 172
Hancock, Winfield Scott, 16, 50, 64, 86,
    122, 124, 126, 128, 134, 136, 164, 178,
    180, 186, 187, 189, 213, 215
  appointed Second Corps commander, 104
  background and character, 104–5
  and Birney, 181, 182
  and Burnside, 68, 191
  and Chancellorsville, 91, 94
  and Cold Harbor, 162
  and Fredericksburg, 68, 71
  and Gettysburg, 115–16, 117, 118, 119,
    120
  and Gibbon, 193, 199
  and Grant, 162, 192
  injury forces him to relinquish command,
    166, 167–68
  and Meade, 110, 115, 187, 193
  and Petersburg assault, 166
  relieved as Second Corps commander,
    192–93
  return as Second Corps commander, 150
  and Spotsylvania, 160, 161
  subsequent career, 193
  and Wilderness, 154–55
Hanover Courthouse, Battle of, 18
Hardie, James, 108–9, 111

Harper's Ferry, Virginia, 41, 46, 53, 106, 125, 186
Harrison's Landing, Virginia, 23, 25, 27, 28, 29
Harrison's Landing Letter, 25, 54
Hatcher's Run, 201
Hays, Alexander, 126, 156
Hays, William, 129, 137, 214
    appointed Second Corps commander, 126
    background and character, 126–27
    relieved as Second Corps commander, 127
    subsequent career, 127
Hazel Grove, 93
Heintzelman, Samuel, 16, 18, 25, 26, 30, 32, 53, 66, 131, 159, 214, 216
    appointed Third Corps commander, 10, 12–13
    background and character, 11–12
    and Fair Oaks, 21, 22
    and Hooker, 55–56
    and Keyes, 13, 28
    left behind in Washington, 40
    and McClellan, 13, 19, 28, 40, 52
    and Pope, 33
    removed as Third Corps commander, 52
    and Sumner, Edwin, 13
    and Second Bull Run, 33
    and Slocum, 51
    subsequent career, 52
Helena, Arkansas, 122
Hincks, Edward, 165
"Historicus," 135, 136
Holly Springs, Mississippi, 73
Hooker, Joseph, 1, 2, 23, 35, 40, 48, 52, 59, 60, 81, 121, 125, 129, 134, 137, 138, 146, 147, 155, 181, 199, 208, 210, 212, 213, 214, 217
    and Antietam, 41, 43, 45
    appointed Army of the Potomac commander, 79
    appointed Central Grand Division commander, 62–63
    appointed First Corps commander, 38–39
    background and character, 20, 79, 82–83
    blames others for defeat at Chancellorsville, 98–101
    and Burnside, 61, 63, 70, 72, 76, 77–78
    and Butterfield, 75–76, 101, 123
    cabinet's doubts about, 97–98

and Couch, 94, 101, 103–4
and Chancellorsville, 90–97
and Chase, 55, 79, 82, 98, 106, 134
evaluation of, 107
and Franklin, 80
and Fredericksburg, 68, 70, 71, 72
and General Orders Number Eight, 77
and Halleck, 79, 82, 105–6, 109
and Heintzelman, 55–56
and Howard, 99, 101, 130
and Kearny, 20
and Lincoln, 82–83, 90, 98, 105–6, 130
    Lincoln's efforts to make one of Meade's corps commanders, 130
    lobbies for command of the Army of the Potomac, 55–56, 70
and McClellan, 20–21, 28, 30, 38–39, 42
and Meade, 55, 66–67, 75, 84, 101, 102–3
    officer corps' doubts about, 83-84, 101–4
    part of efforts to supplant Meade, 134–37
and Pleasonton, 85, 100, 105
and Pope, 33, 39
    relieved as Army of the Potomac commander, 105–6, 109
    reorganizes Army of the Potomac, 85–90
    revitalizes the Army of the Potomac, 84–85
and Reynolds, 101, 102
and Sedgwick, 100–101
and Sickles, 86
and Sigel, 88
and Slocum, 100–101, 130–31
and Smith, William, 87
and Stanton, 70, 79, 105–6
and Stoneman, 99–100
    subsequent career, 131, 136
and Sumner, Edwin, 80
    targeted by General Orders Number Eight, 77
    transferred out west, 123, 130–31
and Williamsburg, 16
    wounded at Chancellorsville, 93–94
Howard, Oliver Otis, 50, 102, 103, 104, 118, 121, 122, 129, 147, 214, 218
    appointed Eleventh Corps commander, 89
    background and character, 89–90
    and Chancellorsville, 91, 92–93, 96, 97
    and Fredericksburg, 71
    and Gettysburg, 112, 115–16, 119

and Hooker, 99, 101, 130
subsequent career, 131–32
transferred out west, 130–31
Howe, Albion, 135
Humphreys, Andrew, 46, 118–19, 128, 129,
  161, 200, 201, 204, 207, 210, 218
appointed Meade's chief of staff, 111, 124
appointed Second Corps commander,
  193–94
and Appomattox campaign, 205
background and character, 124–25
and Birney, 182
and Burnside, 124
and Fredericksburg, 71, 72
and Gibbon, 194–95
and Grant, 162, 194
and Meade, 110
offered Tenth Corps command, 179–80
and Petersburg breakthrough, 205
subsequent career, 220
and Warren, 127
Hunt, Henry, 93, 136
Hunter, David, 63

Island Number Ten, 16, 25, 31
Iuka, Battle of, 47

Jackson, Mississippi, 192
Jacob's Ford, Virginia, 132
James River, 14, 23, 24, 29, 55, 73, 152, 165,
  166, 168, 189, 200
Jerusalem Plank Road, 167, 192
Jetersville, Virginia, 205
Julian, George, 8

Kearny, Philip, 1, 2, 22, 23, 29, 40, 52, 59,
  65, 86, 89, 104, 138, 217
background and character, 19
and Birney, 181
death of, at Chantilly, 34
and Gibbon, 199
and Hooker, 20
and McClellan, 20–21, 28
and Pope, 33
Kelly's Ford, Battle of, 123
Keyes, Erasmus, 16, 18, 25, 26, 30, 50, 212,
  215, 216
appointed Fourth Corps commander, 10,
  12–13
background and character, 12

and Fair Oaks, 21, 22
and Halleck, 32
and Heintzelman, 13, 28
and Lincoln, 32
and McClellan, 13, 30, 32
and Stanton, 32
stranded on the peninsula, 32
subsequent career, 32
and Sumner, Edwin, 13
Kilpatrick, Judson, 148
Knoxville, Tennessee, 151, 192

Lacy Meadow, 153
Laurel Hill, 161
Ledlie, James, 189, 190
Lincoln, Abraham, 5, 15, 40, 57, 58, 118,
  124, 145, 148, 149, 174, 180, 184, 185,
  187, 191, 194, 195, 198, 200, 204, 206,
  209, 212, 213, 216
appoints Burnside as Army of the
  Potomac commander, 60–61
appoints first corps commanders, 10, 12–13
appoints Grant as general in chief,
  144–45
appoints Halleck as general in chief,
  25–26
appoints Hooker as Army of the Potomac
  commander, 1, 79
appoints Meade as Army of the Potomac
  commander, 106
and Burnside, 27–28, 62, 67, 73–75
and Butler, 170, 177, 178, 196–97
criteria for appointing corps commanders,
  4
and Eleventh Corps, 88–89
and Franklin, 73, 80
and Grant, 144–45, 185
and Halleck, 26, 34
and Hooker, 82–83, 90, 98, 105–6, 130
and Keyes, 32
and McClellan, 9, 10, 15, 16–17, 24–25,
  53–55
and Meade, 121, 123, 130, 134, 136
orders Porter's court martial, 57–58
reaction to Chancellorsville, 98
reaction to Gettysburg, 121
reinstates McClellan as Army of the
  Potomac Commander, 34–36
relieves Burnside as Army of the Potomac
  commander, 78–79, 80

Lincoln, Abraham, *continued*
  relieves Butler as Army of the James
    commander, 196–97
  relieves Franklin, Griffin, and Porter, 36
  relieves Hooker as Army of the Potomac
    commander, 105–6
  relieves McClellan as Army of the
    Potomac commander, 56
  relieves McDowell after First Bull Run, 6
  relieves McDowell after Second Bull Run,
    37
  relieves Pope, 36–37
  reserves right to appoint corps
    commanders, 4
  and Sickles, 86, 118
  and Stanton, 26
  and Stoneman, 100
Little Round Top, 119
Lookout Mountain, Battle of, 131

Malvern Hill, Battle of, 23, 24, 28, 29
Manassas, Virginia, 6, 67
Manchester, Maryland, 116
Mansfield, Joseph, 45, 51, 203, 213
  appointed Twelfth Corps commander,
    39–40
  background and character, 39–40
  death of, at Antietam, 43
Marcy, Randolph, 24–25
Martindale, John, 181
Marye's Heights, 71, 94–95, 97
Maryland campaign, 30–47
McClellan, George, 1, 5, 60, 61, 89, 98, 106,
    107, 110, 121, 129, 130, 137, 159, 165,
    174, 175, 184, 204, 209, 211, 212, 213,
    215, 216, 217, 218
  and Antietam, 41–47
  appointed Army of the Potomac
    commander, 6
  appointed general in chief, 8
  Army of the Potomac removed from his
    command, 32–33
  background and character, 6–7
  and Brooks, 174
  and Burnside, 27–28, 42, 53
  and Chase, 6, 9, 34–35, 54
  and Couch, 50–51
  and Cox, 42, 54
  divides the Army of the Potomac into
    wings, 40

evacuates Army of the Potomac from
    peninsula, 31–32, 33
  evaluation of, 57, 58–59
  and Fair Oaks, 21
  fears being removed as Army of the
    Potomac commander, 53
  and Franklin, 18, 30
  gets Franklin, Griffin, and Porter restored,
    38
  and Gibbon, 199
  and Halleck, 26–27, 29, 32–33
  and Harrison's Landing, 25, 26–27
  and Heintzelman, 13, 19, 30, 40, 52
  and Hooker, 20–21, 28, 30, 38–39, 42
  and Kearny, 20–21, 28
  and Keyes, 13, 30, 32
  leaves the Army of the Potomac, 56–57
  and Lincoln, 9, 10, 15, 16–17, 24–25,
    53–55
  lobbies to become general in chief again,
    53–55
  and march into Maryland, 37–41
  and McDowell, 13, 15
  and Meade, 43, 48–49, 57
  and officer corps, 18
  and Parke, 191
  and Peninsula campaign, 13–30
  and Preliminary Emancipation
    Proclamation, 53–54
  and Pleasonton, 100
  and Pope, 33, 36
  and Porter, 18, 29–30, 36, 52–53
  and Radical Republicans, 8–9, 9–10
  relieved as Army of the Potomac
    commander, 56–57
  relieved as general in chief, 10
  and Reno, 40
  reorganizes army after Second Bull Run,
    35–36, 37–38
  restored to Army of the Potomac
    command, 34–35, 37–38
  rests army after Antietam, 47–48
  and Reynolds, 48–49
  and Scott, 8
  and Seven Days Battle, 23–24
  and Smith, William, 29–30
  and Stanton, 9, 24, 29, 34–35, 54–55, 56
  and Stoneman, 65, 85
  subsequent career, 57
  and Sumner, Edwin, 13, 22, 30, 50

view of original Army of the Potomac
  corps commanders, 13, 16
and Williamsburg, 16
and Yorktown, 15, 16
McClellanites, 5, 58, 77, 110, 111, 124, 134,
  138, 147, 181, 192, 197, 215–16, 217
McDowell, Irvin, 6, 9, 10, 15, 21, 23, 31, 33,
  198, 214, 216
  appointed First Corps commander, 10,
    12–13
  background and character, 10–11
  and McClellan, 13, 15
  and Meade, 43
  relieved as First Corps commander, 37
  and Reynolds, 49
  subsequent career, 37
McMahon, Martin, 158, 159
McPherson, James, 131
McPherson's Ridge, 114
Meade, George, 23, 48, 65, 77, 81, 99, 104,
  107, 128, 163, 164, 168, 184, 195, 200,
  204, 206, 207, 208, 209, 211, 212, 213,
  214, 215, 217, 218
  and Antietam, 43
  appointed Army of the Potomac
    commander, 106, 108–9
  appointed Fifth Corps commander,
    66–67, 75
  and Appomattox campaign, 205
  background and character, 109–10
  and Birney, 119, 137, 182
  and Burnside, 66–67, 75, 164, 188,
    190–91
  and Butterfield, 75, 110–11, 112, 123,
    134–37
  and Chancellorsville, 91, 94, 96, 97
  and Committee on the Conduct of the
    War hearings, 135–36
  considered as Burnside's replacement, 79
  considered for Shenandoah Valley
    command, 185–86
  conspired against, 134–36
  and the Crater, 189, 190
  and Doubleday, 115
  evaluation of 137–38
  and Fredericksburg, 70
  and French, 132, 133
  and Gettysburg, 112, 114–20
  and Gibbon, 110, 115, 187, 199
  and Grant, 145–47, 162, 164, 185–87

and Halleck, 121, 123, 134
and Hancock, 110, 115, 187, 193
and Hooker, 55, 66-67, 75, 84, 101, 102–3
and Humphreys, 110
and Lincoln, 121, 130, 136
lobbies for Fifth Corps command, 66–67
and McClellan, 43, 48–49, 57
and McDowell, 43
and Mine Run, 132–34
and Newton, 117
offers to resign Army of the Potomac
  command, 121, 135
officer corps' view of, 102, 110, 121–22,
  128, 134
and Petersburg assault, 166–67
passed over as First Corps commander,
  48–49
and Pleasonton, 128, 135–36
and Porter, 43
reorganizes Army of the Potomac, 147–51
and Reynolds, 48–49, 110, 112
and Ricketts, 43, 159
and Sedgwick, 150–51
and Sheridan, 157
and Sickles, 111, 115, 118, 126, 134–37
and Smith, William, 66, 176
subsequent career, 220
and Sykes, 111
unhappiness under Grant's command,
  164, 186–87
view of his subordinates, 121–22, 128,
  129, 164
and Warren, 111, 133–34, 164, 167,
  187–88, 201, 203
and Wilderness, 153, 154, 155, 156
and Wright, 159–60, 164
Mechanicsville, Battle of, 23
Meigs, Montgomery, 10, 173
Middle Division, 186
Mine Run campaign, 132–34
Missionary Ridge, 149
Mobile Bay, 195
Morrell, George, 40, 49, 65–66, 87
Morris Island, 171
Mud March, 76–77
Mule Shoe, 160

Nashville, Battle of, 104, 195
Nashville, Tennessee, 15, 25, 73, 146
New Bern, North Carolina, 15

New Market, Battle of, 88
New Orleans, Louisiana, 16, 52
Newton, John, 95, 119, 121, 125, 129, 137,
    150, 210, 214, 215
    appointed First Corps commander, 116–17
    background and character, 117
    criticizes Burnside, 74
    and Franklin, 117
    and General Orders Number Eight, 78
    and Meade, 117
    relieved as First Corps commander, 147–48
    and Sedgwick, 117
    subsequent career, 148
New York City, New York, 123
New York Herald, 135, 173–74
New York Times, 133
New York Tribune, 178
Norfolk, Virginia, 39
Norfolk and Petersburg Railroad, 188
Norfolk Naval Yard, 159
North Anna River, 162

Oak Grove, Battle of, 23
Olustee, Battle of, 152
Opportunists, 5, 217–18
Orange and Alexandria Railroad, 132
Orange Plank Road, 154, 155
Orange Turnpike, 153, 154
Ord, Edward, 189, 190, 200, 204, 206, 213,
    214, 218
    appointed Army of the James commander,
    198
    appointed Eighteenth Corps commander,
    180
    appointed Twenty-Fourth Corps
    commander, 183
    and Appomattox campaign, 205, 206
    background and character, 180
    and Grant, 180
    and Petersburg breakthrough, 205
    subsequent career, 220
    and Weitzel, 198
Order Number 28, 169
Overland campaign, 151–68

Pamunkey River, 162
Parke, John, 49, 151, 194, 204, 207
    appointed Ninth Corps commander, 191
    background and career, 191–92
    and Burnside, 191

    and Fort Stedman, 200
    and Grant, 191
    and McClellan, 191
    and Petersburg breakthrough, 205
    and Porter, 192
    and Sherman, 191
    subsequent career, 220
Parker, Ely, 165
Patrick, Marsena, 84
Pea Ridge, Battle of, 15, 66
Peck, John, 22
Peninsula campaign, 13–30
Perryville, Battle of, 47
Petersburg, Siege of, 127, 183–200, 204
    assault on, 165–68
    breakthrough, 204–5
Petersburg, Virginia, 26, 171, 184, 186, 192,
    195, 199, 200
Pillow, Gideon, 20
Pipe Creek, 112, 114, 135
Pittsburgh Commercial, 187
Pittsburg Landing, Tennessee, 16, 144
Pleasants, Henry, 188
Pleasonton, Alfred, 105, 112, 121, 134, 214
    appointed Cavalry Corps commander,
    100, 128–29
    background and character, 100
    and Hooker, 85, 100, 105
    and McClellan, 100
    removed as Cavalry Corps commander,
    148–49
    and Sickles, 100
    and Slocum, 100
    subsequent career, 149
    and Meade, 128, 135–36
Plymouth, North Carolina, 152
Political generals, 5, 216–17
Pope, John, 16, 25, 60, 79, 134, 204
    appointed Army of Virginia commander,
    31
    background and character, 31
    and Heintzelman, 33
    and Hooker, 33, 39
    and Kearny, 33
    and McClellan, 33, 36
    relieved of command, 37
    and Reno, 40
    and Reynolds, 49
    and Second Bull Run campaign, 26
    subsequent career, 37

Porter, David, 196
Porter, Fitz John, 17, 21, 25, 26, 28, 32, 40,
    58, 63, 111, 211, 214, 215
  appointed Fifth Corps commander, 17
  background and character, 18
  and Butterfield, 65
  court martial of, 58
  and McClellan, 18, 29–30, 36, 52–53
  and Meade, 43
  and Parke, 192
  and Pope, 33
  reinstated to Fifth Corps command, 38
  relieved as Fifth Corps commander after
    Antietam, 57–58
  relieved as Fifth Corps commander after
    Second Bull Run, 36, 37
  and Reynolds, 49
  and Second Bull Run, 33–34
  and the Seven Days Battle, 23
  and Slocum, 51
  and Stoneman, 65
  subsequent career, 58
Port Hudson, Louisiana, 122
Port Royal Expedition, 159
Potomac River, 37, 47, 52, 105, 120, 121,
    180
Potter, Robert, 189
Preliminary Emancipation Proclamation, 47,
    53–54, 59
Prince, Henry, 133

Radical Republicans, 8–10, 13, 55, 59, 65,
    79, 82, 88, 98, 105, 106, 124, 134, 147,
    169, 173, 181, 189, 212, 217
Rapidan River, 90, 91, 99, 132, 133, 152,
    156, 163
Rappahannock River, 14, 31, 67, 68, 71, 72,
    73, 75, 76, 90, 91, 94, 95, 96, 97, 98,
    99, 105, 112, 133
Rappahannock Station, Battle of, 123, 128
Rawlins, John, 179
Ream's Station, Battle of, 192–93
Red River campaign, 152
Reno, Jesse, 32, 33, 213
  appointed Ninth Corps commander, 40
  background and character, 40
  and Burnside, 40
  and McClellan, 40
  and Pope, 40
  death of, at Turner's Gap, 41

Reynolds, John, 23, 58, 64, 103, 104, 107,
    108, 116, 122, 128, 159, 213
  appointed First Corps commander, 48–49,
    64
  background and character, 49
  and Chancellorsville, 96, 97
  death of, at Gettysburg, 114
  and Franklin, 49
  and Fredericksburg, 68
  and Gettysburg, 112–14
  and Hooker, 101, 102
  and McClellan, 48–49
  and McDowell, 49
  and Meade, 48–49, 110, 112
  and Pope, 49
  and Porter, 49
  and Smith, William, 49
  turns down Army of the Potomac
    command, 79, 102, 106
Richardson, Israel, 40, 45, 50, 87, 104
Richmond and Danville Railroad, 205
Ricketts, James
  and Antietam, 43
  background and character, 48
  efforts to gain command of First Corps,
    48, 49
  and Meade, 43, 159
  and Spotsylvania, 159
Roanoke Island, North Carolina, 15, 27, 60
Rodman, Isaac, 46
Rosecrans, William, 73, 79, 122, 130, 131

Salem Church, Virginia, 95
Savage's Station, Battle of, 23
Savannah, Georgia, 195
Sayler's Creek, Battle of, 205
Schurz, Carl, 88–89, 93, 99, 129
Scott, Winfield, 6, 8, 10, 12, 18, 19, 20, 25,
    111, 125, 144
Secessionville, Battle of, 159
Second Bull Run campaign, 31–34
Sedgwick, John, 23, 40, 50, 63–64, 67, 89,
    102, 103, 110, 125, 128, 134, 199, 213,
    216
  and Antietam, 45
  appointed Sixth Corps commander, 87
  background and character, 87–88
  and Brooks, 174
  and Chancellorsville, 93, 94–95, 96, 97
  death of, at Spotsylvania, 157–59

Sedgwick, John, *continued*
  and Gettysburg, 116, 119
  and Grant, 158
  and Hooker, 100–101
  and Meade, 150–51
  and Mine Run, 133
  and Newton, 117
  offered command of Twelfth Corps, 39
  and Spotsylvania, 157
  Stanton's efforts to remove from
    command, 150–51
  turns down Army of the Potomac
    command, 106
  and Wilderness, 153, 154, 155
Seven Days Battle, 23–24
Seven Pines, Battle of, 21–22
Seward, William, 9, 35, 39
Sharpsburg, Maryland, 46
Shenandoah Valley, Virginia, 23, 31, 48, 56,
    62, 105, 151, 152, 180, 184, 185, 186,
    187, 195, 200, 201, 203, 204
Sheridan, Philip, 160, 164, 167, 185, 187,
    195, 200, 204, 206, 213, 214, 218
  appointed Cavalry Corps commander,
    149–50
  appointed commander in the
    Shenandoah Valley, 186
  and Appomattox campaign, 205
  background and character, 149–50
  and Five Forks, 200–203
  and Grant, 149–50, 157, 185–86
  and Meade, 157
  and Petersburg breakthrough, 205
  and Spotsylvania, 157
  subsequent career, 220
  and Warren, 201, 202–3
  and Wright, 201
Sherman, William, 73, 131, 145, 151, 152,
    162, 184, 187, 191, 195, 197, 199
Shiloh, Battle of, 16, 25, 144
Sickles, Daniel, 28, 107, 110, 122, 138, 146,
    148, 181, 209, 210, 212, 213, 214,
    217
  appointed Third Corps commander,
    85–87
  background and character, 85–87
  and Chancellorsville, 92, 93, 94, 96
  efforts to reclaim Third Corps command,
    126
  and Gettysburg, 114, 115, 116, 117–18

  and Hooker, 84, 86, 101
  and Lincoln, 86, 118
  and Meade, 111, 115, 118, 126, 134–37
  and Pleasonton, 100
  subsequent career, 136–37
Sigel, Franz, 31, 33, 40, 62, 67, 151, 152,
    180, 212, 214, 216, 217
  background and character, 66
  and Halleck, 66
  and Hooker, 88
  relieved as Eleventh Corps commander,
    88
  subsequent career, 88
Slinker's Neck, 73
Slocum, Henry, 28, 40, 41, 46, 49, 58, 62,
    87, 103, 107, 212, 214, 215
  appointed Twelfth Corps commander, 51
  background and character, 51–52
  and Chancellorsville, 91, 93, 96, 97
  and Franklin, 51
  and Gettysburg, 116, 119, 120
  and Heintzelman, 51
  and Hooker, 84, 101–2, 130–31
  and Pleasonton, 100
  and Porter, 51
  subsequent career, 131–32
  transferred out west, 130–31
Smith, Caleb, 34
Smith, William "Baldy," 16, 28, 40, 46, 49,
    66, 87, 107, 138, 206, 213, 214, 215
  appointed Eighteenth Corps commander,
    170
  appointed Sixth Corps commander, 64
  background and character, 64–65, 170
  and Bermuda Hundred campaign, 171,
    173
  and Brooks, 175
  and Burnside, 73–74, 76–77
  and Butler, 170, 172, 173, 176
  and Cold Harbor, 162
  and Franklin, 64, 66
  at Fredericksburg, 68, 70, 72
  and General Orders Number Eight, 78
  and Grant, 145, 176, 178–79
  and Hooker, 87
  and McClellan, 29–30
  and Meade, 66, 176
  and Petersburg assault, 165–66
  relieved as Eighteenth Corps commander,
    178–79

relieved as Sixth Corps commander, 87
and Reynolds, 49
subsequent career, 179
South Mountain, 41
Southside Railroad, 184, 186, 200, 202, 205
Spotsylvania, Battle of, 156–61
Spotsylvania Courthouse, Virginia, 156, 157
Stahel, Julius, 88–89
Stanton, Edwin, 16, 22, 27, 36, 38, 48, 58,
    63, 66, 74, 75, 76, 86, 98, 100, 103,
    108, 124, 126, 128, 131, 136, 147, 148,
    149, 150, 151, 162, 169, 185, 191, 193,
    197, 199, 201
  background and character, 9
  and Brooks, 175
  and Hooker, 70, 79, 105–6
  and Keyes, 32
  and Lincoln, 26
  and McClellan, 9, 24, 29, 34–35, 54–55,
    56
Steinwehr, Adolph von, 88–89
Stevens, Isaac, 34, 63
Stone, Charles, 84
Stoneman, George, 49, 52, 81, 82, 103, 104,
    210, 214, 215
  appointed Cavalry Corps commander, 85
  appointed Third Corps commander, 65
  background and character, 65
  and Birney, 181
  and Chancellorsville, 91, 95
  and Halleck, 65, 100
  and Hooker, 99–100, 101
  and Lincoln, 100
  and McClellan, 65, 85
  and Porter, 65
  removed as Cavalry Corps commander,
    99–100
  subsequent career, 100
Stone's River, Battle of, 73, 79
Sturgis, Samuel, 71, 78
Suffolk, Virginia, 39
Sumner, Charles, 66
Sumner, Edwin, 16, 18, 23, 26, 28, 30, 31,
    35, 40, 51, 52, 60, 76, 77, 79, 214, 216
  and Antietam, 45–46, 47
  appointed Right Grand Division
    commander, 62–63
  appointed Second Corps commander, 10,
    12–13
  asks to be relieved after Antietam, 49–50

background and character, 11
and Fair Oaks, 21
and Fredericksburg, 68, 71, 72
and Heintzelman, 13
and Hooker, 80
and Keyes, 13
and McClellan, 13, 22, 30, 50
and McDowell, 13
relieved as Second Corps commander, 80
subsequent career, 80
and Williams, 51
Swift Creek, 171
Sykes, George, 64, 86, 91, 104, 115, 116,
    117, 119, 125, 129, 137, 150, 214
  appointed Fifth Corps commander, 111
  background and character, 111–12
  and Meade, 111
  relieved as Fifth Corps commander, 148
  subsequent career, 148

Taneytown, Maryland, 112, 116
Terry, Alfred, 171, 182, 183, 197
Thomas, George, 131, 147, 195
Totopotomoy Creek, 162
Turner, John, 171
Turner's Gap, Battle of, 41, 42, 48

United States Ford, Virginia, 94, 95, 96
Upton, Emory, 160
Urbanna, Virginia, 13, 14

Vicksburg, Mississippi, 73, 122, 144, 192
Virginia Central Railroad, 95

Wade, Benjamin, 8, 98, 136
Wadsworth, James, 60, 120–21, 156
War Democrats, 20, 54, 56, 59, 169, 211,
    215, 216
Warren, Gouverneur, 23–24, 96, 129, 136,
    189, 190, 192, 200, 207, 209, 211, 213,
    214
  appointed Fifth Corps commander, 148
  appointed Second Corps commander, 127
  background and character, 127–28
  and Five Forks, 201–3
  and Gettysburg, 119
  and Griffin, 204
  and Grant, 128, 148, 161, 162, 163, 164,
    167, 188, 201, 203
  and Humphreys, 127

Warren, Gouverneur, *continued*
  and Meade, 111, 133–34, 164, 167,
    187–88, 201, 203
  and Mine Run, 132–34
  offered position as Meade's chief of staff,
    111
  and Petersburg assault, 166–67
  psychological problems, 126, 163
  relieved as Fifth Corps commander, 202–3
  and Sheridan, 201, 202–3
  and Spotsylvania, 157, 161
  subsequent career, 203
  and Wilderness, 153, 154, 155, 156
Warrenton, Virginia, 61, 67
Washburne, Elihu, 144
Webb, Alexander, 194
Weitzel, Godfrey, 197, 200
  appointed Twenty-Fifth Corps
    commander, 183
  background and character, 183
  and Butler, 183, 196
  and Fort Fisher, 196
  and Ord, 198
  subsequent career, 220
Weldon Railroad, 167, 184, 192
Welles, Gideon, 9, 35, 40, 97, 134, 169, 196
West Point, Virginia, 15
West Woods, 45
Whipple, Amiel, 52
White House Landing, Virginia, 22, 23
White Oak Swamp, 184
Wilderness, 90, 92, 152, 156
Wilderness, Battle of, 152–56
Willcox, Orlando, 61, 78, 189, 190, 191,
    209, 214
  appointed Ninth Corps commander, 63
  background and character, 63–64
  and Fredericksburg, 68, 71, 72

and Gibbon, 199
  removed as Ninth Corps commander, 87
Williams, Alpheus, 52, 65, 119, 203, 209,
    211, 212, 214, 216
  and Antietam, 43, 45
  background and character, 51
  and Banks, 51
  becomes Twelfth Corps commander, 43
  relieved as Twelfth Corps commander, 51
  subsequent career, 51
  and Sumner, Edwin, 51
Williamsburg, Battle of, 16
Williamsport, Maryland, 120, 121
Wilmington, North Carolina, 195, 196, 199
Wilson, Henry, 76, 171, 173
Wilson, James, 164–65
Winchester, Battles of, 105, 186
Windmill Point, Virginia, 165
Wright, Horatio, 162, 167, 185, 200, 207,
    213, 218
  appointed Sixth Corps commander, 159
  and Appomattox campaign, 205
  background and character, 159–60
  and Butler, 177
  and Cold Harbor, 162
  and Grant, 162, 164, 205
  and Meade, 159–60, 164
  and Petersburg breakthrough, 204–5
  and Sedgwick, 159
  and Sheridan, 201
  and Spotsylvania, 160, 161
  subsequent career, 220
  and Wilderness, 153, 155–56

Yellow Tavern, Battle of, 157
York River, 14, 165
Yorktown, Virginia, 15, 29, 32
Yorktown, Siege of, 15–16, 18